Kant, Global Politics and Cosmopolitan Law

Why is there so much attention on Kant's global politics in present day law and philosophy? This book highlights the potential fruitfulness of Kant's cosmopolitan thought for understanding the complexities of the contemporary political world. It adopts a double methodological strategy by reconstructing a genealogical conceptual journey showing the development of international law, as well as introducing an interpretation of cosmopolitanism centred on Kant's theory of a metaphysics of freedom. The result is a novel focus on Kant's notion of the world republic. The hypothesis here defended is that the world republic stands as a way of thinking about international politics where the possibility of progression towards peace results from its use as a regulative idea.

Claudio Corradetti is Associate Professor of Political Philosophy at the University of Rome Tor Vergata. He has been a lecturer at the University of Oslo, Norway and at Karl Franzens Universität, Graz, Austria. In previous years he has been a visiting scholar at McGill University, the University of Oxford, the European University Institute and the Wissenschaftszentrum in Berlin. In 2019 he was awarded a Fulbright Research Scholarship at the Philosophy Department, Columbia University, NY.

Routledge Research in Constitutional Law

Series Editor: David Marrani

This series features thought-provoking and original scholarship on constitutional law and theory. Books explore key topics, themes and questions in the field with a particular emphasis on comparative studies. Where relevant, titles will engage with political and social theory, philosophy and history in order to offer a rounded analysis of constitutions and constitutional law.

Available titles in this series include:

Philosophy, Obligation and Law
Bentham's Ontology of Normativity
Piero Tarantino

Constitution-making and Human Rights in the Sudans
Edited by Mohamed Abdelsalam and Lutz Oette

Constitutional Politics and the Judiciary
Decision-making in Central and Eastern Europe
Edited by Kálmán Pócza

EU Law, Fundamental Rights and National Democracy
Eduardo Gill-Pedro

Constitution-making and Human Rights in the Sudans
Edited by Lutz Oette and Mohamed Abdelsalam Babiker

Constitutional Law, Religion and Equal Liberty
The Impact of Desecularization
Azin Tadjdini

Kant, Global Politics and Cosmopolitan Law
The World Republic as a Regulative Idea of Reason
Claudio Corradetti

For more information about this series, please visit: www.routledge.com/Routledge-Research-in-Constitutional-Law/book-series/CONSTLAW

Kant, Global Politics and Cosmopolitan Law

The World Republic as a Regulative Idea of Reason

Claudio Corradetti

Routledge
Taylor & Francis Group
LONDON AND NEW YORK

First published 2020
by Routledge
2 Park Square, Milton Park, Abingdon, Oxon OX14 4RN

and by Routledge
605 Third Avenue, New York, NY 10017

First issued in paperback 2021

Routledge is an imprint of the Taylor & Francis Group, an informa business

Publisher's Note
The publisher has gone to great lengths to ensure the quality of this reprint but points out that some imperfections in the original copies may be apparent.

British Library Cataloguing-in-Publication Data
A catalogue record for this book is available from the British Library

Library of Congress Cataloging-in-Publication Data
A catalog record for this book has been requested

ISBN 13: 978-1-03-223681-0 (pbk)
ISBN 13: 978-0-367-03050-6 (hbk)

DOI: 10.4324/9780429020087

Typeset in Galliard
by Apex CoVantage, LLC

To Carlo, with love

Contents

Acknowledgments

This work has accompanied me for the last six years from Oslo to Rome. It was born out of a context where the idea of 'going back to Kant' was in countertendency to mainstream scholarship. Yet, in the unfolding of the project I met several like-minded scholars. I'm indebted to all of them for the conversations and exchanges that have followed. Sections of this work have been presented extensively on different occasions as particularly at PluriCourts, the Centre of Excellence of the University of Oslo where I worked from 2013 to 2016 with A. Føllesdal and G. Ulfstein and at the Wissenschaft Zentrum zu Berlin/Humboldt University where I spent a period as a visiting fellow in 2015 with M. Kumm. Other chapters have been discussed at either European or American conferences. Among the most significant events is the workshop I co-organized at the EUI on "Global Constitutionalism without Global Democracy (?)", then, partially published in the EUI Working Paper LAW 2016/21. In 2015, I attended a workshop on Kant's Perpetual Peace organized by Asker Sørensen at Aarhus University in Copenhagen. This was an excellent opportunity to discuss Kantian issues with Asker himself, P. Niesen, and B. Milstein. Later, in 2018, I was invited as a visiting scholar to the Clough Center of the Study of Constitutional Democracy, Boston College. In Boston I had the opportunity to present my work also at U-Mass. I thank N. Eisikovits and V. Perju for the discussions on earlier drafts. Last but not the least, the whole central book section on the idea of the world republic was presented at the Venice Conference on "Republic and Republicanism. Theory and Practice" (Venice, 3–5 May 2019), as well as at the 13th International Kant Congress "The Court of Reason" (Oslo, 6–9 August 2019). The final version of the book has been submitted in part to the audience of the Colloquium in Philosophy at Columbia University, NY, where I moved as a Fulbright Scholar for the year 2019–20 as well as to Indiana University, Bloomington. I thank F. Neuhouser and W. Scheuerman for these important occasions of discussion.

Scholars with whom I have engaged in conversation on Kantian issues are far too many. They all have contributed in different ways to develop my interpretation of Kant's legal and political philosophy. With few though, I have maintained a constant intellectual engagement. My gratitude goes in particular to L. Pes,

P. Pettit, R. Maliks, M. Saul, G. Zyberi, D. Tonelli, J. Karlsson Schaffer, A. Wood, C. Lafont, P. Eleftheriadis, A. Aportone, G.W. Brown, H. Williams, G. Sadun-Bordoni and N. Sanchez Madrid, A. Stone-Sweet, M. Kumm, and G. Cesarale.

***

The following chapters have been originally published elsewhere. Nevertheless, there are fundamental revisions that I have introduced in the versions here republished. I thank the publishers for allowing the reproduction of these works. Reprints include: C. Corradetti, "Kant's Legacy and the Idea of a Transitional *Jus Cosmopoliticum*", *Ratio Juris*, 29(1), 2016, pp.105–121; C. Corradetti, "Constructivism in Cosmopolitan Law: Kant's Right to Visit", *Global Constitutionalism*, 6(3), 2017, pp.412–441; C. Corradetti, "Thinking with Kant 'beyond' Kant. Actualizing Sovereignty and Citizenship in the Transnational Sphere", A. Sørensen (ed.), *Danish Yearbook of Philosophy*, 50, 2017, pp.59–82.

Method of citation of Kant's works

All citations of Kant's works are in square brackets and follow the letter and numbering of the standard edition of *Kant's gesammelte Schrften*, published by the Royal Prussian Academy of Sciences. In the case of the *Critique of Pure Reason* [1781–7], citations follow the pagination of Kant's first [A] and second edition [B].

English title	*German title*	*Vol:Page numbers*
Of the different races of human beings	*Von den verschiedenen Rassen der Menschen*	[2:427–443]
Anthropology from a pragmatic point of view	*Anthropologie in pragmatischer Hinsicht*	[7:119–333]
An Answer to the Question: What is Enlightenment?	*Beantwortung der Frage: Was ist Aufklärung?*	[8:35–42]
Determination of the concept of a human race	*Bestimmung des Begriffs einer Menschenrasse*	[8:89–106]
Critique of Pure Reason	*Kritik der reinen Vernunft*	[A ii-A 855/B 883]
On the use of teleological principles in philosophy	*Über den Gebrauch teleologischer Prinzipien in der Phillosophie*	[8:158–184]
Groundwork of Metaphysics of Morals	*Grundlegung zur Metaphysik der Sitten*	[4:385–463]
Idea for a Universal History with a Cosmopolitan Purpose	*Idee zu einer allgemeinen Geschichte in weltbürgerlicher Absicht*	[8:17–31]
Moral Philosophy Collins	*Moralphilosophie Collins*	[27:243–471]
Metaphysics of Morals	*Die Metaphysik der Sitten*	[6:205–493]
Metaphysics of Morals	*Die Metaphysik der Sitten*	[27:479–732]
Vigilantius	*Vigilantius*	[4:255–383]
Prolegomena to any Future Metaphysics	*Prolegomena zu einer jeden künftigen Metaphysik*	[6:3–202]
Religion within the Boundaries of Mere Reason	*Die Religion innerhalb der Grenzen der blossen Vernunft*	[6:205–355]
The Doctrine of Right (first part)	*Metaphysiche Anfangsgründe der Rechtslehre*	
Reflections on the Philosophy of Rights	*Reflexionen zur Rechtsphilosophie*	[19:442–613]

English title	*German title*	*Vol:Page numbers*
The Conflict of the Faculties	*Der Streit der Fakultäten*	[7:77:94]
Preparatory Works on the Doctrine of Virtue	*Vorarbeit zur Tugendlehre*	[23:371–420]
Anthropology Busolt	*Vorlesungen Wintersemester 1788/1789 Busolt*	[25:1435–1531]
Anthropology Collins	*Wintersemester 1772/1773 Collins*	[25:7–227]
Natural Right Feyerabend	*Wintersemester 1784/5 Feyerabend*	[27:1317–1394]
Menschenkunde	*Vorlesungen Wintersemester 1781/1782 Menschenkunde, Petersburg*	[25:853–1203]
	Vorlesungen	
	Vorlesungen	
Anthropology Mrongovius	*Wintersemester 1784/1785 Mrongovius*	[25:1207–1429]
Anthropolgy Pillau	*Wintersemester 1777/1778 Pillau*	[25:733–847]
	Vorlesungen	
On the Common Saying: That may be correct in theory, but it is of no use in practice	*Über den Gemeinspruch: das mag in der Theorie richtig sein, taugt aber nicht für die Praxis*	[8:275-313]
What is Orientation in Thinking?	*Was heißt sich im Denken Orientieren?*	[8:131–148]
Toward Perpetual Peace: A Philosophical Sketch	*Zum ewigen Frieden. Ein philosophischer Entwurf*	[8:343–386]

When not indicated otherwise, English translations are from the *Cambridge Edition of the Works of Immanuel Kant*, edited by P. Guyer and A. Wood, Cambridge University Press, 1992.

Introduction

In the late 1980s at Princeton University a sign appeared on the office door of G. Harman saying: "Just say no to the history of philosophy!".[1] The paper was promptly removed a few days later but the affirmative stand prompted debate and reactions. In a blog-page, still accessible today on the Princeton web page, T. Sorell explains what happened when he asked Harman to give reasons for his act. Even though the reply was dismissive, Harman insisted firmly on two points: he signalled the danger of treating "historical texts as sacred documents [. . . thus avoiding] what Walter Kaufmann called 'exegetical thinking'",[2] and he pointed out forcefully that: "There are no perennial philosophical problems",[3] meaning that the issues debated by philosophers in the past are not the same as those we debate today.

Some forty years on, we can judge now whether a certain way of conducting historical philosophy is to be considered as something definitely dead, or, if instead it still deserves a committed intellectual engagement.

First of all, the dangers of exegetical approaches Harman pointed out cannot be considered only as typical of so-called continental philosophy. On the contrary, they are intrinsic to philosophy itself, including analytic philosophy (the approach Harman privileged as the most appropriate) which has enthroned his heroes and paradoxically prompted exegetical studies as well. This means that one can distinguish between 'good' and 'bad' philosophy as such, and not one between analytic philosophy 'as sharp philosophy' and historical philosophy as supposedly 'a fuzzy and conceptually imprecise one'.

Secondly, Harman's conviction of no perennial problems is a rather problematic statement. Certainly, it is the case that no serious philosophical debate today would be preoccupied with discussing the theory of phlogiston. Yet, this is not the same as with the case, for example, of recently renewed interests in ontology, naturalism, and so on.

1 T. Sorell, *The Eighties: a Snapshot*, available online at https://philosophy.princeton.edu/about/eighties-snapshot (accessed on 1.10.2019).

2 Ibid.

3 Ibid.

What is relevant, in all these latter cases, is that no conceptual shifts are serious if conducted in the absence of consideration of early modern, and even ancient, conceptions of ontology and metaphysics. So it seems that at least some central philosophical categories *have the ambition* of being perennial, and that this is why we go back to the history of philosophy. If we take this point to be true, then, we come to appreciate a more intimate connection between analytic and historical philosophy. It all depends on *how* we conduct research on the history of philosophy and according to which *purposes*. If past writings are read with the idea that they are in fact suggesting a provisional solution to commonly shared philosophical problems, then, the divide between analytic and historical philosophy becomes much thinner. History of philosophy comes to belong to analytic thinking, but also analytic reflection comes to pertain to historical philosophy.

The appreciation of the contribution of history of philosophy to analytical thinking is even more decisive if one sees how further layers of investigation can be added to strict philosophical conceptualizations. To give an example, when we cannot make sense of certain arguments or philosophical positions, whether they are current or belong to the past, it might be useful to have to look at the intellectual context of debate of the author. In such cases, historical philosophy could help in contributing to the 'philosophical therapy' that Wittgenstein himself – certainly not a representative of historical philosophy – assigned to speculation.

Looking to society or other non-philosophical sources of information is a way to clear the table from conceptual misgivings that sometimes affect even enlightened philosophers. In debating this issue, particularly with regard to the ideas of friendship and ethics in the ancient world, M. Frede once pointed out the fact that: "One cannot understand why Plato and Aristotle subordinate ethics to politics unless one recognizes that the relation between the individual and the political community was very different in classical Greece from what it is now and, correspondingly, that it was conceived of rather differently."[4]

Thus, we can approach the historical side of the history of philosophy in two ways: either by considering whether certain ideas and arguments are sound and can be held true today, or by observing whether they can be clarified in the light of historical-social circumstances wherein they arose. One is motivated to delve into the historical shades of a philosophical concept only if the concept is ill-grounded or if one is in need of support of external proofs that are unavailable from textual analysis.[5]

4 M. Frede, "Introduction", *Essays in Ancient Philosophy*, University of Minnesota Press, Minneapolis 1987, p.xviii.

5 Similarly, Kenny affirms that: "The link between philosophy and its history is a far closer one. The historical task itself forces historians of philosophy to paraphrase their subjects' opinions, to offer reasons why past thinkers held the opinions they did, to speculate on the premises left tacit in their arguments, and to evaluate the coherence and cogency of the inferences they drew. But the supplying of reasons for philosophical conclusions, the detection of hidden premises in philosophical arguments, and the logical evaluation of philosophical inferences are themselves full-blooded philosophical activities. Consequently, any serious history of philosophy must itself be an exercise in philosophy as well as in history." In, A. Kenny, "The

There is no doubt that the position here defending the history of philosophy bears important implications for the significance of philosophy itself and, particularly here, for the study of political philosophy in Kantian terms. If one considers the recurrence of certain questions which prominently define the quintessential nature of the philosophical enterprise, then, the study of classics – at the least – paves the way for understanding the time we live in, either because the past is persistently influencing the present, or because we are experiencing disruptively new times.

Ultimately, the question of whether philosophy should be conceived in analytical or historical terms, turns into a demand for clarification of what philosophy is as a discipline, that is, what is the conceptual status of philosophy and whether we find its historical characterization as a useful way to access its concepts.

It might be worth reflecting on whether the study of political philosophy, once framed under the terms sketched above, is something more than just a simple collection of views on practical thinking or on the proper institutional instantiations of social values. Accordingly, the interpretation of Kant that I propose goes very much in the direction of a view of political philosophy as a domain strictly dependent on fundamental metaphysical assumptions. Political philosophy is never only a reflection on mere practices, as if it were only a kind of *philosophia ultima*. By connecting political practices, laws, and even principles to the questions posed by a *philosophia prima*, as it is usually defined, metaphysics, political theory and practices are confronted with the big philosophical questions of the Being, the World, God, Freedom, the Soul. These are the puzzles Kant explicitly engages with in the *Dialectic of Reason* of the *First Critique*. I consider the solutions he provides as valuable also for his reflections on global politics and justice.

Understanding political philosophy in these more complex terms is to recognize that practical categories – the core concern of analytic philosophers – are tools placed in a web of philosophical dimensions that cannot avoid responding to fundamental questions. This is the type of mindset and philosophical concern that I attempt to reconstruct by reference to Kant's political theory of peace.

But what is peace?

Toward Perpetual Peace opens with the satirical signboard on the door of the Dutch innkeeper where peace is depicted as a graveyard of humanity. Kant questions whether peace is "only for philosophers, who dream that sweet dream",[6] and presents his *clausula salvatoria*, placing himself beyond reproach from criticism. Kant separates the practical tasks of the politician who "takes the stance of looking down [. . .] on the theoretical politician",[7] and that of the "academic who, with his ineffectual ideas, poses no danger to a state".[8] After all,

Philosopher's History and the History of Philosophy", T. Sorell and G.A.J. Rogers (eds.), *Analytic Philosophy and History of Philosophy*, 2005, p.20.

6 I. Kant, "Toward Perpetual Peace", M. Gregor (ed.), *Immanuel Kant. Practical Philosophy*, Cambridge University Press, Cambridge, 1999, 8:343, p.317.

7 Ibid.

8 Ibid.

philosophers should not overstep their role and wear the dresses of kings. Yet, were this all for philosophical reflection, how could it be possible to explain the realistic tone in which Kant constantly presented peace as a political project rather than simply as a utopia?

Peace is nothing extrinsic to the coercive scheme of justice and it represents rather "the entire final end of the doctrine of right within the limits of mere reason".[9] For Kant, property – the mine and the thine – as well as the external freedom attached to this is guaranteed only "under *laws* living in proximity to one another".[10] This requires a cosmopolitan dimension of peace. The problem, though, is that it would seem rather difficult to recognize both states' sovereignty and the subordination of their will to cosmopolitan justice. It is across such type of asymmetry that Kant formulates a sophisticated theory of global justice by distinguishing what is required by the theory and what is instead practically feasible.

There is indeed a different and more complex account that should be considered when one interprets Kant's relation between theory and practice, the ideal and the real, and finally, the political reconciliation of moral values and institutional facts. The theory-practice divide poses a deeply compelling challenge to Kant's normative theory. Differently from his immediate predecessors like Hobbes, Locke, and Rousseau, Kant believes that there must be a recognition of a minimal threshold of global justice, something he defines in terms of cosmopolitan right.

But it is at the fracture between the domestic and the international level that a paradox of sovereignty arises with regard to the autonomy of states, on the one hand, and the duties they have towards other states' entities and cosmopolitan citizens, on the other. Whereas the problem of domestic justice can count on the coercive force of a sovereign, a people and its representative institutions, the cosmopolitan affirmation of justice cannot resort to such a scheme.

Kant considers that the justification of one's exit from a natural condition by means of cosmopolitan authority implies an all-encompassing standpoint based on a grounding will establishing a system of law.

When one reconstructs the views of a thinker like Kant, it cannot be ignored the complexity and systemic interdependencies of his thought, particularly, his political tenets. In the interpretation here advanced, Kant's political theory is understood in light of his metaphysics. More specifically, it is considered Kant's 'practical turn' of metaphysics as that which he proposes for liberty understood as a regulative idea of reason. Indeed all political concepts are not only normative and institutional instantiations of the practical-metaphysical idea of freedom, but they are also to be understood in regulative terms. As discussed in the *Dialectic of Reason* of the *Critique of Pure Reason* the relation is here one between the unconditioned and the conditioned.[11] Kant's political philosophy

9 I. Kant, "The Metaphysics of Morals (1797)", M. Gregor (ed.), *Immanuel Kant. Practical Philosophy*, Cambridge University Press, Cambridge, 1999, 6:355, p.491.

10 Ibid.

11 I. Kant, *Critique of Pure Reason*, P. Guyer and A. Wood (ed. and trans.), Cambridge University Press, Cambridge, 2000 [1781–7], A338/B396, p.409 ff.

aims ultimately to reconcile nature and freedom by closing the gap between the noumenal idea of freedom and the natural deterministic chain of causation.

There are four core ideas supporting this view:

a) the idea of a world (state) republic as an idea of reason and as a regulative standard for legitimate politics.
b) the idea of a 'transitionality' of law in approaching the ideal of perpetual peace (as with the distinction between peremptory and provisional rights).
c) Kant's 'critical philosophy' as a philosophy of freedom through the definition of the relation between the theory and practice divide (here the regulative takes the form of immanent criticism, that is, of reformative politics as the only emancipatory transformation of the status quo).
d) The idea of a 'cosmopolitan constitution' as a solution for the theory/practice problem and the legitimacy of the global order (part of this overall picture is the juridical constructivist role of 'the right to visit' as a quintessential element of cosmopolitan right). More specifically, in *Toward Perpetual Peace*, he lists *three types* of constitutions attached to each of the definitive articles and generating a multilevel set of constitutional rings:

> [. . .] any rightful constitution is, with regard to the persons within it, (1) one in accord with the *right of citizens of a state,* of individuals within a people *(ius civitatis)*, (2) one in accord with the *right of nations,* of states in relation to one another *(ius gentium),* (3) one in accord with the *right of citizens of the world,* insofar as individuals and states, standing in the relation of externally affecting one another, are to be regarded as citizens of a universal state of mankind *(ius cosmopoliticum)*. This division is not made at will* but is necessary with reference to the idea of perpetual peace.
>
> (I. Kant, "Toward Perpetual Peace (1795)", 8:349, p. 322)

By assuming this framework, the quest for peace does not rely so much on whether this is a real or a fictional hope, that is, "whether we are not deceiving ourselves in our theoretical judgment when we assume that it is real".[12] Rather, as Kant affirms, peace becomes a necessary concept in order to make sense of our practical actions so that: "we must act as if it [peace] is something real, though perhaps it is not".[13]

But then the problem turns on the following question: how to proceed on the path towards peace? Here Kant seems to hold faith with the view that revolutionary breaks and changes of regimes are never a good strategy to bring about a higher level of freedoms and civil emancipation. The reason is that in all such attempts to overthrow an inadequate constitution "there would then be an intervening moment in which any rightful condition would be annihilated",[14] so that

12 I. Kant, "The Metaphysics of Morals (1797)", 6:355, p.491.
13 Ibid.
14 Ibid.

the cure, so to say, would be more damaging than the illness itself. The alternative which Kant considers in order to avoid the risks of creating a legal vacuum is to promote "gradual reform in accordance with firm principles".[15] Political reformism is the only viable way to "continual approximation to the highest political good, perpetual peace".[16]

Through all these elements, we come to understand the significance of Kantian peace in terms of a realistic utopia, that is, as an ever approximating goal which could bring us continually closer to a civil status. Here, the ever achievable end of an all-embracing peaceful condition is constantly accompanied by the spinning force of freedom as a disenfranchisement from political domination.

Such an apparently aporetical end of history is depicted in Kantian terms by the constant unsolved asymmetry of what is right 'in thesi' – as a normative ideal – from what is realizable 'in hypothesi', that is, as something practically feasible. It is at this juncture that cosmopolitan right plays its constructivist role in mediating between natural law and the positive instantiations of a global civil condition.

The outcome of the realization of such rightful condition is what Kant labels in different occasions under the idea of a "cosmopolitan constitution" (*Weltbürgerliche Verfassung*),[17] and which he assigns, according to the interpretation here defended, a quintessential structuring role for international relations and justice. Peace and the cosmopolitan constitution are co-dependent notions. The more nations proceed along republican lines – within and among themselves – the more there appears a chance to solve conflicts through the law and thus in peaceful terms. It is for this reason, therefore, that Kant can affirm that "we must work toward establishing perpetual peace and the kind of constitution that seems to us most conducive to it (say, a republicanism of all states, together and separately)".[18]

When transferred on to the institutional side, the plethora of political entities Kant envisages (as with the idea of a Congress of states, a league etc.) is reconciled with the ideal of the multistate confederation: a multistate confederation of peoples (the *Völkerstaat*) understood in regulative terms. It is 'as if' one has to consider the possibility to move from a unilateral system of appropriations of the state of nature (culminating into a plethora of political state and international alliances) that the legitimacy of the international order is made to depend on the incorporation of the standard of an omnilateral will (the general united will) to which the *Volkerstaaat/Weltrepublik* gives an institutional form. Ideas of reason are guiding concepts for political emancipation as they ground the dynamics of reformative progress. This means that the way in which regulative ideas come to be realized historically is not through peremptory force but by means of public negotiation. This is the realm of permissive rights and politics, the contingent

15 Ibid.
16 Ibid.
17 I. Kant, "Toward Perpetual Peace (1795)", 8:358, p.329.
18 I. Kant, "The Metaphysics of Morals (1797)", 6:354–5, p.491.

formulation of which Kant considers to be the proper task of a public international reason.

In the present study I introduce a new methodological approach for the interpretion of classical philosophical scholarship. One of the aims here is the overcoming of the obsolete divisions between historical reconstructive approaches and analytical – but historically insensitive – interpretations, as mentioned more generally in the opening sections. The suggestion is to proceed with an integrated approach, one starting from textual analysis but resorting to the appeal of the historical debate of the time whenever it is impossible to find enough textual support for a conceptual hypotheses. With regard to textual interpretation, the idea has been defended of a coherent unity between Kant's writing on *Toward Perpetual Peace* (1795) and the section on the *Doctrine of Right* of the *Metaphysics of Morals* (1797). This is not a novel standpoint in Kantian scholarship and is in line with other interpretations.[19] Yet, here, the reading is one based on the persistent relevance – in both writings – of the idea of a cosmopolitan general will whose antecedent is to be found ultimately in Diderot rather than in Rousseau.

This book opens with a reconstruction of the fundamental political paradigm-shift that has accompanied the entrance into modernity. I start from the idea of universal monarchy – represented in antiquity and medieval times by the Roman emperor, first, and by the pope next – moving then to the debate over the Indios by the Salamancan school. It is in this context of discussion that there appears, for the first time in the history of political thought, the notion of a subject of rights as the ultimate level of justification of the law. It is also in this context that concepts arise that become fundamental in Kant's political thought. These include de Vitoria's discussion of 'the right to travel' (*ius peregrinandi*), 'the right to communicate' (*ius communicationis*) as well as a long lasting discussion on the principles justifying war and territorial acquisition. I conclude this first part by reconstructing the tradition of international pacifism and its influence on Kant's cosmopolitan theory. In particular, I suggest the view that Kant maintains a critical stand towards Rousseau's idea of the general will and that he is rather more keen to interpret it along the lines of Diderot's. This explains the cosmopolitan turn of Kant's general will.

In the second part of the book, I discuss the right to international warfare and colonization as they unfold in the XVII and XVIII century. Kant, who opposed both the idea of a 'just war theory' as well as of a legitimate claim to colonization labels the defenders of such views as only "sorry comforters"[20] (*leidige Tröster*).

19 See O. Eberl and P. Niesen, "Kommentar", O. Eberl and P. Niesen (eds.), *Immanuel Kant, Zum ewigen Frieden und Auszüge aus der Rechtslehre*, 2011, pp. 89–416, in particular pp.100–4 and pp.125–266. H. Williams has defended the thesis that the *Doctrine of Right* may have been drafted before the publishing of *Toward Perpetual Peace*. This would confirm the conceptual hypothesis here defended of an overall unity of Kant's political theory. See H. Williams, *Kant and the End of War: A Critique of Just War Theory*, 2012, pp 52–54.

20 I. Kant, "Toward Perpetual Peace (1795)", 8:355, p.326.

Grotius, Pufendorf, and Vattel are just consolatory intellectuals since they do not foresee a system of legitimate coercion progressing towards peace.

It is curious, though, that among these people Kant does not include Wolff. This exception has motivated my investigation on Wolff's idea of the *civitas maxima* and on its influence on Kant's notion of *civitas gentium*.

The third and fourth part of the book presents the core philosophical innovation introduced by Kant through a reinterpretation of classical metaphysics and its impact on the definition of global justice and cosmopolitan law.

The key idea concerns Kant's interpretation of the world (state) republic in terms of an idea of reason, in analogy to the metaphysical ideas of reasons discussed in the *First Critique*. To this end, I explain what are for Kant the ideas of reason. The view I defend emphasizes Kant's practical turn to inherited metaphysics. Accordingly, I develop the view that Kant's political thought is deeply informed by a link between the regulative role of freedom and the regulative role of the world (state) republic seen as its institutional instantiation. In particular, Kant reinterprets the theoretical concept of freedom by transforming it into a regulative idea of reason.

Since, as part of the core interpretive thesis defended here, the legal and political consequences of Kant's metaphysical turn are of capital interest, I proceed next to the investigation of what appears as the conceptually very promising distinction between provisional and peremptory rights.

Kant's juridical reasoning is developed more extensively throughout the fourth part of the book. Here I engage more closely into the investigation of the significance of cosmopolitan thinking along 'transitional' lines of interpretation. Understanding such rationale involves providing a view of the critical relation between natural right – of which the cosmopolitan right to visit is a quintessential component – and the constitutionalization of interstate relations. At this juncture it becomes possible to find a solution to Kant's asymmetry between a domestic republican sovereign state and an international constitutional dimension protected by adjudicatory mechanisms.

The final part also applies the contemporary debate to a world constitution as recently proposed by the Habermasian theses on the idea of double sovereignties within an international domestic politics. The relevance of Kantian thought for the contemporary debate on the EU and the legitimacy of international law is beyond doubt. Therefore, further lines of investigation on contemporary cosmopolitanism should take stock of Kant's theory.

The work published here has benefited from exposure to several international research groups and discussions. The early methodological phase of elaboration, although not directly related to Kant, dates back to the time when I was an undergraduate student at the University of Oxford. After nearly twenty-five years, I now see the results of this study time come to fruition. I express a sincere recognition to my former supervisor Professor Michael Frede, Chair in History of Philosophy. He adopted a clearly Socratic method of education in philosophical training. The memory is still vivid of how privileged I felt when we met at Café

Rouge spending long hours discussing Aristotle's theory of language. From such discussions I have learned a lot about reading the classics.

The writing of books takes several phases sometimes of acceleration and sometimes of dead ends. In this case, the most important sections and almost half of the book have been written within nine months. This has been just the time my first son, Carlo, came to life. Nature again showed itself to be such a "great artist (*natura daedala rerum*)"[21] to which humans can never equate.

This book is dedicated to him.

21 I. Kant, "Toward Perpetual Peace (1795)", 8:360, p.331.

Part 1

Kant and the legacy of modernity

§1 From universal monarchy to global authority

Global authority as a concept is a prismatic notion reflecting at times different historical, contextual, and political-ideological conceptions of power and the world. It is a notion which can be dated back to Alexander the Great and to his historical enterprise. Aristotle in his letter to Alexander speaks of a "day when men will agree to constitute one rule and kingdom. [A day when] They will cease from wars and strife [. . .]".[1] No matter whether the writing is apocryphal or not, the idea there expressed is compatible both with the unique capacity of the Greeks to rule the world and with the maintenance of the autonomy of the city states under one ruler. Furthermore, the idea of the unity of the human being was not unknown at the time of Aristotle. Indeed, it was certainly expressed by Sophocles,[2] but, perhaps even more significantly, it arose as a notion only as a result of the awareness of uniformity – even if not yet of unity – of human mankind already according to the Homeric tradition.[3]

In the following sections I propose a research hypothesis considering how the notion of world authority underwent across time different transformations shaping the definition of the legitimacy conditions of natural law as well as of the idea of a modern *ius gentium*. To anticipate the most relevant steps: if, in the classical age, the Greek man of the *polis* arose out of the universal measure of authority reaching an apex with the first cosmopolitan leader – Alexander the Great – it was with the Roman Emperors that the *logos* of the Stoics turned into a proper universal political authority, then shifting into the spiritual *urbis et orbis* authority of the Popes.

Modernity began, on the one hand, from the intersection between the eschatological personification of Christ on Earth leads and the recognition of a metaphysical equality of humankind (where men are seen as sons of the same God). Right after Columbus' discovery of America, as soon as the Second Scholastics attempted to answer to the crisis of conscience of the Spanish crown and of

1 The long version of the letter is reproduced and discussed in S.M. Stern, *Aristotle on the World State*, Cassirer, Oxford, 1968, pp.7 ff.

2 See Stern, *Aristotle on the World State*, p.40.

3 H.C. Baldry, *The Unity of Mankind in Greek Thought*, Cambridge University Press, Cambridge, 1965, p.8.

Europe at large, the most important outcome consisted in moving beyond a conception of human equality (understood in merely metaphysical terms) and framing such a concept along a moral and political dimension. Francisco de Vitoria's idea of the dignity of the Indios as equal human beings resisted the prejudice that they lacked the knowledge of the word of Christ. The totality of all the visitable world became apparent.[4] Yet, if the world became smaller, the conceptual realm, including the moral one, became universal.[5] It does not come as a surprise, then, that with Kant the recognition of a full equal standing for all human beings was understood on moral and juridical terms. In Kant, indeed, the unity of humankind was with no exceptions based on substantive and unmodifiable prerequisites going beyond the individual moral will.

Yet, in the archaic times of Greece, the unity of mankind was still conceived in epic narratives, only in terms of an allegiance to one standard of human sameness. Deviating from such a standard was to be a non-human, as the Cyclops were considered.[6] This "biological approach"[7] for the definition of humanity as a homogeneous whole was followed quickly by Heraclitus' idea of a common *logos* as a principle of rationality in virtue of which human beings were considered as part of one and the same family.[8] This concept unfolded further along the fifth and fourth century BC until it became, with Protagoras, the idea of shared norms and then, in Socrates, the idea of a "good life".[9] It followed with Plato and Aristotle that a separation between the Greeks and the barbarians was matched to a territorial division between the inner and the outer *polis*. It followed that slavery was considered an institution in accord with nature, so that no contrary position was expressed against it.[10]

It was only with the Cynics that an idea of cosmopolitanism as universal citizenship appeared. The *kosmopolitēs* was not yet the contemporary cosmopolitan citizen linked to humankind in virtue of brotherhood or world state membership. He was, instead, someone enjoying a status of membership of the universe.[11] Whereas the Cynics did not look for any political and social transformation in the direction of a cosmopolitan political entity, limiting their principles only to individuals, Peripatetics such as Theophrastus conceived of a natural resemblance of humankind in ways that are different from the hyper-individualism of the Epicureans for whom there was no society.[12] It was only with the Stoics that the idea

4 As Schmitt defines the link between law and the earth: "the earth is bound to law in three ways. She contains law within herself, as a reward of labor; she manifests law upon herself, as fixed boundaries; and she sustains law above herself, as a public sign of order. Law is bound to the earth and related to the earth", C. Schmitt, *The Nomos of the Earth*, 2006, p.42.

5 On this crucial point and more in general on the encounter with the other see T. Todorov, *The Conquest of America. The Encounter with the Other*, Harper & Row, New York, 1984.

6 Baldry, *The Unity of Mankind in Greek Thought*, p.10.

7 Ibid., p.25.

8 Ibid., p.26.

9 See, respectively, Baldry, *The Unity of Mankind in Greek Thought*, p.43 ff. and p.53.

10 Ibid., p.85 and particularly p.87 ff.

11 Ibid., p.108.

12 Ibid., p.147.

of a unity among fellow human beings gained significant momentum as with the idea of universal rationality/*logos* inscribed in each human being.[13] The whole of humankind became inscribed into one single rational order commonly shared.

A division between a 'civilized inside' and an 'unregulated outside' reappeared with the decline of the Roman *imperium* and the resurgence of a *limes*, a physically excluding political boundary. The juridical space of the *romanitas* was thus about to be transformed into an empire with no limits.[14] The *imperium* was radically opposed to something totally external and inimical to itself, namely, to barbarianism. If within the ancient Greek *polis* the foreigner could also be seen as a subject *internal* to the city walls (*xenos*), for Rome only the *barbaroi* were the non-recognizable alien subjects.[15] In the Roman empire, thus, the political order was interiorized within a form which aimed to be universal and all-inclusive. Since the empire contained nothing outside itself threatening its own identity, all it could admit externally was only the idea of an *ordo barbaricum*, a 'disorderly arranged order' with no real power or sovereignty.

The *imperium* was the only political ideal capable of assuring an international peaceful condition, the so-called *pax romana*. From the merely contemplative views of the Stoics there followed a political instantiation of the cosmopolitan ideals.

Epictetus and the emperor Marcus Aurelius were the last Stoics to testify to an hyperrationalist contemplative vision. For Marcus Aurelius there was only one single law keeping together the cosmos: the law of reason.[16] In such law was inscribed the metaphor of the cosmos and the city.[17] Marcus Aurelius incorporated

13 For a detailed analysis if this phase, see Baldry, *The Unity of Mankind in Greek Thought*, p.151.

14 An "*imperium sine fine*", in L.Scuccimarra, *I confini del mondo. Storia del Cosmopolitismo dall'Antichità al Settecento*, Il Mulino, Bologna, 2006, p.83.

15 On these points see D. Heater, *World Citizenship and Government. Cosmopolitan Ideas in the History of Western Political Thought*, Palgrave Macmillan, London, 1996, pp.1–26 and Baldry, *The Unity of Mankind in Greek Thought*.

16 "There is one substance, one law, and one reason common to all intelligent beings, and one truth; as there must be one sort of perfection to all beings, who are of the same nature, and partake of the same rational power", Marcus Aurelius, *The Meditations of the Emperor Marcus Aurelius Antoninus*, M. Silverthorne and J. Moore (eds.), F. Hutcheson and J. Moor (trans.), VII, 9, Liberty Fund, Indianapolis, 2008 [II AC], p.84.

17 "The intellectual part is the same to all rationals and therefore that reason also, whence we are called rational, is common to all. If so, then, that commanding power, which shews what should be done or not done, is common. If so, we have all a common law. If so, we are all fellow-citizens: and if so, we have a common city. The universe, then, must be that city; for of what other common city are all men citizens? Hence, therefore, even from this common city, we derive our intellectual power, our reason, our law; as my earthly part is derived to me from some common earth, my moisture from some common element of that kind, my aerial part from its proper fountain, and the warm or fiery part from its proper fountain too. For, nothing can arise from nothing, or return into it. Our intellectual part hath also come from some common fountain of its own nature", Marcus Aurelius, *The Meditations of the Emperor Marcus Aurelius Antoninus*, 2008 [II AC], pp.48–49.

a non-mediated union between his identity as emperor and as a Roman citizen.[18] Yet, such immediate unity was considered to be realizable only within the boundaries of the *romanitas*, that is, only within the geographical and political limits of the empire and according to the scheme of a rationality conceived in accordance with nature. Thus, it was not a case of administering the empire according to a stoic cosmopolitan ideal, but contrariwise, it was the case of living the inspirational drives of the *civitas* in accordance with a cosmopolitan order becoming history and power. From such a political conception it appeared already clear that the spinning force of the empire had lost its momentum, transforming itself into an individual action compliant to a standard of rationality.

The apex of the dichotomy between the universal *civitas* of the empire and the cosmopolitan ideals was then reached during Caracalla's edict of the *Constitutio Antoniniana* of 212 AC where citizenship was extended to all residents of the Roman empire with the sole exception of the *dediticii*. The cosmopolitan ideal of peace and unity of the human race was considered to coincide with Roman imperial power.[19]

Yet, with the end of the empire, world citizenship was soon transformed into Christian earthly citizenship. The individual became a member of the universal Christian *cosmopolis*.[20] Also the Pauline notion of a Church (*ecclesia*), in such respect, did not absorb political people within a supraordinate political collectivity. On the contrary, the Pauline ecclesia was without autonomy. The ecclesia, therefore, could realize the much welcomed unity only in a mystic form, that is, through the consideration of its own affiliates as followers in the faith in Christ.[21] The outcome of the theological transfiguration of the earthly *polis* led to the celestial realization of the cosmopolitan ideal.[22]

Augustine formalized then such duality of Christian affiliation, the terrestrial and the celestial city in the *De Civitate Dei* (*City of God*),[23] the place where the affiliation of those who believe in a Christian eschatology that goes behind the

18 "My natural constitution is that of a rational being, fitted for civil society. My city and country, as I am Antoninus, is Rome; but, as I am a man, 'tis the universe", in Marcus Aurelius, *Meditations of Marcus Aurelius*, p.80.

19 The *dediticii* were considered a class of human beings who did not lose their freedom but 'surrendered unconditionally' (*deditio*) to the Roman empire and therefore could not be entitled to universal citizenship. They were neither former Roman citizens nor slaves nor Latins but politically subjugated subjects of the Roman empire. On the definition of the civil status of the *dediticii* see O. Hekster, *Rome and Its Empire, AD 193–284*, Edinburgh University Press, Edinburgh, 2008, p. 47.

20 "One state we know, of which all are citizens – the universe [Unam omnium rempublicam agnoscimus mundum]", Tertullian, *Apology* and *De Spectaculis*, T.R.Glover trans., Loeb Classical Library, n.250, Harvard University Press, Cambridge, Mass., 1931, XXXVIII, 3, pp.172–173.

21 Paul, *Paul's Letter to the Philippians*, D. Gordon (ed.), Eerdmans Publishing, Grand Rapids, Mich., 1995.

22 As Scuccimarra has aptly synthesized, rather than cosmopolitans, Christians became "uranopolitans citizens of the celestial kingdom", Scuccimarra, *I confini del mondo*, note 32, p.102.

23 Augustine of Hippo, *City of God*, 2004.

terrestrial world is realized. The bishop of Hippo formalized also the theme of double citizenship as according to the earthly and celestial one. In the first one, all Christians were considered citizens, whereas in the second one, only a form of universalism without citizenship could be conceived.[24] Thus, the Christian subject was left in the condition of being a *peregrinus* on earth. Never considered as a proper citizen politically, Christians awaited indefinitely to find their own place on Earth and, in parallel, their own citizenship in the celestial kingdom. The universal Christian society envisaged by Augustine was meant to manifest itself at the end of all times. Yet, the *vita activa* of the followers imposed the idea that a terrestrial union was to be achieved among all those identifying themselves in the figure of Jesus Christ. The ultimate celestial union required a political-theological union – the *ecclesia christianorum* – a transitional entity in view of the afterlife peace. Terrestrial peace, differently from the *pax romana*, became instrumental to the reach of the true peace at the end of times, namely, with the advent of the celestial kingdom. The sacralization of the Roman empire nullified the territorial *limes* (boundary) of the *imperium* and its expanding character while domesticating the *xenos* as a 'domestic foreigner' – a subject of faith and thus worth of living in the *Res Publica Christiana*. The Church of Rome transfigured the political and territorial limit of the empire into the unification of the affiliation of humankind through Christ under which it became the only republic for all Christians.[25]

Nevertheless, the apparent horizontality of cosmopolitan citizenship in the *Res Publica Christiana* stood in a relation of subordination to a transcendent God revealed through Christ. It was only with the transferring of such a relation into what was, according to the theological doctrine the representative of Christ on earth – the Pope – that cosmopolitan citizenship was transformed into a true form of political-religious power identified in the terrestrial possibility of a universal Christian state.

With Constantine and the birth of the Byzantine empire, the emperor gained the salvific role on the world in accordance with a Christian ideal: the "*autokrator* assigned to the government of the 'world' as if it were God in person".[26] This one, in so far as he assumed the task of reunifying all peoples through the faith, became the "*kosmokrator*",[27] a ruler of the world under one single faith. The *sacrum imperium*, according to the Roman jurists commenting on the *Digest*, was kept united by the *dominus mundi*. But already starting from the comments to the *Decretum Gratianii*[28] there appeared the idea of a pretended universal *dominium* by the imperial power. It was not surprising therefore that already Pope Nicholas asked that the Popes were considered princes *urbis et orbis*.[29] With

24 Scuccimarra, *I confini del mondo*, p.109.
25 Scuccimarra, *I confini del mondo*, p.114.
26 Scuccimarra, *I confini del mondo*, p.117. My translation.
27 Ibid.
28 Gratianus, *Decretum Gratianii*, Bayerische StaatsBibliothek [1142]. Available online at http://geschichte.digitale-sammlungen.de/decretum-gratiani/online/angebot (accessed on 28.06.2018).
29 Scuccimarra, *I confini del mondo*, note 96, p.120.

Innocent IV, then, such universalist recognition of the monarchical-papal power was finally formalized. As a result, it opened a competitive dichotomy between the *sacerdotium* and the *imperium* with reference to a political domain, namely, who was entitled to govern the world. Both the *sacerdotium* and the *imperium* assumed the role of universal authorities, arriving therefore at the level of realization of a Christian global society which remained, notwithstanding, in competition with the secular power of the kings. It is in such a late medieval phase of the thirteenth and fourteenth century that took shape the idea of a universal monarchy contended between the pope and the emperor.[30]

When in this phase reference is made to universal *dominium* and to the *Res Publica Christiana*, in reality it indicates solely Europe, that is, the geopolitical area considered as the only civilized one. Both the papacy and the empire re-established within the European *limes* the boundary of the universality of the *Christianitas* as having the Church of Rome as its absolute regent.[31]

Innocent III spoke of *terrae christianorum*, a concept that for the fathers of the Church like Augustine could have never been assimilated to the notion of *possession*, if not for the realization of the kingdom of Cain.[32] With Innocent IV, next, in the turning phase of the second millennium, the idea of a *monarchia universalis* finally appeared. Even if not yet a fully formed political project, universal monarchy was certainly conceived as a legitimate entity, something grounded upon the pontifical ideology of the universal church. Yet, the geopolitical translation of Christian universalism transformed itself into a conquering force, pushing away and assimilating to itself the pagan world through subordination and transformation of newly occupied territories. Yet, to a pyramidal model, there was opposed the view of a horizontal-federative arrangement, a league of all Christian states united under the aim of maintaining peace. Dubois anticipated the idea of instituting an International Court of Arbitration with the aim of solving the controversies among the states and the Pope who maintained the role of ultimate arbiter as a guarantor of the *Pax Christiana*.[33]

This partially real and partially imaginary world of mutually checking powers entered into crises with Columbus' discovery of American territories in 1492.[34]

30 I will expand on this point later with reference to Dante's theory. For a general overview on this topic see F. Bosbach, *Monarchia Universalis. Ein politischer Leitbegriff der frühen Neuzeit*, vol. 32, Schriftenreihe der Historischen Kommission bei der Bayerischen Akademie der Wissenschaften, Vandenhoeck & Ruprecht Gm.,1997.

31 On the idea of the Schmittian *katéchon* opposing power to anomy and as the only political model applicable to this phase see M. Cacciari, *Geofilosofia dell'Europa*, Adelphi, Milan, 1994, p.117.

32 Scuccimarra, *I confini del mondo*, note 110, p.124.

33 On the presentation of early proposals of an international court of arbitration see T.W. Balch, *The Proposed International Tribunal of Arbitration of 1623*, 1907, pp.302–311. Available online at https://archive.org/stream/jstor-983742/983742_djvu.txt

34 On this crucial shift in the conception of universal authority see J.B. Scott, *The Catholic Conception of International Law*, 2007, 5 ff.

Columbus was indeed both an ethically controversial figure as well as a fascinating one. Moved more by a spirit of 'Christianization' of indigenous people rather than by acquisition of gold, he held an ambiguous attitude towards the Indios. He was the one to introduce the institution of the *encomienda* in Hispaniola in 1499 where the Indios were provided with housing, protection and a small salary in exchange for their work.[35] Columbus' notes and letters testify to his initial appreciation of the new encounters, defined as good people; but this attitude soon turned into a feeling of contempt and labelling of inferiority. Christian equality was thus substituted by an internal division and discrimination between those Indios who could be converted to Christianity and those who were ineradicably savage and to be used only as slaves. This opened a profound moral and intellectual crisis within the most advanced society of that time, to the extent that as early as 1495, Isabel I Queen of Castile stopped a sale of slaves sent by Columbus to Seville "because we wish to be informed by civil lawyers, canonists and theologians whether we may, with a good conscience, sell these Indians or not",[36] as reported by Chacón y Calvo in his *Cedulario Cubano.*

Columbus failed to recognize the subjectivity of the Indios. This failure, together with the political attitude that it inspired, was at the root of understanding the contradiction between the genocidal approach of the *conquistadores* in the American lands and the colonialist, but not 'enslavist' attitude of the Spanish crown and the Papacy. Whereas the first approach was responsible for the largest holocaust in history, the second one, in defending assimilation, led to colonialism.[37] The debate over the legitimacy of the conquest of America by the Spaniards, something conducted through the submission and extermination of the Indios, prompted a long-lasting legal and philosophical debate which reframed the paradigms of law, authority, and justice. As a result of such an epochal event, the conception of the unity of the world was reconceived together with a reconceptualization of the normative world of antiquity.

The discovery of America in 1492 began therefore with the widest planning in scale of genocide.[38] It was only after a crisis of conscience in the Spanish crown

35 A. Pagden, *The Fall of Natural Man. The American Indian and the origins of comparative ethnology*, Cambridge University Press, Cambridge, 1990, p.34.

36 Pagden, *Fall of Natural Man*, p.31.

37 On the reconstruction of Columbus' complex attitude towards native Americans and on the consequences that this ambivalence had on later colonialism see Todorov, *The Conquest of America*, pp.14–50.

38 On this point, Stannard observes with regard to the thesis of a holocaust after Columbus' arrival: "Just twenty-one years after Columbus's first landing in the Caribbean, the vastly populous island that the explorer had re-named Hispaniola was effectively desolate; nearly 8,000,000 people – those Columbus chose to call Indians – had been killed by violence, disease, and despair. It took a little longer, about the span of a single human generation, but what happened on Hispaniola was the equivalent of more than fifty Hiroshimas and Hispaniola was only the beginning". In D. Stannard, *American Holocaust. The Conquest of the New World*, Oxford University Press, New York, 1992, p.x. See also B. Madley, "Reexamining

and a long-lasting debate by Spanish theologians, lawyers, and intellectuals that a paradigm-shift occurred in the conception of law, authority, and justice. A Copernican revolution of sorts, which shook the moral-legal unity of the ancient Roman world. The up-to-then undivided confidence in a *civitas romana* together with its direct successor, the Christian papacy separating an internal reign of law, faith and justice, on the one hand, and an external anarchical chaos as a space of uncivilized barbarians, on the other hand, underwent an identity crisis. At the intersection of such epochal fractures, something like telluric moments in the formation of new orders, appeared the idea of a universal human being as the ultimate source of right among nations. History turned an epochal page. If 12 October 1492 was not the date of a 'discovery' in the proper sense, it was certainly the date of a conquest. This was reinforced by the two papal bulls *Inter cetera* which were proclaimed soon after the return of Columbus on 3 and 4 May 1493 by pope Alexander VI. In such bulls, the pope revised a treaty between Spain and Portugal conferring on the first a domain over the Atlantic islands together with their inhabitants. Upon the insurgence of Portugal, the two countries signed the Treaty of Tordesillas in 1494 which regulated the mutual spheres of control on the base of the meridian "la raya" near Cape Verde: the west lands to Spain, the east lands to Portugal.[39]

Shortly after the arrival in America, the Spaniards established the domestic practice of the *encomienda*. This consisted in concessions of portions of territory or cities to noteworthy people. The colonization of American territories had begun: Hernán Cortés conquered the reign of the Aztecs during the years 1519–1521, Francisco Pizarro subjugated the Incas from 1532 onwards and other *conquistadores* yet further territories including today's Florida, Panama, and more.

New unilateral provisions were introduced to give an appearance of legitimacy to the action of occupation and conquest. The Burgos injunctions (1512) included the so-called *requerimiento* (request) a document consisting in the notification to the Indios of the confiscation of their lands by the Castilian crown.[40]

---

the American Genocide Debate: Meaning, Historiography and New Methods", *American Historical Review*, 120(1), 2015, pp.98–139.

39 On the strict interconnection between law and either pre-modern or modern geographical representation of the Earth, see C. Schmitt: "For centuries, humanity had a mythical image of the earth, but no scientific understanding of it as a whole. There was no concept of a planet, of human compass and orientation common to all peoples. In this sense, there was no global consciousness and thus no political goal oriented to a common hope. Thus, a *jus gentium* [international law] capable of encompassing the whole earth and all humanity was impossible. If one speaks of a *jus gentium* in this age, it is only in terms of differing spatial structures, but not in terms of what later, after the emergence of planetary and global concepts, was called the law of nations, *jus gentium*, or international law." In Schmitt, *Nomos of the Earth*, p.50.

40 Todorov provides us with historical and interpretive views on this practice. He mentions, among others, the sarcastic comments made by de Las Casas. The *requerimiento* was intended as a public reading addressed to the Indios to legitimize the conquest of their territories. It was introduced in 1514 by the jurist Palacios Rubios and started with a short history of humanity culminating into the figure of Christ as a supreme sovereign of humanity. From

It was on this occasion that a first debate over the Indios took place, with regard to the discussion of whether they had to be considered as free men or as natural slaves. King Ferdinand asked his two lawyers, Juan López de Palacios Rubios and Matías de Paz, to express their views on the matter.[41] The result was surprising. In the *Libellus de insulanis oceanis*, one of the first documents we have assessing the merits of the American conquest, Palacios Rubios justified authority and enslavement of the Indios on the basis of their natural inferiority.[42] Or, more precisely, it was argued that while the Indios were free men before the Spanish conquerors arrived, they lost their independence with the encounter with "natural masters".[43]

The Spanish crown tried to limit the violence of the *capitanes* by establishing the Council of Indies in 1523 and the captains were required to be accompanied by two priests during their expeditions and assume moral responsibility for the actions against the Indios.

Starting from such conservative premises, a new progressive paradigm of law arose with the recognition of equality among fellow human beings matched by the idea of a global universal authority. Following the ethical and juridical issues raised with the Spanish conquest of the New World and with the instauration of the regime of the *encomiendas*, the clerics spread in the American territory began to testify to the atrocities of the *conquistadores*, raising fundamental issues of an ethical-juridical nature. It was in particular with the School of Salamanca, a representative movement of the philosophical interests raised by the Second Scholastics, that were formulated the first theological-philosophical theses on whether Spaniards had a legitimate title to the occupancy of the American territory, or whether this had rather to be considered an instance of just war (*bellum iustum*) based on a legitimate title to *dominium*.

§1.1 The debate over the Indios and the School of Salamanca

The first strategies of justification for the occupancy of the American territory considered that the land and its product fell under the category of *res nullius* and thus required only approval by the Spaniards following the legitimation conferred by the universal authority, as a monarch, of the Pope. This was the justification brought forth by Columbus and based on the idea that the discovered lands did not belong to anyone. Accordingly, the Indios were not recognized to have any legitimate title of possession. Or, admittedly, even if they had acquired them following the arrival of the *conquistadores* and the announcement of the word of Christ, they had then lost them. In the thirteenth century, Alanus Anglicus

Christ then the power was passed over to Saint Peter and next to the Popes until the Spanish Crown. See T. Todorov, *Conquest of America*, p.146 ff.

41 Pagden, *The Fall of Natural Man*, p.50.

42 Ibid., p.51.

43 Ibid., p.55.

had defended the doctrine according to which the legitimate administration of the temporal possessions depended upon the condition of grace of the cleric and that only Christians could be the true possessors of earthly goods as the only legitimate descendants of Christ under the Church of Rome. Such a doctrine was proposed again also by Henry of Susa (*Hostiensis*), who considered that the infidels were incapable of any domain on things and that such prerogative was thus recognized to them only in virtue of ecclesiastic concession – *ex tolerantia ecclesiae* – in order to avoid conversion being used only in order to maintain one's own goods.[44] It happened that in Constance those same colonizing positions, more recently advanced by Wyclif, were prohibited.[45] Yet, the appeal to the *requerimiento* helped the first *conquistadores* to shield themselves from the possible charge of violating the decisions adopted in Constance. Even whenever it was possible for the Indios to recognize a possession of the goods in their territory, this was no longer sufficient to guarantee a title of legitimate jurisdiction on such territory upon the arrival of the Spaniards. This was because the political power and thus the *iurisdictio* could be conferred only by the religious power of Christianity, the Pope.

Yet, the brutality with which the Indios were treated prompted the reaction, first, of the missionaries and, then, of the Castillian crown as well as of the papacy. A famous episode was the speech that Antonio de Montesinos gave at Hispaniola to the Spanish occupants warning that their sinful behaviour towards the locals would put them out of salvation together with the infidels.[46]

The dispute over the Indios testified also to a deeper conceptualization for a new foundation of Christianity following the Lutheran reformation as a result of the 95 theses of 1517. In such a context was proclaimed the papal bull *Veritas ipsa* of 1537 (named also *Sublimis Deus*), published in 1539, the same year as when de Vitoria wrote the first part of the *De Indis*, in which Paulus III openly opposed the enslavement of the Indios considering them as "true men" (*veros homines*)[47] and thus capable not only of understanding the message of the Christian faith but also capable of exercising their own liberty and a possession over things.

The official position undertaken by the Pope was favoured by the philosophical speculations of some of the representatives of the School of Salamanca. Indeed, Domingo de Soto in his *Relectio de Dominio* delivered in the spring of 1535

44 L. Milazzo, *La teoria dei diritti di Francisco de Vitoria*, Edizioni ETS, Pisa, 2012, pp.65–66.

45 J. Muldoon, *J.Wyclif and the Rights of the Infidels: The Requerimiento Re-Examined*, The Americas, 36(3), 1980, pp.301–316.

46 Pagden, *The Fall of Natural Man*, p.30.

47 As stated in the papal bull: "the Indios, who are true humans, are not only capable of receiving the Christian faith but even more, from what We have seen, come rapidly to embrace this faith [. . .] We decide and declare [. . .] that the said Indians and all other peoples whom Christians might come to know, even if they live outside the faith, can freely and legitimately use, possess and enjoy freedom and the ownership of their goods, and shall not be enslaved", Paulus III, *Veritas Ipsa*, Secret Vatican Archive, Arm.XXXVII, 15 f.145rv, *America Pontificia. Primi saeculi evangelizationis 1493-1592. Documenta Pontificia ex registris et minutis praesertim in Archivio secreto Vaticano existentibus, collegit, edidit* J. Metzler, Libreria Editrice Vaticana, Città del Vaticano, vol.1 (2 vols.), n.84, 1991, pp.364–366.

answered the question of whether it was just that a man became the lord of another man.[48] De Soto distinguished between private and public domain. With regard to the first, namely, to the possibility of appropriating something for personal use, this was admitted only for reasons of natural occurrence, that is, either as the result of a war of punishment or as a voluntary sale of one's liberty or, finally, as a voluntary enslavement. In all cases, liberty remained safeguarded. From such distinction de Soto drew one of the most important conceptual transformations of the time operated by the School of Salamanca: the refusal of Aristotle's conception of natural slavery.

With regard to the public domain, instead, namely to jurisdictional power, de Soto asked whether the emperor was to be considered as the lord of all world. To this question he gave a negative answer. The imperial title was not considered as a sufficient title to the *urbis et orbis dominium*, namely, to the jurisdictional pretence on the world. Thus, "the emperor does not hold any right nor a *dominium* on the lands of the infidels, if not on those that were previously ours [. . .]".[49] Similarly inspired was the reflection of the Dominican scholar Francisco de Vitoria in his *Relectiones de Indis* (respectively, *prior* and *posterior*, the latter known also as *On the Law of War*), his reflections on the illegitimacy of the expropriations of the goods of the Indios, and the limitation of the reasons to support the just war theory.

Indeed, as soon as the legitimacy of territorial possession ceased to be a received attribute from the Pope, it opened the reflection on the reasons for the just war. According to Francisco de Vitoria, the Pope did not have any *auctoritas universalis*, that is, he could not legitimize the Spanish conquest nor could he assign the territories. To this respect, de Vitoria in the *Relectio de Indis Posterior*, *On the Law of War* [1539] established that the just war theory amounted to defining a relation of violation of a right (*iniuria*). De Vitoria asked: what justifies the right of the Spaniards to subjugate the Indios? Which power has the Spanish Royal crown over the Indios in temporal and civil matters? And, more generally, which are the legitimate titles to the conquest? Which are instead the illegitimate ones?

In the first part of the *Relectio*, de Vitoria answered positively to the question of whether the Indios had a title to dominate their own lands before the arrival of the Spaniards, namely, whether such a title did not cease to be valid, either because they were sinners, or because they were non-believers, irrational or whatever. De Vitoria listed those illegitimate titles that have instead justified historically the assignment of the American lands to the Spaniards. He excluded the possibility of justifying the possession of American lands on the base of either a right of discovery, a "*ius inventionis*", which was what Columbus had claimed originally as a justification of territorial occupancy and exploitation, or because of the refusal by the Indios to accept the faith in Christ notwithstanding the Bible had been preached to them, or again, that war was to be considered just in virtue

48 See D. de Soto, "Relecci6n «de dominio»", J. Brufau Prats (ed.), Editorial San Esteban, Salamanca 1955 [1535].

49 De Soto, "Relecci6n «de dominio»", J. Brufau Prats (ed.), *Relecciones y opúsculos*, vol. 1, Editorial San Esteban, Salamanca 1955, [1535], p.156.

of the sins committed by the barbarians. Finally, the idea was also rejected that the Indios, by receiving the Spaniards sent by the Castilian crown, had with that accepted to their dominion over their lands, not to mention the idea that the Spaniards had received the American lands as a special gift from God.

According to de Vitoria, the reasons excluding the legitimacy of Spanish conquest started from the right to natural society and to free circulation (*ius naturalis societatis et communicationis*) in reference of which was derived the right to migration (*ius peregrinandi*) and the right to commercial exchange (*ius commercii*).[50]

First, de Vitoria held that there was a natural society of Republics (*Republicae*) that formed the *communitas orbis* and that was regulated by the *ius gentium*.[51] The society of states was the subject of an international right of peoples where republics and their princes were bound to deliver the good to their citizens.[52] The ultimate subjects of the universal society of republics, though, were not states but rather humanity as a whole. It is in the name of "the authority of the whole world" (*totius orbis auctoritate*)[53] that the international order was understood as impartially adjudicated and the natural rights of the *ius gentium* derived accordingly.

Second, for de Vitoria such all rights pertained to the domain of the *ius gentium*, something he modified in collective terms starting from Roman individual premises; yet, ultimately it reflected a principle of natural law according to which things on earth were to be held in common.[54] In these passages, one can find synthetically expressed the foundation of modern *ius gentium* that then led directly to Grotius and Kant, namely with the idea of (a) the right to travel/visit, (b) the qualified right to trade (in so far as harm is not caused), (c) the right of sojourning. All such rights could have never been conceived by de Vitoria without a preliminary statement on the freedom of the seas, something that became a crucial theme in Grotius' seminal work *The Free Sea* (*Mare Liberum*) [1609].[55]

These forms of structuring of the law of the peoples were next to be transformed along constructivist lines by Kant who showed, implicitly, that he was

50 F. de Vitoria, "On American Indians", A. Pagden and J. Lawrance (eds.), *De Vitoria Political Writings*, Cambridge University Press, Cambridge, 2017 [1537], p.278.

51 L. Ferrajoli, *L'America, la conquista, il diritto. L'idea di sovranità nel mondo moderno*, Meridiana, 15, 1992, p.23.

52 I don't agree here with Ferrajoli with regard to an equation between 'doing the good' for one's people and introducing 'a democratic principle'. See Ferrajoli, *L'America, la conquista, il diritto*, p.24.

53 F. de Vitoria, "On Civil Power", A. Pagden and J. Lawrance (eds.), *De Vitoria Political Writings*, Cambridge University Press, Cambridge, 2017 [1528], p.40.

54 As Scott correctly asks himself: "Upon what is this right of the Spaniards based, and also the like right of the Indians? Upon none other than the law of nations (*ius gentium*). And what is this law? It 'either is natural law or is derived from natural law'; and what is the authority for this statement? The *Institutes* (I.2.1) of Justinian: 'What natural reason has established among all nations is called *jus gentium*' (*Quod naturalis ratio inter omnes gentes constituit, vocatur jus gentium*)", Scott, *Catholic Conception*, p.18.

55 H. Grotius, *The Free Sea*, D. Armitage (ed. with an introd.), Liberty Fund, Indianapolis, 2004 [1609]. See Scott, *Catholic Conception*, p.22.

fully aware of such conceptual and historical development.[56] In de Vitoria there occurred a fundamental transformation from the Roman law idea of *ius gentium* as applicable law to non-citizens and to their positive status as slaves, to an idea of *ius gentium* as a universal and natural paradigm of law, reconstructed by gaining the perspective of a collective society of peoples as a whole.[57] De Vitoria not only assumed a global perspective for the ultimate justification of the law, but he also claimed that this was enforceable law. *Ius gentium* therefore took precedence over positive local constituencies. Together with standards of natural law it defined the universal parameters of international civil coexistence.

This scheme rightly assumed the perspective of "a whole world, which is in a sense a commonwealth".[58] This impartial perspective of adjudication arose from the abandoning of a condition of original ownership by all through a "virtual consent of the whole world" (*virtuali consensu totius orbis*).[59]

The double roots of the global order as based on the combination of natural law and positive *ius gentium* defined the premises for the construction of a system of global law which followed from the right "of natural partnership and communication".[60] The bonds of sociality, as natural affiliations among human beings, revealed the original anthropological and theological commitment of de Vitoria: men are in a natural tie and share of the earth.[61] Hospitality is therefore due to foreigners in a society of peoples since no one could have rationally given up a right to visit following the division of the Earth.[62]

De Vitoria's argument articulated itself along the following steps: Indios are capable of understanding the possibilities of a good administration by the Spanish ruling as well as the advantages derived from mutual commerce. In the hypothesis that they did not get the advantages of Spanish administration, Spaniards could exercise their natural right to communication and commerce, first peacefully, and then, if resisted by the Indios, through appeal to just war. For de Vitoria the natural right to communication was absolute and it could not be prevented. Whoever did so, violated the fundamental presuppositions of international *ius gentium* and therefore he became a legitimate addressee of a just war. Therefore,

56 See, for instance, Pagden's consideration on the "perish" of the natural law tradition in Kant and Hegel, in A. Pagden, "Introduction: Francisco de Vitoria and the Origins of the Modern Global Order", J.M Beneyto and J.C. Varela (eds.), *At the Origins of Modernity. Francisco de Vitoria and the Discovery of International Law*, Springer, Dordrecht, 2017, p.2.

57 On a similar point see also Pagden, "Introduction", 2017, pp.5–6.

58 De Vitoria, "On Civil Power", p.40.

59 F. de Vitoria, "Commentarios a la Secunda secundae de Santo Tomas", Ediciòn preparada por el R. P. Vicente Beltrán de Heredia, D.P., Tomo III: *De Iustitia*, q. 57, n. 5, Salamanca, 1934 [1533–4 and 1536–7], p.16.

60 De Vitoria, "On American Indians", p.278.

61 This notion was already in Justinian's Digest (I.I.3), as de Vitoria knows: "Nature has established a bond of relationship between all men [. . .] it is contrary to natural law for one man to dissociate himself from another without good reason". Cited in Scott, *Catholic Conception*, p.23.

62 As de Vitoria claims: "in the beginning of the world, when all things were held in common, everyone was allowed to visit and travel through any land he wished", de Vitoria, "On American Indians", p.278.

Indios could be attacked and subjugated whenever they did not accept the commercial exchange with Spaniards. Paradoxically, the type of rights defining de Vitoria's *ius gentium*, rather than solving the unjust discriminations of the New World, offered in fact a justification for the wars of colonization that would later define international politics and international rights during the following centuries. Only later would one of the other modern fathers of the law of nations, Emer de Vattel, defend a qualified view on trade as an imperfect right and obligation.[63]

For de Vitoria there was a clear recognition of the right of humanitarian intervention into the affairs of the *Indios*, not only in view of trade, but also whenever they committed acts of cannibalism and the murdering of innocents.[64] From such ambivalence, one might conclude that the basis on whether the Indios were capable of judgment was left uncertain by de Vitoria. Certainly, though, for de Vitoria, there could be no valid justification for the exclusion of the Indios based on the denial of a legitimate control, a *dominium* over their territories. Only serious injury – not any sort of harm –[65] could justify just war.

This was already a reduction to one of the three reasons for justifying just war that were already present in Thomas Aquinas – the *auctoritas* of the prince, the reasons for the war, and the right intention. Aquinas, in such circumstance, was reinterpreting the theory of just war in Augustine and the canonists of the *Decretum Gratiani*.

But what were such serious crimes leading to injustices (*iniuriae*) and therefore justifying intervention for humanitarian reasons?

De Vitoria dedicated an entire work, the *Relectio On Dietary Laws, or Self-Restraint* (also known as *On Dietary Laws*), to analyse the reasons 'for and against' war.[66] To begin with, de Vitoria adduced a theological reason: to eat human flesh is against divine law as stated in the Bible "But flesh with the life thereof, which is the blood thereof, shall ye not eat (Gen.9: 3–4)".[67] This possibility had to be excluded also in case of an extreme necessity of survival. Indeed,

63 E. de Vattel, *The Law of Nations. Or, Principles of the Law of Nature, Applied to the Conduct and Affairs of Nations and Sovereigns, with Three Early Essays on the Origin and Nature of Natural Law and on Luxury*, R. Whatmore and B. Kapossy (eds.), Liberty Fund, Indianapolis, 2008 [1797], p.275.

64 For an analysis of the issue of anthropophagy by the School of Salamanca see A. Pagden, "The Forbidden Food: Francisco de Vitoria and José de Acosta on Cannibalism", *Terrae Incognitae. The Journal of the Society for the History of Discoveries*, vol.13, 1, 1981, pp.17–29.

65 "it is not lawful to start war for every reason of injury". In F. de Vitoria, "On the Law of War", A. Pagden and J. Lawrance (eds.), *De Vitoria Political Writings*, Cambridge University Press, Cambridge, 2017 [1539], p.304.

66 F. de Vitoria, "On Dietary Laws, or Self-Restraint", A. Pagden and J. Lawrance (eds.), *De Vitoria Political Writings*, Cambridge University Press, Cambridge, 2017 [1537], pp.205–230. On an interesting, but partially diverging interpretation of this argument from my reconstructions see G. Cavallar, *The Right of Strangers. Theories of International Hospitality, The Global Community and Political Justice since De Vitoria*, Ashgate, Aldershot, 2002, p.103.

67 De Vitoria, "On Dietary Laws", p.208.

it would not be possible to justify such practice: "whether it is lawful to feed on human flesh *in extreme necessity*? [. . .] the probable conclusion is *that it is not lawful to feed on human flesh in any kind of necessity*".[68]

But, then, the question shifted to another point: even if we admit that eating human flesh is not permissible, would it be the same with making "*human sacrifice*"?[69] This was a practice condemned not only by divine law but also by natural law. The reason was that, since we are not masters of other people's lives, we cannot, as instead we are allowed with the animals, sacrifice other people's lives for the sake of a divinity.[70]

But then, given all the reasons above, is there a legitimate claim to justify war on the basis of anthropophagy or human sacrifice?[71] The answer was that while "*non-Christian princes can force their own subjects to give up their rituals* [. . .]",[72] this could not be imposed by Christian princes on unbelievers.[73] Nor could they wage war on the base of natural sins and crimes against nature.[74] Yet de Vitoria identified one reason justifying humanitarian war based on the injustice of such intolerable practices: "No one can give another the right to kill him, whether it be to eat him or to sacrifice him".[75] Therefore, concluded de Vitoria, the reason was not so much that anthropophagy and human sacrifices were against natural law, but rather, that they "involve[d] injustice (*iniuria*) to other men".[76] This is "the reason why the barbarians can be conquered",[77] even if intervention should be finalized and proportionate to the committed injustice.[78] This view on war seen as a means for sanctioning injustice inaugurated a new legal doctrine which spanned over the centuries up until Kelsen.[79]

All in all, the debate over the Indios was very articulated and included a variety of positions. Some among the most influential ideas were the theses proposed by de Covarrubias, another representative of the School of Salamanca, who considered in his *De iustitia belli adversus indos* whether the Indios had a title to a war of resistance against the Spaniards. For de Covarrubias, it was in virtue of natural right that the Indios had a right to their land. This meant that the Spaniards lacked a right to occupation justifiable either with reference to the idea of a natural right, a *ius gentium*, or even by divine right. It followed that the Indios had a right to prohibit the *ius commercii* of the Spaniards on their territory

68 Ibid., p.211.
69 Ibid., p.212.
70 "Now since a sacrifice should be made from our own goods which we offer to God, it is clear that we cannot make a sacrifice of a human life", de Vitoria, "On Dietary Laws", p.214.
71 Ibid., p.217.
72 Ibid., p.219.
73 Ibid., p.223.
74 Ibid., p.224.
75 Ibid., p.225.
76 Ibid.
77 Ibid.
78 Ibid., p.226.
79 Ferrajoli, *L'America, la conquista, il diritto*, p.29.

and that therefore the entire *ius gentium* rested on a different rationale than the one de Vitoria accounted for.[80]

§1.2 Disclosure of modernity: Francisco de Vitoria's theory of global authority and the right to travel (*ius peregrinandi*)

The modernity of de Vitoria consisted in having understood the *ius gentium* primarily as a universalistic hypothesis for all mankind.[81] As no positive legislator was necessary to enact the laws of peoples, similarly no world government nor any actual gathering of the peoples should have been postulated for the definition of the principles of *ius gentium*. Only a reconstruction of the rational presuppositions of what could have been consented "by the greater part of the world"[82] sufficed to justify the notion of *ius gentium* as a positive legal domain partially independent from natural law. As de Vitoria clearly put this: "the law of nations (*ius gentium*) [. . .] has the validity of a positive enactment (*lex*)".[83] Accordingly, it is "the whole world, which is in a sense a commonwealth",[84] that which "has the power to enact laws which are just and convenient to all men".[85]

Francisco de Vitoria conceived the legitimacy of international law ultimately, but not exclusively, in terms of a virtually reconstructed consent by the majority of peoples. Therefore, no one, neither a commonwealth nor an individual, could be exempted from being bound by international law. Yet, lacking overarching

80 "One should consider rightly that Indios could prohibit to the Spaniards the extraction of gold from such lands [. . .] they could rightly prohibit entrance to foreigners" [Illud tamen advertendum est posse juste indos prohibere hispanos in illis provinciis aurum effodere [. . .] juste poterunt prohibere exterorum ingressum], in D. de Covarrubias, *De iustitia belli adversus indos*, Salamanca University Library, MS M.2043, Also translated in part into Spanish by V.L. Pereña (trans. and ed.), *Misión de España en América (1540-1560)*, Consejo Superior de Investigaciones Científicas, Madrid, 1956, p.363. English translation is mine.

81 On the necessity to recognize in de Vitoria a number of inviolable human rights for the exercise of global authority see A. Wagner who observes that in de Vitoria: "The protection of their (fundamental) rights is the ground for the global commonwealth, and these rights are not at the disposal of any political potestas or auctoritas, however universal these may be", providing also textual evidences. In A. Wagner, "Francisco de Vitoria and Alberico Gentili on the legal character of the global commonwealth", *Oxford Journal of Legal Studies*, 31(3), 2011, pp. 571–572.

82 De Vitoria, "On American Indians", p.281.

83 De Vitoria, "On Civil Power", p.40.

84 Ibid.

85 Ibid. As Pagden remarks: "What this implied was that the law of nations should be understood as that law which could have been agreed upon by 'the consent of the greater part of the world' had anyone been in a position to discover what its collective reasoning might be. Such a law did not, however, actually require, as De Vitoria's pupil and successor, D. de Soto put it, 'a meeting of all men in one place' to decide what this was, because 'reason dictates what are its particularities.' It was then enacted, if only ex hypothesis, by what De Vitoria famously called the *respublica totius orbis* – 'the republic of the whole world'". In Pagden, "Introduction", p.6.

international authorities entitled to define the content of such principles, the enforcing of a universal *ius gentium* relied on the good will of princes and the domestic commonwealths.[86] It remains an open question to define the consensual institutionalization of international adjudicative subjects with regard to controversial cases, as well as to determine the application of the relevant principles.[87] The prince, or an elected representative of a majority of states, is that which has authority not only to defend its own territory, but also to impede that other princes commit harmful actions. Indeed, the prince is allowed to act so by "the authority of whole world".[88] For de Vitoria, it is as if it was "the whole world [. . . that which] has the power to enact laws".[89] Once constrained within a 'court of conscience', the problem of international adjudication, on the one hand, remained attached to an inner moral dimension, whereas, on the other hand, it suffered from the absence of an impartial adjudicator, an international court, either temporary or permanent.[90]

Concerning the definition of a general standard of global authority, de Vitoria introduced the revolutionary idea of a modern conception of law and authority for which men and peoples are to be considered all equal by nature and law.

De Vitoria drew a clear distinction between having *control on everything* ("*dominium super omnia*"),[91] as a capacity to use all available things, and being a *dominus* in the sense of being in control of something (a "*dominus omnium rerum creatum*").[92] For de Vitoria, one's original right to use all things is constrained by the same right held by another man. This requires a transitioning to the notion of possession/property. The latter is justified only upon the condition that no harm is made either to himself or to the others ("*non noceret aliis hominibus vel sibi*").[93] To avoid harm, common resources are to be rationally used and owned, that is, distribution should comply with a principle of economy, arguably, in view of individual necessity. The relation that de Vitoria established with the original distinction between having *dominium* and being a *dominus* bears important consequences in the definition of rights, both internationally and domestically. First, individual property – the relation between a subject and an object of property established in a regime of power – was made to depend on the fulfilment of a preliminary intersubjective condition, one where the exercise of a right to use of all things was conceived intersubjectively as a primordial interconnection to all members of the human family. Indeed, only once it was assumed that there

86 De Vitoria, "On the Law of War", p.301.

87 As Scott notices in this regard: "what is his [de Vitoria's] government by majorities except government by consent? And therefore within his state, as between nations, there is consent – which is not a command – and between states there are agreements, which negative a command [. . .]", Scott, *Catholic Conception*, p.88.

88 De Vitoria, "On Civil Power", p.40.

89 Ibid.

90 Scott, *Catholic Conception*, p.43.

91 De Vitoria, "Commentarios", 1934 [1533–4 and 1536–7], p.74.

92 Ibid.

93 Ibid.

held such an original intersubjective dimension did there follow the possibility of formulating a constraining principle limiting the number of possible appropriations with regard to the consideration of the others.

Next, following this general criterion, the shift from the idea of an original use of all things to the idea of limited ownership, required an appeal to the notion of consent of the others, a standard which could be justified only against a background notion of rational acceptability. De Vitoria justified the shift from use to property by presuming a hypothetical and interpretive consent.[94] The Dominican scholar proposed therefore a conjectural view of the original condition of appropriation which depicted a point of equilibrium between a plurality of interests, namely, with the establishing of the rationality and justice of positive laws. This argument, though, relied on the interpretation of natural law as something *permitting* not as something *obliging* that goods on earth belong to all.[95] In so far as men are all *domini* on the things on Earth, it followed that Earth could be also legitimately divided and possessed. Since natural law should concede that Earth was originally given in common, it followed that each was free to renounce to part of his *dominium* and allowed others to appropriate privately some of its portions.

It is precisely starting from this pattern of reasoning, and particularly from the idea of an interconnection between a *ius naturale* and a *lex naturale*, that it become also possible to set a limiting condition of resources appropriation and, finally, to recognize a right to visit as a foreign citizen. This dynamics of justification paved the way to the debate over the intersection between domestic and international law (as well as between natural and positive law).

Later arousal of political certainty showed an often too easily dismissed debt to de Vitoria's arguments, as for Hobbes' distinction in the *Leviathan* [1651] between natural right ("the liberty each man hath, to use his own power"), and natural law ("a precept, or general rule [. . .] by which a man is forbidden to do [. . .]"), in providing a justification for exiting the state of nature.[96] But this same legacy was, to my view, also apparent in Locke's two provisos that concern the argument on property, as namely, the 'sufficiency' and the 'spoilage' proviso, not to mention Kant's understanding of cosmopolitanism as the third pillar of public law grounded on the right to universal hospitality (or, as alternatively called, the right to visit).[97]

It is crucial, therefore, to reconstruct part of de Vitoria's views on authority and international justice in order to capture the new themes that arouse at the birth of modernity. It is not accidental, indeed, that following from de Vitoria's construction of modern *ius gentium*, something based on a right to move freely

94 "ex consensus virtuali et interpretative [. . .] non consensus certo et formali", in de Vitoria, "Commentarios", p.79.

95 De Vitoria, "Commentarios", pp.76–77. On this point see also Milazzo, *La teoria dei diritti*, p.85.

96 T. Hobbes, *Leviathan*, J.C.A. Gaskin (ed.), Oxford University Press, New York, 1998 [1651], [64] 1–3, p.86.

97 See, respectively, "Property", J. Locke, *Second Treatise of Government*, R.H. Cox (ed.), Harlan Davidson, Inc., Wheeling, Ill.: 1982 [1690], pp.17–31 and Kant, "Toward Perpetual Peace (1795)", 8:357, p.328 ff.

(*ius peregrinandi*), there followed a long lasting discussion keeping at its core precisely the consideration of the extent to which such right had to be considered.

To this regard, Melchor Cano replied to de Vitoria's argument by observing that even if there could be established a universal natural right as a traveler, one could not consider the Spaniards as simple visitors to America. Rather, they went there as colonizers. Similarly, one could consider that "Alexander the Great" was not "a peregrinus".[98]

Later, Pufendorf in 1672 reacted against de Vitoria's fusion of the concept of hospitality with that of property, so that one could not avoid considering the weight that all such natural law tradition had in Kant's treatment of cosmopolitan right in order to appreciate his conceptual innovations. It was presumably following Pufendorf's intuition that it consolidated the view of an irreconcilability between a positive *ius gentium* decided by peoples (and not by individuals in the state of nature), and the idea of such a primacy over the will of the prince. This shift could not be easily accepted and the problem Kant had to address was precisely one of interpretating how to continue some of Pufendorf's lines of reasoning.[99] This required a new reassessment of the relation between natural law, the law of peoples, and domestic positive law – something to which Kant made his original contribution.

In the following sections, I argue that de Vitoria's arguments, as presented in several of his writings, inaugurated a new modern conception of the legitimacy of public authority: as introduced already, this is what de Vitoria called "the authority of whole world".[100] This notion bore fundamental implications for the detection of the legitimacy conditions of the *ius gentium* and for the structuring of international justice more in general. It also justified the point of view from which retributive processes after a just war might have been legitimately applied.[101]

Starting from the notion of an original "natural partnership and communication",[102] de Vitoria derived the idea of a universal "right to visit [*ius peregrinandi*] and travel through any land"[103] as an unrebuttable right to move, inhabit, and trade globally, one which cannot be abridged but only accommodated

98 "nisi vocetur Alexander peregrinus", in M. Cano, *De Dominio indorum*, V.L. Pereña (trans. and ed.), *Misión de España en América (1540–1560)*, 1956, p.142, also quoted in A. Pagden, "Introduction", p.10.

99 Ibid.

100 "No Kingdom may choose to ignore the law of nations, because it is given by the authority of the whole world (*est latum totius orbis auctoritate*)", de Vitoria, "On Civil Power", p.40. I follow here the modified English translation proposed by Wagner, "Francisco de Vitoria", p.563.

101 "[. . .] after the victory has been won and property restored to its rightful owners, and peace and security are established, *it is lawful to avenge the injury done by the enemy, and to teach the enemy a lesson by punishing them for the damage they have done*. For the proof of this point it should be noted that the prince has the authority not only over his own people but also over foreigners to force them to abstain from arming others; this is his right by the law of nations and the authority of the whole world", de Vitoria, "On the Law of War", p.305.

102 De Vitoria, "On American Indians", p.278.

103 Ibid.

for in specific cases. Illegitimate attempts to infringe upon such right gave rise to "just war [*bellum iustum*]"[104] since they amounted to committing an *offence – iniuria* – against the commonwealth as a whole.

As I show in later sections, the *ius peregrinandi* squared the circle between the idea of an original freedom – one based on sociability and communication to move and occupy any land on Earth – and the reasons that could be put forward in justifying a legally just condition via a theory of *iustum pretium*. The right to be received with hospitality provided therefore the linchpin between what should have flowed from natural law to the law of peoples in order to make sure that a just international order did not revert into injustice and, ultimately, to (legitimate) acts of sedition. But also a violation of such inalienable right to travel could give a title to just war. Indeed, for de Vitoria, in the case where the Indios prevented the Spaniards from making trade "without trickery or fraud",[105] they could be legitimately attacked and their territories occupied. But here, to be coherent with all that has been claimed so far, for de Vitoria the justification for war would not be based on the specific commercial interests of the Spaniards, but rather on the consideration of the overall benefit of the commonwealth. Determination of such effects would cohere with Aquinas' "right intention",[106] the third requirement he added to Augustine's notions of legitimate authority and just cause for defining a war as just. Spaniards should certainly first "remove any cause of provocation",[107] but was this not enough, they should wage war in order to regain "their rights (*ius suum*)".[108]

For de Vitoria there seemed to hold a symmetry between just price as something benefiting the entire commonwealth and unjust price as something that, while applying to individuals or groups, extended to the entire commonwealth. This meant, accordingly, that were the Indios to prevent Spaniards from trading, they would have perpetrated an injustice (*iniuria*) against the commonwealth as a whole. Thus, the justification of war.

All in all, with regard to the modern re-foundation of international law, de Vitoria adopted a two-fold strategy: on the one hand, he conceived the status of the Indians as legitimate subjects of international law (differently from how the Saracens were treated before), on the other hand, he defined "a novel system of universal natural law".[109] The divine system of law, previously informing international relations under the authority of the Pope, was replaced by a new scheme of justification. This avoided a religious grounding in favour of the idea of a global commonwealth linked to the juristic hypothesis of a world emperor. It was

104 De Vitoria, "On the Law of War", p.303.
105 De Vitoria, "On American Indians", pp.283–284.
106 See on this point G. Cavallar, *Kant and the Theory and Practice of International Rights*, University of Wales Press, Cardiff, 1999, p.94.
107 Ibid.
108 De Vitoria, "On American Indians", p.282.
109 A. Anghie, *Imperialism, Sovereignty and the Making of International Law*, Cambridge University Press, Cambridge, 2007, p.19.

starting from the idea of a new *ius gentium* based upon rational principles that natural law could gain pre-eminence. This shift became possible only as a result of the recognition of the rational capacities of the Indians and their conferral of a status as equal subjects of the law.

The hypothesis I consider here moves from such premises and it explores the significance of the right to travel. The conclusion is that the right to travel, contrary to a *prima facie* universally recognized freedom, paves the way to the legitimation of the Spaniard presence in the America.

The following chapter, accordingly, analyses the problematic consequences of de Vitoria's arguments as well as it reveals the internal layers of argumentation – economic, moral, and juridical ones – that sit uncomfortably with the possibility of conceptualizing the notion of just war. The conclusion is that de Vitoria's idea of the authority of a whole world – the global commonwealth – in so far as it attempts at protecting the rights of the humankind, ends up in legitimizing practices of territorial occupation and resource-exploitation that, ultimately, pave the way to arguments justifying colonization.

§1.2.1 De Vitoria's conception of power and authority

De Vitoria's contribution to the philosophy of international law was surely characterized by an attempt to modernize the received tradition of the Middle Ages. De Vitoria's overall task replaced the authority of divine law with that of a "secular natural law".[110] In de Vitoria's understanding, the Pope could not be seen anymore as a universal commander conferring powers on the kings. This meant that for de Vitoria, Pope Alexander VI's bulls *Inter Caetera* of 1493 – conferring to the Castilian crown domain over the American territories – did not represent a juridically legitimate act of transferring power and territorial control over America. De Vitoria's contribution intersected an epochal legal-philosophical shift, one reframing some of the fundamental questions on international law and justice.

Interesting signs of such telluric shifts came also from the late publication of Lorenzo Valla in 1517 on the *De falso credita et ementita Constantini donatione declamatio* (*Discourse on the Forgery of the Alleged Donation of Constantine*),[111] originally written in 1440. In this writing, the Italian Renaissance philologist proved that the *Donation of Constantine*, conferring all Western territories of the Roman Empire to the Pope, was in fact an apocryphal.

De Vitoria showed clearly to be in favour of a 'non-papist' understanding of world authority when he referred to the writings of Silvestro Mazzolini da Prierio. This was an Italian theologian who defended the thesis of an exchange of lands between Constantine and the Pope, as well as other similar 'papist theses'.

110 Anghie, *Imperialism*, p.18 ff.

111 L. Valla, *Discourse on the Forgery of the Alleged Donation of Constantine*, C.B. Coleman (trans.), Yale University Press, New Haven, Conn. 1922 [XV sec./pub.1517]. Available online at Hanover Historical Texts Projects, https://history.hanover.edu/texts/vallapart2.html, pp.20-183 (accessed on-line 19.1.2017).

De Vitoria defined such views as asserted "in even more foolish and idle vein".[112] For de Vitoria, the Pope was neither the owner of American lands nor had he a temporal power over the Indios or other infidels.[113]

For de Vitoria, then, not only the Pope, but also the emperor did not have the authority over the world and, specifically, over the newly discovered American territories. Indeed, de Vitoria argued that even if the emperor was considered to be the owner of the whole world, then his right would have been received directly from God's authority and, thus, justified by divine law. Yet, there was no such a trace of authority-transferring, as noticed by de Vitoria,[114] and even if there was, it would not have sufficed to justify the emperor's appropriation of the lands of the Indios.[115] The Indios were instead to be regarded as the legitimate masters and possessors of the lands they inhabited and as the possessors of the public and private goods upon such soil.[116]

Once a notion of global authority on the Earth attributed to either the Pope or the king was excluded, it became all important to excavate de Vitoria's characterization of domestic power and authority. In the writing dedicated to the legitimacy of the civil state, *On Civil Power* [1528], he proposed a fundamental distinction between *auctoritas* and *potestas.* De Vitoria said that whereas *auctoritas* was transferred to the sovereign by the commonwealth – a factual constitution of public authority – power could never be conferred to the sovereign by the civil commonwealth. This latter came directly from God: "Let us conclude [. . .] that *royal power is not from the commonwealth, but from God himself* [. . .] that is to say, the commonwealth does not transfer to the sovereign its power (*potestas*), but simply its own authority (*auctoritas*)".[117]

The clarification of what this distinction amounted to was offered by de Vitoria in two different writings, namely, in the *Commentary* on Aquinas' *Secunda Secundae*, and in the meditation (*Relectio*) *On the Power of the Church.*[118] According to the Commentary and the *Relectio On the Power of the Church*, the term *potestas* had two meanings: (a) as capability and (b) as adjudicative power, or as a power to declare war. The latter notion consisted in "the 'authority or jurisdiction' which is conferred upon the magistrates, priests, and empires by the community".[119] In this second meaning "public power is the authority or right of government over the civil commonwealth".[120] Yet, the connection with divine power-conferral was still maintained even though without covering *all* forms of government. Indeed, in monarchy, which was for de Vitoria the perfect form of

112 De Vitoria, "On American Indians", p.259.
113 Ibid., p.258.
114 Ibid., p.252.
115 Ibid., pp.257–278.
116 Ibid., p.250 ff.
117 De Vitoria, *On Civil Power*, p.16.
118 See Pagden, *Relection I*, pp.45–108.
119 See Pagden, "Introduction", p.xix.
120 De Vitoria, "On Civil Power", p.18

government,[121] power-ruling was conferred on the sovereign by God, whereas in other forms of civil government, as in the case of aristocracy or timocracy (whose degeneration according to the Aristotelian classification was democracy),[122] power was seen as conferred to the regent(s) by the civil commonwealth: "civil power [. . .] is from the people".[123]

Power played also a specific societal-formation function. For de Vitoria, in all these cases, power represents a constitutive presupposition for society: without the former, the latter cannot even exist. It appeared that the transformation of the multitude into a political community was dependent upon power as a constitutive principle. If power informing the perfect political entity came from God, and if society could be conceived as a political whole only upon a constitutive condition of power, then society was ultimately a society derived from God. But this emptied the political capacity of the collectivity to self-determination.

The solution to this problem was for de Vitoria straightforward: the capacity of majorities to deliberate on the common good closed the gap between the coming into being of political collectivity through a transfer of public power to the monarch and the possibility for the society to express its own political views.

Even in the case of a society ruled by a prince, the political identity of a community came from the majority of the united wills of individuals that, in so doing, performatively created the unity of the social community by establishing the principle of *potestas civilis*: "Once the commonwealth assumes the right to administer itself, and once the principle of majority rule is established, it may adopt whatever constitution it prefers."[124]

Power, in this view, differentiated itself into the power of the ruler, as a socially constituting power, and the civil power of the people, one based on the majority rule and oriented to self-ruling. But if this were so, then, the source of power would be inherently divided and contrary to an overarching divine grounding. De Vitoria rejected the idea of two autonomous definitions of power by stating that "there is no question of two separate powers, one belonging to the sovereign and the other to the community [. . .]".[125] On the contrary, he added, "we must say about royal power exactly what we have asserted about the power of the commonwealth, namely that it is set up by God and by natural law".[126] The ultimate unity of power in God's conferral to the monarch did not prevent de Vitoria from considering the majority principle as an internal principle of civil determination within the political community. If this was the way to interpret de Vitoria's understanding of power, then, it should have been concluded that the ultimate source of power was itself external to the process of self-constitution of

121 Ibid., p.19.
122 Ibid., note 43.
123 De Vitoria, "On Dietary Laws", p.218.
124 De Vitoria, "On Civil Power", p.32.
125 Ibid., pp.16–17.
126 Ibid.

the community. Accordingly, this would have run away from any contemporary understanding of the democratic principle informing civil power.

These initial points on the characterization of power and its metaphysical grounding into divine will were all important for understanding how de Vitoria conceptualized the legitimate conditions for international law, whether the Indios were legitimately ruled and, finally, which principles global power should have been based on.[127]

With regard to this last point, one thing was clear from the start: for de Vitoria there held a symmetric relation between the majorities of Christian-wills in forming the commonwealth and the election of "a single universal monarch" by the "majority of Christians".[128] Indeed, for de Vitoria, as the king was bounded by his same laws as a member of the commonwealth,[129] also the different commonwealths were compelled to obey to international law (*ius gentium*). The latter ones did not consist simply of "the force merely of pacts or agreements between men",[130] but they had rather "the validity of a positive enactment (*lex*)".[131] De Vitoria's extension of the domestic analogy to the international realm required that a further collective subject had to be introduced, namely, the idea of a global commonwealth encompassing within itself all politically and territorially constrained kingdoms or republics. Such a commonwealth, as de Vitoria called it, was the legislating point of view which could be adopted with reference to "the whole world".[132] This all-encompassing legal reference had a privileged perspective in so far as it represented "the power to enact laws which are just and convenient to all men".[133]

One could wonder whether such a perspective gained from the commonwealth could add anything to a metaphysical understanding of what was the human good judged from a purely divine perspective. De Vitoria substantivized humanity and used it as a reference point for adjudicating 'the global good'. Yet, de Vitoria's notion of humanity sprang directly from the Christian view according

127 This view, though, does not prevent de Vitoria from considering "that the heathens have legitimate rulers and masters", in de Vitoria, "On Civil Power", p.18. Yet, a clear argument is missing and perhaps it cannot even be drawn from what he argued in the early writing of the *De Potestate Civilis* delivered in 1528. It is for such lack of clarity, and in some cases, incoherencies on full capacity of indigenous self-determination that de Vitoria has been seen as legitimating Eurocentric views on international law. A strong thesis on this is formulated by A. Anghie who concludes: "there are two essential ways in which sovereignty relates to the Indian: in the first place, the Indians excluded from the sphere of sovereignty; in the second place, it is the Indian who acts as the object against which the powers of sovereignty may be exercised in the most extreme ways". In A. Anghie, *Imperialism*, p.27. Notwithstanding the merits of this analysis, it is doubtful that de Vitoria endorses an idea of "state" as Anghie claims.

128 See de Vitoria, "On Civil Power", pp.30–31.

129 "A king does not cease to be a member and part of the commonwealth just by becoming a king", de Vitoria, "On Civil Power", p.40.

130 Ibid.

131 Ibid.

132 Ibid.

133 Ibid.

to which the good was also meta-ethically predefined on the base of a certain metaphysical view. It is interesting to notice, in passing, how Kant, instead, later referred to the "*republican* constitution [as the only one] completely compatible with the right of human beings",[134] defending a moral perspective out of which universal rightness, cosmopolitan right/justice would take logical precedence over universal goodness, that is, to the good of individual citizenries and polities. It was in this sense that Kant could conclude that "the right of human beings must be held sacred"[135] and, while being positive, it had to be always congruent with moral precepts.

A further element concerns here the clarification of the terms in which de Vitoria claimed that international law was positive law (*lex*). The suggestion is that, in de Vitoria, the positive/natural law conundrum for the status of international law could be interpreted as connected to the institutional origins and to the content of the law, respectively.[136] This might allow us to make sense of why, for de Vitoria, it was by positive law that "the law of nations"[137] was made.

This way of conceiving the positive nature of international law had as a consequence that of justifying the punitive effects attached to the infringements of international law. In all such cases, for de Vitoria, the violator "has the sanction [by authority] of the whole world",[138] and the "prince"[139] authorizes potential violators to refrain from committing international injustices (*iniuriae*).

The problem, though, was that differently from the case of kingdoms or a coalition of Christian kingdoms united under a universal king, the global commonwealth did not have a power-entity representative but it was rather itself a law-constituting collectivity. From this vantage point, one could derive the idea that the global commonwealth was a natural law source of global public law, a normative entity overarching the constitutional framework of the interests of the humankind and structuring both the internal and the external legal legitimacy of states. This element explains also why, for de Vitoria, international law did not amount simply to a relation among states based on contracts or agreements, but was primarily framed by fundamental principles of *ius cogens*. So one had to argue that, when de Vitoria answered the question of "*whether the laws of tyrants are binding*"[140] by considering that this depended on whether the tyrant "serves the commonwealth's purposes",[141] he held implicitly the idea that, in addition to the interests of the majority, there was also a generalizable natural law interest of the commonwealth which belonged to the humankind as a whole. This being the case, the majority principle adopted by de Vitoria represented a litmus

134 I. Kant, "Toward Perpetual Peace (1795)", 8:366, p.335.
135 Ibid., 8:380, 1999, p.347.
136 G. Cavallar, *The Rights of Strangers*, 2002, p.91.
137 De Vitoria, "On Civil Power", p.40.
138 Ibid.
139 De Vitoria, "On the Law of War", p.305.
140 De Vitoria, "On Civil Power", p. 42.
141 Ibid.

test for detecting variable community interests, but it did not help defining the rational universalizable commonality of the interests of humanity. It followed that whatever was the construction of majority interests spread along different kingdoms, these could never contradict the belonging to a world's community. The normative presupposition of the global commonwealth, therefore, made use of a legitimate instrument of validation on the empirical side through the majority principle. Variable preferences of historically differentiated commonwealths were justifiable only as falling into a predefined set of generalizable interests, both within the realm of domestic and global borders and in relation to the commonwealths among themselves.

It is along these lines, I reckon, that for de Vitoria the legitimate transferring of authority was traced back to the hypothesis of a global commonwealth. Certainly, this pattern of justification provided only the conditions for understanding the subjective aspect of natural law principles in relation to which the validity of international norms was assessed. But, according to the distinction de Vitoria traced between *potestas* and *auctoritas* this did not suffice to establish the objective validity of the norms.

One might argue therefore that, once the authority of the Pope and the Emperor as the lords of the world were excluded, the idea of a supreme authority was replaced by a *juristic hypothesis.* This meant that an idea of *impartiality* was introduced within the reasoning on the *ius gentium* and that a juristic presumption was adopted in view of the definition of a genealogical "method of succession",[142] one which accompanied the division of the world "into various countries and kingdoms",[143] guaranteeing therefore an independent point of adjudication.

§1.2.2 *Shifting paradigms of law: equality of men and impartiality of* ius gentium

The fundamental question that the Spanish theologians came to answer, therefore, was whether and under which conditions the Spanish conquest was justified. For de Vitoria, to offer an argument in this respect required, first, to rebut the Aristotelian thesis for natural slavery, one equating slaves to '*barbaros*' and namely to all not-civilized Greeks.[144] Secondly, it meant to rebuild a paradigm of law where domestic and international voluntary contracts and agreements were subordinated to the non-rebuttable conditions of individual equality among men and peoples. It was, next, for such substantive conditions beyond the will of powers and individuals that a notion of authority by all people could be established.

142 De Vitoria, "On American Indians", p.252.

143 Ibid. For the idea that de Vitoria is here introducing a notion of *presumptio iuris* see Wagner, "Francisco de Vitoria", p. 570. My only caveat here is that this level is not yet the most fundamental one since it needs first to achieve an impartial normative standpoint.

144 "Among the barbarians [. . .], the female and the slave occupy the same position [. . .] – the assumption being that barbarian and slave are by nature one and the same", Aristotle, *Politics*, E. Barker (trans.), Oxford University Press, Oxford, 1995, 1252b §4, p.3 ff.

All subsequent issues concerning just war, fair treatment of the Indios, and the use or confiscation of their properties were seen as being dependent upon such argument.

The idea of a universal equality among human beings represented a turning point in providing de Vitoria with new reflections upon international law and justice. The Indios could not be considered inherently as natural slaves; on the contrary, they showed several man-like features and rational capacities. Yet, they manifested also psychological weaknesses, so that inability to will what is morally correct and their capacities to engage in rational thinking were considered as two separate qualities.

For de Vitoria, the myth of 'a natural man' had perished a long time ago and namely with the Flood and the advent of a post-diluvian society.[145] The Indios had rather missed to understand this new epochal shift, failing to adjust themselves from a natural to an exploitative system of subsistence. Yet this did not mean, for de Vitoria, that they could not be instructed accordingly. Indeed, men were free by birth: "homines non nascuntur servi, sed liber".[146] Therefore, whenever they showed 'unnatural behaviors', the Spaniards were justified in promoting their growth from a status of childhood and slavery to one of adulthood and self-determination.

De Vitoria's modernity in thinking about the law and justice started, therefore, from the idea of a universal equal standing of all human beings. De Vitoria's rejection of natural slavery inaugurated a point of departure from Aristotelianism. In so doing, it defended a principle of natural equality among human beings by showing how Aristotle's account for natural slavery was incoherent.[147] Starting from the general Aristotelian principle for which nature never made anything incomplete and vain, since it always pursued a *telos*, de Vitoria concluded that the Indios could not be said to be only intellectually able, on the one hand, but incapable of mastery over themselves or others, on the other, and thus conclude that they were slave by nature. De Vitoria rejected Aristotle's views by demonstrating that if American Indians were naturally deficient beings, then God and nature would have "created something 'incomplete' and 'in vain'".[148] So, for de Vitoria, to consider that men were in a condition of equal standing meant that they were in an original capacity of dominion on everything (***dominium omnium***).

This conferred on the people a special kind of authority. The point was, next, to show on which grounds one could legitimately conceive the abandoning of such 'domain on all things' of the world. For de Vitoria, this had to be by "consent of all world" (*consensus totius orbis*),[149] an agreement that he defined as "*virtual*" (*ex virtuali consensu*).[150]

145 Pagden, *Fall of Natural Man*, p.74 ff.

146 "Humans are not born enslaved, but free". My translation. In de Vitoria, "Commentarios", p.228.

147 See the reasoning along the lines of de Vitoria's reply to *Question 2, Art.1* in de Vitoria, "On American Indians", p.254 ff.

148 Cavallar, *Rights of Strangers*, p.88.

149 De Vitoria, "Commentarios", p.16.

150 Ibid.

The principles that accompanied the transferring of authority on possessions were justified in the name of the 'whole world', or, as de Vitoria said, it was the whole world that had the power to bring about the law ("Totius orbis habet potestatem legis ferenda").[151] De Vitoria's grounding of the authority of international law in the virtual authority of a global commonwealth traced a link between his views and the stoic cosmopolitan idea of sociability, one from which a global legal order was justified. De Vitoria's idea of a "natural partnership and communication"[152] among men, a social-communicative scheme justifying the intersubjective character of rights, stood in continuity with the stoic-cosmopolitan notion of sociability.

Cicero in *De legibus* had already established a connection between the cosmic-rational order of the universe and the *lex naturae*. The latter ones were taken as the last parameter of validation for any law and human legislation for all beings endowed with reason (*ratio*) and wisdom (*sapientia*).[153] In the *De Officiis*, Cicero reminded us of the general precept of faithfulness to the rules of universal society of human kind, professing himself in favour of the principle of universal sociability through the commands of reason.[154] He affirmed, though, that such principle must have been reconciled with different duties of partial affiliation that were articulated at communitarian levels: the family, the nation, the *gens* etc. Therefore, from the family to the *urbs*, a gradient of progressive socialization was inscribed within a principle-duty of universal sociability. With regard to the negative and radical opposition between the *polis* and the *cosmopolis*, the internal and the external side, Cicero established forms of *scalar negations* between the universalist and the decontextualized principle of sociability which together defined the degrees of affiliations among the individuals.

Reasoning from an impartial standpoint allowed de Vitoria to claim that Christian and non-Christian princes were alike and that "if Christian princes can punish unbelievers or wage war on them, by the same token unbelievers can punish Christians [. . .]. A Christian prince has no more power over an infidel prince than over another Christian".[155] The recognition of equal standing was extended from the individuals in the original scenario to the princes under international law. This move bore relevant consequences with regard to both the definition and the political-legal implications of the concept of *iniuria*, that is, a

151 De Vitoria, "On Civil Power", p.40.

152 Ibid., p.278. It must be noted that for de Vitoria the right to communication in the context of the controversy on the Indios amounted mostly to the right to evangelization: "*My first proposition in support of this is that Christians have the right to preach and announce the Gospel in the lands of the barbarians*". In de Vitoria, "On American Indians", p.284.

153 See Baldry, *Unity of Mankind*, p.194 ff.

154 "it follows, in accordance with that same nature, that there are interests that all men have in common. And if this is true, we are all subject to one and the same law of nature; and if this also is true, we are certainly forbidden by nature's law to wrong our neighbour", Cicero, *De Officiis*, W. Miller (trans.), The Loeb Classical Library, III, 6, 27, William Heinemann Ltd., London, 1913, p.295.

155 De Vitoria, "On Dietary Laws", p.219.

legal offence justifying war, particularly since Spanish *conquistadores* like Cortes attempted to masquerade massacres of indigenous people through the view that Spaniards were acting in self-defence.[156] De Vitoria's standpoint of a global commonwealth against which international law standards were to be accounted for introduced a multilevel dynamics between *cosmopolitan* sources for international law and *domestic levels* of compliance to such norms.[157]

§1.2.3 **Ius peregrinandi** *(right to travel) and* **iustum pretium** *(theory of just price)*

In *On American Indians* [1537], de Vitoria argued that, before the original division, "when all things were held in common",[158] there was no limitation in travelling and visiting "any lands [one] wished".[159]

By agreeing on leaving such condition one had reasonably to presuppose that "this right was clearly not taken away by the division of property (*divisio rerum*)".[160] From the point of view of conjectural reasoning, the right to travel could not be reasonably forfeited. To argue to the contrary, would be to argue against the starting conditions of a natural social partnership among fellow human beings, a society of communication, as the only valid starting point one can reasonably conceive in the attempt to define the legitimate conditions of international law and justice. De Vitoria, thus, derived from the idea of natural partnership the Spaniard's "right to travel and to dwell in those countries"[161] – America – as well as the idea that they "cannot be prevented [. . .] from doing so".[162] It followed, as he said, that: "Amongst all nations it is considered inhuman to treat strangers and travelers badly without some special cause, humane and dutiful to behave hospitably to strangers".[163]

Complications and difficulties arouse, though, when de Vitoria connected the right to travel and to communicate to the right to trade as well as to the

156 G. Cavallar, *Rights of Strangers*, p.95. On the definition, based also on reliably reconstructed population data, of the conquest of America as the first and largest cultural and ethnic genocide in history see T. Todorov, *Conquest of America*, p.5 and more in detail at pp.127–146. Cortes was a complex figure: besides his criminal responsibilities in the conquest of America he was also the first who attempted an interpretation of the linguistic-cultural symbols and the internal political divisions of the Indios. For a detailed account on these points see Todorov, *Conquest of America*, pp.98–126.

157 On the epistemic role of domestic commonwealths see Wagner, "Francisco de Vitoria". p.573: "The normative authority of particular commonwealths – or even of their governments – on the municipal level is transformed into an epistemic authority on the international level and cannot decide on, but can effectively contribute to, the recognition of rules of *ius gentium*".

158 De Vitoria, "On American Indians", p.278.

159 Ibid.

160 Ibid.

161 Ibid.

162 Ibid.

163 Ibid.

corresponding duty of the addressees of the trade not to refuse commercial exchanges, unless these were detrimental to their well-being. The right to trade, therefore, implied that "no harm to the citizens"[164] resulted to whom commerce was directed. The conclusion was thus that "the Spaniards may lawfully trade among the barbarians, so long as they do not harm to their homeland [. . .] they may import the commodities which they lack and export the gold, silver, or other things which they have in abundance".[165]

Indeed, according to de Vitoria's formulations the right to travel, while granting a fundamental freedom to commerce which cannot be infringed upon because it is derived from an original scenario, also justifies respect of a limiting clause on appropriation that applies also to economic exchanges: "In necessitate extrema quilibet potest capere alienam, quando aliter non potest habere".[166] In this second meaning, I submit that the expected function of the right to travel should be seen as a tool of justification of an international scheme of justice based on the premise of a natural equal status for all. For de Vitoria, therefore, the *ius peregrinandi* instantiated the idea for the abandoning of a *dominium* of all on all. On the contrary, the right to travel freed space to the possibility of accessing the division of earth in accordance to a general scheme of justice. The overarching principle informing such reasoning was one where individual unfair losses derived from commercial visits were sufficient motives to limit the right to travel. Thus, the only title the Spaniards had to wage war on the Indios depended upon their right to travel and engage in commerce. The war waged in the name of the right to travel was said to be *just* except in those cases where the conditions of the addressees of the trade were worse had a commercial interaction established.[167] But the point at stake was: under whose authority did the Spaniards, as well as others, have a legitimate right to travel and not be prevented from trading with the Indios?

The difficulty with this view turned next to examine how to define the normative and economic conditions under which it could be said that a population, or commonwealth, was damaged simply by engaging into a certain trade. This led to understanding trade and the exchanged goods in light of an economic theory based on the value of the things exchanged. This was indeed the view that informed de Vitoria's reasoning, something connecting the *ius peregrinandi* with the theory of *iustum pretium*.

To understand the theory of *iustum pretium* and, accordingly, the conditions of fair trade that accompanied de Vitoria's inalienable right to travel, one should go back to the scheme of reasoning that he adopted in discussing the problem of self-determination and territorial occupancy. The question was: how would it be possible to distinguish a convenient exchange from a non-convenient one? Was there a shifting point of view informing de Vitoria's conclusions on the *iustum*

164 De Vitoria, "On American Indians", p.279.
165 Ibid.
166 De Vitoria, "Commentarios", p.339.
167 De Vitoria, "On the Law of War", p.314 ff.

pretium and thus on the eventuality of a justified war? It seemed that the two questions were to be regarded in a mutual connection and that the definition of what was a convenient exchange depended on the point of view that was adopted to define the economic terms of its convenience. How to conduct an overall assessment from the point of view of 'the whole of humanity'? For de Vitoria this was answered by the theory he had on what represented a just price of the goods exchanged, the so-called theory of *iustum pretium*.

First of all, to understand how just price is established one should refer to the maxim by Aquinas that there is no injustice to that who wills (as according to the *dictum* "volenti non fit iniuria").[168] Therefore, the reconstruction of the presumptive will informing the selling of one's goods, whenever postulated in the absence of the constraints of necessity, generates always a legitimately binding norm. On the contrary, in a condition of indigence, the sale of primary goods that are necessary for survival is always illegitimate, even when apparently 'willed'. In such cases there can be no sincere manifestation of the will, remaining always something involuntary in the exchange: "aliquid de involuntario".[169]

Secondly, it must be possible to establish an equivalence between the things that are exchanged under an overall economic scheme of price-value. In this second case, one has to choose whether the just price is established either by reference to individual estimations of the goods exchanged sensitive to local markets, or, by appealing to the value assigned to goods on the base of considerations based on aggregate value of competitive markets. A theory of *iustum pretium* has to take a decision between one of these two mutually exclusive criteria in order to define how to establish a just price on goods.

For de Vitoria, individual estimations of the prices of goods could not be reliable since they varied and, therefore, were not objective. Instead, assessments made by public competitive *fora*, with the exception of non-competitive conditions of indigence, as i.e. those of famines, could provide an objective standard for establishing just equivalences among goods. A just price is the result of a global public market assessment. Following the words of de Vitoria: just price is the result of a common estimate, as if it had occurred in a public square: "secundum communem aestimationem in foro, a cómo vale en la plaza".[170] It seems therefore that this type of common assessment has to assume the point of view of the authority of the whole world, if it wants to advance an aggregate value calculation of the market and therefore an assessment of the individual values of the goods that are exchanged. This reasoning committed de Vitoria to the idea of a global open market out of which the interests of individual populations were assessed from the perspective of a global commonwealth consideration. De Vitoria's hypothesis, according to which the legitimacy of international law stood upon a geographically unconstrained freedom of movement and trade across all territories,

168 De Vitoria, "Commentarios", p.31. On this connection see L. Milazzo, *La teoria dei diritti*, pp.54 ff.
169 De Vitoria, "Commentarios", p.122 and p.123.
170 Ibid., p.118.

depended upon the unjustified presumption that a globalized economic model would be non-arbitrary, benefiting both European and indigenous people alike. The hypothesis might have been one based on trickle-down global economic effects, one might argue, rather than one based on a community-based economy responding only to local needs.

Unfortunately, though, this scheme of reasoning leaved local populations with no power of deciding how to direct their own economic and development policies. The Dominican scholar, therefore, by sacrificing political and commercial self-determination of independent communities to "the authority of the whole world" ("totius orbis auctoritate"),[171] ended up deprived of intellectual resources to counteract practices of economic or territorial exploitation and colonization. One might concede a *bona fide* attitude as the inspiring criterion of de Vitoria's theory of international law. Yet, if not of sophistry, this did not dispense de Vitoria's positions from the suspicion of political naivety. Indeed, the trickle-down effects on global economy implied the view that in de Vitoria's cosmopolitanism there is no guarantee of a fair redistributive scheme of global wealth. Notwithstanding the overall step forward he made in conceiving international law well beyond the vernacular limits of the European subject, perplexities remain on whether de Vitoria's proposal really succeeded in overcoming asymmetric forms of power domination, territorial exploitation and, finally, the colonization of indigenous peoples.

It is well known that subsequent theories of international and cosmopolitan law reconsidered the right to travel in terms of a right to temporararily visit. Later, Kant will transform this point into a pillar for his cosmopolitan theory. Yet, he turned upside down such a perspective and claimed that the right to visit did not extend also to the right to settlement in case of non-cooperative behavior by the visited countries. Differently from de Vitoria, for Kant, the hosting communities had full authority to reject the visitors as well as to decide whether to engage in commercial exchanges. The only limits were when one's life was endangered upon return in his land. Therefore, for Kant, the criterion of autonomous sovereignty manifested by states defined a standard of domestic protection from possible attempts at colonial actions.

Despite such weaknesses, de Vitoria's modernity stands out in having set up the modern conditions of *ius gentium*. In so far as it introduced the law as a set of positive and coercive obligations, *ius gentium* laid out the presuppositions for coordinating public institutional action, not only in the absence of an international overarching power, either a universal monarch or the Pope opening the space to international authority, but also in compliance with the principle of equality as a fundamental basis of international law, as well as under a qualified right-claim to territorial action. These three elements de Victoria introduced became structural pillars of international law valid also today.

171 De Vitoria, "On Civil Power", p.40.

§1.3 Reacting to colonization: the debate of Valladolid (1550–1)

It was precisely in answering the lesson given by de Vitoria that the counsel of the royal crown, Sepúlveda, constructed his counter arguments presented in his *Democrates Secundus* (or *Alter*), a text dated 1544 but published later.[172] The book was received with mixed feelings and its approval for publication was initially denied by the Council of the Indies and then by the universities of Salamanca and Alcalà (probably due to the influence of de Las Casas according to the author).[173] The book was thus anticipated by the *Apologia for Democrates secundus*, a synthesis of the dialogues, published in Rome in 1550.

In such texts Sepúlveda argued for an unremediable intellectual inferiority of the Indios accompanied by servilism (*tarditas*). The Indios were said to be quasi-men, *homunculi*, and as hardly showing any possession of humanity.[174] The basic Aristotelian thinking here attested a clash with the new perspective presented by de Vitoria with regard to the perfectibility of the cultural disadvantage of the Indios through contamination with Spanish civilization. Sepúlveda recognized that it was possible to enter into a relation of proximity and even of friendship with the Indios, but he never showed the correct way to those who were mistaken, but also that he had to save from the precipice those who did not wish to understand the correct way.

In 1542 the Spanish crown opened a new phase in the process of colonization of America. The complaints brought forth by de Las Casas with regard to the atrocities of the Indios convinced the Spanish Castilian crown on the opportunity of examining the Council of the Indies, the main administrative body established by Charles V to manage the commercial relations with the Americas and the Philippines. This anticipated the promulgation of the 'New Laws (Leyes Nuevas)' in 1543. The king wanted to begin a new course of action after the cruelties that followed with Columbus' administration of America. A new politics was meant to abolish, first, the slavery of the Indios and, secondly, the repressive regime of the *encomiendas* even if recognizing their governmental autonomy.

The project was meant to realize a form of colonization in line with the respect of the minimal rights of the Indios. Yet such a political operation failed because there followed several refusals of application of the Leyes Nuevas. These were finally revoked in 1545. Next, a commission of examination for the operation of the Council of the Indies and the Spanish politics in the Americas was formed in

172 J.G. Sepúlveda, *Democrates segundo o de las justas causas de la guerra contra los Indios*, A. Losada (ed.), Madrid, Consejo Superior de Investigaciones Científicas, Instituto Francisco de Vitoria, 1984; also in J.G. Sepúlveda, "Democrates segundo. Apologia en favor del libro sobre las justas causas de la guerra", A. Losada (ed.), *Obras Completas*, revision de A. **Moreno,** Pozoblanco, Ayuntamiento de Pozoblanco, 3, 1997 [1544].

173 Pagden, *The Fall of Natural Man*, p.110 ff.

174 Cf. Sepúlveda, *Democrates.*

Valladolid in 1550. The so-called Junta de Valladolid was characterized by a fierce debate between de Las Casas and Sepúlveda in the years 1550–1. This occasion revitalized the interest with regard to the dignity of the Indios. The result of the debate justified in 1573 the decision by Philip II to proclaim the *Ordenanzas* as a way to modify the general attitude towards the Indios. The start of the new phase was opened by the linguistic shift of the word "conquest" (*conquista*) with "pacification" (*pacificación*).[175] Along the different phases that accompanied the *junta*, de Las Casas, 'the defensor of the Indios' replied accurately to the theses brought forth by Sepúlveda in favour of the subordination of the American territory and population. The debate of Valladolid opened with a speech by Sepúlveda who exposed the main points of the theses of his as yet unpublished *Democrates secundus*.[176] Here he developed some arguments on the just war theory that were in line with the Christian doctrine and which he had expressed already in the *Democrates primus seu de convenientes militaris disciplinae cum christiana religione dialogus*, published in Rome in 1535.

There Sepúlveda defended the idea of a just war as a result of a received injustice (*iniuria*) and in such context he admitted also the possibility of waging a preventive war with the purpose of discouraging possible future *iniuriae*. In the *Democrates secundus*, he admitted the possibility of subjugating the Indios, since they were naturally placed under the condition of obedience.[177]

There were four causes of just war which Sepúlveda's *Democrates* believed could have been adduced as justifications for the war of the Spaniards against the Indios: the first appealed to the barbarous character as well as to the natural enslavement. According to the right of nature, this required that inferior creatures are subordinated to those superior. The second and the third right of nature appealed, instead, to the respect of the divine command which aimed to impede the adoration of devils and the perpetration of injustices against innocent peoples.[178]

To these arguments de Las Casas replied in Valladolid for five consecutive days.[179] Following an initial confrontation between the two, de Soto a Dominican philosopher of the School of Salamanca, was asked to draft a synthesis of the arguments structured according to a Summary (*Sumario*).[180]

175 S. Di Liso (ed.), *Bartolomé de Las Casas, Juan Ginés de Sepúlveda, La controversia sugli Indios*, Edizioni di Pagina, Bari, 2016, p.65.

176 Sepúlveda, *Democrates*.

177 "Sunt et aliae justi belli causae [. . .] quorum mihi videris patrocinium suscepisse, ut armis, si non patet alia via, in ditionem redigantur, Id, quorum ea conditio naturalis est ut aliis parere debeant, si eorum imperium recusent. Hoc enim bellum justum lege naturae philosophorum maximi testantur", Sepúlveda, *Democrates*, p.53.

178 Sepúlveda *Democrates*, pp.83–85.

179 B. de Las Casas, "Apologia", 1989 [1550–1]. See on this point also Bartolomé de Las Casas, Juan Ginés de Sepúlveda, *La controversia sugli Indios*, S. Di Liso (ed.), Edizioni di Pagina, 2016, p.53.

180 D. de Soto, "Sumario", J. Brufau Prats (ed.), *Relecciones y Opúsculos*, vol. I, Editorial San Esteban, Salamanca 1995, [1552], pp.199–233.

In April 1551 the second session began. Sepúlveda formulated 12 counter-objections based on de Soto's *Sumario*. De Las Casas replied in turn.

De Las Casas' reflections on the human quality of the Indios is all evident in his *Apologética historia* and the *Argumentum apologiae* which he published in 1552, namely, in the wake of the debate of Valladolid. Here, de Las Casas defended a non-deterministic explanation for the behaviour of indigenous people, one which demonstrated that the American Indians actually fulfilled all the Aristotelian requirements of civility and allowed, at the same time, an understandin of their cultural difference from the European societies.[181]

Particularly in the *Argumentum apologiae*, de Las Casas discussed four categories for the notion of 'barbarian', and considered which one applied to the case of the American Indians. This was their being non-Christians and their behaving in irrational terms.[182] The discussion on the barbarous state of the Indians and thus of their condition as slaves followed from these hypotheses.

All in all, de Las Casas analysed the conditions under which the occupation of the American territories was to be considered legitimate and, in particular, whether it was indeed a legitimate move that the Castilian crown could declare war on the Indios even before they had received the word of God.

Most importantly, though, de Las Casas replied to the four theses formulated by Sepúlveda in the following way: first of all, the sin of idolatry could not be seen as a sufficient reason to wage war to the Indios because this could not result from the Sacred texts, namely, from those passages where God punishes the Canaanites.[183] Secondly, the hypothesis of a justified use of force against the apostates cannot concern the Indios who did not know God and his word before the Spanish arrival. Third, the emperors had never been legitimated by the popes in the use of force against idolatry, and this could be explained by the fact that the Church – fourth – did not have a jurisdiction over the Indios and over all those who did not manifest a Christian belief, since this could advance only rights over baptised subjects.[184]

How to deal with the crucial theme of the 'humanitarian intervention' of the Church for the purpose of protecting the innocent victims of human sacrifices? To this difficult problem, de Las Casas answered by drawing a differentiation between those who became guilty of apostasy and those who, like the Indios, erred due to the lack of knowledge. For de Las Casas, the action of the Church and the propagation of the faith could not occur through the use of violence. Following de Soto's summary, it appeared that de Las Casas rejected violence under any means, both in view of the removal of the obstacles of faith and of the missionary enterprise, as well as, moreover, in view of conversion.[185]

181 Pagden, *The Fall of Natural Man*, p.121.

182 Ibid., p.135.

183 De Las Casas, "Apologia". See on this point also Di Liso (ed.), *Bartolomé de Las Casas*, p.55.

184 Ibid.

185 "He [de Las Casas] concluded this article by saying that they are wrong who think to the contrary when they say that these wars are not made to force the faith, but to suggest/ and

The denial of resorting to violence occupied also the third thesis of Sepúlveda, that which concerned the just punishment for cannibalism. In such respect, de Las Casas reinforced the idea of the forbiddance of punishment of the Indios for their lack of awareness of Christian faith. He reminded also how analogous facts occurred in antiquity where unaware populations sacrificed to God their best belongings.[186]

Finally, coming to the fourth thesis of Sepúlveda, that concerning natural slavery, de Las Casas replied that the word 'barbaric' had three meanings, differently from what Aristotle believed. It referred to those groups that showed unusual behaviours or uncultivated people because deprived of written language or, it referred to those people incapable of living in society and, therefore, showing an animal character.[187] Concerning the Indios, de Las Casas claimed that while it could be said that these fell rightly into the first two categories, it was not correct to project to them into the third, natural slavery. Contrariwise, they manifested characters of civility without there subsisting a right of subjugation through force. According to the 'apostle of the Indios', as de Las Casas was called, the Indios had an absolute autonomy and subjectivity and therefore could rightly be considered not only as equals to the Europeans, under the perspective of affiliation to the human species, but also as having a title to full sovereignty to their communities. The theocratic aspirations and the imperial power must have halted in front of such evidences.

It appears here that with regard to the notions of 'alterity' and 'otherness', the ideas that were discussed initially, as with the notion of a *limes* for the Roman world, or with the negation of one's identity and unity, had to be seen as a form of alterity for other beings, either as not fully humans or as non-Christians, indigenous man. De Las Casas' comparative ethnology operated a further negation: it negated the negation of human quality to the Indios that Sepulveda had in turn defended. De Las Casas' comparative ethnology programme continued with José de Acosta and his *Historia natural y moral de las Indias*. With this new contribution there occurred also a shift in the Spanish universities discussing the issues of the Indios: from the Dominicans and the School of Salamanca there followed the order of the Jesuits,[188] but this did not mean to remain aligned to the considerations of de Las Casas.

For Acosta, the target was not anymore Aristotle's philosophy. Rather, it was a certain way of considering the "primacy of experience"[189] in order to rule out all those false beliefs circulating about the Indios. Acosta was less well-disposed and benevolent than de Las Casas towards the Indios. He considered them as

---

to preach them. Since truth is not only this indirect force, but immediately direct, because they say that in these wars you have to intend to preach after the faith", de Soto, "Sumario", p.225. English translation is mine.

186 De Soto, "Sumario", pp.229–230.

187 See on this point also S. Di Liso (ed.), *Bartolomé de Las Casas*, p.62.

188 Pagden, *The Fall of Natural Man*, p.146 ff.

189 Ibid., p.153.

having low intellectual qualities and a weak will. The discussion over the different meaning of being 'barbarian', whether for religious reasons, lack of understanding and so on, was for Acosta to be measured by the degree of development and refinement of the language. In the case of the Indios, the absence of abstract and articulated reasons certainly did not play in favour of their civility.[190] Thus, for Acosta, the Mexicans fell within "the third and highest category of barbarians".[191] This classification was for Acosta a way to organize in steps the progression towards the civil society, that is, the Christian polity. Indians were just about to be part of the advanced world. There was nothing inherently preventing them from entering the civilized world, even if progression had still to be realized in their customs, knowledge and beliefs. Such historical change was in the hands of God and his teleological plan of history. Yet, besides such metaphysical explanation on the progression towards civilization, Acosta recognized the cultural relativity of the different stages achieved by the peoples in the world, in particular with nomadism and the construction of cultural identities. The level of civilization depended on the interaction these populations had with all others versus their isolation or inhospitable conditions of living that prevented human flourishing. This immigration theory contained one important but dangerous consequence: while it allowed seeing the possibility of progression through civilization, it also recognized that something primitive and uneducable was ineradicably part of our societies.[192]

190 Ibid., p. 181.
191 Ibid., p. 189.
192 Or, as Pagden puts it: "Primitive 'natural man' [. . .] lives within us all". In Pagden, *The Fall of Natural Man*, p.196.

§2 The tradition of internationalist pacifism before Kant

Utopia or cosmopolis?

When Kant begins writing *Toward Perpetual Peace*, published then in 1795, the discussion on the possible models of peace among states was already at an advanced phase of debate. Forerunner of internationalist pacifism, even though from within the perspective of a religious discourse, was Erasmus of Rotterdam who in 1521 wrote a text titled *The Complaint of Peace*, where he wishes a peaceful coexistence of peoples under an ideal of Christian brotherhood.[1]

It is certainly Rousseau, though, who will most inspire mostly the Kantian reflection on perpetual peace. Rousseau, indeed, had already dedicated the *Abstract of Monsieur the Abbé de Saint-Pierre's Plan for Perpetual Peace* [1761],[2] to the critical understanding of one of the most illustrious interpreters of pacifist projects of his time. This occasion provides to Rousseau the opportunity to elaborate also a personal vision regarding the conditions of realization of a world peace. To be sure, even if formulated at the same time as the *Abstract*, but published later, the writing titled *Judgment of the Plan for Perpetual Peace* depicts clearly the characters of the Rousseauian proposal through an explicit critique of Saint-Pierre.[3] The *Abbé*, according what to Rousseau says in the *Judgment*, has been naïve in thinking that a long lasting union could be based on the benevolent nature of enlightened princes of the European courts, rather than on the coercing force of the law, as it will be then for Kant.

Yet, Rousseau does not think that the project of the *Abbé* is deprived of a foundation but rather that it is inadequate with regard to the proposed means of

1 D. Erasmus (of Rotterdam), *The Complaint of Peace. Translated from the Querela Pacis*, The Open Court Publishing Co, Chicago and London, 1917 [1521].

2 J.J. Rousseau, "Abstract of Monsieur the Abbé de Saint-Pierre's Plan for Perpetual Peace", C. Kelly and J. Bush (trans.), C. Kelly (ed.), *Jean-Jacques Rousseau. The Plan for Perpetual Peace, On the Government of Poland, and other Writings on History and Politics*, University Press of New England, Dartmouth College Press, 2005 [1761], pp. 27–49.

3 On this point see B. Bachofen and C. Spector, "Le Project de la paix perpétuelle: de Saint-Pierre à Rousseau", B. Bernardi and G. Silvestrini (eds.), *Principes du droit de la guerre, Ecrits sur le Project de Paix Perpétuelle de l'abbé de Saint-Pierre*, Vrin, Paris, 2008, pp.229–294. J.J. Rousseau, "Judgment of the Plan for Perpetual Peace", C. Kelly and J. Bush (trans. and ed.), *Jean-Jacques Rousseau. The Plan for Perpetual Peace, On the Government of Poland, and other Writings on History and Politics*, Dartmouth College Press, University Press of New England, 2005 [1782], pp.53–60.

realization. Rousseau in the *Judgment*, indeed, concludes that the evaluation of Saint-Pierre warning that "Let it not be said, then, that if his system has not been adopted, it is because it is not good; on the contrary one should say that it was too good to be adopted; for the evil and the abuses from which so many people profit find their way in by themselves; but what is useful to the public hardly finds its way in except by force, considering that private interests are almost always opposed to it."[4]

Saint-Pierre, to be fair, had already enjoyed an important diplomatic experience as a secretary of Polignac during the signature of the treatise of Utrecht of 1713 and therefore he was experienced enough to observe with lucidity the utopian elements of pacifist theories before him: from Penn's idea of 1693 to form a European Dyet formed by representatives (not only sovereigns) in a proportional number to the annual revenue of their respective countries,[5] to that of Bellers of 1710 who, on the base of a cost/benefit calculus, had hoped for a federal agreement among European peoples without excluding, though, the possibility of an authoritarian unification from above.[6]

Saint-Pierre is for a Union, but of sovereign Christian states and not solely of peoples or state representatives at large, as in the case of Penn and Bellers.[7] To that purpose, the exclusion of Turkey from the European gathering limited significantly the universalist scope of the peace project of the *Abbé*. This fact can be explained with the disenchanted attitude of Saint-Pierre with regard to the proposal advanced by Crucé in his influential work *The New Cyneas* of 1623, regarding the institution of a general assembly of states – a proposal in many respects anticipating the contemporary General Assembly of the United Nations.[8]

The Union foreseen by Saint-Pierre is geographically more constrained but not weaker on this account since it is considered that the presence of an army is a guarantee of the respect of the covenants and the decisions that are adopted by its members. Furthermore, as will also be the case of Kant's *Toward Perpetual Peace*, Saint-Pierre conceives of the *Project* of 1713 as a treatise structured into articles that hint at the possibility of its realization.

From his side, Rousseau in the *Abstract* goes even further than the proposal of Saint-Pierre of an agreement among sovereigns, suggesting that international peace proceeds, first of all, by the pre-institutional consolidation of confederal unions, that is, by the formation of transnational solidarities among European peoples constructed on the base of a sharing of economic interests and a similarity

4 Rousseau, "Judgment of the Plan", p.60.

5 W. Penn, *An Essay towards the Present and Future Peace of Europe by the Establishment of an European Dyet, Parliament, or Estates (1693)*, available online at http://www.fredsakademiet.dk/library/penn.pdf (accessed on 17.07.2018).

6 J. Bellers, "Some Reasons for an European State (1710)", J. Bellers, *His Life, Times and Writings*, G. Clarke (ed.), Routledge and Kegan Paul, London, 1987, pp.177–220.

7 Saint-Pierre formulates his project of a perpetual peace for Europe along several writings. For an overview of his contributions see D. Archibugi and F. Voltaggio, *Filosofi per la pace*, 1991, in particular pp.40–42 and bibliography.

8 E. Crucé, *The New Cyneas*, T.W. Balch (ed.), Allen Lane and Scott, Philadelphia, 1909, reprinted by Forgotten books, London, [1623] 2017.

of traditions. Rousseau alludes in this way to the idea of a European civil society, a "society of the Peoples of Europe",[9] as he calls it, namely, a socio-cultural substrate starting from which a confederation is constructed. It is this further trait, more clearly public and political, which characterizes distinctively the vision of a union among peoples, first in Rousseau, and then also in Kant.

The idea of a union among the peoples of Europe united under the aegis of a confederal political association is in the *Abstract* kept well-distinguished from that of a supranational state, as evidenced by the handwriting corrections made by the same author.[10] Rousseau evidences two interconnected problems with the solution proposed by Saint-Pierre: on the one hand, the insufficient guarantee offered by the mere appeal to the enlightened will of sovereigns to search for the good of one's own state, and therefore to avoid war; on the other hand, the relative independence of the states in exercising their reciprocal sovereign powers, that is, the absence of an international general will in respect of which it is necessary to subordinate the singular state preferences. Even though this last weakness of the thesis of the *Abbé* is not remediable, since it faces the costs of an inadmissible loss of autonomy of the states, the appeal to a mere disinterested will or reason [*lumières*] requires further levels of synthesis of the public interests of the peoples among themselves such that as a confederation

> it have a judicial Tribunal, which can establish laws and rule that must oblige all the members; that it have a compulsory and coercive force to constrain each State to submit to the common deliberations [. . .] so as to keep the Members from separating from it at their will as soon as they believe they see their particular interest contrary to the general interest.
>
> (Rousseau, "Abstract", p.36)

Not the least is for Rousseau the presence of a naturalistic element, so to say, on the balance of powers; an element not only supported by considerations concerning the physical-geographic conformation of Europe, but based also on the political role as point of equilibrium between the Germanic Body "which keeps all the other parts in check".[11] Such balance of forces, inspired by the Westphalian system, even if it guarantees an appearance of stability – "no Potentate will have to fear being dethroned by another"[12] – in so far as this depends on the mediation of private interests, it ends up in determining a condition of "continuous agitation"[13] among states, rather than of perpetual peace. An association of states, "a solid and durable confederation"[14] would "put all its Members into such a

9 Rousseau, "Abstract", p.29.
10 Bachofen and Spector, "Le Project", p.234.
11 Rousseau, "Abstract", p.35.
12 Ibid.
13 Ibid.
14 Ibid., p.36.

mutual dependence",[15] lacking which "each would be really independent under an apparent subjection".[16]

It would seem therefore that the essence of Rousseau's proposal, starting from the *Abstract* until the reflections expressed in the *Judgment*, consisted in the realization, on the one hand, of the European evils as a prevailing of private interests, and on the other hand in recognizing this fact as a necessary evil, so to say, for the purpose of conceiving a European project of confederal peace.[17] Such a shift requires nevertheless an overturning of the interests: from private to public. This is indeed the crucial point in respect to which stands the possibility of limiting wars until their progressive extinction. This is also the point of major distance of Rousseau from the theses of the *Abbé de Saint-Pierre*. This implies though that to the purpose that the public interests prevail upon private calculations it becomes necessary that the component members of the confederation endorse a regime of democratic government. On this point Rousseau does not express himself unequivocally leaving implicit such supposition. Indeed, only through a Union formed by democratic states does it become possible to externalize also on the international plane the element of common public interest. Yet, for Rousseau, as it is widely acknowledged, only the general will is capable of providing the results that conform to an idea of common good.[18] One can, therefore, legitimately ask what are the available instruments to the realization of peace. That is, what remains at hands to the theoretician of the perpetual peace once the possibility of an appeal to human nature has been excluded, or to the benevolent and disinterested intelligence of the princes? Rousseau considers that the issue is rather of a political and juridical nature than of an anthropological character. He mentions, without developing it, the idea that the goal of perpetual peace requires a certain development of international public right, the only remedy to the war among states. Thus, neither the idea of an empire that subjugates to itself the individual and divergent sovereign wills, nor a balancing of the powers among European states is capable of guaranteeing the progressive ascent of the ideal of peace. But not even the spirit of commerce can, according to Rousseau, by itself, stabilize interstate relations. On the contrary, in the *Abstract*, the spirit of commerce is identified as at the origin of the war among peoples, where this becomes the

15 Ibid.

16 Ibid.

17 In an extremely lucid passage, Rousseau summarizes his position in the following way: "Three incontestable truths result from this exposition. First, that except for the Turk, there reigns among all the Peoples of Europe a social relation, imperfect, but closer than the general and loose knots of humanity. Second, that the imperfection of this society renders the condition of those who compose it worse than the privation of all society among them would. Third, that these first bonds, which render this society harmful, at the same time render it easy to perfect; so that all its Members could draw their happiness from what at present constitutes their misery, and change the state of war that reigns among them into an eternal peace", ibid.

18 On the idea of the democratic principle as a *trait d'union* in Rousseau between the *Judgment* and the *Social Contract*, see Archibugi and Voltaggio, *Filosofi per la pace*, p.118.

manifestation of private interests. The opposition between public and private is not irremediable. On the contrary, if only the sovereigns "consulted their true interests",[19] they would become able, for Rousseau, to overcome such opposition by adopting a model of European confederation. But to take such step requires that the will of the government is subordinated to the will of the political community. This is what Madison will observe showing sympathy but also recommending an integration to Rousseau's theory:

> He [Rousseau] should have said, whilst war is to depend on those whose ambition, whose revenge, whose avidity, or whose caprice may contradict the sentiment of the community, and yet be uncontrolled by it [. . .]. As the first step towards a cure, the government itself must be regenerated. Its will must be made subordinate to, or rather the same with, the will of the community.
> (J. Madison, *The Writings of James Madison*, Gaillard Hunt (ed.), New York, G.P. Putnam's Sons, 1900, https://founders.archives.gov/documents/Madison/01-14-02-0185 (accessed on 19.07.2018))

This article was published in *The National Gazette, 2* February 1792. It is not unrealistic to suppose that Kant might have read Madison and used his democratic views to justify the non-belligerent character of republics due to the self-safeguard of citizens' interests in *Toward Perpetual Peace*.[20]

This is the tradition of international pacifism that prevailed till Kant. There is no doubt that among such authors, certainly it was Rousseau who exerted the most influence on Kantian cosmopolitanism. In some respects, unexpectedly, some of the central themes of the Kantian cosmopolitan conception take up precisely the threads of the reasoning traced by Rousseau not only in the *Abstract* but also in the *Judgment*. It appears though that Kant had never read Rousseau's *Judgment*, notwithstanding that this work, written between 1758 and 1759, was published only in 1782.[21] Thus the sceptical attitude with which Kant recognizes also in Rousseau a certain degree of utopianism must be understood as ascribable uniquely to the positions that he expressed in the *Abstract*.

In this writing, indeed, the conclusive paragraph is relevant where Rousseau notes that the realization of the European confederation implies a unifying political action of an enlightened sovereign as a novel Henri IV, but that he brings

19 Rousseau, "Abstract", p.48.

20 "When the consent of the citizens of a state is required in order to decide whether there shall be war or not (and it cannot be otherwise in this constitution), nothing is more natural than that they will be very hesitant to begin such a bad game, since they would have to decide to take upon themselves all the hardships of war". In Kant, "Toward Perpetual Peace (1795)", 8:350 p.323. On this point see also Archibugi and Voltaggio, *Filosofi per la pace*, p.210.

21 See M. Mori, *La pace e la ragione. Kant e le relazioni internazionali: diritto, politica, storia*, Il Mulino, Bologna, 2008, p.49.

with himself "means that are violent and formidable to humanity".[22] Therefore, the avoidance of occurrence of violent events is presented as a consolation for the lack of its realization. This reflection opens the problem of how to conceive the realization of a European peace, that is, if it has to proceed by stages, as it will be argued for the case of Kant in the following chapters.

More in general, the points of connection in the perspectives of the two philosophers proceed both from the public character of externalizable interests that, from the consideration of a public European law oriented to their coordination, that is, to the democratic-republican vocation of the states as component members of an international confederation. It is starting from such elements, indeed, that Kant will introduce his major innovation in the field of *ius publicum*. The introduction of cosmopolitan right as a third pillar of public right, after state constitutional right and international right, is a proof.

Differently from Rousseau, though, for Kant the perpetual is not so much the juridical statute of the agreement among states, nor the institution that is adopted for the best satisfaction of such condition. Given the impossibility, even if in the ideal desirability, of a world (state) republic (*Weltrepublik*),[23] perpetual is the moral, political, and juridical tension towards the realization never ultimately acquirable of a pacification among the peoples. Where to start one's moves in the direction of such an arduous task? The anti-utopian element that Kant introduces as a distinctive trait of his position in regard to the inherited tradition consists in assuming as a starting point a degree of proximity with the actual political reality. States must be in the position of considering likely the type of confederal institutional link that it is proposed. It is in such sense, thus, that the "league of states" (*Völkerbund*) is assumed as a starting stage in order to proceed to the stabilization of interstate relations. But it is with the idea of a progressive juridical fusion among states, namely, of what Kant will call "the cosmopolitan constitution" (*Weltbürgerliche Verfassung*),[24] that the league of peoples, on the one hand, and the cosmopolitan right, on the other hand, realize. According to the interpretation that is provided in the following chapters, for Kant the institutional form of the *Völkerbund* becomes insufficient whenever state interests are progressively transformed by international and cosmopolitan public right. This would explain the ideal-normative element of the world republic that is destined to remain so with regard to its factual realizability.

For Kant, there is no easy solution in this direction, being that of superimposing an international order, coercively, and against the will of the states. On the contrary, this is not admitted unless states' autonomous sovereignty is violated. The problem to which Kant must provide an alternative solution, therefore, is one of showing how to overcome a condition deprived of justice and coercive laws at the international level. It is therefore to this specific point that an explanatory argument is required.

To this deadlock, there is for Kant only one way out: to transform along regulative *a priori* lines the Rousseauian idea of a will that is "*omnilateral*" and given

22 J.J. Rousseau, "Judgment of the Plan for Perpetual Peace", 2005 [1782], p.60.
23 Kant, "Toward Perpetual Peace (1795)", 8:357, p.328.
24 Ibid. p.329.

a priori, from which originates a legitimate global polity solving the conflicts in the state of nature;[25] and *pace* Rousseau and Hobbes, to resort to such notion of an *a priori* omnilateral will in terms of fundamental conditions of authority in light of which all state sovereign powers can claim individual legitimacy.

It is therefore in the scenario defined by a cosmopolitan constitution that the possibility of a peace among peoples manifests itself. That is, the *institutional form* that is mostly adequate to the realization of the ideal of a cosmopolitan constitution does not appear to Kant a relevant question, at least not so much as the need to clarify the *practical* cosmopolitan picture within which states must conceive of themselves as subjects of a global juridical order. In such sense, thus, the accusation of utopianism moved by Kant against Rousseau and Saint-Pierre is directed rather to the desirable practical-institutional realizations. According to the thesis advanced here, peace for Kant remains, instead, a regulative ideal towards which to strive. As such, this communicates the hope of an approximation that proceeds asymptotically ("constantly approaching perpetual peace").[26] From his side, the regulative principle upon which public right relies, guarantees for Kant precisely that element of publicity that transforms private interests of individuals into extensible interests to a collectivity. Since, according to the principle of publicity, subjective maxims seeking to realize public good must result from an accord between right and politics – "only in this is the union of the ends of all possible") – [27] it follows that "this is the proper task of politics".[28]

This regulative vision of the ideal of peace is an integral part of the institutional reference that Kant places on the ideal of guidance of the confederal state of peoples (*Völkerstaat*) whose form of maximal expansion and positive realization is represented by the world republic (*Weltrepublik*). As regulative institutional forms, the *Völkerstaat*, together with its positive world instantiation in a *Weltrepublik*, configure a scheme of practical reasoning of a moral, political, and juridical nature. The two expressions, while referring to *the same* institutional object, possess *two different modes* of signification: whereas the *Völkerstaat* identifies the traits of the individual constituent subject (as with the plurality of states), with *Weltrepublik* it captures the republican form of the government. The partial difference in the mode of signification that distinguishes the two terms is also in the static and final character of the *Weltrepublik* versus the dynamical and unfulfilled character of the *Völkerstaat* where the form of government, the political identity of the institutional entity, remains unspecified. All in all, it is on the basis of the distinction between these ideal final stages of institutional development from the provisional character of the league of state that a 'transitional'

25 "a unilateral will (and a bilateral but still *particular* will is also unilateral) cannot put everyone under an obligation that is in itself contingent; this requires a will is *omnilateral*, that is united not contingently but a priori and therefore necessarily, and because of this is the only will that is lawgiving". In Kant, "The Metaphysics of Morals (1797)", 6:263, p.415.

26 Kant, "Toward Perpetual Peace (1795)", 8:360, p.331,

27 Kant, "Toward Perpetual Peace (1795)", 8:386, p.351.

28 Ibid.

interpretation is justified. 'Transitional' here indicates the character of asymptotic institutional and juridical progression towards the ideal of perpetual peace. This means that the peremptory *a priori* character of right, for the purpose of conciliating with historical temporality, must find a mediation into transitional forms. The continuum that is given by the movements of progression towards the political-constitutional ideal of the world republic (or the confederation of peoples), is self-determined in steps of progressive pacification of interstate relations. As a criterion of classification of the forms of government, the idea of a *Weltrepublik* does not represent an absolute novelty. In the distinction between republican and monarchic form is reflected, indeed, part of the definition that Montesquieu had traced with regard to the types of governments.[29]

The reference to a world state republic as a model for defining the conditions of international society date back in history to the point of disjuncture between the Stoic visions of the rationality of a universal logos and the institutionalization of power-discourses in the Roman empire. As shown in the previous chapter, the continuation of such an institutional model was then reflected in the spiritual transformation of the power of the Roman empire into the idea of the Pope as a universal monarch endowed with *auctoritas universalis*. With the fall of a renewed foundation of the Roman *ius gentium* into the universal authority of the Pope, an event which coincided with the conquest of America, the Spanish theologians, and in particular de Vitoria, proceeded to re-centre international law into a new form of universal authority by introducing the idea of "the whole world [. . . as] a commonwealth [endowed with] power" (*totius orbis auctoritate*).[30] De Vitoria's contribution to the Spanish-American Indian controversy signalled that a new concept of authority had to be found, one appealing to some form of human commonality and exercising legitimate global power. But this view could not solve once and for all the problem of an ultimate foundation of international law. The necessity of rethinking an ultimate foundation of the *ius gentium* reappeared again with the formation of the modern state. It is starting from such political premises and intellectual legacy that Kant began reflecting upon the newly transformed conditions of the international order. These included the far reaching processes of colonization and exploitation of the New World and other territories. It is not surprising therefore that in response to such hegemonic relations among peoples, Kant considered it necessary to rethink the tradition of modern international law from its roots: the idea of the *ius peregrinandi* ('right to travel'), as de Vitoria called it. For Kant, it became unjustifiable to hold the view of a temporally unconstrained stay as a foreign visitor. For Kant, the right to travel had to be transformed into a 'right to visit' (*Besuchtsrecht*) or 'to hospitality', that is, as being hosted with dignity. Kant's *Besuchtsrecht* was conceived precisely to contrast both de Vitoria's view of an unlimited right to commerce as well as to react

29 C.L. (de) Montesquieu, *The Spirit of the Laws*, A.M. Cohler, B.C. Miller, H.S. Stone (eds.), Cambridge University Press, Cambridge, 1989 [1748], pp.21 ff.

30 De Vitoria, "On Civil Power", p.40.

to the Hobbesian idea of an anarchical international society. The natural right to present one's requests as a foreign visitor expressed degrees of non-conditionality ranging from a state's compulsory obligations to discretion. It is in light of such differentiation that even while rooted in natural right, the right to visit shifts into the positive dimension of international and cosmopolitan law and becomes coercive. The cosmopolitan right, thus, reintroduces distinctively the idea of a unity of the international legal order, since it applies to all human beings, and it recast the view of a world state order in purely regulative terms. What Kant decidedly excludes is the opportunity of a "universal monarchy" since this would constitute a despotic form of power.[31] Kant does not mention it explicitly but certainly it cannot be excluded that behind his position there is also Dante's idea of a universal monarchy as a guarantee of peace. When Dante writes the *De Monarchia* in 1310–13, he defends the historical-political opportunity to realize a universal monarchy founded on two distinct powers – not only on a world's papal power, nor on a supremacy of the Emperor over the Pope, as instead the Guelph and the Ghibellines, respectively, wished.[32] He, instead, becomes the promoter of a personal and original thesis, that is to say, the idea of a separation of the spheres of authority between the imperial power and the power of the Pope. Following the *De Monarchia*, Dante will reconsider this thesis in the Canto XVI of the Purgatory in the *Divina Commedia* through the theory of "the two suns", that is, the idea of an equal but separate authority that is to be recognized both to the temporal power as well as to the spiritual one. This presents itself as a political hypothesis that is to be preferred to those theories considering one power as dominating on the other – the so-called theories of "the sun and the moon". A testimony of this thesis is the passage where Dante affirms that "[. . .] the shepherd who is leading you / can chew and cud but lacks the cloven hoof",[33] that is, where it is affirmed that the shepherd of the Church, the Pope, can ruminate, that is, predicate the verb, but he does not have sharp nails. Thus, he is not in the position of having a grip on reality and thus of exercising power on the world.

Dante wants therefore to contrast the idea that the emperor lives of a reflected light, that he is "enlightened" by the papal wisdom. The two power domains remain distinct because respondent to different functions. In the third book of the *De Monarchia*, Dante focusses on the meaning of the two missions: while the universal sovereign must preoccupy himself with conducting men to happiness through the respect of the law and the subjugation of all other sovereigns, the Pope, on his hand, must conduct men to celestial happiness through the doctrinal teachings and the faith. For Dante, universal monarchy is the only form of

31 Kant, "Toward Perpetual Peace (1795)", 8:367, p.336.

32 Dante Alighieri, *Tutte le opere. Opere minori. Il convivio, Epistole, Monarchia, Questio de acqua et terra*, F. Chiappelli, E. Fenzi, A. Jacomuzzi, P. Gaia (a cura di), UTET, Turin, 1997, pp.471–781.

33 Dante Alighieri, *The Divine Comedy, Purgatory*, Harmondsworth, Penguin, London, 1985. The original is the following: "[. . .] 'l pastor che procede, rugumar può, ma non ha l'unghie fesse", Dante Alighieri, Purgatorio, in "Divina Commedia", Canto XVI, 98–99, N. Sapegno (ed.), La Nuova Italia, Firenze, 1990, 179.

government that is capable of assuring peace and stability among the peoples. The restoration of peace is part of a sort of eschatology of Providence and of a return to the *Pax Romana*, namely, to that long period of relative quietness that began in 29 BC with the Emperor August and which terminated in 180 AC with the death of the Emperor Marcus Aurelius.

Kant forcefully rejects such a solution. This is not an acceptable one because imperial despotism establishes too high a price, namely, the loss of individual liberty. It is instead through the *Völkerstaat* as a paradigm of state self-reflection that the possibility of a process of transnational constitutionalization is realized. But which form of coercion is possible to conceive between those states whose wills of political self-determination must remain autonomous? Kant defines juridical coercion of the transnational level as a distinct type in respect to the one that is exercised within state-juridical boundaries. Behind each typology are juridical facts of a distinct nature. Kant speaks of a difference in the "*status iuridicus*"[34] that whereas for the states is defined through the idea of a social contract among individuals, in case of the juridical relations among states depends on "some kind of pact" ("aus irgend einem Vertrage hervorgehen").[35]

Kant does not tell us more on the normative statute of this form of transnational covenant, but one thing is clear: "even if it [read: original external acquisition] is solved through the original contract, such acquisition will always remain only provisional unless this contract extends to the entire human race".[36]

What one can reconstruct, though, is that it establishes itself as a standard of orientation of the relations of the states among themselves and not instead as a determining form of realization of an ultimate juridical status. It follows the impossibility of considering the hypothesis of a centralized regime of government that guarantees the effectiveness of right. For Kant, therefore, cosmopolitan right has rather the aim of maintaining constant the tension towards the emancipatory process of the right in general, beginning from an association of free States.

This element introduces the Kantian vision with regard to universal history in accordance with a cosmopolitan point of view: a theme to which Kant dedicates attention in several writings and even an entire essay as with the *Idea for a Universal History with a Cosmopolitan Aim* [1784].[37] With regard to what has been said above concerning the purely regulative statute of the coercion among states, how is the progression of the conditions of peace among states themselves to be understood? For Kant the answer lies even here in assuming an equally regulative attitude of the judicial reflection, namely, 'as if' it was possible to reconstruct conceptually a historical progression toward perpetual peace. Translated into different terms, according to Kant there would be nothing in nature *to obstruct* the

34 Kant, "Toward Perpetual Peace (1795)", 8:383, p.349.

35 I. Kant, *Immanuel Kant Zum Ewigen Frieden. Ein Philosophischer Entwurf*, O. Eberl and P. Niesen (ed. and comm.), Suhrkamp, Berlin, 2011 [1795], p.62.

36 Kant, "Metaphysics of Morals (1797)", 6:266, p.418.

37 I. Kant, "Idea for a Universal History with a Cosmopolitan Aim (1784)", G. Zöller and R.B. Louden (eds.), *Anthropology, History and Education*, Cambridge University Press, Cambridge, 2011, pp.107–120.

realizability of a peace among states. In another writing, namely in the second section of *The Conflict of the Faculties* [1798],[38] Kant manifests even a certain optimism with regard to the consideration that peace constitutes an ideal that can be approximated positively through the history of humankind. This increment of trust in human possibilities for regulating the relationships through right, rather than through the use of force, suggests the consideration of what can be thought for a historical progression towards peace: from the consideration of those factors that constitute a non-impediment, to the *possibility* that peace is realized through historical happenings of distinct meaningfulness. In such regard for Kant the French Revolution would assume an emancipatory value not only for those who have made it happen, the French revolutionary, but also for all the peoples of Europe that have been inspired by this.

There is a sense of pedagogical preoccupation informing the relation that holds in Kant between history and human political emancipation. To become a citizen of the world, for Kant is certainly to become, first a republican citizen in one's state, but it extends also to the enjoyment of such status within the international realm. The educational function of history, therefore, is not in Kant limited to a moral transnational education leading, at the end, to a sense of "'love of humanity'" as in Rousseau.[39] The moral republican education that the republics can allow to their citizens is not enough for Kant to deactivate the egoism of the citizens clashing against the common good. It is yet a point of departure which was hinting already in Rousseau at a preliminary phase of legal cosmopolitanism.

Yet Rousseau's "thin moral cosmopolitanism"[40] represented by the "'peaceful spirit'"[41] of Emile assumes a structured and systemic legal form. For Kant, indeed, the cosmopolitan project, in so far as it aims to avoid the hypocrisy and the naivety of his predecessors, certainly reconstruct a legal-political dimension starting from a moral commitment: the republican practices of states conjoin with the *a priori* general will that justifies the entrance into a scenario regulated by an international rule of law. Morality, though, is not left behind. On the contrary, the regulative character embedded in the construction of a cosmopolitan society bifurcates into (a) a moral regulative commonwealth of humanity, and (b) a legal-institutional dimension of a regulative cosmopolitan community. These two dimensions define what Kant calls in a reflection as the "*respublica noumenon*".[42] This notion is paralleled to the idea of what Kant calls an "invisible church"[43]

38 I. Kant, *The Conflict of the Faculties. Der Streit der Fakultäten*, M. Gregor (trans. and introd.), Abaris Books, New York, 1979 [1798], pp.141–171.

39 G. Cavallar, *Kant's Embedded Cosmopolitanism*, 2015, p.80. See also G. Cavallar, *Pax Kantiana. Systematisch-historische Untersuchung des Entwurfs »Zum ewigen Frieden« (1795) von Immanuel Kant*, Böhlau, Wien, Wien/Köln/Weimar, 1992.

40 G. Cavallar, *Kant's Embedded Cosmopolitanism*, p.84.

41 Ibid.

42 I. Kant, *Kant's Gesammelte Schriften*, Preussische Akademie der Wissenschaften (ed.); Deutsche Akademie der Wissenschaften zu Berlin (ed.), Akademie der Wissenschaften der DDR (ed. until 1991) and Akademie der Wissenschaften zu Göttingen (ed.), de Gruyter, Berlin/ Leipzig, 1900 ff., vol. xix, refl.8077, 30–33, p. 609,

43 Kant, *Gesammelte Schriften*, vol. xix, refl.8076, 14–21, p.603.

towards which he considers that a "visible church"[44] stands in a relation of a never solved approximation.[45] Form the hiatus between the ideal and the real dimension of political justice follows the notion of 'transitionality' in political history. This allows for non-ideal compromises and even political solutions, in so far as they contribute to the progressive realization of peace. The regulative analogy that holds in the relation between the idea of a *respublica noumenon* and its approximation through the *respublica phaenomenon* justifies "some form of pacts" aimed at bringing under public laws states' political practice with the principles of right and morality. This framework through which international and cosmopolitan right must be understood is certainly the most significant contribution that Kant has introduced in the modern debate on justice among nations.

§2.1 Innovating Rousseau's general will

In order to understand the points raised in the previous paragraphs, I propose to consider the Kantian reinterpretation of Rousseau's general will along *a priori* and cosmopolitan lines. This interpretive thesis is permitted by Kantian texts and supported, historically, by the flourishing debate of the time concerning the idea of general will in cosmopolitan terms.

From a textual point of view, in *Toward Perpetual Peace*, Kant clearly points to the need to recognize a general will in order to guide politics by means of *a priori* principles of public right. In the *First Appendix*, Kant addresses the issue of political wisdom as a resource for approximating peace. There, Kant clarifies how – just and wise – politics should proceed from the guidance of *a priori* principles of public right ("hence with reference to a politics cognizable a priori"[46]). Attempts to act politically in view of an "advantage whether natural or moral"[47] are nullified by attainment to "the general will given a priori (within a nation or *in the relation of various nations to one another*) [emphasis added]"[48] as the only source for *a priori* determination of what should be considered as right among human beings.

This is Kant's most explicit textual evidence for the idea of a general *a priori* will that is not simply domestic, but ultimately cosmopolitan.

The hypothesis I advance here, accordingly, is one which recognizes a Kantian attempt to renovate the natural law tradition; one requiring, consistently, an overall transformation of Rousseau's interpretive function of natural right by the general wills of the nations. The unification of the particularistic general wills of nations falling under an all-encompassing general will is a necessary step for progressing towards the realization of peace – what Kant calls the "highest good",[49]

44 Ibid.
45 Kant, *Kant's Gesammelte Schriften*, vol. xix, refl. 8077, 3–5, p.612.
46 Kant, *Toward Perpetual Peace*, 8:378, p.345.
47 Ibid.
48 Ibid.
49 I. Kant, "On the common Saying: That may be correct in theory, but it is of no use in practice (1793)", M. Gregor (ed.), *Immanuel Kant. Practical Philosophy*, Cambridge University Press, Cambridge, 1999, 8:279, p.282.

namely, the "universal happiness combined with and in conformity with the purest morality throughout the world".[50] The highest good places itself as an end of moral practical reason but never as a determining reason for the moral will (since only the categorical imperative can be).[51]

Besides the complexities of the practical Kantian framework, what is relevant here is that there is no doubt that Rousseau was for Kant one of the most influential ones with regard to the ultimate justification of cosmopolitan authority (but with an important consideration of Diderot's general will).

Even more so, Kant brought to conclusion the unaccomplished Rousseauian programme on "international law, trade, the law of warfare and conquest, public law, federations, negotiation, treaties etc.",[52] as he admits to have left unaccomplished in the concluding remarks of *The Social Contract* [1762]. According to Rousseau this was indeed an all new area of enquiry still "too far from [. . .] sight".[53] Rousseau therefore never developed a cosmopolitan programme. Yet, he was fully engaged in the debate on cosmopolitan peace as proposed by the Abbé de Saint-Pierre. Rousseau manifested a respectful scepticism to Saint-Pierre's proposals, stating that his views were "too good to be adopted".[54] After all, Rousseau was not convinced by current cosmopolitan projects in which he saw that "we ought to think of those so-called cosmopolitans [as some . . .] who boast of their love for all so as to have the right not to love anyone".[55]

The persistent ambivalence of cosmopolitan attitudes appears in Rousseau both as a form of admiration, as in his *Discourse on Inequality* [1755] – where he expresses the wish for "a few great cosmopolitan souls, who break through the imaginary barriers between peoples and [. . .] include the whole human race in their benevolence",[56] – and as a form of disrespect as in the writings on *Discourse on Political Economy* [1758] and the *Geneva Manuscript* [1756?], where he adopts a much more bitter tone.[57]

50 Ibid. On the reconstruction of the ethical/theological-political debate in Kant between the highest good and peace see R.S. Taylor, "Kant's Political Religion: the Transparency of Perpetual Peace and the Highest Good", *The Review of Politics*,.72(1), 2010, pp.1–24.
51 S. Neiman, *The Unity of Reason. Rereading Kant*, Oxford University Press, Oxford/New York, 1994, p.172.
52 J.J. Rousseau, "The Social Contract", C. Betts (trans., introd. and notes), *Discourse on Political Economy and the Social Contract*, Oxford University Press, Oxford, 2008 [1762], p.168
53 Ibid.
54 Rousseau, "Judgment of the Plan", p.60.
55 J.J. Rousseau, "The Social Contract. Appendix. The General Society of the Human Race", C. Betts (trans., introd. and notes), *Discourse on Political Economy and the Social Contract*, Oxford World's Classics, Oxford University Press, Oxford, 1994 [1762], p.174.
56 J.J. Rousseau, *Discourse on Inequality*, F. Philip (trans.), P. Coleman (ed.), Oxford University Press, Oxford, 2009 [1755], p.69.
57 See, respectively, J.J. Rousseau, "Discourse on Political Economy", C. Betts (trans., introd. and notes), *Discourse on Political Economy and the Social Contract*, Oxford University Press, Oxford, 2008 [1758], pp.1–42, and J.J. Rousseau, "Geneva Manuscript", R. Masters (ed.) and J. Masters (trans.), *On the Social Contract. With the Geneva Manuscript and Political Economy*, Saint Martin's Press, New York, 1978 [1756?], pp. 157–208.

Interestingly, some of the central themes of Kantian cosmopolitan conception develop the threads of the reasoning traced by Rousseau both in the *Abstract* and in the *Judgment*. The *Judgment* was written between 1758 and 1759 but it was published only in 1782 and Kant, apparently, never had the opportunity to read it.[58] In the closing sections of the *Abstract*, Rousseau notes that the realization of the European confederation demands a unifying political action by an enlightened sovereign, a novel Henri IV who will nevertheless adopt "means that are violent and formidable to humanity".[59] It is starting from this reflection that it re-opens the problem of how to conceive the realization of a European peace: whether this has to proceed along stages, or all at once.

Kant suggests adopting a juridically structured plan to such demands. In so doing, Kant will advance Rousseau's programme on the basis of one fundamental innovation: the transformation of the general will as a step out from the state of nature along cosmopolitan lines. This shift impacts on the types of motivating reasons of the citizens,[60] either national or cosmopolitan, also suggesting the idea that the foundation of law is based on, what might be called, a global *Grundwille*.

This Kantian innovation is matched by the idea of cosmopolitan right which, in turn, will account for the residual constraint of natural law in the state of nature. I will show in later sections a reversion in the consideration of what Rousseau defines in terms of "compensating advantages [*ces compensations*]",[61] when referring to entering into the civil condition by means of the covenant (and a parallel loss of natural freedom), and Kant's consideration of the natural right to visit as a compensatory measure for entering into the civil condition.

In general, the points of convergence in the perspectives developed by the two philosophers proceed from consideration of the transitory mode in which (1) the fair social contract comes about and (2) the ways in which the public character of externalizable interests are realizable. With regard to the first point, Kant seems to transfer into juridical categories the Rousseauian sociological scheme organized in phases moving from the state of nature to the civil state, as with the linking phases that can be traced between the *Discourse on the Origin of Inequality* [1755] and *The Social Contract* [1762].[62] Here the shifts depart from a natural phase moving towards a first and a second revolution, appropriation and, finally, from an unfair to a fair social contract.[63] The *Discourse on the Origin of Inequality* ends precisely with the definition of the material conditions that inform the unfairness of the contract, whenever "the rich man [. . . invoked:] 'let us unite'[. . .]'to protect the weak from oppression'".[64] Along a somewhat similar

58 See Mori, *La pace e la ragione*, p.49.

59 Rousseau, "Judgment of the Plan", p.60.

60 On the analysis of the change in the *types* of reasons between the natural and the civil man under the general will, see F. Neuhouser, *Rousseau's Theodicy of Self-Love*, Oxford University Press, Oxford, 2008, p.192 ff.

61 Rousseau, *Social Contract*, p.59.

62 Rousseau, *Origin of Inequality*.

63 Ibid., pp.55 ff.

64 Ibid., p.68.

scheme of approximation, Kant adopts the idea of *leges latae* as normatively impure and intermediate steps before the conditions for a full enforcement of the peremptory character of the right is available (see part 3, §7.2).

In Kant, the adoption of permissive laws is part of a general scheme of juridification of the historical steps necessary for the realization of a coercive scheme of global justice.[65] Kant's cosmopolitan extension of the Rousseauian civil stages requires the idea of an all-comprehensive general will.

It was Arnauld who introduced the expressions *volonté générale* and *volonté particulière* in his almost unknown works collected in 43 volumes.[66] But the concept of *volonté générale* gained momentum particularly with Pascal's *Ecrits sur la grace*, where this notion was confronted with the idea of a *volonté absolue* in order to justify, in the first case, God's conferral of grace for salvation to the meritorious and, in the second case, a power of damnation. Pascal identified the latter, arbitrary, will with Calvinist theology, whereas he linked the first with St. Agustine's disciples who "believed that, before the Fall of Adam, God had a *volonté générale et conditionelle* to save all men".[67]

It was only after the Fall that God willed, by shift into a *volonté absolue*, the salvation of some men only because of His piety.[68] Pascal also developed a distinction between the *volonté générale* and the *volonté particulière* (where the latter subordinates itself to the will supervising the entire political body). Thus, Pascal paved the way to the conception of the particular will in terms of something leading to injustice, self-love, and disorder and to the necessity of subordinating it to a general will under which to seek justice.[69]

Malebranche too suggested a political-theological reading whereby the general will appeared under the form of laws, as will be later the case with Rousseau's. Interestingly, though, the same concept was already present in Montesquieu, as in his partially lost *Traité des devoirs* (1725), where he affirmed, under the influence of Stoicism, that justice establishes a general relation among particular wills.[70]

It is with Diderot, though, that the concept of a general will acquires an extension applicable to the concept of humanity as a whole, that is, as a moral principle of conduct in society and between societies and as a law, properly. Diderot's *volonté générale* becomes a concept connected to the transformation of the international state of nature under the template of the *ius gentium*. Here one finds the expression for which "the general will never errs".[71] Rousseau, as is well known, will limit this idea to the view of a particular will.[72] For Diderot, instead,

65 See in particular the *Second Part* of Rousseau, *Origin of Inequality*.

66 P. Riley, *The General Will before Rousseau. The Transformation of the Divine into the Civic*, Princeton University Press, Princeton, N.J., 2014, p.14.

67 Ibid.

68 Ibid.

69 Riley, *General Will before Rousseau*, pp.18–19.

70 See Riley, *General Will before Rousseau*, p.142.

71 D. Diderot, "Droit Naturel", J. Hope Mason and R. Wokler (eds.), *Political Writings*, *Political Writings*, Cambridge University Press, Cambridge, 1992 [1755], p.21.

72 Riley, *General Will before Rousseau*, p.54.

there holds a relation of mutual legitimation among men and peoples based on an equal right to reciprocal demands of compliance.[73] The general will of human kind grounds a concept of international justice.

This point is widely explained by Diderot in his *Encyclopédie*'s entry "Droit naturel".[74] Here Diderot summarizes his view on the matter in the final sections where he states: "It is for the general will to determine the limits of all duties. You have the most sacred natural right to everything that is not resisted by the whole human race."[75] Such natural rights reside in a host of plural sources as in "the principles of prescribed law of all civilized nations; in the social practices of savage and barbarous peoples; in the tacit agreements obtaining amongst the enemies of mankind".[76] What is crucial, here, is the conceptual function that these notions assume. For Diderot they serve "to compensate for social laws and public retribution".[77] I argue later that Kant, in his characterization of the natural right to visit and constructivist definition of a positive global order, will expand upon this rationale.

To this aim it is all important to keep in mind Diderot's implications following from the idea of an all encompassing general will as an authority source of justice. He mentions nine features such as that (1) man's private will is against the human race, (2) that the general will expresses fellow-men's mutual interests, (3) that it binds the conduct not only of individuals within a society but also of the individuals among different societies, (4) that the bonds of the general will keep all societies bound together including also the criminal ones, (5) that laws are directed to all, (6) that the general will never errs (as already introduced), (7) that natural right never changes, (8) that justice is equity, (9) that reason is the only source of all these notions.[78]

The idea of a basic human equality is also what informs Diderot's considerations for the legitimacy of the first occupants developed in Raynal's *History of the two Indias* of 1770 (cited by Kant in *Toward Perpetual Peace*),[79] a work profoundly engaged with the debate opened by the Second Scholastics and to which, apparently, Diderot provided anonymous comments.[80] For some scholars, thus, it appeared plausible to consider that Kant's cosmopolitan roots belong in

73 Ibid., p.432.
74 Diderot, "Droit Naturel", pp.17–21.
75 Ibid., p.20.
76 Ibid.
77 Ibid.
78 Diderot, "Droit Naturel", pp.20–21.
79 G.T.F. Raynal, *A History of the Two Indies*, P. Jimack (ed.), Routledge, New York, NY, 2006 [1770].
80 On the editorial genesis of *The History of the Two Indias*, see S. Muthu, *Enlightenment against Empire*, Princeton University Press, Princeton and Oxford, 2003, p.72 ff. This is the thesis also of Arayo who affirms that: "Diderot bien pudo abrirle los ojos al ámbito de la política, gracias a ciertos artículos de la *Enciclopedia* y sus contribuciones anónimas a esa *Historia filosófica y política de los establecimientos y del comercio de los europeos en las dos Indias*, firmada finalmente en solitario por el abate Raynal sin mencionar a sus colaboradores. En definitiva, Diderot tendría un gran peso específico en las reflexiones políticas e incluso jurídicas de Kant, sin que este pueda citarle, por ignorar su autoría en esas dos obras colectivas, de

fact to Diderot's indirect influence (as with the right to visit, first occupancy, the civil condition, etc.). This hypothesis plays also in favour of the idea of a more radical support by Kant of the French Revolution than that manifested by other intellectuals of the time.

As recalled, in the *Encyclopédie*'s article called *Droit Naturel* (*Natural Right*), Diderot speaks of "the general will of humanity"[81] in terms of an ethical standard linked to "indignation and resentment"[82] when injustices take place. It is from this vantage point that Diderot criticizes European colonialism on the base of a general physical and moral similarity among human beings. Both the *Encyclopédie* and Raynal's *History* became very popular and discussed works at that time. Kant and Herder had certainly read them.[83] This might help explaining the influence on Kant's position against European imperialism as well as his consideration of moral universality and humanity in light of justification of a cosmopolitan legal order.

Rousseau's definition of the *volonté générale* as well as its distinction from the *volonté particulière* is clearly at a distance from Diderot's views. Furthermore, there remains an undercutting unsolved tension in Rousseau's intersection between the general will of nations and the generality of the natural law.

In the *Government of Poland*, Rousseau emphasizes the distinctiveness of national characters showing also how particular attachments and feelings could never be fully replaceable by cosmopolitan ties.[84] Yet, Rousseau's ambivalence emerges once again in the *Discourse on Political Economy*[85] where he claims that the notion of a general will is connected both to a supra-state level and to the idea of an interpreter of the natural law that applies "to the great city of the world".[86] He comes to this conclusion after having drawn a parallel according to which "the will of the state, although general in relation to its members, ceases to be so in relation to other states and their members, becoming instead, for them, a particular and individual will, the justness of which is governed by natural law".[87] All this suggests that Rousseau, even when mentioning the idea of a general will in terms of an individual way of interpreting natural law precepts, never considers the hypothesis of a generalized legal condition beyond the state level.[88]

To this conceptual limiting condition for the institution of a global condition of the rule of law there is for Kant only one way out: the transformation along

las que nos consta que no le fueron ajenas." R.R. Aramayo, "La Plausible Impronta (Política) de Diderot en Kant", *Ideas y Valores* 66(163), 2017, p.21.

81 Diderot, "Droit Naturel", p.10, quoted in Muthu, *Enlightenment against Empire*, p.77.

82 Ibid.

83 Muthu, *Enlightenment against Empire*, p.121.

84 J.J. Rousseau, "Considerations on the Government of Poland and on its Planned Reformation", C. Kelly and J. Bush (trans.), C. Kelly (ed.), *Jean-Jacques Rousseau. The Plan for Perpetual Peace, On the Government of Poland, and other Writings on History and Politics*, University Press of New England, Dartmouth College Press, 2005 [1782], pp. 167–240.

85 Rousseau, "Discourse on Political Economy".

86 Ibid., p.7.

87 Ibid.

88 Ibid.

regulative lines of the idea of an *omnilateral* will.[89] This move justifies the constitution of a legitimate cosmopolitan polity virtually capable of solving through law the conflicts arising out of the state of nature.[90]

Such Kantian elaborations are made certainly plausible by the Rousseauian distinctions between "sovereignty" [*souveraineté*] as a principle of the general will and "sovereignty" (or "sovereign-authority" [*l'autorité souveraine*]) as its "emanations" [*émanations*].[91] For Rousseau, scholars, by not having distinguished the indivisibility of the principle of sovereignty from its applications, "[. . .] have [gained] no correct idea of the sovereign [. . . taking] manifestations of its authority to be parts of it".[92] They have therefore wrongly equated *an act* of sovereignty with *the law*, as when acts of declaration of war have been mistaken for a legal precept.[93] As analysed in later sections, a similar reasoning also accompanies Kant's reasoning on the regulatory role played by certain key political concepts.

All in all, there is a sense of pedagogical finality that informs Kant's conception of history as a cosmopolitan process of emancipation for the humankind. This view overlaps only slightly with Rousseau's ideas of human improvements through education. For Kant, indeed, the pedagogical function of history is not limited to a moral cosmopolitan education accompanying a sense of "love of humanity"[94] as it is for Rousseau. Moral republican education is not enough for Kant to deactivate citizens' egoism – particularly beyond state borders – where no sense of common affiliation arises. It follows that Rousseau's "thin moral cosmopolitanism"[95] embodied by the "peaceful spirit"[96] of Emile, is transformed by Kant into a cosmopolitan legal project structured around a systemic form. For Kant, the political praxis of republican states conjugates with an *a priori* general will that justifies, in turn, states' entrance into an international rule of law. This position, as will be discussed later more extensively, requires that a cosmopolitan legal order is constructed upon a regulatory principle of a cosmopolitan community, an idea which Kant ties to the view of a regulative notion of cosmopolitan authority.

89 On a reading emphasizing Kant's idea of the social contract as 'hypothetical' and as 'an idea of reason' in analogy with the Platonic ideal, what Kant calls the *respublica noumenon*, see P. Riley, *Will and Political Legitimacy. A Critical Exposition of Social Contract Theory in Hobbes, Locke, Rousseau, Kant, and Hegel*, Harvard University Press, Cambridge, Mass. and London, 1982, pp.125 ff.

90 "a unilateral will (and a bilateral but still *particular* will is also unilateral) cannot put everyone under an obligation that is in itself contingent; this requires a will is *omnilateral*, that is united not contingently but a priori and therefore necessarily, and because of this is the only will that is lawgiving", Kant, "Metaphysics of Morals (1797)", 6:263, p.415.

91 Rousseau, "The Social Contract", p.64.

92 Ibid.

93 Ibid., p.65.

94 Cavallar, *Kant's Embedded Cosmopolitanism*, p.80.

95 See the remarks by Cavallar, *Kant's Embedded Cosmopolitanism*, p.84.

96 Ibid.

Part 2

Kant's critique of just war theory and colonialism

§3 The 'sorry comforters'

Kant's discussion of the tradition of internationalist pacifism proceeds in parallel with his rejection of the classical theory of just war. Along with the discussion of the *Second Definitive Article*, in *Toward Perpetual Peace*, Kant asserts that: "the right *to go to* war is, strictly speaking, unintelligible".[1] The reason being that "it is supposed to be a right to determine what is right not by universally valid external laws limiting the freedom of each but by unilateral maxims through force".[2] This unilaterality of the will is what prevents the overcoming of a lawless condition among states and it is therefore an obstacle to the instantiation of a general rule of law.

It is the case, indeed, that differently from other natural law thinkers, for Kant, the state of nature is characterized by a condition of violence. But in disagreement with Hobbes, for Kant this condition poses a problem with regard to the relation of states among themselves, as in the case of an international state of nature. The difficulty, though, is that no state would ever give up *de facto* its own sovereignty in order to become an "*inferior* (obeying, namely the people)"[3] constituency of a "*superior* (legislating)" polity – call it a world state or an international federal confederation.[4] Yet, the necessity to overcome such a natural condition remains unchanged if international relations are to be regulated in accordance to a rational standard of law. That Kant conceives of the legitimacy of individual and interstate relations as conditions that are valid *a priori* is clear from the replacement of Grotius' "private community [*communio primaeva*]"[5] with the idea of an "original community".[6] Whereas Grotius' community was considered as primary only with regard to a temporal dimension, for Kant, the idea of

1 Kant, "Toward Perpetual Peace (1795)", 8:356, p.328.
2 Ibid.
3 Kant, "Toward Perpetual Peace (1795)", 8:354, p.326.
4 Ibid.
5 Kant, "Metaphysics of Morals (1797)", 6:251, p.405.
6 "This *original* community of land, and with it of things upon it (*communio fundi originaria*), is an idea that has objective (rightfully practical) reality. This kind of community must be sharply distinguished from a *primitive community* (*communio primaeva*), which is a fiction; for a primitive community would have to be one that was *instituted* and arose from a contract by which everyone gave up private possessions and, by uniting his possessions with those of everyone else, transformed them into a collective possession [*Gesammtbesitz*]". In Kant, "Metaphysics of Morals (1797)", 6:251, p.405.

an original community is such only in so far as it represents a rational anticipation of all possible empirical instantiations.

To be sure, Kant included some *a posteriori* elements, such as the idea of a spherical shape of the Earth, the lack of insurmountable natural barriers separating geographical areas etc.[7] These features presented a rationalized view of nature, a condition in which the conflict on individual appropriations required an idea of public authority, namely, a general will.

It is starting from this context of mediation between an external coercive will and a free acceptance by states of a supraordinate order that Kant appeals Grotius, Pufendorf, and Vattel as "only sorry comforters [*leidige Tröster*]".[8]

Why such a severe judgement?

The context in which this judgement is proffered is one where Kant discusses, in a clearly anticolonial spirit, the difference between "the European and the American savages".[9] He claims, ironically, that whereas the first eat their victims, the second know only better how to make a more profitable use of their defeated ones in order to employ them in future wars. It is by virtue of the "malevolence of human nature"[10] that the use of the word "*right*"[11] seems for Kant mostly inappropriate as a way to justify wars.

Why so? The answer, framed in descriptive terms, comes immediately after when Kant states that "their code, couched philosophically or diplomatically, has not the slightest *lawful* force and [even] there is no instance of a state ever having been moved to desist from its plan by arguments armed with the testimony of such important men".[12] Put in prescriptive terms, what Kant affirms is that the persistence of an international natural condition among states is such that no matter which laws are proclaimed, there holds no common compulsory scheme obligating states to exit a condition deprived of justice. The three 'sorry comforters' are thus liable of having proposed theories with no obligating force "since states as such are not subject to a common external constraint".[13]

7 "the spherical surface of the earth unites all the places on its surface". In Kant, "Metaphysics of Morals (1797)", 6:262, p.414.

8 Kant, "Toward Perpetual Peace (1795)", 8:355, p.326. Williams and Cavallar suggest the following reading of the expression: "Georg Cavallar provides a very helpful insight to the meaning of the phrase 'sorry comforter' (*leidige Troester*) in his discussion of Kant's global commonwealth in *The Rights of Strangers*. The phrase takes us to the heart of the issue of the acceptability of war in Kantian theory. Cavallar argues that the term *leidig* has two 'meanings in eighteenth-century German. It may either mean *beschwerlich* (troublesome, but also tiring) or *unangenehm* (unpleasant, inconvenient). Thus Kant either wants to tell us that the doctrines of the mentioned natural lawyers are in fact only subtle justifications of more wars, and as such unconvincing. Or he intends to stress that their treatises are inconvenient in so far as they remind ruthless power politicians of the demands of morality, and cause occasionally some pangs of remorse'. In Cavallar's view, Kant's text plausibly 'supports both interpretations'", Williams, *Kant and the End of War*, 2012, p.60.

9 Kant, "Toward Perpetual Peace (1795)", 8:354–5, p.326.

10 Ibid.

11 Ibid.

12 Ibid.

13 Ibid.

Only a theory postulating the *a priori* status of a general will over the will of the individuals and states is a view capable of redeeming humanity from a condition of perpetual war. As will be later showed, the idea of an international general makes possible the shifting away of states from an international natural condition to an international civil condition, one based on justice. States' compliance with the mandates of such will remains voluntarily, but once accepted, it becomes mandatory on the base of states' commitments to substantive principles of justice.

Kant's overall approach to the just war tradition has therefore two sides: on the one hand, it proposes a negative evaluation of the inherited tradition of international law; on the other hand, it advances a positive suggestion of what should be an appropriate line of reflection on international relations – as I argue – a cosmopolitan vision of individual and interstates relations based on the anticipation of a general will.[14]

With regard to the first point, Kant criticizes all those visions of international relations that remain incapable of overcoming a state of nature among peoples.[15]

Regarding the second point, Kant notices how the expression 'just war' is contradictory. War is an act pertaining only to a natural condition deprived of law and justice. Instead, these latter concepts apply only to the civil order. Therefore, the expression 'just war' constitutes a *contradictio in adiecto*, that is, a contradiction between the name and its attribution. To be sure, for Kant it is not possible to speak of right in any of those cases, and particularly in the case of the *ius in bello*, where war and the law are supposedly proceeding together: "The greatest difficulty in the right of nations has to do precisely with right during war; it is difficult even to form a concept of this or to think of law in this lawless state without contradicting oneself (*inter arma silent leges*)".[16]

Last, as an extension of the incompatibility of reason with war mentioned in the opening of this section, reason is for Kant totally incompatible with conflicts occurring also in other domains than practical thinking. Kant speaks in this regard of a "critique of pure reason as the true court of justice for all controversies of pure reason",[17] something out of which we are left "as it were in the state of nature".[18]

The analogy between a rule-governed solution of theoretical controversies with the practical domain is pushed even further when Kant adds that "what brings the quarrel in the state of nature to an end is victory [. . .] but in the state of law it is the verdict, which [. . .] must secure a perpetual peace".[19]

As reason is incompatible with war in the practical sphere, so conflicts in all practical and theoretical fields are solvable either by compliance to "**due**

14 For an interpretation limited to the observance of only the first prong, see G. Cavallar, "Kant and the 'Miserable Comforters': Contractual Cosmopolitanism", *Imperfect Cosmopolis*, University of Wales Press, Cardiff, 2011, pp.64–84.

15 See Cavallar, "Kant and the 'Miserable Comforters'", p.70 ff.

16 Kant, "Metaphysics of Morals (1797)", 6:347, p.485.

17 I. Kant, *Critique of Pure Reason*, [1781–7], A751/B779, p.649.

18 Ibid.

19 Kant, *Critique of Pure Reason*, A752/B780, p.650.

process"[20] – if through reason – or, by "**victory**",[21] if we remain within a state of nature. Thus, one might conclude that as pure reason must subject itself to criticism in order to diffuse internal conflicts, so practical reasons should be constructed in such a way that respect to a formal principle of morality is granted.

In light of such interpretive hypotheses, Kant would charge Grotius, Pufendorf and Vattel for having inverted a relation between a *de facto* legitimation of power with a *de jure* philosophical and juridical vision. War can never be included within a normatively justified scheme of law, except when this is a punishment for the violation of a right falling under still imperfect conditions of realization of justice. But this would amount to an impure form of remedy among nations, one justifiable only under a permissive interpretation of the right of peoples. Rather, those who pretend to conceive war in strictly legal terms – according to strict laws (*leges strictae*) – turn out to be only 'sorry comforters'.[22]

Such points shed light also on Kant's two fundamental presuppositions holding true for the legitimation of the international order, as namely:

1 The view of a global contract understood in terms of an idea of reason given *a priori* and establishing itself as a presupposition for the international order. This formulation is necessary in order to exit from the state of nature. As Kant explicitly asserts: the idea of a global contract is the only one which allows a transformation of possession from a provisional to a peremptory form. Furthermore, that possession remains provisional not only in the external relations but also within states themselves is something depending on the lack of regulation of states' external interactions under the commands of a general will. Kant refers explicitly to this point when he speaks of an original contract where "acquisition will always remain only provisional unless this contract extends to the entire human race".[23]
2 The idea of perpetual approximations, divided into phases, leading towards peace. This is the movement which I call 'transitional'. It introduces the view of historical developments under a cosmopolitan view, something which we understand in terms of 'as if' progressions.

2.1 As will be showed in later sections, for Kant, war can be tolerated only within an intermediate transitional condition – in accordance with laws of transitions. This idea is explicitly introduced in Kant's "preliminary articles for perpetual peace".[24] According to this view, wars, like armaments, are admissible measures only under imperfect conditions of progression towards cosmopolitan justice. They are included as provisional articles in *Toward Perpetual Peace*, that is, as

20 Ibid.
21 Ibid.
22 The distinction between *leges latae* and *leges strictae* will be addressed more extensively in Part 3 §7.2.
23 Kant, "Metaphysics of Morals (1797)", 6:266, p.416.
24 Kant, "Toward Perpetual Peace (1795)", 8:343, pp.317 ff.

exceptionally admissible rules under imperfect circumstances of approximation to justice. Before the *a priori* system of laws takes over the irrational form in which states solve their diatribes, we need to accept as provisional measures those warfare resolutions that are acceptable only under qualified circumstances. Such laws of war, though, can never become peremptory under a cosmopolitan framework of justice. Wars are tolerable only as temporary exceptions that occur under imperfect conditions of realization of justice. Derogation to law is justifiable only in view of a future rapprochement to an all-encompassing juridical condition.

Let's investigate now, more closely, the arguments by the 'sorry comforters' that Kant rejected so forcefully.

§3.1 Grotius' freedom of the seas and the laws of war

In 1609 it appeared in Leiden an anonymous libel published by Elzevier and called *Mare liberum* (Free Sea). The book was supported by the Zeeland Chamber of the Dutch East India Company following the international crisis opened by the Dutch confiscation of the Portuguese vessel Saint Catharine in the Straits of Singapore in 1603. The goods were sold in Amsterdam for almost the equivalent of the annual revenue of England at that time.[25] The author of the book was a young Grotius who defended the right of the Dutch East Indies Company to the booty as a prize for just war.[26] In *Mare liberum* Grotius theorized the conditions in virtue of which interference in the internal affairs of the states was to be considered legitimate (i.e. when a sovereign was not capable of assuring peace or an internal stability of his own people). This opened a long lasting controversy among international law scholars and philosophers to which John Selden responded by an argument defending 'closed seas' (*Mare clausum*).[27]

The discussion on the opening/closure of the seas was of relevance for the definition of the fundamental pillars of international law. In modernity, with the proclamation of the Charter of the United Nations of 1945 in Art.2, such a principle has been formalized into the principle of "sovereign equality among [. . .] States".[28]

25 R. Tuck, *The Rights of War and Peace: Political Thought and the International Order from Grotius to Kant*, Oxford University Press, Oxford, 1999, p.80.

26 In 1864 during a sale of the de Groot family papers it was discovered that *Mare liberum* corresponded to the twelfth chapter of Grotius' *Commentary on the Law of Prize and Booty* (also known as *De Rebus Indicis*). See D. Harmitage, "Introduction", Grotius, *The Free Sea*, 2004 [1609], p. xiii.

27 On the reconstruction of this debate see, M. Brito Vieira, "*Mare Liberum vs. Mare Clausum*: Grotius, Freitas, and Selden's Debate on Dominion over the Seas", *Journal of the History of Ideas*, 64(3), 2003, pp.361–377; H. Thornton, "John Selden's Response to Hugo Grotius: The Argument for Closed Seas", *International Journal of Maritime History*, XVIII, 2006, pp.105–127; E. Papastavridis, "The Right of Visit on the High Seas in a Theoretical Perspective: *Mare Liberum* versus *Mare Clausum* Revisited", *Leiden Journal of International Law*, 24(1), 2011, pp.45–69.

28 United Nations Charter, art. 2(1). Available at: https://www.un.org/en/charter-united-nations/, (accessed on 18.09.2019).

Grotius' considerations were advanced on the basis of the premise of a pre-political state of nature out of which the laws of nature were derived accordingly. For Grotius, differently than Hobbes, the state of nature was not to be conceived as a hypothetical state, it was rather to be seen as a real and visible scenario, as in analogy to the high seas of the East Indies.

Even though the international state of nature lacked an overarching authority, it possessed nevertheless a system of rights whose obedience was based on natural social instinct. The concept of social appetite was introduced by Grotius right at the opening of the *Prologue of On the Law of War and Peace*, where he recognized that "among the traits characteristic of man is an impelling desire for society, that is, for the social life [. . .] peaceful, and organized".[29]

This point was what "the Stoics called 'sociableness'".[30] The driving question linking Grotius's other natural law thinkers was "how to combine civic integrity with a foundation in nature [. . .] in terms of *right* [?]".[31]

Grotius based his defence of the right to seize booty on natural reason and on the idea that God had given certain things of the world in common use to humanity, thus, commanding abstention from appropriation of others' unless "without damage of all",[32] and by "one's labor and industry to become proper".[33]

These two basic natural laws were sufficient to conjecture that the Portuguese had appropriated illegitimately that which was not theirs by controlling the seas and excluding access to the East Indies. For such reason Grotius considered that the Dutch admiral Jacob van Heemskerk was entitled to keep as compensation the cargo of the carrack Santa Catarina.[34] It was using the development of such argument that Grotius constructed an argument against the Portuguese by making use of the authority of the Salamanca School in order to support his arguments for a freedom of movement and trade of goods. He rejected not only the idea of the East Indies as *res nullius* before the presumed exclusive appropriation by the Portuguese (these belonged indeed to their indigenous residents), or by papal donation, or even on the basis of natural servitude of the local inhabitants. Differently from de Vitoria, Grotius believed that the locals had no obligation to trade.[35] But differently also from what Kant would affirm later, Grotius saw a right

29 H. Grotius, *On the Law of War and Peace*, S.C. Neff (ed. and annot.), Cambridge University Press, Cambridge, 2012 [1625], p.2.

30 Ibid.

31 A. Brett, "Natural Right and Civil Community: the Civil Philosophy of Hugo Grotius", *The Historical Journal*, 43(1), 2002, p.33. For a theological reading of Grotius' law of nature see C. Edwards, "The Law of Nature in the Thought of Hugo Grotius", *The Journal of Politics*, 32(4), 1970, pp.784–807. On a reading evidencing the modernity of Grotius' moral philosophy and its non-reducibility to Aristotelian naturalism see S. Darwall, "Grotius and the Creation of Modern Moral Philosophy", *Archiv f. Gesch. d. Philosophie*, 94(3), 2012, pp.296–325.

32 Grotius, *The Free Sea*, p.6.

33 Ibid.

34 Apparently this was one of Grotius' cousins. See Tuck, *Rights of War and Peace*, p.79.

35 Grotius, *Law of War and Peace*, p.102.

to passage and temporary sojourn with a more extensive force than just as something limited to Kant's *non-refoulement* mandatory reasons.[36] He also rejected the idea of a possible appropriation of the sea which, differently from land, was subject to fluidity and could not be used by excluding the others: "The sea therefore is in the number of those things which are not in merchandise and trading, that is to say, which cannot be made proper [ergo, the sea] 'was so common, that it may be in the dominion of none but God alone'".[37]

Grotius thus rejected the exclusive jurisdiction of the Portuguese on allowing navigation and exclusive trade in East Indies. These were natural rights which belonged to all nations and could not be altered by custom. All those arguments echoed de Vitoria's defence of a *ius peregrinandi et communicationis*; but now the promoters of such rights were the new emerging commercial powers of the time: the Dutch. An open issue remained the consideration of Grotius' solution to the problem of international punishment and commutative justice more in general.

The relation of Grotius to the Second Scholastics remains indeed rather ambiguous. Grotius' humanism allowed for a justification of a principle of international punishment, but this consisted in the pre-de Vitoria's idea that "barbarians or natural slaves might rightfully be appropriated by civilized peoples".[38] All in all, starting from the *Commentary on the Law of Prize and Booty* (*De iure predae*),[39] Grotius transformed the Aristotelian theory of distributive justice into an international theory of corrective justice. This theory was articulated around a notion of just war and namely on the right to punish all those actions pursued exclusively for the sake of self-advantage and in view of the disrespect of the interests and rights of the others.

In 1625 the work which made Grotius internationally famous appeared in Paris, namely the treatise *On the Law of War and Peace* (*De iure belli ac pacis*).[40] The book was essentially an expansion of the arguments he presented in *Mare liberum* which, as recalled, was later found to be the fifth book of *De iure predae*.

In book 1 of the *De iure belli ac pacis*, the influence of the Stoics and particularly of Cicero as well as the Digest is enormous. Following the Aristotelian tradition of the *Nicomachean Ethics*,[41] law is divided in volitional law and the law of nature. Volitional law, in turn, is distinguished into human and divine law. Finally, human volitional law differentiates into municipal law and the law of nations (*ius gentium*). Apparently these divisions distinguished the laws whose obligating force is above the will of the subjects from those laws whose force is peremptory.

36 "permission to pass ought first to be demanded; but, if it is refused, passage can be made by force" Grotius, *Law of War and Peace*, p.100.
37 Grotius, *The Free Sea*, p.30.
38 Tuck, *Rights of War and Peace*, pp.102 ff.
39 Grotius, *Law of Prize and Booty*.
40 Grotius, *Law of War and Peace*. H. Grotius, *De Iure Belli ac Pacis*, B.J.A. de Kanter-van Hettinga Tromp (ed.), Brill, Leiden, 1939 [1625].
41 Aristotle, *Nicomachean Ethics*, T. Irwin (ed.), Hackett Publishing Company, Inc. Indianapolis/ Cambridge, 1999.

Yet, since also the force of obligation of consensual law is derived ultimately by natural law, for Grotius "nature [could be considered] the great-grandmother of municipal law".[42] So, no matter whether *ius gentium* was consensual or not, its binding force was considered to be based on natural law.[43]

Grotius discusses whether war could be said to be in conflict with law, claiming that: "In the first principles of nature, there is nothing which is opposed to war".[44] The aim of war is in "the preservation of life and limb".[45]

In book 2 he lists "the three justifiable causes of war",[46] which he identifies as the right to self-defence, to private property, to have a debt paid.[47] He mentions also the right to punish, but this is a secondary right and its role is explained as a reaction to the violation of one of the first three. Grotius introduces here some conceptual innovations, such as the notion of property and a precise theory of punishment. In the *De iure predae* this point is conceptualized as an idea of acquisition (*occupatio*) and then integrated into the view of tacit agreement (*pactum tacitum*). One could say that well before Locke's exposition of the theory of property through labor, as exposed in the *Second Treatise of Government* (1690), it was Grotius who justified private property as a natural acquisition, absent a civil covenant.

Similar to the notion of private property, Grotius' right to punish is grounded in the state of nature. This right is based on the right to punish which follows from an unlawful act. This could be either a violation of private or of public right as well as either according to positive or to natural law. Regarding the right to punish non-citizens, either individuals or peoples, the source of the right is seen in terms of a natural kind. Grotius' theory of the natural right to punish is constructed upon a multiplicity of sources of states and individual obligations that include not only what today are non-derogable peremptory norms of *ius cogens*, but also *erga omnes* obligations on the international community.

Yet, Grotius never moves beyond the idea of a society of peoples. For the sake of such society he reconstructs a scheme of division of property on the starting premises of a "primitive common ownership",[48] a notion that Kant will consider fallacious. In this context Grotius affirms that those things which do not become private through a possible division of natural resources, do become so through appropriation, thus reaffirming the view that "the sea [. . .] cannot become subject to private ownership".[49]

42 Grotius, *Law of War and Peace*, p.5.
43 Cf. Grotius, ibid., p.32.
44 Ibid., p.35.
45 Ibid.
46 Grotius, *Law of War and Peace*, p.81.
47 Ibid. For an interpretation of private property in Grotius that emphasizes its status as "a man-made institution" see M. de Araujo, "Hugo Grotius, Contractualism, and the Concept of Private Property: An Institutionalist Interpretation", *History of Philosophy Quarterly*, 26(4), 2009, pp.353 ff.
48 Grotius, *Law of War and Peace*, p.93.
49 Ibid., p.94.

Whereas, on the one hand, a notion of distributive justice is excluded from the law of peoples and punishment as commutative justice remains, on the other hand, the only international scheme of remedy,[50] Grotius' conception of the society of peoples falls outside a global process of authority legitimation. As a source of law, Grotius considers the desire for the "maintenance of the social order".[51] In this respect he rebuts the Hobbesian dictum: *homo homini lupus*.[52] Yet, from a Kantian perspective, the unsocial sociability of men requires a system of coercive sanctioning for law-deviating behaviors. Grotius, unfortunately, provides no mechanism for the shift from a mere society of relative independent states to a global civil condition of peoples. Thus, the only consolation he can offer is the one mitigating the harshness of war by recognition of a *ius ad bellum* and a *ius in bello*. For these reasons, Grotius remains for Kant only a 'sorry comforter'.

§3.2 Pufendorf: the state as a subject of international law

After the crisis of the seventeenth century and the thirty-year war, Germany was left with one third of the urban population, a plethora of semi-independent states, and a disastrous economy. This was a post-Westphalian scenario. Samuel von Pufendorf, a prominent intellectual of the time for whom a chair in the law of nature and nations was created for the first time in Heidelberg, elaborated new political notions for the definition of the conditions among Westphalian states.[53] Kant mentions Pufendorf as the second 'sorrow comforter' whose views showed how peaceful coexistence among states was possible in an international state of nature.[54]

For Pufendorf, indeed, there was no asymmetry between a civil condition and – the real and not hypothetical – international state of nature. In opposition to Hobbes, he held that men could act in accordance with God's will and for the sake of increasing common utilities, rather than in view of the maximization of self-interests. Thus, the Hobbesian idea of an international state of nature characterized by a war of all against all was misplaced: "As for the causes adduced by Hobbes for men's desire to hurt one another, they are only particular and therefore by no means sufficient for stirring up a necessary war of all against all among humankind, but only of some against some".[55]

50 Ibid., p.269 ff. For an emphasis on a similar point see also R. Tuck when he writes about Grotius "that corrective justice dealt with rights 'strictly so called. Whereas distributive justice dealt with what was customarily termed 'imperfect' rights, or claims upon other people for their assistance [. . .]'". In Tuck, *Rights of War and Peace*, p.98.
51 Grotius, *Law of War and Peace*, p.3.
52 "For that teaching cannot long prosper which makes a man anti-social with his kind and also hateful in the sight of God", Grotius, *Law of War and Peace*, pp.474–475.
53 See M. Koskenniemi, "Miserable Comforters: International Relations as New Natural Law", *European Journal of International Relations*, 15(3), 2009, p.397.
54 Tuck, *Rights of War and Peace*, p.142.
55 S. Pufendorf, "On the Law of Nature and Nations", C.L. Carr (ed.) and M.J. Seidler (trans.), *The Political Writings of Samuel Pufendorf*, Oxford University Press, Oxford, New York, 1994 [1672], p.145.

Against Grotius, Pufendorf, in his *Elementorum Jurisprudentiae Universalis* (*Elements of Universal Jursiprudence*) [1660],[56] held the view that there was no international right to punish unless a state was directly injured. This was a sort of right to retaliation.[57]

Pufendorf criticized Grotius also on other two basic notions, namely, on the theory of sociability as well as on that of property.

For Pufendorf, sociability derives from safety. As he affirms:

> For sociality, as we understand it here, is not merely a tendency to form particular societies, whose purpose and manner of formation can also be evil, like an association of thieves – as if just any intention for joining oneself to another would do. Rather, we mean by it a kind of disposition whereby a man is understood to be joined to every other man by ties of benevolence, peace, and charity, and therefore by a mutual obligation. And so it is utterly false to claim that the sociality we are introducing is indifferent as to whether a society is good or evil.
>
> (S. Pufendorf, "On the Law of Nature and Nations", p.152)

Whereas for Grotius the duty to commutative justice was based on a negative duty not to harm others, for Pufendorf this amounted to a positive natural duty towards humanity.[58] If for Grotius there held no duty of assistance among nations, nor of redistribution of goods, for Pufendorf, instead: "It is not enough [. . .] not to have hurt another [. . .]. Something good must also be conferred on the other".[59] He defended this view by appealing to an idea of gratitude as a natural instinct of human beings generating an obligation to mutual help.[60]

Concerning property, Pufendorf criticized Grotius' idea on a natural right to property. For Grotius, there was a natural right of all to occupation of any plot of earth left uncultivated. Only a general control (jurisdiction) could be exercised by the local king over the occupants or the seas, demanding thus obedience to its rules.

Pufendorf, on the contrary, claimed that all property required agreement and convention such that no direct limitation clause could be established between

56 S. Pufendorf, "Elements of Universal Jurisprudence in Two Books", C.L. Carr (ed.) and M.J. Seidler (trans.), *The Political Writings of Samuel Pufendorf*, Oxford University Press, Oxford, New York, 1994 [1660], pp.31–94.

57 See Tuck, *Rights of War and Peace*, p.158.

58 Pufendorf, "Law of Nature and Nations", p.164 ff. See also D. Horst, *Moralphilosophie und Naturrecht bei Samuel Pufendorf*, 1972.

59 Ibid.

60 "A person is useful to others in a more definite way if he bestows on certain men something that can bring them some kind of profit. This can often be done without any loss, or bother and labor, to ourselves. To have denied or begrudged another such a thing is considered a detestable malice and inhumanity." In Pufendorf, "Law of Nature and Nations", p.165.

natural needs and consumption.[61] This allowed him to justify private possession and use of sea waters, and thus of state property, contrary to Grotius' views. By not drawing a clear-cut distinction between property and ***dominium***, Pufendorf justified, ***ante-litteram***, an anti-Lockean and anti-colonialist view whereby uncultivated lands also belonged to the authority of the local inhabitants.

Pufendorf's views move away from a theory of global moral authority. They point towards a state view and avoid a restriction, as was customary at that time, to only Christian peoples. As Alberico Gentili had already showed, the Chinese were also considered to be part of the international society and they were right in limiting foreign access to their territory.[62]

These same considerations reappear later in Kant when he defends the right of the state to limit temporary access to a territory as with the recognition of a cosmopolitan right to visit. Kant's view is clearly based on the community duty to self-preservation.[63] But since there was no obligation to allow visiting, a community could promote a selective right to admit some and exclude others, as in the case of the Japanese admittance of only the Dutch to trade, among all Europeans.

As a result of all this, how should we interpret Kant's dissatisfaction with Pufendorf's theory of international law? An indication in this sense comes from Pufendorf's view that there exists an analogy between the moral personality of individuals and that of states, so that no real distinction can be drawn between natural and international law.[64] Lacking such distinction, it appears that any attempt to make international law rely on state's compliance would lack a

61 Tuck, *Rights of War and Peace*, p.156.

62 "There are things contrary to the local religion, others contrary to the moral discipline and so on. Foreigners cannot argue on such issues since they don't have the right to change the institutions or the costumes of another people. What should we say, then, when it access to the internal zones of a region is prevented to merchants and only coming close to the borders is consented to? Britons once acted this way. Today we know that also the Chinese do so. It does not seem to me that, in such cases, one can affirm that commerce has been forbidden. One cannot say, indeed, that a guest has been expelled, when he has not been allowed entrance in every part of one's house. It is permitted to keep hidden the secrets of a reign and to keep distant those who have come to spy or who can only possibly do so." In A. Gentili, *De Iure Belli, Libri III* (1598), Cap.19, 145 p.85-86, available at https://archive.org/details/dejurebellilibri00gent/page/n4 (accessed on 6.07.2019). Author's translation.

63 G. Cavallar, "De Vitoria, Grotius, Pufendorf, Wolff and Vattel: Accomplices of European Colonialism and Exploitation or True Cosmopolitans?", *Journal of the History of International Law*, 10(2), 2008, p.199.

64 "We must also add something now *about the law of nations,* which is to some nothing other than the law of nature, insofar as it is observed among nations not connected with one another by supreme sovereignty, who must in their own manner perform toward one another the same duties that the law of nature prescribes to individuals. There is no reason for us to deal specifically with this here, since the things we are saying about the law of nature and the duties of individuals can easily be applied to whole states and nations that have also coalesced into one moral person." In. Pufendorf, "Elements of Universal Jurisprudence", p.64. See on this point also L. Krieger, *The Politics of Discretion. Pufendorf and the Acceptance of Natural Law*, The University of Chicago Press, Chicago and London, 1965, p.165 ff.

coercive mechanism of enforcement and thus would not be mandatory. Accordingly, Pufendorf's theory could only provide a 'sorry comforter'.

§3.3 Vattel's rejection of Wolff's *civitas maxima*

Whereas Pufendorf's ideas about sovereignty and appropriation in the state of nature were explicitly criticized by Locke, as documented by Barbeyrac,[65] it was with Vattel that a new Lockean line of interpretation opened up. Vattel was also a critic of Wolff, of whom he rejected the idea of a *civitas maxima*, the notion of a universal republic instituted by nature and including the most enlightened peoples.[66] For Vattel, states' obligations were always "imperfect with respect to other people".[67]

Peoples have to contribute to the well-being of all others only to the extent that this does not run against the well-being of one's own community. As a reaction to Wolff's duty to interstate assistance (even if limited by the right to self-preservation), as well as to de Vitoria's theory of *iustum pretium*, Vattel held that refusal to trade did not amount to a right to punishment. Yet, he was more extreme in justifying occupation when a state was unable to preserve itself. It is in such perspective that Vattel justified colonial aggressions and occupations of American territories.[68]

As it will be shown later, what Kant aimed to innovate was Wolff's *civitas maxima* when he introduced the regulative idea of *civitas gentium*. For Kant, the relation between natural and positive law obliged states to recognize reciprocally limited, but perfect, rights for the individual cosmopolitan right of *non-refoulement*. This did not extend beyond other traditional dimensions of cosmopolitan rights, such as trade rights.

What Wolff addressed in terms of a "voluntary law of nations"[69] is justified by Vattel in terms of yet a different foundation. For Vattel, natural law transfers its standards of validations to the positive laws of nations. Vattel assumed that the

65 Tuck, *The Rights of War and Peace*, p.181.

66 For an equation between 'civitas' with 'republic' but not with 'state', see N. Greenwood Onuf, "Civitas Maxima: Wolff, Vattel and the Fate of Republicanism", *The American Journal of International Law*, 88(2), 1994, p.292.

67 E. de Vattel, *The Law of Nations*, 2008 [1797], p.75.

68 "Thus, though the conquest of the civilized empires of Peru and Mexico was a notorious usurpation, the establishment of many colonies on the continent of North America might, on their confining themselves within just bounds, be extremely lawful. The people of those extensive tracts rather ranged through than inhabited them." In E. de Vattel, *The Law of Nations*, 2008 [1797], p.130. On this point see also Cavallar, "Accomplices", p.205.

69 "Since nations, in their transactions with each other, are equally bound to admit those exceptions to, and those modifications of, the rigour of the necessary law, whether they be deduced from the idea of a great republic of which all nations are supposed to be the members, or derived from the sources whence I propose to draw them, – there can be no reason why the system which thence results, should not be called the *Voluntary Law* of nations, in contradistinction to the *necessary*, internal, and consciential law. Names are of very little consequence: but it is of considerable importance carefully to distinguish these two kinds of law, in order

precepts of natural law are self-evident and understandable by all nations, so that adherence can be purely voluntary. The transformation of natural law precepts into the positive law of nations is based only on states' individual will and not, as will be later the case for Kant, on a practice-based conception of justice where 'facts' of cosmopolitan relevance, i.e. visits of various sort, raise the question of what should be transformed into articles of a cosmopolitan constitution of kind.[70]

For Vattel, indeed, the international state of peoples was a natural domain that could not be transformed into a civil state condition: "the body of the nation, the state, remains absolutely free and independent with respect to all other men, all other nations, as long as it has not voluntarily submitted to them".[71] Accordingly, as he notices at the inception of his book – *The Law of Nations* – the idea of a *civitas maxima* is incompatible with the notion of state sovereignty.[72] What regional-supranational polities can achieve is a balance of powers where an equilibrium of forces holds in view of general peace and stability.

The European context was an example of this case.[73] Yet, Vattel had to solve the problem of how states were compelled to obey the principles of natural law, lacking a centralized coercive authority. A possibility was that this was due to man's compliance to basic reasons, such as with "self-love and a desire for the happiness of a perfect soul".[74]

When compared to Grotius and Pufendorf, Vattel certainly appears as a thinker who left us with a much more restricted room of manoeuvre for the individual in international law.[75] States are the sources of positive international agreements. Both the principle of state equality and autonomy emerged clearly as new pillars of *ius gentium*.[76] These cannot be overruled simply by resorting to the presumption of an international state – the *civitas maxima* – out of which binding commands are derived. States have a moral personality, but whereas in the case

---

that we may never confound what is just and good in itself, with what is only tolerated through necessity." In de Vattel, *Law of Nations*, p.16.

70 "Positive laws: These three kinds of law of nations, the *voluntary*, the *conventional*, and the *customary*, together constitute the *positive law of nations*. For they all proceed from the will of nations, – the *voluntary* from their presumed consent, the *conventional* from an express consent, and the *customary* from tacit consent: and as there can be no other mode of deducing any law from the will of nations, there are only these three kinds of *positive law of nations*". In de Vattel, *Law of Nations*, p.78.

71 Ibid, p.68.

72 Ibid., p.14.

73 "The continual attention of sovereigns to every occurrence, the constant residence of ministers, and the perpetual negotiations, make of modern Europe a kind of republic, of which the members – each independent, but all linked together by the ties of common interest – unite for the maintenance of order and liberty. Hence arose that famous scheme of the political balance, or the equilibrium of power; by which is understood such a disposition of things, as that no one potentate be able absolutely to predominate, and prescribe laws to the others." In de Vattel, *Law of Nations*, p.496.

74 De Vattel, *Law of Nations*, p.xvi.

75 Cavallar, "Accomplices", p.207.

76 P.P. Remec, *The Position of the Individual in International Law according to Grotius and Vattel*, Martinus Nijhoff, The Hague, 1960, p.56.

of Wolff's *civitas maxima* this is a top-down process of transferring, for Vattel it remains a bottom-up process.

At the end, for Kant, there will be a more articulated process of construction for an international condition of legitimacy among states. Namely, this will have to combine both a bottom-up process (with the formation of states covenants), and a top-down dynamics, as with the exit from the natural society of peoples by means of "some kind of contract"[77] under the presumption of a global general will.

For Vattel, whereas the original society of humankind is able to account for the validity of natural law, the shift into positive law is exhausted by the creation of states' entities. The positive non-voluntary character of the *civitas maxima* remains for Vattel (a pupil of Wolff) a fiction in need of preservation of the autonomy of states' wills.

In this respect, the moral personality of states is derived from the covenant of the people, the pact they form in the unification of their wills. The reaction of Vattel to Wolff is justified in view of the possible loss of states' autonomy once their legitimacy of action is derived by Wolff in conformity with the idea of an all-encompassing republic (*civitas maxima*).

This point is indirectly accounted for by Kant when he mentioned the possible (performative) contradiction in which states would fall were they to decide to merge into a suprastate order, thus, renouncing to their individual sovereign autonomy.

Vattel attempts to solve the problem by defending the combination between the principle/duty of state preservation, on the one hand, and the idea of an equal responsibility of states derived from their equal standing in international law. This is derived ultimately from a double duty of men in the state of nature: that of protecting themselves while striving for perfection, on the one hand, and that of realizing the offices towards humanity – of stoic and ciceronian origins – on the other hand.[78]

For Vattel the equality of states derives from the notion of an equality of individuals.[79] Differently from what will later be the case with Kant, in Vattel's construction of the validity of law, there holds a domestic analogy between individuals, states, and the international order. Yet, Vattel's conception of the equality of states remains a naturalistic view limited to a state's physical power, something which does not need to resort to an idea of equality under (global) law.[80]

From this view there follows a number of classical problems. First of all, that whenever a state infringes upon those interests belonging to the community as a whole there holds a general interest of prevention. Yet, there remains an incoherence with regard to the lack of a compulsory system of decision-making. The state

77 Kant, "Toward Perpetual Peace (1795)", 8:383, p.349. Translation partially modified.

78 De Vattel, *Law of Nations*, p.261.

79 "Since men are by nature equal, and their individual rights and obligations the same, as coming equally from nature, Nations, which are composed of men and may be regarded as so many free persons living together in a state of nature, are by nature equal and hold from nature the same obligations and the same rights". In DeVattel, *Law of Nations*, p.18.

80 Remec, *Position of the Individual*, p.186 ff.

remains the only subject of international law and an absolute sovereign. Kant will correct this view by introducing yet another normative layer: the notion of cosmopolitan right as one pillar of public right.

Through this innovation, individual subjects become positioned within the international realm both in terms of state citizens as well as of foreign nationals. Accordingly, state sovereignty loses its territorially related character, connecting the validity of domestic jurisdiction to cosmopolitan law. Sovereignty loses its absolute and unrelated character becoming compatible with contemporary forms of (reversible) delegations of power-competences. Yet, this requires that the relation between the natural law principles, such as freedom of movement and appropriation, as well as the constraining force of positive norms of the *ius gentium*, is mediated through cosmopolitan right. Kant will sketch precisely this constructivist view of law by means of the idea of a cosmopolitan constitution.

Unfortunately, in Vattel, such relation remains only external and uncompromised. The unchangeability of the natural law opposes itself to the extreme variability of the voluntary law of nations. Here, there lacks a mediating element which, through cosmopolitan right, allows in Kant the incorporation of natural law moral precepts into the positively binding force of an international law scheme.

Vattel is therefore for Kant only a 'sorry comforter': in so far as states' interpretations of the duties attached to natural law precepts remain subjective and lead to possible conflicting views, there holds no authoritatively suprastate entity, nor any law-constraining possibility to make states comply with international justice. Instead, states remain equally right in defending their respective views and war becomes justified from each state's perspective.

It appears, though, that whereas for Kant the first two 'sorry comforters' lack a proper view of international law as a form of positive biding tool, with regard to Vattel, instead, he fails to draw the logical conclusions with regard to the idea that there is a strict intersection between natural and positive law. It is on this *constructivist hypothesis*, as I will later show, that Kant defines the relation between cosmopolitan right and the positive right of nations. To this purpose, therefore, it is not by chance that Kant saves Wolff from the label of being only a 'sorry comforter'.

§3.4 . . . and Wolff's *civitas maxima*?

The question that is to be answered at this point is the following: why does Kant not include Wolff among the sorry comforters? For Wolff, all moral entities are fictitious. States, as well as individuals, have corresponding imaginary categories on the basis of which their value is assessed. For the case of interstate relations, it is the *civitas maxima* that plays the role of the corresponding notion from which can be derived a voluntary law of peoples. Wolff adds several other features to the idea of *civitas maxima*, such as the popular ruling of humanity, and the idea of the will of nations deriving from a mediation between nature and the use of right reason.[81]

81 Greenwood Onuf, "Civitas Maxima", p.286.

Even more interesting, for the purposes of Kant's later reformulations, is the view that as each nation has a leader (a leader 'superior' with power to rule), so there is a "ruler of the supreme state [*rector civitatis maximae*] who, following the leadership of nature, defines by right use of reason what nations ought to consider law among themselves, although it does not conform in all respects to the natural law of nations, nor altogether differ from it".[82]

It is here clear how the notion of a fictitious ruler mediates between the inapplicability – by itself – of natural law on the one hand, and the arbitrary subjectivity of the wills of individual states, on the other hand.[83]

For Vattel the *civitas maxima* could not be a source of international law. Voluntary laws, indeed, have to be derived from internationally accepted states practices, but the idea of *civitas maxima* conflates voluntary with necessary laws. Vattel, accordingly, modifies the Wolffian scheme for the positive laws of nations,[84] and the idea of *civitas maxima* is rejected in favor of the principle of balance of power. Yet, basing the possibility for European peace only on an equilibrium of power was a too precarious solution for Kant: not only because it was revealed to be an insufficient instrument to restrain states from waging aggressive wars, but also because it appeared an inadequate tool for vindicating a Republican ideal.[85]

To all such controversy, Kant's answer found a middle way between Vattel's and Wolff's lesson.

From Vattel, Kant retained the view that sovereign states – not republics with no statehood component – are the basic building blocks of international relations – this explains the use of the expression "*civitas gentium*"[86] as a replacement for *civitas maxima*.

From Wolff, instead, as will be discussed more at length later, Kant developed the idea of a *Weltrepublik* as a practical guidance – a tribunal of reason – for the creation of interstate valid laws.

In this respect, Kant attempted to learn the lessons from both his two predecessors by considering that the voluntary laws of nations could be conceived only in terms of a regulative idea of reason – 'as if' (*als ob*). In this way he thought it

82 C. Wolff, *Jus Gentium Methodo Scientifica Pertractatum*, J.H. Drake (trans.), Clarendon Press, Humphrey Milfford, Oxford, 1934 [1749], para.22.

83 "Societas and civitas now stand decisively severed, with the rector fictus mediating between them." In Greenwood Onuf, "Civitas Maxima", p.286.

84 "When he began his substantive exposition, Vattel changed this scheme. Voluntary law, conventional law and customary law became 'three divisions' (not two species, one divided) that form together the positive Law of Nations, for they all proceed from the agreement of Nations; the voluntary law from their presumed consent; the conventional law from their express consent; and the customary law from their tacit consent", Greenwood Onuf, "Civitas Maxima", p. 300.

85 "Vattel's time; a generation later it failed catastrophically. Beyond a foundation in the balance of power, what Vattel had in mind for his republic is not at all clear. We could say that he failed to honor the separate senses of the term 'republic': polis, civitas, body politic, on the one hand; politeia, status, form of rule, on the other", Greenwood Onuf, "Civitas Maxima", p.302.

86 Kant, "Toward Perpetual Peace (1795)", 8:357, p.328.

was possible to avoid, on the one hand, the error made by Wolff to blur away the distinction between a natural and a civil society of states, and on the other hand, the same error of naivety made by Vattel with regard to an international society where states have only a feeble duty to overcome their egoistic self-interests.

These conceptual premises played a crucial role in allowing Kant to reformulate the relation between a necessary law of nature and voluntary laws of *ius gentium*.

§3.4.1 Kant, Wolff, and the idea of a civitas gentium

As introduced before, Kant's philosophy is situated at the crossroads of two fundamental shifts in the unfolding process of international law: (a) the progressive formation of states' subjectivity within the international order, and (b) the transformation of international relations from pyramidal to horizontal and state-to-state relations.[87]

Vattel was already the forerunner of the concept of state's self-determination and sovereignty against Wolff's idea of a *civitas maxima*, something prefiguring a globally valid covenant constraining states behind their autonomous will.[88] Wolff's idea was that the *civitas maxima* represented the result of a rationally presumed consensus among individuals and peoples. This explained its rational mandatory force beyond states' wills.

Kant's conception of the legitimacy of the international order was situated in between these two positions.

Even though Kant never demonstrated much enthusiasm for Wolff's metaphysics, it is telling that he continued developing his ideas by keeping Wolff as a constant reference point. It should not seem surprising, therefore, that Kant speaks of a *civitas gentium* in terms of a world state republic. This notion, I argue, is a re-elaboration of Wolff's idea of *civitas maxima*. The modification Kant introduces of the *civitas gentium* reflects some kind of 'critical proximity' to Wolff,[89] through the emphasis he places on the plurality of states as the component parts of a global civil whole. What is perhaps even more important, notwithstanding the differences, is that both Wolff and Kant assume a similar justificatory point of departure, namely, the idea of defining the rational form of right on the assumption of a unitarian view. Wolff and Kant, therefore, both resort to an all-encompassing idea of what it means to obtain legitimate interstate relations in terms of a presumptive regulative consensus.[90]

Whereas Wolff's *civitas maxima* suffices to provide a mandatory platform to harness states' behaviour to a presumed compulsory scheme of globally shared law, Kant's *a priori* rationality of a *civitas gentium* never wants to overrule the

87 Cavallar, *Theory and Practice*, p.44.
88 Ibid., p. 47.
89 Kant, "Toward Perpetual Peace (1795)", 8:357, p.328.
90 See F. Cheneval, "Der präsumtiv vernünftige Konsens der Menschen und Völker – Christian Wolffs Theorie der civitas maxima", *ARSP: Archiv für Rechts- und Sozialphilosophie / Archives for Philosophy of Law and Social Philosophy*, 1999, pp. 563–580.

constituent will of the peoples, certainly not that of the republics, nor that of the minimal threshold of citizen-protections in illiberal states. Yet Wolff's state of positive and compulsory force of international law remains for Kant more desirable than the non-remedial character of the natural law purported by Grotius, Pufendorf, and Vattel.

Significant linguistic traces of Wolff's writings are evident also in a passage where Kant speaks of "the right of nations as [. . .] *status iuridicus*"[91] which "must proceed from some kind of contract" ("aus irgend einem Vertrage").[92] A parallel here, is Wolff's definition of the *civitas maxima* as a "quasi-contract (*quasi-Vertrag*)".[93] The quasi-contract is for Wolff a fictional concept endowed with a heuristic function lacking any negative connotation. Differently from a *consensus expressus*, a contract having actually taken place, or a *consensus tacitus*, an agreement silently reached, the *consensus praesumtus* is a form of covenant that is real but has never occurred in reality. For Kant this is the presumption of a 'will' to enter into a contractual relation but not yet a formulated contract. In so far as it is real, it establishes rights and duties as an explicit covenant, yet it does not require an actual gathering of the wills, but only the conformity to an ideal rationality.[94] The quasi-contract is an anticipation of a rational consensus for all interested peoples deliberating under ideal conditions.[95] It establishes "*a status populari*",[96] that is, a democracy ("*eine Demokratie*")[97] of free and equal states but only – as it will be claimed later by Kant – as a presumption of a universal scheme of justification without a positivist law-making power. As a fictional entity, the *civitas maxima* explains what is in Wolff, and later in Kant, a building-block theory of a society of individuals and states organized around rights as, respectively: a *societas magna* (*civitas maxima*), a society of men in Wolff, and a *civitas gentium*, a society of peoples, in Kant.[98]

The use of fictional legal entities, here, appears mostly appropriate. To conceive of men as subjects of the law requires a conceptual leap-forward. One must think of oneself in hypothetical terms as someone other than just a natural subject. Accordingly, the union of individuals through artificial entities – the state – whereas it can resemble even a monstrous entity as in the case of the Leviathan

91 Kant, "Toward Perpetual Peace (1795)", 8:383, p.348. Translation partially modified.
92 Ibid.
93 As C. Wolff affirms: "[. . .] the quasi-contract [quasi-Vertrag], by which that supreme state is understood to have been formed between nations [. . .]" (translation partially modified), Wolff, *Jus Gentium* §9, p.12.
94 On these distinctions see Cheneval, "Der präsumtiv vernünftige Konsens", p.569. For F. Cheneval the fictional contract is "faktisch aber nicht statfindet", ibid.
95 Most, but not all these features are in Cheneval, op. cit.
96 Cheneval, "Der präsumtiv vernünftige Konsens", p.574.
97 See citation of Wolff in F. Cheneval, op. cit., note 62, p.574: "C. Wolff: JG, §19: 'Die Civitas maxima besteht aus allen Staatsvölkern, die als einzelne frei und unter einander gleich sind [. . .]'".
98 Cheneval, "Der präsumtiv vernünftige Konsens", p.572.

for Hobbes, is for Kant and Wolff to be conceived instead as a moral entity.[99] This explains why Wolff's building-block theory for the definition of the legitimacy of law and Kant's idea of the state republic define state-entities as interdependent wholes whose obligations are ultimately to comply with the idea of a presumptive rational consensus. However, this is a conjecture, and the notion of a *civitas maxima* amounts to the postulation of an institutional presumption for the justification of coerciveness in international law.

Wolff's juristic hypothesis of a presumptive rational consensus is transformed by Kant along regulative-ideal terms and this, as will be demonstrated later, depends on Kant's rethinking of the metaphysical tradition. Kant has a long-structured argument in favour of such a regulative function, one starting from the state of nature.

Differently from Wolff, Kant's rationale for justifying the exiting of the state of nature through a "*general will given a priori* (within a nation *or in the relation of various nations to one another*) [emphasis added]",[100] defines the autonomy of states' sovereignty so that no external coercion is admitted. Through this move, Kant reformulates the theoretical legal basis for Wolff's conception of world state legitimacy. Indeed, if the presumption of a global contract cannot be made coercive *unless* states will it so, its constraining role turns into regulatory terms. As a result of this, Kant solves the stalemate between the theory and the practice of states' politics and their legitimate interconnections within the global order.

The question then turns into the following: how can states remain legitimate entities without eventually contradicting the same presuppositions from which they have been established?

It has been said that only if the world state republic is transformed into a regulative idea does it then become possible to grasp the legitimacy of interstate relations within one single global legal framework. Here, however, lies a profound difference between Kant's and Wolff's theories. Indeed, Wolff considers the hypothesis of a contract to explain his idea of a *civitas maxima*. As he declares: the commonwealth of states is: "as if this has been reached through a separate contract" [*als wenn sie durch einen eigenen Vertrag zu Wege grebracht wäre*].[101] Since, for Wolff, this contract is subject to a presumptive rational consent (*consensus praesumtus*), the compulsory force it displays is one of positive law.[102] The same does not follow from Kant's regulative ideal of the world state republic. Here, the preservation of the free will of states to adhere to international agreements cannot be compromised. Any derogation from such a requirement would run counter to Kant's idea of state sovereignty and the republican ideal of people's free will for legislative self-determination. It becomes then an open question

99 Ibid., p.567.

100 Kant, "Toward Perpetual Peace (1795)", 8:378, p.345.

101 C. Wolff, "Grundsätze des Natur und Völckerrechts etc.", *Gesammelte Werke*, vol.19, Olms Verlag, Halle [1754] 1980, §1090.

102 On this interpretation see Cavallar, *International Rights*, 1999, p.59.

to define in Kant by what nature comes to have global constitutional law when not backed by the enforcement of the threat to punish.

The answer to this point derives again from the highlighting of the different functions that the two justificatory platforms of international law assume, respectively, in Wolff and Kant. Indeed, each legal strand identifies a specific type of relation: the first, Wolff's *civitas maxima* qualifies the idea of an earthly society of states stepping out of which would incur the violation of a positive contract; the other, Kant's *civitas gentium* (or *Völkerstaat*)[103] qualifies a political entity that, while unachievable constitutively, turns into an object of practical reason for the definition of legitimate relations among states that are also in accordance to an *a priori* scheme of right.

Kant's disambiguation and regulative transformation of the constitutive legal status of Wolff's *civitas maxima* shows itself to be incompatible with the possibility of "forc(ing) consent [of the] unwilling"[104] states in the name of a global covenant. Kant, through this move, maintains two elements at once: he saves the free will of states in self-determining their own destiny and foreign policy (in accordance with the republican principle of self-legislation and autonomous sovereignty), while keeping open the possibility of a natural duty to enter a juridical condition regulated by the principles of justice.

All in all, Kant's theory of international law and justice pulls together two different and apparently irreconcilable strings of an overall unitary system of peoples and cosmopolitan men. Both subject entities define jointly the peremptory conditions of global peace. Presupposing a world state republic as a regulative idea means to find a median term, an Archimedean point of juncture between such two poles.

Kant is a true reformist. In various passages, he holds the view that states should undergo gradual reforms in light of an approximation to republican ideals. Progressive enlargement of civil freedoms has to go hand in hand with the same gradual affirmation of an enlightenment project – a project realizing the emancipation of human beings through history: a "perfect republic [. . .] governed by the principles of justice".[105] Unlike Locke, however, Kant shows himself to be opposed to the idea of a constitutional right to rebellion. This conviction

103 Kant, "Toward Perpetual Peace (1795)", 8:357, p.328. The German text draws an explicit association between the terms: "Völkerstaat (*civitas gentium*)". In I. Kant, *Zum Ewigen Frieden*, 2011 [1795], 8:357, p.29.

104 As Wolff says: "And since it is understood in a civil state that the tutor is compelled to act, if he should be unwilling to consent of his own accord, but that even when the agreement is extorted by a superior force that does not prevent the tutelage from resting upon a quasi-agreement; why, then, is it not allowable to attribute the same force to the natural obligation by which nations are compelled to enter into an alliance as is attributed to the civil obligation, that it is understood *to force consent* even as from one unwilling? [emphasis added]". In Wolff, *Jus Gentium*, §9, p.13.

105 As Kant affirms: "civil freedom can no longer be so easily infringed without disadvantage to all trades and industries [. . .] this freedom is gradually increasing [. . .] And thus enlightenment gradually arises." Cited in Cavallar, *International Rights*, 1999, p.39.

is due to the contradiction that it would engender by holding a people as judging unitedly "under a general legislative will [of a] supreme authority"[106] and the possibility of judging unitedly but independently from such constituted legislative power-unity. Nevertheless, as a moral prerogative, Kant admits to the possibility of criticizing the executive power either through direct parliamentary action of elected representatives or through the public use of reason of philosophy academics having the duty to reform by signalling the wrongness and the incoherencies of governments.[107] This view would cohere with the only non-institutional possibility that Kant admits, that is, the idea of "people acting as a mob"[108] as a non-organized form of collective subjectivity reacting against a legitimately constituted power.

106 Kant, "Metaphysics of Morals (1797)", 6:317, pp.461–462. In this respect, Guyer speaks of an argument arguing for "some sort of ontological impossibility for a people to rebel", P. Guyer, *Kant*, Routledge, London/New York, 2006, p.285.
107 See Guyer, *Kant*, p.289 ff.
108 Kant, "Metaphysics of Morals (1797)", 6:340, p.480.

§4 Kant's rejection of just war theory

The tradition of just war theory is older than the debate led by Grotius, Pufendorf, and Vattel. As mentioned in previous sections, the discussion had already begun in Augustine's *City of God*,[1] and it continued with Aquinas' definition on the conditions for just war, as namely, with the notion of right authority, just cause, and right intention.[2] It is from such tradition that the modern views on just war theory appear later in Grotius and others, as with the distinctions between a *ius ad bellum*, *in bello* and *post bellum*.[3]

Even if Kant saved Wolff from the list of the 'sorry comforters', most probably due to Wolff's views on the *civitas maxima* expressed in his 1750 book on *Ius Gentium*,[4] the thesis on a right to war appeared clearly four years later in his work on the *Principles of Natural and International Law*.[5] For Wolff, the *civitas maxima* could justify military intervention for the sake of the safeguard of the international states' community and never simply for the defence of individual

1 Augustine, *City of God*.

2 "In order for a war to be just, three things are necessary. First, the authority of the sovereign by whose command the war is to be waged. For it is not the business of a private individual to declare war, because he can seek for redress of his rights from the tribunal of his superior [. . .] Secondly, a just cause is required, namely that those who are attacked, should be attacked because they deserve it on account of some fault [. . .] Thirdly, it is necessary that the belligerents should have a rightful intention, so that they intend the advancement of good, or the avoidance of evil." In St. Thomas Aquinas, *Summa Theologica*. Catholic Way Publishing, London, 2014, pp.1813–1814. As Pagden notices, "Wars are 'just', St Augustine had written, in what was one of the most frequently cited passages in support of this view, 'which revenge the injuries caused when the nation or *civitas* with which war is envisaged has either neglected to make recompense for illegitimate acts committed by its members, or to return what has been injuriously taken.' [the citation is from *Quaestionum in Heptateuchem*, VI.X.]" In A. Pagden, "The Law of Continuity: Conquest and Settlement within the Limits of Kant's International Right", K. Flikschuh and L. Ypi (eds.), *Kant and Colonialism*, Oxford University Press, Oxford, 2014, p.29.

3 On a thoughtful discussion of the development of the *ius post bellum* concept see C. Stahn, J.S. Easterday, and J. Iverson, *Jus Post Bellum: Mapping the Normative Foundations*, Oxford University Press, Oxford, 2014.

4 Wolff, *Jus Gentium*, pp.5–19.

5 Wolff, *Grundsaetze des Natur- und Voelkerrechts*, Halle (Saale) [1754], Available online at: http://www.deutschestextarchiv.de/book/view/wolff_voelckerrecht_1754?p=5.

state's interests.[6] Kant shared this overall point of view, but he also provided a more nuanced reading on how to incorporate warfare from the perspective of a globally instituted civil condition to peace as a juridical condition.[7]

Kant holds an apparently ambivalent position on war. On the one hand, he considers it as a necessary instrument of nature in so far as the latter provides a guarantee for perpetual peace; on the other hand, he appears as the most forceful opponent of any theory of just war, as is shown in his sarcastic comments on the works of his predecessors.

In the opening of the first supplement of *Toward Perpetual Peace*, Kant claims that nature, as a "great artist (*natura daedala rerum*)"[8] makes "concord [to] arise by means of the discord between human beings even against their will".[9] This reveals a "mechanical course [of] purposiveness"[10] of nature, something that we might call "*providence*".[11] Nature's astuteness "by *war* it has driven them [humans] everywhere, even into the most inhospitable regions, in order to populate these";[12] but also "by war it has compelled them to enter into more or less lawful relations".[13]

Through war not only can we make sense of the spreading of human beings around the globe, but also of their forming social groups and mutually conflicting states. With a clear aesthetic appreciation, Kant observes "that the sandy wastes contain salt for the *camel*, which seems *as if created* for traveling in them, so as not to leave them unused, is already *wonderful* [emphasis added]".[14] It is an act of reflective judgment, one might argue, which allows us to see the teleology of nature and the disposal of human beings within its contours as something well-conceived. Yet, concludes Kant "what *drove* them *into* those regions, however, was presumably nothing other than war".[15]

There is a limiting point at which all this process comes to a halt, as when even "*military courage* [. . . as well as the sense of] an inner *dignity*"[16] is confronted with "the *spirit of commerce*, which cannot coexist with war".[17]

Furthermore, Kant suggests a point of convergence between a natural teleological plan and the obligations justifiable under a moral perspective.

As he puts it: "Even if a people were not forced by internal discord to submit to the constraint of public laws, war would still force them from without to

6 See Williams, *Kant and the End of War*, p.166.
7 See on this point I. Maus, *Menschenrechte, Demokratie und Frieden*, 2015. For an earlier discussion refer to H. Saner, *Kants Weg vom Krieg zum Frieden*, 1967.
8 Kant, "Toward Perpetual Peace (1795)", 8:360, p.331.
9 Ibid.
10 Ibid.
11 Ibid.
12 Kant, "Toward Perpetual Peace (1795)", 8:363, pp.332–333.
13 Ibid.
14 Ibid.
15 Ibid.
16 Kant, "Toward Perpetual Peace (1795)", 8:365, p.334.
17 Ibid., 8:368, pp.336–337.

do so, inasmuch as [. . .] each people would find itself in the neighborhood of another people pressing upon it, against which it must form itself internally into a *state* in order to be armed as a *power* against it".[18] Therefore, for Kant the plan of nature and the duties that can be reconstructed as morally coercive on us do not conflict at all, and "The problem of establishing a state, no matter how hard it may sound, is *soluble* even for a nation of devils."[19]

Coming to the critical stand of Kant's views on just war theory, an initial interpretive puzzle concerns the apparent irreconcilable contradiction between the position expressed in *Toward Perpetual Peace* and the one, more open to war, defended two years later in the *Metaphysics of Morals*, section on the *Doctrine of Right*.

Such apparent textual uncertainties have led scholars to suggest two radically different interpretations considering Kant either as yet another just war theorist (Byrd and Hruschka, Teson, Orend, Shell and others),[20] or alternatively, as an anti-just war theorist based on an ideal continuity of *Toward Perpetual Peace* to the *Metaphysics of Morals* (Gregor, Williams).[21]

The diatribe amounts essentially on how to interpret the concession that Kant allows to preventive war in the case of the threat of a 'rough state', what he calls a "*potentia tremenda*",[22] that is, a state mining the security of the international order and of state citizens. An analogous case is that of the so-called "unjust enemy",[23] which Kant labels so probably with a dose of irony, if one considers its pleonastic sense.

Taking into account Kant's overall system of global politics, it seems that the view of a thematic unity between *Toward Perpetual Peace* and the *Metaphysics of Morals* is the most plausible interpretation to adopt.

It might certainly be the case, as Williams notices, that some of the crucial passages of the *Metaphysics of Morals* were written in advance of the publication of

18 Ibid., 8:365–8:366, p.335.

19 Ibid, 8:366, p.335.

20 B. Orend, *War and International Justice: A Kantian perspective,* Wilfrid Laurier University Press, Waterloo, 2000; F. Teson, *Humanitarian Intervention: An Inquiry into Law and Morality,* Transnational Publishers, Irvington-On-Hudson, NY, 2005; S. Shell, "Kant on Unjust War and 'Unjust Enemies' reflections on a pleonasm", *Kantian Review* 10(1), 2005; S. Byrd and J. Hruschka, *Kant's Doctrine of Right: A Commentary,* Cambridge University Press, Cambridge, 2010, p.15 and p.195. Cited in H. Williams, *Kant and the End of War*, p.54.

21 As Williams frames such a diatribe: "In contrast to Byrd and Hruschka, there is every reason to believe, as Mary Gregor indicates, that 'thematically *Toward Perpetual Peace* takes up where *The Doctrine of Right* ends.' Gregor sees the shorter book as building upon the more schematic outlook presented in the book on right. Thus despite the shorter book appearing before the treatise on right, Gregor maintains it has a similar systematic priority." Williams, *Kant and the End of War*, p.55.

22 Kant explains the case in the following way: "This is a wrong to the lesser power merely by the *condition* of the *superior power,* before any deed on its part, and in the state of nature an attack by the lesser power is indeed legitimate. Accordingly, this is also the basis of the right to a balance of power among all states that are contiguous and could act on one another." Kant, "Metaphysics of Morals (1797)", 6:346, p.484.

23 Kant, "The Metaphysics of Morals (1797)", 6:349, p.487.

Toward Perpetual Peace.[24] But in order to make sense of why "Perpetual Peace should be regarded as Kant's most fully worked out treatment of the question of just war",[25] it is crucial to lay out the overall structure and transitions that, supposedly, he had in mind.

The suggestion is therefore to consider that Kant thought of the international order as something structured along *three transitional phases*. These should be seen as spanning from: 1. an international state of nature among peoples, 2. a condition of interstate regulations brought about in accordance to international law, and 3. the establishment of a global civil condition under the premises of a cosmopolitan constitution.

Under this framework, Kant claims not only that states are allowed to engage in wars of self-defence, but also that there should hold a maxim according to which "there is to be no war".[26] Hesitance, with regard to Kant's interpretation of the notion of *potentia tremenda* or unjust enemy, depends entirely on which phase of transition we are considering. The more we progress towards a global civil condition, the less these are meaningful categories.

Things are complicated by Kant's use of the expression "*right to go to war*"[27] adopted in the *Metaphysics of Morals*. If a state of nature is a state deprived of law (so that war is admissible due to the lack of other legitimate resources), then, why the term 'right' be used? In fact, adds Kant, "this [vindication of a wrong] cannot be done in the state of nature by a lawsuit (the only means by which disputes are settled in a rightful condition)".[28]

One useful indication comes from the preceding §55 where Kant had defined such a right in terms of an "original right that free states in a state of nature have to go to war with one another".[29] What Kant has in mind here is a natural right to defend oneself when under physical attack. It is not an established right, something positively defined by an instituted public authority. Yet, an appeal to self-defence is legitimate in those state contexts where there is not yet a legal frame under which it is yet possible to solve international controversies.

If Kant thought that the international natural state was all we had, then, certainly we could consider this as a theory of just war. But Kant never thought that the natural state among nations was the final stage of historical development. On

24 Williams, *Kant and the End of War*, p.52 ff.

25 Ibid., p.51. Williams, to be sure, proposes the more general view for which "One other possible way of resolving the conflict between the two passages in Kant's writings is to suggest that the two rules apply for Kant to two different conditions. The rule which is presented in *Perpetual Peace* as part of the 'transcendental formula of public right' (8: 381/347) applies, it is argued, to the relationships that exist between states that have already emerged from the state of nature amongst themselves (who form part of a federation of free states) and so can be accepted to abide by commonly agreed reciprocal rules – and the rule that is presented in *Metaphysics of Morals* applies to states in their more normal condition of unregulated independence." In Williams, *Kant and the End of War*, p.100.

26 Kant, "Metaphysics of Morals (1797)", 6:354, p.491.

27 Ibid., 6:346, p.484.

28 Ibid.

29 Ibid., 6:344, p.483

the contrary he thought that this condition should have been overcome on the base of states' mutual sustenance: "Since a state of nature among nations, like a state of nature among individual human beings, is a condition that one ought to leave in order to enter a lawful condition [. . .]";[30] and again, when speaking of the ius post bellum – "right after war",[31] Kant explicitly affirms that: "there is also a right for states to constrain each other to leave this condition of war and so form a constitution that will establish lasting peace".[32] From all these indications it arises an "irresistible veto: there is to be no war, neither war between you and me in the state of nature nor war between us as states".[33]

But then the problem remains *how* to move from 1. an international state of nature, to 2. a condition of interstate relations regulated under international law. Here Kant points clearly to the idea that international alliances among states "serve for continual *approximation* to it [toward perpetual peace]".[34] This goal is "a task based on duty and therefore on the right of human beings and of states [. . . which] can certainly be achieved".[35] But the establishment of positive law regulations among states as well as the creation of supranational entities must coexist with partial conditions of non-compliance of those states that still refuse to embrace law and reason as a form to solve conflicts. Since states, differently from individuals, cannot be forced to enter into interstate relations that are in agreement with an international rule of law, the former must still be safeguards readily available for a transitioning under conditions of instability (as with free riders).

Such safeguards resembling law (but in fact only tolerable exceptions to peremptory norms) are called by Kant 'provisional norms'. An example is given in the *Preliminary articles* of *Toward Perpetual Peace* where Kant lists as provisional laws those temporary measures necessary to defend state entities from unexpected state aggressions. Provisions such as those allowing state armies, the acquisition of new states through contracts or marriages, or also state's financial debts held in the hands of foreign powers are rules derogating provisionally to the application of strict norms for the law of peoples. These can be tolerated only on the basis of a given imperfect progression towards a condition of full peace and justice. Such measures, though, would never be admissible under a peremptory regime of the law of nations. It is not surprising, therefore, that Kant affirms that "any rights of nations [. . .] which states can acquire or retain by war, are merely *provisional*".[36]

To conclude, Kant was not a just war theorist but neither was he a utopian pacifist. Indeed, he admitted the possibility of humanitarian intervention as a form of 'wide' ethical duty in assisting non-nationals when their liberties were

30 Ibid., 6:350, p.487.
31 Ibid.
32 Ibid.
33 Ibid., 6:354, p.491.
34 Ibid.
35 Ibid.
36 Ibid., 6:350, p.487.

violated.[37] Yet, as we have seen, he also considered it an "original right"[38] for states to wage war if under military threat. Furthermore, he considered that in an initial phase characterized by a natural condition among states, war could "perhaps [. . .] establish a condition more closely approaching a rightful condition".[39]

Certainly, though, this could not be the final stage that one would be ready to accept under the rational presuppositions of politics and society. Therefore, one will have to wait until a final and fully fledged civil condition is established among states before it becomes possible to put aside war as a means of resolution of interstate conflict and adopt instead juridical means of the pacification of international controversies.

37 Ibid., 6:390, p.521. Against a perfect duty of intervention in Kant see H. Williams, *Kant and the End of War*, p.140. A very thought provoking contribution (often not enough considered) is Maus, *Menschenrechte*.

38 As an "original right that free states in a state of nature have to go to war with one another", Kant, "Metaphysics of Morals (1797)", 6:344, p.483.

39 Ibid.

§5 Kant on race and colonialism

Kant's views on race and colonialism raise perplexities among interpreters. Undeniably, he makes a number of unambiguously racist considerations on non-European populations in the course of his various lectures on anthropology. In the late 1770s he affirms that: "The Negroes [. . .] are [. . .] no longer susceptible of any further civilizing; but they have instinct and discipline, which is lacking in the Americans";[1] whereas ten years later he admits that "The Negro race [. . .] acquire culture, but only a culture of slaves; that is, they allow themselves to be trained".[2] Such assertions are accompanied by a good dose of Eurocentrism when judging "a regular course of improvement of state constitutions",[3] which "in our part of the world [. . .] will probably someday give laws to all the others".[4]

1 I. Kant, "Anthropology Pillau (1777–8)", A. Wood and R.B. Louden (eds.), *Lectures on Anthropology*, Cambridge University Press, Cambridge, 2012, 25:844, p.276. See also, I. Kant, "Anthropology Mrongovius (1784–1785) [complete]", A. Wood and R. Louden (eds.), *Lectures on Anthropology*, Cambridge University Press, Cambridge, 2012, pp.335–510.

2 I. Kant, "Menschenkunde (1781–2)", A. Wood and R.B. Louden (eds.), *Lectures on Anthropology*, Cambridge University Press, Cambridge, 2012, 25:1187, p.320.

3 I. Kant, "Idea for a Universal History with a Cosmopolitan Aim (1784)", 2011, p.119, 8:29–30. For a clarification of 'race' and Kant's various observations on a race hierarchy, Louden observes that "Race [which on Kant's view is not a social construction but a natural kind – albeit one that develops "only over the course of generations" (*On the Use of Teleological Principles in Philosophy* 8: 164)] is a prime example of what nature makes of the human being, rather than of what the human being 'can and should make of himself' as a free acting being" (see 7: 119). Nevertheless, the race issue looms large in three separately published essays included in this volume [*Of the Different Races of Human Beings* (1775), *Determination of the Concept of a Human Race* (1785), *On the Use of Teleological Principles in Philosophy* (1788)], and other versions of Kant's classroom lectures on anthropology and geography contain much more explicit and controversial discussions of race (see, e.g., *Menschenkunde* 25: 1187–1188, *Physical Geography* 9: 311–320). Additionally, related discussions of "civilized (i.e., western) Europeans" and "uncivilized natives" also feature prominently in several of the history writings included in this volume [see, e.g., *Idea for a Universal History with a Cosmopolitan Aim* (1784) 8: 21–22; *Review of J. G. Herder's Ideas for the Philosophy of the History of Humanity* (1785) 8: 64–65]". In R.B. Louden, "General Introduction", G. Zöller and R.B. Louden (eds.), *Anthropology, History and Education*, Cambridge University Press, Cambridge, 2011, pp.6–7.

4 Kant, "Universal History", 2011, 8:29–30, p.119.

How could the defender of human emancipation and universal rationality proclaim such degrading judgments? The debates over the exploitation of non-European peoples as well as of the injustices of global commerce were already part of a flourishing discussion among several intellectuals of the Enlightenment.[5] Adam Smith had published in the 1770s his *Enquiry into the Causes of the Wealth of Nations*, where he reacted to the injustices of western trades prefiguring, next, a rebalancing of powers between east and west in view of global market adjustments.[6]

Furthermore, the Abbé Raynal published a 10-volume work of the French edition of his *A History of the Two Indies in* 1770 which included anonymous anti-slavery and anti-imperalist contributions by leading scholars of the time, such as Diderot.[7]

The puzzle becomes even more challenging since no traces of Kant's former considerations are left in the published work he finally dedicates to anthropology – *Anthropology from a Pragmatic Point of View* [1798].[8] Similarly, and even more telling, is that *Toward Perpetual Peace* [1795] assumes an explicit anti-colonialist stand, which is maintained also in the *Metaphysics of Morals* [1797].

In *Toward Perpetual Peace*, indeed, Kant criticizes "the *inhospitable* behavior of civilized, especially commercial, states in our part of the world, the injustice they show".[9] The trickery with which western occupants presented themselves as visitors transformed instead into a conquest and perpetration of horrible actions.[10] So, Kant approves the protectionist attitude and filtered closure to foreign commerce of China and Japan "which had given such guests a try [but then] wisely [placed restrictions on them] allowing them access but not entry".[11]

5 A comprehensive presentation is in B. Kapossy, I. Nakhimovsky, R. Whatmore (eds.), *Commerce and Peace in the Enlightenment*, Cambridge University Press, Cambridge, 2017.

6 "Hereafter, perhaps, the natives of those countries may grow stronger, or those of Europe may grow weaker, and the inhabitants of all the different quarters of the world may arrive at that equality of courage and force which, by inspiring mutual fear, can alone overawe the injustice of independent nations into some sort of respect for the rights of one another. But nothing seems more likely to establish this equality of force than that mutual communication of knowledge and of all sorts of improvements which an extensive commerce from all countries to all countries naturally, or rather necessarily, carries along with it." In A. Smith, *An Inquiry into the Nature and Causes of the Wealth of Nations*, R.H. Campbell and A.S. Skinner (eds.), W.B. Todd (text ed.), vol.2, Liberty Fund, Indianapolis, 1981, pp.626–627.

7 See S. Muthu, "Conquest, Commerce and Cosmopolitanism in Enlightenment Political Thought", S. Muthu (ed.), *Empire and Modern Political Thought*, Cambridge University Press, Cambridge, 2012, p.210. For a thorough reconstruction of the rejection by the Enlightenment of imperial designs, see S. Muthu, *Enlightenment Against Empire*, 2003.

8 I. Kant, "Anthropology from a Pragmatic Point of View", G. Zöller and R.B. Louden (eds.), *Anthropology, History and Education*, Cambridge University Press, Cambridge, 2011 [1798], pp.227–429.

9 Kant, "Toward Perpetual Peace (1795)", 8:358, p. 329.

10 Ibid.

11 Ibid., 8:359, pp. 329–330.

Kant speaks of the "unsocial sociability"[12] of peoples and nations as one of the essential components for progression. Nevertheless, the increase of global commodity exchanges as well as the assumption of the spreading of civilization is not per se a sign of *moral progress.* It is true that "*the spirit of commerce*"[13] deters nations from engaging in war by establishing mutual monetary interests, but this is no guarantee of peace. In order to really move forward, the international scene has to construct antagonism among peoples "in accordance with principles of outer freedom",[14] that is, as according to external laws with the law of peoples whose cosmopolitan right is an essential component.

Instead, in the absence of an international system of cosmopolitan rights and justice – which alone can favour moral progression – we can at most praise ourselves for 'mere civilization'. But this is an ephemeral satisfaction: "We are *civilized* [. . .] but very much is still lacking before we can be held to be already *moralized*".[15] For Kant, the human being is not meant only to civilize himself, but also to cultivate and, most importantly, to moralize himself through the arts and the sciences.[16]

Yet, moralization of external freedom requires law without which no peace is possible. Kant's view, instead, is that violations of international justice – and of cosmopolitan rights – are perpetrated primarily by "the civilized, especially commercial, states in our part of the world".[17]

Considering that Kant lectured on anthropology from 1772 until his retirement in 1796 and that from the last student's transcripts we have of his courses until 1788–1789 (*Anthropology Busolt*),[18] as well as the "last lecture series [. . .] dating from 1791 to 1792 (VA Ko 362–5)",[19] the hypothesis here made is that a change of mind on races is to be placed in between 1792 and 1793, namely, with the publication of *On the Common Saying: This May Be Correct in Theory, But It Is of No Use in Practice* [1793].[20]

12 Kant, "Universal History", 8:20, p.111.
13 Kant, "Toward Perpetual Peace (1795)", 8:368, p. 336.
14 Kant, "Metaphysics of Morals (1797)", 6:347, p. 485.
15 Kant, "Universal History", 8:26, p.116. For a discussion of this point see also S. Muthu, "Conquest, Commerce and Cosmopolitanism in Enlightenment Political Thought", 2012, p.224. S. Muthu (ed.), *Empire and Modern Political Thought*, Cambridge University Press, Cambridge, 2012, p.224.
16 The same concept recurs also in other texts: "The sum total of pragmatic anthropology, in respect to the vocation of the human being and the characteristic of his formation, is the following. The human being is destined by his reason to live in a society with human beings and in it to *cultivate* himself, to *civilize* himself, and to *moralize* himself by means of the arts and sciences", I. Kant, "Anthropology from a Pragmatic Point of View", 2011 [1798], 7:324–325, p.420.
17 Kant, "Toward Perpetual Peace (1795)", 8:358, p.329.
18 I. Kant, "Anthropology Busolt (1788–1789) [excerpts]", A. Wood and R. Louden (eds.), *Lectures on Anthropology*, Cambridge University Press, Cambridge, 2012, pp.511–524.
19 P. Kleingeld, "Kant's Second Thoughts on Colonialism", K. Flikschuh and L. Ypi (eds.), *Kant and Colonialism*, Oxford University Press, Oxford, 2014, p.64.
20 I. Kant, "On the Common Saying", pp.273–310. I leave to further speculation here the possibility that such timing reflects a paradigmatic shift brought about also for the anthropological conception of the human race by the French Revolution.

This thesis excludes those hypotheses sustaining a Kantian line of continuity on racial inferiority and slavery as "one of those evils that contributed to the advance of the human race through the diffusion of European culture, a part of its 'civilizing mission'".[21] On the contrary, it supports and specifies further the conviction of those scholars, like Kleingeld, whose hypothesis is one of Kant's second thoughts on race starting from the 1790s.[22]

In the following sections, I provide an interpretation of what might have pushed Kant towards a change of mind on colonialism and races. The general thesis is that the more Kant matured the idea of cosmopolitanism as a human emancipatory project, the more he felt the need to revise his previous views on the hierarchy of races.[23] Even if it is the case that Kant never equates views on the hierarchies of races with inherent moral differences, so that he "regarded the 'moral characterization' of the races as an issue that was entirely distinct from a discussion of the concept of race as a 'physical' notion";[24] it is also the case that the abandoning of the earlier conception on racial hierarchy coincides with a shift in the view of the capacity of group peoples to realize an autonomous emancipatory process.

Whereas in the writing *Of the Different Races of Human Beings* (1775),[25] as well as in the *Determination of the Concept of a Human Race* (1785),[26] Kant establishes an anthropological vision in support of a cosmopolitan theory of history where Europe would eventually give laws to the rest of the world ("one will discover a regular course of improvement of state constitutions in our part of the world (which will probably someday give laws to all the others)");[27] from 1793 onwards, it becomes clear that a truly cosmopolitan process of human emancipation requires the engagement and inclusion of *all peoples*. Under this premise, it no longer becomes possible to think of nature as something which limited empirically the possibility for each race to contribute to human approximation to the good. This newly designed connection between cosmopolitanism and

21 T. McCarthy, *Race, Empire and the Idea of Human Development*, Cambridge University Press, Cambridge, 2009, p.64.

22 As the author affirms: "I argue in favor of [. . .] the view that Kant defended European colonialism during the 1780s and early 1790s, and that he started to criticize it only during the 1790s [. . .]. The texts display a chronological pattern indicating that Kant radically changed his views on colonialism in the mid-1790s". Kleingeld, "Kant's Second Thoughts on Colonialism", p.45.

23 I. Kant, "Of the Different Races of Human Beings (1775)", G. Zöller and R.B. Louden (eds.), *Anthropology, History and Education*, Cambridge University Press, Cambridge, 2011, pp.82–97. As Kant makes explicit: "from a *cosmopolitan* perspective (with a view to the well-being of the *human race* as a whole and insofar as it is conceived as progressing toward its wellbeing in the series of generations of all future times)." Kant, "On the Common Saying", 8:278, p. 281.

24 P. Kleingeld, "Kant's Second Thoughts on Colonialism", p.63.

25 Kant, "Different Races", pp.82–97.

26 I. Kant, "Determination of the Concept of a Human Race (1785)", G. Zöller and R.B. Louden (eds.), *Anthropology, History and Education*, Cambridge, Cambridge University Press, 2011, pp.143–159.

27 Kant, "Universal History", 8:29, p.119.

human political emancipation requires the support of a vision of the relation between nature and history as something *non-impeding* the possibility of political collective self-determination. Yet, this conformity to ends of the human races could only be established, from a cognitive point of view, by use of a regulative teleological judgment. There is nothing objective in the teleological appearance of a cosmopolitan progression of the human race. In the writing *On the Use of Teleological Principles in Philosophy* (1788),[28] Kant distinguishes among three uses of teleological principles, as namely, between the natural teleology of natural sciences, that of a teleology of moral freedom, and finally, that of transcendental philosophy, as that of a teleology of nature considered under the purposive realization of freedom, later developed in the *Critique of the Power of Judgment* [1790], namely, in the *Power of Teleological Judgment.*[29]

Rather, the consideration that instinctual behaviours that activate natural predispositions are led by "unsocial sociability"[30] (personal ambitions, desire of wealth, power and so on) triggers social transformations 'as if' there was a providential design – an all purposive intelligent nature - accompanying these processes. In such respect, nature would turn the unsocial sociability of human beings into a collective action for human emancipation.

In the footnote to paragraph *III. of Theory and Practice – On the Relation of Theory to Practice in The Right of Nations Considered from a Universally Philanthropic, that is, Cosmopolitan Point of View* – Kant anticipates that the presuppositions of human species to reach the condition of a cosmopolitan constitution cannot be based purely on a philanthropic sense of amelioration, but on something more demanding, through which it will be possible to achieve a cosmopolitan progression and well-being of the human race.[31] Since, if there is something inherent in the human species, such that it can progress towards the good, then, we can still maintain a reasonable hope of "love of the race [. . .] whatever might be said to the contrary by the affectations of universal philanthropy".[32] Were there something ineradicably evil in humanity, "especially in deliberate mutual violation of the most sacred human rights",[33] we could never feel a sense of love for our fellow beings and even, one might add, for ourselves. But since "omnilateral violence [. . .] brings a people to decide to subject itself to the

28 I. Kant, "On the Use of Teleological Principles in Philosophy (1788)", G. Zöller and R.B. Louden (eds.), *Anthropology, History and Education*, Cambridge, Cambridge University Press, 2011, pp.192–218.

29 See Zöller, "Editor's Introduction", G. Zöller and R.B. Louden (eds.), p.193.

30 As Kant introduces this notion in the fourth proposition of the Idea: "*The means nature employs in order to bring about the development of all its predispositions is their* ***antagonism*** *in society, insofar as the latter is in the end the cause of their lawful order.* Here I understand by 'antagonism' the *unsociable sociability* of human beings, i.e. their propensity to enter into society, which, however, is combined with a thoroughgoing resistance that constantly threatens to break up this society." In, Kant, "Universal History", 8:20, p.111.

31 Kant, "On the Common Saying", note *, 8:307, p.304.

32 Ibid., p.305.

33 Ibid.

coercion that reason itself prescribes [. . .] and to enter into a *civil constitution* [. . .] so too must [. . .] states [. . .] even against their will [. . .] enter into a *cosmopolitan constitution*".[34]

As will be thoroughly discussed to make apparent this final stage of human emancipation it is required that cosmopolitan right – the right to temporary visit – is conceptualized. This implies, in turn, that the way in which Kant arrives at the conceptual necessity of introducing cosmopolitan right becomes a position grounded on anti-colonialist stands.

Colonialism is for Kant connected essentially to unfair commercial terms, territorial occupation or, finally, war of conquest. Yet, international trade is for Kant also a sign of progression towards peace. Also in the absence of a third party arbiter, a condition demanding the establishment of an overall civil relation among states, bilateral trades, even when not fair, can be judged under a teleological perspective as "*provisionally right* [since] they foreshadow the civil condition in which right is publically administrated".[35]

Judged by a cosmopolitan perspective, bilateral trade-relations *might* indicate the possibility of an upcoming cosmopolitan transition where peoples' trade rights could find tutelage. Yet, for Kant, mere commercial interaction, per se, is *not* a sign of approximation towards peaceful relations. It is only when this is judged *a posteriori* from an already achieved civil condition, i.e. what Kant indicates with the notion of a league of states or a *Foedus Pacificum*,[36] that it becomes possible to reconstruct, retrospectively, how such welcoming result had been achieved.

In this respect, therefore, any commercial relations leading to territorial colonization should be rejected. Interdependence and commercial interaction can be thought of as fully legitimate only if inscribed within an international system of laws. The latter, not surprisingly, emerge as necessary solutions for interstate commercial controversies, similarly, one might say, to those controversies over possessions of objects as those arising among individuals in a state of nature.

All in all, even if commerce between individuals and states can be judged *a posteriori* as one of the elements that define a litmus paper for cosmopolitan progressions, per se, commerce is not a sign of moral progression whenever it appears. Therefore, Kant is far from being an ultraliberal thinker who sees in commerce a new faith for the spreading of liberal peace. On the contrary, humanity's moral progression towards the good can be measured only through political steps of instantiation of the conditions of international right. These only can make us approximate towards perpetual peace. These steps, though, are mindful of the inherent pluralism of cultures co-participating to the unfolding of historical justice. Global commerce, therefore, remains entrapped in the paradoxical relation for which human sociability favours a search for communicative

34 Ibid., p.307.

35 L. Vanhaute, "Colonists, Traders or Settlers? Kant on Fair International Trade and Legitimate Settlement", K. Flikschuh and L. Ypi (eds.), *Kant and Colonialism*, Oxford University Press, Oxford, 2014, p.142

36 Kant, "Toward Perpetual Peace (1795)", 8:356, p.327.

exchange and interconnection among peoples whereas, unsociability, instead, maintains separateness and relative isolation guaranteeing an overall condition of justice.

It is also for this reason that Kant not only rejects the idea of a world monarchy, as we will later see, but he also favours pluralist international regimes made of differentiated types of political entities and social groups, ideally embracing republican ideals of autonomy and civil rights.

When discussing war and colonization, Kant excludes categorically the possibility that a conquered state is transformed into a colony. If this were the case, one would allow for the possibility of depriving the losing state of its civil freedom and constitution, an act which could not be tolerated.[37] Additionally, there is no consequential reason which might justify the fraudulent acquisition of territories "in order to establish a civil union with them and bring these human beings (savages) into a rightful condition (as with the American Indians, the Hottentots and the inhabitants of New Holland) [. . .]. Such a way of acquiring land is therefore to be repudiated".[38]

It must also be recognized that possession as use is a category that Kant considers as a form of legitimate reason to exclude colonizers from expropriating one's territory. To this purpose Kant writes that:

> If the settlement is made so far from where that people resides that there is no encroachment on anyone's use of his land, the right to settle is not open to doubt. But if these people are shepherds or hunters (like the Hottentots, the Tungusi, or most of the American Indian nations) who depend for their sustenance on great open regions, this settlement may not take place by force but only by contract, and indeed by a contract that does not take advantage of the ignorance of those inhabitants with respect to ceding their lands.
>
> (Kant, "Metaphysics of Morals", 6:353, p.490)[39]

There is yet another sense of 'colony', or 'colonists', one referred to as a "social sense of an ethnic settlement"[40] when foreigners are admitted by "a local lord of the land"[41] into a portion of land which does not infringe upon the right of private properties, *or use*, of an already established social group.

37 Kant, "Metaphysics of Morals", 6:348, p.486.

38 Ibid., 6:266, p.417.

39 Kant, "Metaphysics of Morals", 6:353, p.490. On the asymmetry between the option open to non-state peoples to sell their lands through contract and the lack thereof by state immigrants (due to an inseparable connection between territory and the 'moral person' of the state), see Pagden, "Law of Continuity", p.36.

40 On this point see the observations by Kleingeld, "Kant's Second Thoughts on Colonialism", p.59.

41 "The *lord of the land* has the right to encourage *immigration* and settling by foreigners (colonists), even though his native subjects might look askance at this, provided that their private ownership of land is not curtailed by it". In Kant, "Metaphysics of Morals (1797)", 6:338, p.478.

This is the only admissible form of colony for Kant. The reference is evidently to the Indian territories, particularly the Americas and to the issue of European colonization. With this observation we close in full circle the debate opened by the Salamancan School of theology on the legitimate policy of the Spaniards over the Indios and the American territories. Kant, in this respect, is shown to be an acute innovator of de Vitoria's *ius peregrinandi* and *ius communicationis* as well as of the later debate developed by the Second Scholastics. Perhaps he has in mind precisely such tradition when he affirms that "it is easy to see through this veil of injustice (Jesuitism), which would sanction any means to good ends".[42] The purposes of civilizing other cultures for the sake of humanity are "supposedly good intentions [which] cannot wash away the stain of injustice in the means used for them".[43]

Humanity, for Kant, in its juridical instantiation, is no longer an abstract notion, as in de Vitoria, leading to the paradoxical legitimation of oppressive market practices of colonization. Instead, it becomes through the idea of cosmopolitan right, a 'concrete universal', embracing a plurality of forms of living and cultural practices. Kant arrives at this shift by reformulating de Vitoria's concept of the 'authority of the all world', and by turning such a concept from a metaphysical into a civic notion, by means of the introduction of a globalized 'general will' (as I have shown, an old debated concept since Paul, Augustine, Malebranche etc. until its restrictive interpretation in Rousseau).

In this respect, the interaction and unsocial sociability that Kant identifies starting from the imaginary state of nature, turns into a conceptual tool for the realization, through collective practices, of co-participating historical anti-imperialist and anti-oppressive developments. As Kant defines clearly such historical dynamics among peoples progressing towards a cosmopolitan peace:

> [. . .] the ills that arise out of this necessitate our species to devise to the in itself salutary resistance of many states to one another arising from their freedom a law of equilibrium and to introduce a united power giving emphasis to that law to introduce a cosmopolitan condition of public state security, which is not wholly without *dangers* so that the powers of humanity may not fall asleep, but it is at least not without a principle of *equality* between its reciprocal *effect* and *counter-effect*, so that they may not destroy each other.
>
> (I. Kant, "Idea for a Universal History with a Cosmopolitan Aim (1784)", 8:26, pp.115–116)

For Kant the realization of an ultimate moral historical accomplishment, what he calls a "Kingdom of Ends", admits a variety of cultural forms – a *pluriversum* – of legitimate ethical practices all virtually capable of satisfying the demands of

42 Ibid., 6:266, p.418.
43 Ibid, 6:353, p.490.

morality. Accordingly, there is no need to hold firm thoughts on racial inferiority, nor eventually to surrender to the conceptual impossibility of reconciling racial inferiority of natural predispositions with equality in morality as some interpreter has argued.[44] The universal singularity of practical moral reason is not questioned by the plurality of cultural practices. In principle, there is no conflation between a universalist singular moral code and a multiplicity of arrangements of the social and political life, as long as freedom, in all these interactions, is maintained as an ultimate value for civil cohesion.

In *Toward Perpetual Peace* and in the *Metaphysics of Morals*, as will be discussed more extensively later, Kant introduces the right to visit in terms of a quintessentially anti-colonialist right, an understanding of global justice from an impartial point of view, as with the original rights to earth one can derive from a state of nature. Individuals from all races and continents, but at this point the distinction is irrelevant, are recognized as possessing a juridical status in virtue of their right to temporal visit of a foreign state. Furthermore, it is on the premise of a cosmopolitan right that a *reformist approach* is introduced into international relations (something placed in substitution for an approach in support of a just war theory, or even to those invoking revolutionary emancipations). The latter case, indeed, in so far as it leads outside a regime held under a rule of law, brings within itself a contradictory purpose leaving us in a status of juridical vacuum.

Enlightened reformism, though, is not without counter indications. If sociopolitical intuitions are conceived simply along pure globalist lines, the result would be an undesired destruction of local cultures and economies.[45] Kant stood against such an ultraliberalist form of cosmopolitanism and maintained states' republics, together with their differentiated conceptions of the goods, as the building-blocks for a shareable notion of global justice.

44 T. McCarthy, *Race, Empire and the Idea of Human Development*, 2009, p.66 and p.68.

45 On this point see also, S. Muthu, "Conquest, Commerce and Cosmopolitanism in Enlightenment Political Thought", S. Muthu (ed.), *Empire and Modern Political Thought*, Cambridge University Press, Cambridge, 2012, p.209.

Part 3

Theory and practice

The world (state) republic as a regulative idea of reason

§6 Freedom, nature and right

The interconnection between freedom and right is at the core of Kant's practical thought.[1] A 'critical turn' in the analysis of right was already present in Kant's lectures on *Natural Right* [1784], also known as *Naturrecht Feyerabend*.[2] These were lectures given three years after the first edition of the *Critique of Pure Reason* [1781] and before the *Critique of Practical Reason* [1788] and the *Critique of Judgment* [1790].[3] A critical approach becomes explicit only in 1786, in the writing *What is Orientation in Thinking?* [1786].[4] Here, Kant defends the centrality of reason as a reference mark for orienting ourselves in thinking. Only by pointing to the possibilities and the limits of reason can we define scientific knowledge and practical imperatives. Freedom is a central concept in so far as a free use of reason stands as a prerequisite for the analysis of reason itself. We have to presume our acting as free individuals in order to ascribe rationality and independence of our actions. But what dimension of freedom is here the relevant one? Is it the internal moral or the external political one? Freedom without any further specification should be considered both in terms of the moral as well as the practical-political dimension of our autonomy.[5] The two domains become, ultimately, co-dependent variables. Accordingly, if we aim to engage in a free use of reason, we need to defend also a third aspect of freedom, namely,

1 On this fundamental interconnection, see W. Kersting, *Wohlgeordnete Freiheit. Immanuel Kants Rechts- und Staatsphilosophie Mit einer Einleitung zur Taschenbuchausgabe 1993: Kant und die politische Philosophie der Gegenwart*, Suhrkamp, Frankfurt am Main, 2016, p.116 ff.; F. Kaulbach, *Der Begriff der Freiheit in Kants Rechtsphilosophie*, 1973, pp.78–91.

2 I. Kant, *Gottfried Feyerabend. Kant's Natural Right.* Read in the Winter of the Year 1784, English Translation by L. Vinx; available online at http://www.academia.edu/5541693/

3 For Guyer, a critical stand was already present since 1764, that is, in the essay *An Inquiry Concerning the Distinctness of the Principles of Natural Theology and Morality*, which obtained a second prize from the Academy of Sciences in Berlin. See P. Guyer, *Kant on Freedom, Law and Happiness*, Cambridge University Press, Cambridge, 2000, p.18.

4 I. Kant, "What is Orientation in Thinking?", H.S. Reiss (ed.), *Kant Political Writings*, Cambridge University Press, Cambridge, 2012 [1786], pp.235–249.

5 On some related aspects to these views see H.J. Paton, *The Categorical Imperative. A Study in Kant's Moral Philosophy*, Hutchinson's University Library, London, 1947, p.217 ff.

that of thought and communication by public debate and reason in order to orient ourselves in thinking along political lines.[6]

For Kant, the "*freedom of thought* should remain inviolate",[7] even when freedom of speech and writing is limited by civil authority. Such freedom is vital in so far as it "signifies the subjection of reason to no laws other than those *which it imposes on itself*".[8]

All in all, Kant's rejection of Mendelssohnianism is an objection to the dominant Leibnizian-Wolffian tradition for the promotion of the critical-regulative method.[9]

Kant's critical view on right, more specifically, is all important as a step forward in the natural law debate of the time. It suggests an original standpoint against a mere opposition between natural and positive rights, such as the one reflected by the *French Declaration of the Rights of Man and of the Citizen* [1789].

For Kant, a solution in this sense can come only with a reconciliation between nature and freedom, that is, between the deterministic causality of nature and the unconditioned causality of the free will.[10] This tension is reflected in Kant's conception of rights and their balancing, a dynamics leading to the construction of a civil constitution starting from natural law.

It should be noted that already starting from Feyerabend's lectures on natural right Kant establishes a connection between legitimate coercion and freedom: "Coercion is rightful if it furthers universal freedom. A law of actions that we can force someone to perform is a coercive law, and the right attached to it is coercive right. A right that is not coercive right is equity. The latter is *ius late dictum*, the former *ius stricte dictum*."[11] On the basis of such premises, the overcoming of the opposition between natural and positive right opens the space for transitional politics and provisional right in so far as it is concerned with the distinction between provisional and peremptory rights (*ius late dictum* and *ius stricte dictum*).

Temporal progression towards a peremptory civil condition, both domestically and internationally, is what defines a philosophical-historical trajectory for the approximation of peace among peoples. There remains here a persistent tension between nature and freedom.

6 "a purely rational belief is the signpost or compass by means of which the speculative thinker can orient himself on his rational wanderings". In Kant, "What is Orientation in Thinking?", p.245.

7 Kant, "What is Orientation in Thinking?", p.247.

8 Ibid.

9 Guyer, *Kant on Freedom, Law and Happiness*, p.19. The importance of Kant's Natural Right is in support of a historiographical reconstruction of the idea of freedom which for some would begin only with the *Groundwork*. On this point see G. Sadun Bordoni, "Introduzione", I. Kant, *Lezioni sul diritto naturale (Naturrecht Feyerabend)*, G. Sadun Bordoni and N. Hinske (eds.), Bompiani, Milano, 2016 [1784], note 56, p.26.

10 O. Höffe argues that the hypothesis of "Ein »antinaturalistischer Kognitivismus« is schon deshalb plausibel". In O. Höffe, *»Königliche Völker«*, 2001, p.20.

11 Kant, *Gottfried Feyerabend*. 27:1328, p.13.

The idea of history as an end of a cosmopolitan world is understood by Kant in terms of the postulates of practical reason, not as a theoretical claim of natural history that will, someday, come about as a result of natural mechanisms.

It is rather through the free adoption of the principle of morality that men will eventually be able to bring about the political conditions for the exercise of freedom.[12] The end of history, as well as politics, becomes the realization of freedom through the coercive laws of justice. These, together, realize civil liberty and the dignity of men as a value in itself: "the rights of humanity [*das Recht der Menschen*]"[13] acquire thus maximal respect.

The ultimate standard upon which one can judge equality among human beings is not through instrumental rationality – rationality as a means to achieve ends – but rather through the recognition of man's capacity to be an end in itself. This means for men to be able to act on the basis of unconditioned values rather than on natural determination. It follows, therefore, that it must be possible to enact a process of becoming aware of such practical independence in reasoning. This is what the moral imperative teaches us about our freedom.

This last step defines man's exit from the natural condition and his entrance into a historical dimension, one characterized by freedom as well as by "unsocial sociability".[14] Here morality and nature dwell for the affirmation of a dimension of cosmopolitan peace. Moral imperatives struggle to affirm themselves with natural tendencies to a form of egoist self-fulfillment.

It would be a mistake, though, to understand the relation of nature to peace only in constitutive terms. Instead, if morality has to prompt progression towards peace, the reconciliation of the moral imperative with nature should be established on the base of a *regulative dimension.*

Nature must be conceived 'as if' it did not present an impediment to the realization of the duties of justice and 'as if' peace was possible even when reality showed contrary tendencies. This relation is expressed by Kant in several writings spanning across the 1790s. Nature is assumed by Kant as a supplement to the moral duty to achieve peace. Not only is nature not an obstacle for our achievement of peace, but it allows us to judge historical approximation towards peace in terms of a subjective principle for the finality of human endeavors.

12 See Guyer, *Kant on Freedom, Law and Happiness*, p.13.

13 Kant, *Gottfried Feyerabend*, p.43. I share Sadun Bordoni's observation here with regard to the impossibility of equating Kant's notion of the rights of humanity (which refers to a collective category as a whole), with the contemporary idea of human rights as individually subjective. The concept is further clarified in the example of the promise to a thief which, if betrayed, does not infringe upon his rights and yet it infringes upon the rights of humanity which has a not-strict right to the respect of pacts. See G. Sadun Bordoni, "Introduzione", G. Sadun Bordoni and N. Hinske (eds.), I.Kant, *Lezioni sul Diritto Naturale (Naturrecht Feyerabend)*, Bompiani, Milan, 2016 [1784], note 86, p.34.

14 Kant, "Universal History", 8:20, pp.111 ff.

§6.1 The inherent value of freedom

Kant's moral philosophy is at the basis of his conception of positive law and thus of his views on politics. Yet, often, scholars have failed to notice that the interlinking concepts between all these spheres are given by a certain notion of freedom that Kant defines in opposition to Hobbes. Whereas for Hobbes freedom is a space open to subjective will where the law remains silent, for Kant, freedom is always connected to law, either moral or positive coercive law.[15]

Freedom for Kant is a value in itself. As a value – not as a fact – it grounds our capacity to act in accordance with the moral imperative.[16] For Kant, it is freedom and not reason that stands as the justification of the concept of human beings seen as ends in themselves. Certainly, men can be at times the means of nature. In the *Metaphysics of Morals*, Kant traces the distinction between rational (*Vernunftwesen*) and reasonable being (*vernünftiges Wesen*),[17] where rationality is defined through freedom, and reasonability amounts to 'having reason' more in general, including only theoretical reason with regard to a merely living being.

In the already mentioned lecture on natural law – *Naturrecht Feyerabend* – Kant expresses this idea at different times, as for instance when he states that: "While only reasonable beings can be ends in themselves, they can be ends in themselves not because they have reason, but because they have freedom. Their reason is only a means";[18] or when he affirms that: "But reason is not yet the cause: since man is an end in itself, he has a dignity that cannot be replaced by any equivalent. But reason does not give us this dignity";[19] or, again when it is claimed that: "It is freedom, and freedom alone, which makes that we are ends in themselves."[20]

Freedom, as internal moral freedom, is thus the explicit ground for why humanity should be never considered as a means but only as an end, as according to (one of) the formulations of the categorical imperative of the *Groundwork*. Indeed, acting in accordance with universalizable maxims is to treat everyone in respect to their freedom and therefore to dignity.

Freedom, therefore, constitutes a metaphysical presupposition of our moral agency, not its factual outcome. Accordingly, the way in which we can conceptualize freedom is not in theoretical terms – this could only grant for the possibility of the freedom of the will – but in a practical way, that is, as an inference of our moral obligations. Freedom and the moral law are mutually related: freedom is the substance to the moral law and the moral law is its form.[21]

15 The most comprehensive study on the role of freedom in Kant's legal and political thought remains that by Kersting, *Wohlgeordnete Freiheit.*

16 Guyer, *Kant on Freedom, Law and Happiness*, p.5. On an overview of the notion of freedom as independence in Kant's first Critique see, K. Ameriks, *Kant's Theory of Mind. An Analysis of the Paralogisms of Pure Reason*, Clarendon Press, Oxford, 2000, p.189 ff.

17 On the textual reference and discussion of this point see G. Sadun Bordoni, "Introduzione", p.26.

18 Kant, *Gottfried Feyerabend*, p.5.

19 Ibid.

20 Ibid., p.6.

21 Guyer, *Kant on Freedom, Law and Happiness*, p.8.

What is the more specific link between the two concepts? Guyer suggests reading the moral imperative in Kant's *Groundwork* in accordance with a shift from the universal formula of the moral law to the law of humanity: "freedom in form of humanity is the fundamental aim and the condition of the possibility of the categorical imperative".[22] The kingdom of ends is the successful application of the categorical imperative to every human being as, namely, with the realization of the highest good.

In the *Lectures on Ethics*, Kant defines freedom as the *summum bonum*, the inner value of the world.[23] Through our obligation to the categorical imperative, freedom becomes part of the phenomenal world by showing effects in the real world.[24] Moreover, the stipulation of freedom as the highest good is compatible with individual free choices. As a result, the Kantian deontological definition of freedom as a good per se gets connected with teleological reasoning, that is, with the maximization of the outcome of choice.

The distinction ultimately disappears. Indeed, adherence to the rationality of the moral law is the way to preserve freedom on all future occasions. Freedom and the moral law stand together in a synthetic unity rather than in an analytical one.[25] The implication is that human beings are ends in themselves on the basis of their inherent freedom, not of their reason. One can act according to a moral will only if the act is free. If one is able to act only in accordance with reason, even in the case of a universal type, it can be inferred only that nature – not morality – would be the ultimate ground of our agency. Rather, human agents are capable of setting autonomously moral significant ends only as free human beings.

Unfortunately, for Kant, freedom is strictly speaking undemonstrable. Kant recognized this already in 1762 in the writing on *An Inquiry Concerning the Distinctness of the Principles of Natural Theology and Morality*, written for the philosophical competition of the Berlin Academy.[26] The assumption to which Kant maintains faith also in later writings is that if we want to make sense of human beings as ends in themselves, and thus of the worthiness of their moral value, we need to assume that the freedom of the will – even if it cannot be proved – must be presupposed.

The possibility of obeying the moral law, in turn, consists in that human beings are virtually capable of acting absent the conditioning of sensible inclination, but only if action is conducted in virtue of the moral law; yet, that hypothesis is not an

22 Ibid., p.10.

23 "But the inner worth of the world, the *summum bonum*, is freedom according to a choice that is not necessitated to act. Freedom is thus the inner worth of the world." In I. Kant, "Moral Philosophy: Collin's Lectures Notes", *Lectures on Ethics*, P. Heath and J.B. Schneewind (eds.), Cambridge University Press, Cambridge, 1997 [1784], 27:344, p.125. A similar definition occurs also in later lecture transcriptions – as *The Moral Mrongovius*, according to Guyer. See Guyer, *Kant on Freedom, Law and Happiness*, p.96.

24 Cf. Guyer, *Kant on Freedom, Law and Happiness*, p.131.

25 Ibid., p.55 and p.153.

26 Ibid., p.130.

account for such possibility.[27] Practical reason can show that we all have a free will, but it cannot provide the reason – it cannot explain – why and how this is so.[28]

The next step is for Kant to establish the conceptual essence of the moral law once it has been recognized that any determination of the will, in order to be morally significant, has to do without any sensible cause but only in virtue of a formal practical law. Accordingly, Kant speaks in this respect of the moral law in terms of "a fact of reason",[29] that is, as a form of consciousness of our moral obligations under the conditions of freedom of the will.[30] Moral duties make us conscious of the fact that we are free agents, but metaphysically we can conclude that we are capable of moral actions just because we are free. To acquire consciousness of our freedom through awareness of the moral commands induces a sense of happiness, in so far as we see that our decisions are not necessarily determined by nature. Certainly, happiness cannot be thought in terms of a principle of state justice, nor it can be thought as an *a priori* principle. It expresses "an empirical condition",[31] a sensation and not a concept.

Again, this argument reinforces the idea that only if freedom is postulated as an absolute and indemonstrable value per se, then, can one assess the significance of happiness as a result of the awareness of our independence from the physical world. It is not, rather, the case that we are free because of our sense of happiness.[32]

Freedom and moral worthiness are thus inseparable notions and moral freedom, the capacity to act according to universal moral laws, belongs to every human being by virtue of his/her humanity. Humanity has for Kant a normative standing. It also plays the role of a springboard for the possibility of restricting rights. Yet, such a standard operates through the respect of a universalizable condition of freedom that puts on a balance individual choices. Ponderation and judgment are needed to assess those cases where the use of force against an agent's rational choice is justifiable in respect of the safeguard of greater freedom. Thus, freedom comes before the moral justification of human worthiness. Indeed, it is in virtue of moral freedom that a legitimate justification of moral worthiness can be even formulated.

As Guyer notices in his review to the re-edition of the Feyerabend lectures, Kant is here indicating two things: "First, freedom is a necessary condition of being an end, because without freedom a being could not set ends, they could only be a means for some other beings; but second, freedom is a sufficient condition for being an end in itself, the source of the value or dignity (*Würde*) of the human being."[33]

27 Ibid, p.137.
28 Ibid. p.138.
29 I. Kant, "Critique of Practical Reason (1788)", 1999, 5:31, p.164.
30 Guyer, *Kant on Freedom, Law and Happiness*, p.136.
31 Kant, *Gottfried Feyerabend*, p.8.
32 On this problematic relation see Guyer, *Kant on Freedom, Law and Happiness*, p.98.
33 P. Guyer, "Stellenindex und Konkordanz zum *Naturrecht Feyerabend*, Teilband I: Einleitung des *Naturrechts Feyerabend*", *Ratio Juris*, 25(1), 2012, p.114.

To achieve such a final end in the chain of causes appears as a necessary point. Admitting something as a means implies that there must always be something else to be regarded as an end in itself. In the natural concatenation of means to ends, freedom is what puts an end to such infinite connections. Something should necessarily be conceived "at the end of the progression [. . .]. Otherwise, the progression would not have an end."[34]

Finally, if it is the case that there must be a necessary end in an otherwise infinite chain of progressions, then, this something must be characterized by having an inherent value. For Kant, such *fundamentum inconcussum* is freedom, namely, the necessary presupposition that man has an autonomous will: "The freedom of man is the condition under which man himself can be an end".[35] Men as final ends are independent from sensitive determinations. Animals also have a will but this is not free and therefore they are used as instruments dependent on men's wills.[36]

The decisive step comes when Kant distinguishes between the laws of nature and the laws of freedom. Was freedom "subjected to a law of nature [. . . it would not be] freedom".[37] If we want to conceive laws of freedom, then, these cannot fall under nature: "Freedom must, if is it to be under laws, give its laws to itself".[38]

Yet, adds Kant, "this cannot be done through natural laws since in this case man would not be free".[39] There one comes to the only apparently paradoxical conclusion that right is the restriction of one's freedom and that this takes the form of a duty.[40] Freedom is a constraint under a universal law: "I may sit wherever I want to sit, and he may sit wherever he wants to sit. But if he is sitting, I cannot be sitting at the same time. Accordingly, there has to be a universal rule under which the freedom of both can exist."[41]

Unconstrained freedom must be restricted, otherwise a conflict of the wills would be irremediable. Furthermore, if anyone was free in the absence of a law then "nothing more horrible can be thought of than a state in which everyone is free without law. In such a state, everyone would do to the other whatever he wanted, and as a result no one would be free."[42]

All in all, the reconstructed argument on Kant's theory of freedom shows that if one moves from internal moral freedom to its external dimension, there holds a parallel role between the constraining force of the categorical imperative – as a rule to the moral will – and the coercive force of the external laws to human choices.

34 Kant, *Gottfried Feyerabend*, 27:1321, pp.4–5.
35 Kant, *Gottfried Feyerabend. Kant's Natural Right*, 27:1319, p.3.
36 Ibid.
37 Kant, *Gottfried Feyerabend*, 27:1322, p.6.
38 Ibid.
39 Kant, *Gottfried Feyerabend*, 27:1321, p.4.
40 Ibid.
41 Kant, *Gottfried Feyerabend*, 27:1320, p.3.
42 Ibid.

In *Kant's Lecture on Natural Right* of 1784 (*Naturrecht Feyerabend*), it is made explicit that all duties in general derive from an intrinsic value of freedom of humanity: "An action that is directed according to a universal rule of freedom is right; if it is in disagreement with freedom according to a universal rule an action is unjust, regardless of what the intention may have been."[43]

To conclude, neither moral obligation, as I have shown, nor political obligation, as it appears, can be formulated absent a reference to the regulatory grounding notion of freedom. Freedom is the reason why we can consider humanity to be an end in itself. Thus, to treat rational agents as ends means to safeguard their rationality as a capacity to set independent ends as targets of their actions.[44] Once this condition is extended to all others, the same preservation of rational agency applies through the exercise of coercion – the limitation of individual freedom – in order to make the liberty of each coexist with that of the others. This means that rationality, either in oneself or in others, is not destroyed, i.e. with suicide or murder, but also with lies. To such perfect duties, as Guyer notes, applies for Kant also the "duty to do what one can to *advance* the successful exercise of rational agency in oneself and others",[45] whose neglect does not infringe upon the "*preservation* of humanity as an end in itself",[46] even though it does not favour its moral "*advancement*".[47]

43 Kant, *Gottfried Feyerabend,* 27:1328, p.13.
44 Guyer, *Kant on Freedom, Law and Happiness*, p. 149.
45 Ibid.
46 Kant, "Metaphysics of Morals (1785)", 4:430, p.81.
47 Ibid.

§7 The illusions of reason

Freedom as a regulative idea

In the *Dialectic of Reason* of the *First Critique*, Kant defines transcendental ideas in terms of those views of whose "object [. . .] we have no concept, even though [these are] generated in an entirely necessary way".[1] Those are ideas of which "we can have a problematic concept of it".[2] In order to show what this problematic stands for, Kant engages in a double task: on the one hand, he provides a 'negative' critique as a way to show the "transcendental illusion[s]",[3] whenever intellectual pretences extend understanding beyond the limits of experience; on the other hand, he gives a positive definition of the tasks of reason, thus redefining its transcendental role in regulative vs. constitutive terms. Reason falls into a self-deceiving activity whenever it assumes its ideas as objective statements of existence. The shift of subjective principles into objective ones is what makes us fall into a dialectical error.[4]

Whereas regulative principles apply to what ought to be the case, constitutive principles apply to what falls under spatio-temporal constraints. Regulative ideas are followed asymptotically. What ought to be the case can never be a property identifiable with an existing thing, nor can regulative ideas be deducible as the categories of the intellect in the *Transcendental Analytic*.[5] Regulative ideas are for Kant of a special kind since "one may never concede them objective reality (existence)",[6] rather, "they provide indispensable standard for reason (A569– B598)".[7] Such a standard is an idea of unity for all empirical determinations, something Kant shows reason needs necessarily. This standard arises out of a demand of reason when confronted by the justification and use of the ideas of reason. Here reason resorts, necessarily, to an unconditioned mode in order to account for the conditioned. It follows that the regulative use

1 Kant, *Critique of Pure Reason*, A338/B396, p.409.
2 Ibid.
3 Ibid., p.384.
4 J. Bennett, *Kant's Dialectic*, Cambridge University Press, Cambridge, 2016, p.271 ff.
5 Kant, *Critique of Pure Reason*, A664-665/B691–692, p.600 ff. For an earlier treatment, see H.J. Paton, *Kant's Metaphysics of Experience*, George Allen & Unwin Ltd, London, 2 vols., 1936.
6 Louden, "General Introduction", p.12.
7 Ibid.

of the ideas of reason is a result (not a starting hypothesis) of the antinomies or paralogisims of reason.[8]

The ideas of reason Kant discusses are those concerning God, the soul, and the world. Some illustrations follow from each case. In psychology, as Kant explains, we "connect all appearances, actions, and receptivity of our mind to the guiding thread of inner experience **as if** the mind were a simple substance",[9] that is, something persisting notwithstanding change. Similarly, in cosmology, "we have to pursue the conditions of the inner as well as the outer appearances of nature through an investigation that will nowhere be completed, **as if** nature were infinite in itself and without a first or supreme member".[10] Finally, concerning theology, we have to consider "**as if** the sum total of all appearances (the world of sense itself) had a single supreme and all-sufficient ground outside its range, namely an independent, original, and creative reason".[11]

Regulative ideas help us with thinking but they can never provide knowledge since they never have objects of experience to organize.

A regulative idea is therefore a "*focus imaginarius*" which even if placed "outside the bounds of possible experience – nonetheless still serves to obtain for these concepts the greatest unity".[12]

Reason, by unifying the cognitions of understanding into a single principle, embraces the idea that "the unity of reason is the unity of a system".[13] In presupposing its own unity, reason becomes self-critical with regard to the orientation of thinking on particular cognitions.

The use of reason, accordingly, becomes "hypothetical"[14] since the universal is assumed only "**problematically**".[15] It follows that in the regulative adjudication of the particulars, one does not conclude for "the truth of the universal rule".[16] On the contrary, the regulative use of reason helps at "bringing unity into particular cognitions as far as possible and thereby **approximating** the rule to universality".[17]

When transferred into the political terrain, this means that the plurality of political entities that we encounter in the international realm is the phenomenological datum which our regulative use of reason can bring into unity in so far as it only approximates the ideal of the noumenal republic as the world (state)

8 M. Grier, *Kant's Doctrine of Transcendental Illusion*, Cambridge University Press, Cambridge, 2004, p.295.
9 Kant, *Critique of Pure Reason*, A672/B700– A673/B701, pp.606–607.
10 Ibid.
11 Ibid.,
12 Kant, *Critique of Pure Reason*, A644/B672, p.591. On this point see W.H. Walsh, *Kant's Criticism of Metaphysics*, Edinburgh University Press, Edinburgh, 1997, pp.248–249.
13 Kant, *Critique of Pure Reason*, A 680/B708, p.610.
14 Kant, *Critique of Pure Reason*, A646/B674– A647/B675 p.592.
15 Ibid.
16 Ibid.
17 Ibid.

republic. This remains a universal concept which helps thinking about the unity of the political transnational pluralism by unification of "particular cognitions".[18] But the type of "systematic unity"[19] that is here reached "is only a **projected** unity",[20] one that is not "given in itself, but only as a problem".[21]

For Kant, there holds a fundamental difference "whether something is given to my reason as **an object absolutely**",[22] or whether this "is given only as an **object in the idea**".[23] Whereas in the first case concepts are used to "determining the object",[24] in the second case one has "only a schema for which no object is given [. . .] but which serves only to represent other objects to us, in accordance with their systematic unity, by means of the relation to this idea".[25] This connection institutes a type of indirect relation between objects and ideas, a scheme for the thinking about the unity of the given particulars.

For Kant, the definition of the positive objectives of metaphysics is part of an overall critique of reason, something driving towards a general reassessment of the classical views of the ideas of reason. The overall definition of the appropriate use of reason emerges only after Kant engages in a critical investigation of the natural human tendency to apply reason beyond the sensible limits of experience. The sensible realm of the intellect "is the land of truth [. . .] surrounded by a broad and stormy ocean".[26] There are therefore limits to the extension of scientific knowledge like those Kant had defined along the sections of the *Transcendental Analytics.* The pretences of a transcendental use of reason lead to the illusion that an objective knowledge of the ideas of reason is attainable. This was the position of the classical metaphysical ideas on rational psychology, cosmology, and theology. But for Kant, reason cannot speak of the truth and knowledge of supersensible objects: "The principles of pure understanding [. . .] should be only of empirical and not of transcendental use, i.e., of a use that reaches out beyond the boundaries of experience."[27]

Since the ideas of reason represent a totality without a corresponding sensible intuition, they do escape existential conditions as empirical objects of experience. Such *a priori* wholes are unconditional ideas required by reason to bring into unity the conditioned of the cognitions. These forms allow to understand the unlimited chain of the conditioned by presupposing an *unconditioned*, something which in later developments of German idealism will be labelled as visionary and

18 Ibid.
19 Kant, *Critique of Pure Reason*, A647/B675, pp.592–593.
20 Ibid.
21 Ibid.
22 Kant, *Critique of Pure Reason*, A670/B698, pp.605–606.
23 Ibid.
24 Ibid.
25 Ibid.
26 Kant, *Critique of Pure Reason*, B295, p.354.
27 Ibid., A296/B252–3, p.386.

transformed into other metaphysical foundations.[28] This speculative interest of reason, which adds itself to the practical one, is what allows us to "comprehend the derivation of the conditioned, starting with the unconditioned".[29] There is thus a regressive process through which "the principle of reason is only a **rule**, prescribing a regress in the series of conditions for given appearances in which regress is never allowed to stop with an absolutely unconditioned".[30] The reconstruction of the way in which the dynamism of such a recursive chain of causal determinations "**is to be instituted**"[31] is what "attains to the complete concept of the object".[32]

The critical screening of what reason cannot achieve turns next into the characterization of the illusory use of reason; but the solution of the paralogisms and antinomies of reason reopens the possibility for metaphysics as something in need of renovation along practical terms.[33]

If not for knowledge what are these ideas useful for? For Kant, they serve to achieve *a priori* the greatest unity of knowledge together with its greatest extension. Reason "cannot think this systematic unity in any other way than by giving its idea an object".[34] As determinations are essential to knowledge (so that sensible things of the experience are defined cognitions of human understanding), equally, there is a compelling necessity to the unity of reason. Ideas are thus presupposed *a priori* by reason in order to achieve a systematic unity.

In this respect, the regulative use of reason gives the lines of direction for our thinking. This is a necessary condition for reason. Furthermore, this is certainly a subjective form of unification, a principle, one establishing an horizon of sense which "points the way toward systematic unity".[35]

All in all, Kant's practical shift of metaphysics has ancient roots, as with particularly the critique of Plato's ideas. Kant embraces in part the Platonic definition of ideas as a totality, an archetype of reason, which therefore can never be a sensible object of an intuition. Like Plato, ideas for Kant prompt action as

28 On these developments, see K. Ameriks, "The Critique of Metaphysics: The Structure and Fate of Kant's Dialectic", P. Guyer (ed.), *The Cambridge Companion to Kant and Modern Philosophy*, Cambridge University Press, Cambridge, 2006, p.291 ff.
29 Kant, *Critique of Pure Reason*, A467/B495, p.498.
30 Ibid., A508/B536, p.520.
31 Ibid., A510/B538, p.521.
32 Ibid.
33 On a metaphysical revival in interpreting Kant's politics see the rich collection of essays in S. Baiasu, S. Pihlström, H. Williams (eds.), *Politics and Metaphysics in Kant*, University of Wales Press, Cardiff, 2011. In emphasizing Kant's practical reinterpretation of classical metaphysics, I expand upon the views of V. Gerhardt, *Immanuel Kant. Vernunft und Leben*, Reclam, Stuttgart, 2002; ; V. Gerhardt, *Immanuel Kants Entwurf »Zum ewigen Frieden«. Eine Theorie der Politik*, Wiessenschaftliche Buchgesellschaft, Darmstaadt, 1995; P. Keating, *The function of ideas of reason in Kant's political philosophy*, PhD Thesis, submitted to the School of Philosophy, University of New South Wales, Oct. 2007, pp.14 ff.; on a more sceptical view see Walsh, *Kant's Criticism of Metaphysics*, pp.174 ff.
34 Kant, *Critique of Pure Reason*, A681/B709, p.611.
35 Ibid., A668/B696, p.604.

"efficient causes (of action and their objects)".[36] As for Plato, as well as in Kant virtue, morality etc. are ideas that can never find exhaustive representation in the empirical world of human experience. Yet, Kant rejects the ontological metaphysics of Plato, whereas he maintains the idea of a critical distance from reality. The dichotomy between the real and the ideal, though, is nothing like "a dream of perfection that can have its place only in the idle thinker's brain".[37] It rather amounts to the relation that can be established between reason and its objects.

Yet, differently from Plato, the Kantian Republic is not a being of perfection placed in a self-standing realm. The republican ideal amounts rather to the terms of "a constitution providing for the *greatest human freedom* according to laws that permit *the freedom of each to exist together with that of others*".[38] This is "a necessary concept of reason [which] consider[s] all experiential cognition as determined through an absolute totality of conditions".[39]

For Kant, it is clear that the practical turn of transcendental metaphysics implies a multilevel structuring of external freedom in accordance with constitutionalization processes at the national, international, and cosmopolitan level.[40]

The *Dialectic* represents therefore Kant's turning point in the redefinition of classical metaphysics. Through the discussion of the antinomies of reason – that is, contradictory statements whose falsity cannot be demonstrated – Kant achieves a new perspective in the conceptual clarification of freedom, as it is clear with the recognition of its regulative role. Kant calls an idea of reason as "*ens rationis ratiocinatae*",[41] an entity that is never to be found in experience but which "is rather taken as a ground only *problematically* (because we cannot reach it through any concepts of the understanding) [emphasis added]".[42]

This is an entity for which practical reason only can determine objective reality. Connections among objects provide a ground "for the systematic unity over all experience",[43] that is, 'as if' the world of experience was organized in a certain way.

Whereas knowing is an activity applying only within the boundaries of experience, thinking is a way of looking at certain matters 'as if' these were the case.

36 Ibid., A317/B374, p.397
37 Ibid.
38 Ibid.
39 Kant, *Critique of Pure Reason*, A327/B384, p.402.
40 This point reinforces Gerhardt's when he affirms: "[. . .] wenn wir sehen, wie Kant die Beschäftigung mit den Vernunftbegriffen motiviert und welche Erwarungen er mit dem ausdrücklich von Platon entlehnten Begriff der *Idee* verbindet, dann ist klar, dass schon der zweite große Teil der Transzendentalen Logik der Beantwortung der Frage *Was soll ich tun?* Gewidmet ist". In V. Gerhardt, *Immanuel Kant*, Reclam, Stuttgart, 2002, pp.183–4.
41 Kant, *Critique of Pure Reason*, A681/B709, p.611. On the reconstruction of the distinction between *ens rationis ratiocinatae* and *ens rationis ratiocinantis* from Suarez and Baroque-Age scholastics by Novotny till the German Enlightenment metaphysics and reception by Kant, see C.A. Andersen, "*Ens rationis ratiocinatae* and *ens rationis ratiocinantis*: Reflections on a New Book on Beings of Reason in Baroque-Age Scholasticism", *Questio, Annuario di storia della metafisica*, 14, 2014, pp.315–327.
42 Kant, *Critique of Pure Reason*, A681/B709, p.611.
43 Ibid.

The distinction between knowing and thinking overlaps with the view for which the metaphysical ideas of reason are not defined in constitutive terms. Whereas constitutive principles are part of a process of knowing, in so far as they organize what is brought to intuition, regulative ideas are orienting principles framing our reflections. Under the constitutive principles of understanding, the limits of experience are the limits of knowing; instead, under the regulative conditions of reason, the unity of our cognitions is the orientation to thinking of the ideas.

In the discussion of the third antinomy of the second transcendental idea of reason,[44] Kant has to solve the puzzle of whether "all the appearances of the world can be derived"[45] either from a causality according to the laws of nature or from freedom. These are dialectical oppositions. For Kant there is a distinction between analytical and dialectical oppositions, since in the latter "the two judgments dialectically opposed to one another could both be false, because one does not merely contradict the other, but says something more than is required for a contradiction".[46] Dialectical oppositions lead to "transcendental illusion"[47] in so far as they make us believe, for the case of cosmological ideas, that the world is "a thing in itself".[48] Kant presents the two opposing statements concerned with natural or free causality in the following way.

According to the *thesis*, empirical appearances do not all derive from a causality of nature, but they admit also an explanation of a causality based on freedom. The *antithesis*, in turn, affirms that "there is no freedom",[49] and that "everything in the world happens solely in accordance with laws of nature".[50] The solution to the antinomy implies that this is shown to be "a mere illusion, and that nature at least **does not conflict with** causality through freedom – that was the one single thing we could accomplish, and it alone was our sole concern".[51]

Here freedom is defined not only *negatively* as independence from sensible determination, but also *positively* as a free causality of events. Whereas the proof of the thesis is grounded in the idea of freedom as a first uncaused cause – provisionally, in the transcendental notion of freedom – the antithesis advances the pretence that everything falls along the spatio-temporal dimensions of an infinite causal chain of finite determinations.

The solution Kant sees to this antinomy is one defending a form of compossibility and mutual strengthening between freedom and nature. But this requires seeing transcendental freedom shifting into practical freedom. This is due to the fact that a theoretical proof of our transcendental freedom cannot be given. When we try to provide a deduction of transcendental freedom as a first uncaused cause

44 I. Kant, "The Antinomy of Pure Reason. Third Conflict of the Transcendental Ideas", *Critique of Pure Reason*, [1781–7], A444/B472, p.482 ff.
45 Ibid.
46 Kant, *Critique of Pure Reason*, A504/B532, p.518.
47 Ibid.
48 Ibid.
49 Kant, *Critique of Pure Reason*, A 445/B473, p.485.
50 Ibid.
51 Kant, *Critique of Pure Reason*, A558/B586, p.546.

of a chain of determinations, we instantly fall into the assumption of freedom as a presumption of normative agency.[52] Thus, we assume freedom as regulatively necessary for a non-deterministic orientation of ourselves in the natural realm. Freedom becomes a notion to be used by practical agency and not a concept of the understanding.

This requires, in turn, a shift of metaphysics from theoretical to a practical-regulative use, so that free causality and freedom more in general are normatively safeguarded in thinking.

Kant discusses extensively the regulative role of freedom as an idea of reason. The metaphysical discussion of freedom is crucial to Kant's political theory. As he explicitly affirms: "It is especially noteworthy that it is this **transcendental** idea of **freedom** on which the practical concept of freedom is grounded."[53] It is only by limiting freedom according to universal principles that it is possible to speak of a legitimate global political order. Politics and law are all about finding proper terms of restriction of one's liberties in light of all others'.

The regulative role of freedom remains a notion compatible with the causal determinations of nature. Our self-understanding as free beings "**does not conflict with**" it,[54] since it allows us to conceive of ourselves as both entities inscribed in the laws of nature as well as free agents. The possible co-occurring of the laws of causal freedom with natural determination leads us to think of ourselves 'as if' we were free human agents even if we cannot know whether we are in fact free.[55]

Yet, acting as presupposing the same possibility of our free choices is compatible with the causal determinations of nature, as with the possibility of being both a natural and a moral being. The regulative interpretation of freedom solves such dualism by allowing to posit ourselves as noumenical and phenomenological subjects. When we act under the practical assumption of being free beings, we endorse both the idea that we are caused by uncaused freedom, regulatively interpreted, as well as that we are causally ruled by the laws of nature. In practical agency these two causal assumptions coexist in so far as we achieve our free goals within the rules of the natural realm.

Human agency is the only one which is driven by intelligible causality and takes place in the phenomenological world, thus, being respondent to a sensible causality. This finds a reconciliation in Kant's freedom and necessity, that is, in the regulative role of the laws of liberty with the constitutive role of the laws of natural determination.

The reconciliation of such two domains is all important in order to understand Kant's grand theory of global politics, particularly in its relation to history. Indeed, whereas the ideas of freedom, as I will show in later sections, are at the root of

52 On the relation between right and transcendental freedom as resulting from the transformation of moral and legal philosophy see Kersting, *Wohlgeordnete Freiheit*, p.134 ff.

53 Kant, *Critique of Pure Reason*, A533/B561, p.533.

54 Kant, *Critique of Pure Reason*, A558/B586, p.546.

55 Ibid., A556/B584, p.545.

the constructions of the international constitutional order, the causality of nature not only does not impede the historical approximation towards perpetual peace, but seems even to further it.

In this respect, Kant speaks in the eight proposition of the *Idea for a Universal History with a Cosmopolitan Aim* of a philosophical "chiliasm".[56] This means for Kant that "one can regard the history of the human species in the large as the completion of a hidden plan of nature to bring about an inwardly and **to this end**, also an externally perfect state constitution, as the only condition in which it can fully develop all its predispositions in humanity".[57]

§7.1 The world (state) republic and the unity of theory and practice

Thinking about world politics along regulative terms requires assuming the principles of reason "as heuristic principles".[58] In the *Metaphysics of Morals* one finds a trace of such regulative understanding of the political idea of the world (state) republic when Kant speaks of an "*approximation*"[59] towards perpetual peace "of entering into such alliances of states".[60] As the ideal of peace as such remains always "unachievable",[61] the plethora of alliances among states requires an idea which also cannot be empirically realized.

The way in which Kant defines the political-institutional process of approximating peace is therefore strikingly similar to the way in which he defines the nature of the regulative ideas in the *Critique of Pure Reason*, whose principles – reason – "in the empirical use [. . .] can follow only asymptotically".[62]

The world (state) republic is therefore an idea for thinking the legitimacy of the world politics and not a concept of knowledge.

Lacking a closing concept of experience in a chain of determinate causes to which one could appeal in conceiving the political unity of the whole world (as knowledge), what is left is the regulative presupposition for thinking, under the idea of a whole, the plurality of transnational entities populating the institutional realm. There is here assigned clearly a regulative function to the idea of the world (state) republic as something which allows us to think of the legitimacy of the international order in terms of its formal unity.

One cannot know what the world (state) republic is since there is never an empirical case connected to this concept, as I have recalled before for the case of regulative ideas. The world (state) republic is instead an idea that reason gives to itself in order to think, freely, the normative constraints of the international order.

56 Kant, "Universal History", 8:27, p.116.
57 Ibid.
58 Kant, *Critique of Pure Reason*, A663/B691, pp.601–602.
59 Kant, "Metaphysics of Morals (1797)", 6:350, p.487.
60 Ibid.
61 Ibid.
62 Kant, *Critique of Pure Reason*, A663/B691, pp.601–602.

To think according to the regulative standard of freedom is to think by the laws of morality, and namely by the categorical imperative. The world state republic instantiates therefore the demands of freedom through the compliance of the mandates of the categorical imperative.

In the following sections I investigate what it means for Kant to hold the view that the world (state) republic is a regulative standard along the lines of the ideas of reason (*Vernunftideen*). In the proposed account, the regulative role of the world (state) republic works in tandem with the regulative role played by other ideas such as, particularly, the idea of freedom and peace.

This view integrates the praiseworthy conceptions of Ellis and Keating of political regulatory ideas in Kant which still fall short of the consideration of the world (state) republic as an overarching political idea of reason.[63] This political ideal is to be considered in purely regulatory terms and never as a positive, empirical instantiation. Connected to the view of the transcendental illusions of reason is therefore the discussion of the positive idea of the world state as a metaphysical deception. This falls prey to the same illusion of extending the principles of knowledge beyond empirical application.

The reading I propose reinforces therefore the assumption that, for Kant, law and politics are legitimate in so far as they reflect the ideals of moral freedom. Since freedom according the *Critique of Pure Reason* is an idea of reason (and thus it is regulative),[64] I conclude that the world (state) republic – in so far as it institutionalizes freedom for global politics – is an idea of reason holding a regulative function.

Let's reconsider this conceptual puzzle by reference to the famous paragraph of *Toward Perpetual Peace* where Kant draws a distinction between what is right in theory (*in thesi*) – as with the desirability of a world republic/multistate confederation (note that here Kant uses the term *Weltrepublik*) – and what is instead right in practice (*in hypothesi*), as with the realization of the federation/league of states seen as a negative, second best, surrogate.

63 E. Ellis, *Kant's Politics. Provisional Theory for an Uncertain World*, Yale University Press, New Heaven and London, 2005, pp.112 ff. and P. Keating, *The Function of Ideas of Reason in Kant's Political Philosophy*, 2007, p.58 ff.

64 According to P. Keating "Thus, there is an important disanalogy between the laws of nature and the laws of freedom, because the latter are regulative and not determinative, that is, action guiding and not action determining [. . .]. This explains Kant's strange passage in the second edition Preface about how the human soul is both free and determined. (Bxxvi–xxx) The soul is thus free, not because it is capable of a dualism, but rather, because it is the site of unification for the laws of freedom with the laws of nature. Kant gives the example of a free action in the conditional: If (for example) I am now entirely free, and get up from my chair without the necessarily determining influence of natural causes, then in this occurrence, along with its natural consequences to infinity, there begins an entirely new series [. . .]. For this decision and deed do not lie within the succession of merely natural effects and are not a mere continuation of them [. . .] (A451/B479). So when we view ourselves as capable of freedom (the intelligible standpoint) we assign free choice to our actions". Keating, *Function of Ideas of Reason,* pp.63–64.

If, according to the ideal standard of practical reason, the world (state) republic is the solution to adopt, but nations "in accordance with their idea of the right of nations [. . .] do not at all want this, thus rejecting *in hypothesi* what is correct *in thesi*",[65] then, a suboptimal solution becomes legitimate only in so far it maintains itself compatible and open to the normative demands of the defined ideal. In other words, the practical rejection of the ideal standard of global politics by states is justifiable *pro tanto* only if it shows that the second-best solution does not contradict the ideal of the practical demands of reason as those presented by the model of the world (state) republic. The normative demand for a *formal congruence* between theory and practice persists.

Accordingly, just as the league of states, in order to result in a normatively significant entity (not just as a brute fact!) has to incorporate within its suboptimal institutional arrangement the normative ideal of the world (state) republic, similarly, the concept of a global arrangement of world politics has to turn itself into a regulative ideal. It is exactly at this textual juncture that Kant's elliptic introduction of the conceptual possibility for the idea of the league of states 'as if' it was a world (state) republic should be seen.[66] But this, in Kantian terms, requires a consideration of the relation between the league of states and the world (state) republic in a way similar to the relation between the regulative ideas of reason and the empirical occurrences of experience.

Such a point opens the problematic issue of how to conceive the relation between theory and practice in Kant's global politics. Some passages are indicative of this difficulty.

First, in the just-mentioned text of *Toward Perpetual Peace*, just before the introduction of the distinction between theory and practice Kant explains that the international state of nature among states can be abandoned in no other way

65 Kant, "Toward Perpetual Peace (1795)", 8:357, p.328.

66 The expression "*Völkerbund als Weltrepublik*" belongs to G. Geismann, "Kants Rechtlehre vom Weltfrieden", *Zeitschrift für philosophische Forschung*, 37(3),1983, p.377. Unfortunately, the author either abandoned or did not develop this view any further and in later writings shifted, instead, into a standard interpretation based on the idea of a linear progression from a league of states to a positive instantiation of a world (state) republic. In G. Geismann, *World Peace: Rational Idea and Reality on the Principles of Kant's Political Philosophy*, available online at https://www.researchgate.net/publication/27518143_World_Peace_Rational_Idea_and_Reality_On_the_Principles_of_Kant's_Political_Philosophy (accessed on 27.2.2018). Originally published in H. Oberer and G. Seel (eds.), *Kant. Analysen – Probleme – Kritik*; Königshausen und Neumann, Würzburg, vol. ii; 1996, pp. 265–319. But see also the brief but very pertinent article by H. Dreier, *Kants Republik*, 2004, pp. 745–804. A more extensive treatement is in I. Mauss' remarks: "Kant, dessen Rechtsbegriff zur Realisierung der Republik als faktischer Gesetzgebung des Volkes kategorisch verpflichtet, intensiviert im Hinblick auf den Frieden zwischen Staaten mit unterschiedlichen Verfassungssystemen die Konstruktion des »als ob« der bloß republikanischen »Regierungsart«". In Mauss, *Menschenrechte,* p.39. On the idea of Kant's 'subsidiary cosmopolitanism' ("komplementärer und zugleich subsidärer Kosmopolitismus"), which does not consider the forfeiting of sovereignty by states, see Höffe, *»Königliche Völker«*, p.234.

"but war",[67] similarly to the way in which individuals are forced to leave "their savage (lawless) freedom".[68]

Yet, the possibility that "an (always growing) *state of nations* (*civitas gentium*)"[69] would arise and "finally encompass all the nations of the earth"[70] is prevented by the will of states who will never freely subordinate themselves to a superior power. Therefore, one might conclude, "if all is not to be lost",[71] the world (state) republic can be assumed only as a conceptual guidance for the arrangement of interstates relations. The distinction Kant draws between what is correct *in thesi* and what is instead feasible in practice, should be interpreted in relation to a regulative role of the idea of theoretical correctness.

By suggesting the view that the world state republic provides practical guidance to the structuring of international relations, Kant safeguards the unity of theory and practice through the hope that peace among nations is a realizable ideal.

In the writing *On the Common Saying*, Kant had already affirmed that "such a universal state of nations [. . .] is possible *(in praxi)* and [. . .] it *can be*".[72] Yet, in *Toward Perpetual Peace*, he reminds us that only by subordinating politics to public right under the guidance of the world (state) republic can we hold "a well-founded hope [that] *perpetual peace* [. . .] is no empty idea but a task that, gradually solved, comes steadily closer to its goal".[73]

To confirm the interpretation provided above, it is worth recalling one decisive passage where Kant addresses explicitly the point on the regulative role of the world (state) republic.

In *Religion within the Limits of Mere Reason* (1793),[74] Kant draws an analogy between the objective unity of religion as a rational idea and "the political idea of the right of a state [*der politischen Idee eines Staatsrechts*] in so far as this right ought, at the same time, to be brought into line with an international law which is universal and *endowed with power*".[75]

For Kant we cannot have much "hope"[76] for an empirical peaceful realization of such a trajectory. As he immediately exemplifies, whenever we look back to history and on how states have ever tried to approximate such an ideal, one cannot fail to notice that this has occurred by "subjugat[ing]

67 Kant, "Toward Perpetual Peace (1795)", 8:357, p.328.
68 Ibid.
69 Ibid.
70 Ibid.
71 Ibid.
72 Kant, "On the Common Saying", 8:313, p.309.
73 Kant, "Toward Perpetual Peace (1795)", 8:386, p.351.
74 See I. Kant, *Religion within the Boundaries of Mere Reason. And Other Writings*, A. Wood and G. Di Giovanni (eds.), R. Merrihew Adams (intro.), Cambridge University Press, Cambridge, 1998 [1793], 6:124, pp. 128–129.
75 See Kant, *Religion within the Boundaries*", 6:124, p.129.
76 Ibid.

all others to itself and achiev[ing] a universal monarchy".[77] Yet, soon after, this did not last long and disintegrated "to split up from within into smaller states".[78]

Similarly, affirms Kant, we cannot nurture much hope for achieving the empirical unity of the church, that is, a unity realized within one single "visible church".[79] Rather, such unity should be conceived in terms of an "*idea* [. . .] *of reason* [*eine Idee* [. . .] *der Vernunft*] [emphasis added]"[80] that is, as a "practical regulative principle [*als praktisches regulatives Prinzip*]".[81]

Unity as a rational idea does not mean to surrender to an unmodifiable status quo but to activate a transformation of the political reality under the guidance of publicity and practical reason. As a regulative principle, it "has nonetheless the objective reality [*objektive Realität*] required to work towards this end of unity".[82]

Noumenical unity is connected to the visible church in so far as it provides its same normative presuppositions. The phenomenological unity of state and international law appears alongside interstate relations in the unfolding of the different stages of approximations to the ideal.[83]

This connection is testified also in the preparatory drafts of the *Rechtslehre – Reflections on the philosophy of right* [1764–] – where Kant asserts that "**there is no salvation outside the republic.** – A world republic [is] one where no individual state would have enough forces to fight the great republic if necessary."[84]

Clearly, the relation between the noumenical and the phenomenological world remains in a perennially unsolved tension. This point is raised again for the domestic domain in the writing of *The Conflict of the Faculties.* Here Kant observes that: "The Idea of a constitution in harmony with the natural right of man [. . .] signifies a Platonic Ideal (*respublica noumenon*) [and] is not an empty chimera".[85]

Accordingly, "a civil society organized conformably to this ideal [. . .] (*respublica phaenomenon*) [. . .] can only be painfully acquired after multifarious hostilities and wars; but its constitution [. . .] is qualified as the best among all

77 Ibid.
78 Ibid.
79 Ibid.
80 Ibid.
81 Ibid.
82 Ibid.
83 This is the distinction between *respublica noumenon* and *respublica phaenomenon* (built on the parallel to that of the invisible church as the original image of the visible church). As Cavallar remarks: "Kant refers to the *respublica noumenon,* to the concept of a completely pure state constitution (XIX, refl.8077, 609, 30–33)". Cavallar, *International Rights*, p.77. See also on this point Kersting, *Wohlgeordnete Freiheit*, p.428 ff.
84 I. Kant, "Reflections on the philosophy of right", F. Rauscher and K.R. Westphal (eds.), *Lectures and Drafts on Political Philosophy*, Cambridge University Press, Cambridge, 2016 [1764–], §807, p.68.
85 Kant, *Conflict of the Faculties. Der Streit der Fakultäten*, 1979 [1798], pp.163–165.

others".[86] Yet, the ideal side directs the process of political transformation. It is not by chance that such remarks fall in the paragraph *Concerning the Difficulty of the Maxims Applying to World Progress with Regard to Their Publicity* where Kant argues that "the prohibition of publicity impedes the progress of a people toward improvement".[87] Freedom of speech and the public use of reason are at the bottom of the collective process of political self-emancipation through a critical use of reason.

In view of this picture, the dichotomy between the noumenical and the phenomenological leaves room for a transitional understanding of international politics – a condition in which gradual reform of the status quo is conducted under the *a priori* guidance of the regulative principles of global politics.

All this informs us of a crucial point: whereas Kant's theory leads to ideal standards, it does not aim to reach a perfectionist conception of right and morality. The divide between the ideal and the real – the theory and the practice – can be brought back into unity under the idea of transitional stages of approximation. Kant is, in such respect, a truly critical and reformist thinker.[88]

§7.2 Thinking the contradiction between provisional and peremptory rights

The controversy in understanding the problematic relation between permissive (provisional) and peremptory (strict) laws concerns the proper place the former have in respect to the latter. According to Kant's Categorical Imperative – the founding matrix of right – laws can be either necessary (*leges praeceptivae*) or prohibitive (*leges prohibitivae*). Thus, he adds, it has been rightly questioned whether "there could also be *permissive rights (leges permissivae)* of pure reason".[89]

The proper understanding of permissive rights is a core aspect of politics and more in general of the overcoming of the divide between theory and practice through historical progression.[90]

Provisional laws are thus a difficult aspect of Kant's legal and political theory, but one having the potential to reveal the deeper structure of a theory of justice. Kant deploys different formulations to refer to provisional rights, calling them at times either permissive rights or, also, *leges latae* ('wide laws'), in opposition to *leges strictae* ('strict laws'). This was a notion already present in the Roman Digest

86 Ibid.

87 I. Kant, *Conflict of the Faculties*, p.161.

88 As affirms C. Horn: "Kant ist kein Perfektionist, sondern Liberaler; er vertritt einen *deontologischen Liberalismus*." In C. Horn, *Nicht Ideale Normativität. Ein neuer Blick auf Kants politische Philosophie*, Suhrkamp, Berlin, 2014, p.332.

89 Kant, "Toward Perpetual Peace (1795)", 8:348, p.321. On this problem see R. Brandt, "Das Problem der Erlaubnisgesetze im Spätwerk Kants", O. Höffe (ed.), *Zum Ewigen Frieden*, Akademie Verlag, Berlin, 2004, pp.69–86.

90 See on this R. Brandt, "Das Erlaubnisgesetz, oder: Vernunft und Geschichte in Kants Rechtslehre", R. Brandt (ed.), *Rechtsphilosophie der Aufklärung*, 1982, p.233 ff.

as well as in the *Decretum Gratiani* where law was divided into prohibiting, permitting, and punishing law.

Permissive natural laws, from the twelfth century onwards, were also at the basis of the justification of property rights.[91] The debate on permissive natural laws continued in the Second Scholastics and particularly, as we have seen in earlier sections, in de Vitoria's idea of common possession of humanity and the shift to private property and popular government. Such standard problems of justification of the civil condition also reappeared later in Kant with regard to move legitimately from a state of nature (where things are held in common) into a civil division of the Earth. Permissive rights retain a special role in the debate Kant inherits.

Indeed, also eighteenth-century jurists as Christian Wolff and Gottfried Achenwall (whose treatise *De iure naturae* Kant adopts as a course book) were preoccupied in finding the appropriate place for such laws. Wolff, for instance, considered that under the obligation to progress towards perfection, permissive natural laws allowed for the possibility of choosing the route one preferred, the *licitum* (licit).[92]

To this occurrence of the concept, Achenwall added a second understanding. He considered the distinction between laws as distinguishing determined actions (commanded or prohibited act – *obligatoria*), and laws allowing for undetermined acts (*indifferentia*).[93] Achenwall, later echoed by Kant, considered that the first occupant, by the same act of *occupatio*, was legitimated to appropriate a *res nullius* and to put under constraint all others (not to appropriate the same).

This view was not compatible with Grotius' idea of a community *primaeva* where things were held as commonly owned, not just possessed. This required a consent to all others on the pain of infringing a natural right of humanity. Yet, since this was not the starting condition out of which, in Achenwall, possession came to be justified, then, provisional rights of unilateral appropriation were an inherent part of the process of justification of private property. This also became the case for Kant's justification.

Kant's notion of an original community differs in fundamental ways from historical accounts of primitive communities (Grotius' *communio primaeva*) in so far as, in Kant, this is an heuristic hypothesis of reason. For Kant, this notion represents a more fundamental concept, since empirical accounts have to presuppose their same institutionalization and thus "a contract by which everyone gave up private possessions [. . .] but it is contradictory to claim that such a procedure is an *original* taking possession".[94]

91 B. Tierney, "Permissive Natural Law and Property: Gratian to Kant", *Journal of the History of Ideas*, 62(3), 2001, p.383 ff.

92 Ibid., p.393.

93 Tierney, "Permissive Natural Law", p.395. For a detailed analysis of Achenwall see J. Hruschka, *Das deontologische Sechseck bei Gottfried Achenwall im Jahre 1767. Zur Geschichte der deontischen Grundbegriffe in der Universal jurisprudenz zwischen Suarez und Kant*, Joachim Jungius-Gesellschaft der Wissenschaften e.V. Hamburg 4, 1986/2.

94 B. Tierney, "Kant on Property: the Problem of Permissive Right", *Journal of the History of Ideas*, 62(2), 2001, p.306.

All such connotations are present in Kant's scattered but fundamental treatments of the *leges permissivae* presented in both the section of the *Doctrine of Right* in the *Metaphysics of Morals* and in *Toward Perpetual Peace.*

For Kant, permissive rights stand to strict rights only as a "limiting condition".[95] Their contingent formulation is connected to the duty posed on public authorities to bring reforms. Accordingly, the postponement of a reform is necessitated by that same duty whenever contingencies prevent the realization of the purported practical scope. There appears therefore no contradiction in natural law between the *a priori* command of strict laws and the contingent postulation of a provisional postponement for the realization of the same objective.[96]

I propose here to interpret Kant in accordance with a unitary theory of law and politics, one where permissive rights are closer to 'political' measures. To argue for a deeper operational level of the two components of law is to recognize a *pragmatic a posteriori* and a necessary *a priori* interlink in the Kantian system of relation between rights and politics. By understanding an inherent connection between law and politics, *leges strictae* and *leges latae* it becomes possible to account for the generation of a system of distributive justice combining both prudential and moral peremptory conditions of right.

This overall rationale helps make sense of how permissive rights justify a pragmatic unity of law and politics: by postponing in the name of prudential reasons

95 "I wanted only to draw the attention of teachers of natural right to the concept of a *lex permissiva,* which reason presents of itself in its systematic divisions, especially since in civil (statutory) law use is often made of the concept, but with the following difference: the prohibitive law stands all by itself and the permission is not included in that law as a limiting condition (as it should be) but is thrown in among exceptions to it. Then it is said that this or that is prohibited, *except* for number 1, number 2, number 3, and so forth indefinitely, since permissions are added to the law only contingently, not in accordance with a principle but by groping about among cases that come up; for otherwise the conditions would have had to be introduced *into the formula of the prohibitive law,* and in this way it would have become at the same time a permissive right." In Kant, "Toward Perpetual Peace (1795)", 8:348, p.321.

96 "Whether, in addition to commands (*leges praeceptivae*) and prohibitions (*leges prohibitivae*), there could also be *permissive rights* (*leges permissivae*) of pure reason has hitherto been doubted, and not without grounds. For laws as such involve a ground of objective practical necessity, whereas permissions involve a ground of the practical contingency of certain actions; thus a *permissive right* would involve necessitation to an action such that one cannot be necessitated to do it, and, if the object of the law had the same meaning in both kinds of relation, this would be a contradiction. But in the permissive right here, the prohibition presupposed is directed only to the future way of acquiring a right (e.g., by inheritance), whereas the exemption from this prohibition, i.e., the permission, is directed to the present status of possession, which in the transition from the state of nature to the civil condition can continue as possession that, though not in conformity with rights is still *possession in good faith* (*possessio putativa*) in accordance with a permissive right of natural right, although a putative possession, as soon as it has been cognized as such, is prohibited in a state of nature, just as a similar way of acquiring is prohibited in the subsequent civil condition (after the transition has been made), and this authorization to continue in possession would not occur if such an alleged acquisition were to take place in the civil condition; for then, as soon as its nonconformity with rights were discovered, it would have to cease, as a wrong." In Kant, "Toward Perpetual Peace (1795)", 8:348, p.321.

the juridical construction of positive laws in conformity to an *a priori* system of strict rights, it is possible to advance politically, step-by-step, towards a condition of perpetual peace.

The distinction between legal and political rights responds to the view that the former are rights *stricto sensu* in so far as they conform closely to the *a priori* formal standard of the *Innate Principle of Morality* as well as to the *Universal Principle of Right*. Political rights respond, instead, to the demands of pragmatic considerations. Nevertheless, political rights are justified only with reference to *a priori* rights. Indeed, they are rights derogating from the object of strict laws in view of a postponement for its future realization.

Kant is cautious in clarifying immediately that deferrals can never be "*ad calendas graecas*, as Augustus used to promise".[97] Concessions to postponement have to be justified both in light of contingent considerations of a status quo and in view of the practical aim that is to be realized.

In the following sections I provide an overview analysis of the three significant areas of law in which provisional rights are justified in accordance to a practical assessment. I discuss, initially, the significance of provisional rights for private right; next, I move to the consideration of public right and, respectively, to constitutional and cosmopolitan right.[98] I leave out of analysis the idea of permissive rights as the morally licit, that is, as morally indifferent actions that mandatory laws leave to the free choice of the actor.

All in all, the view that emerges is one where the intersection of provisional and peremptory rights is such that the congruence of political justice to *a priori* standards of rights requires the pragmatic mediation of provisional rights. The necessity to account for Kant's internal dynamism between juridical and political rights is a problem already raised by Fichte in his *Review* of *Toward Perpetual Peace* who notices, significantly, that the league of nations can be only an "intermediate" condition.[99]

I conclude by discussing whether provisional rights are to be considered in accordance with either natural or positive rights, that is, whether they hold an *a priori* or *a posteriori* status, or, finally, a mix thereof. The problematic definition of the nature of provisional rights contributes to the further definition of the role of the world (state) republic as a regulative idea of reason. In the final sections, I clarify, therefore, the elements connected to this point.

97 Kant, "Toward Perpetual Peace (1795)", 8:347, p.321

98 R. Vierhaus (ed.), *Eigentum und Verfassung*, 1972. On the Kantian notion of "supreme proprietorship of the soil" as a category justifying all right (both private and public), see Schmitt, *Nomos of the Earth*, p.46.

99 As Fichte affirms on this point: "just as individuals unite in a civil state, so these warring states must unite in a state of nations, in which their conflicts will be decided in accordance with positive laws. – This, anyway, is the decision of pure reason, and the federation of nations [*Völkerbund*] proposed by Kant for the preservation of peace is no more than an *intermediary* condition [emphasis added]", G. Fichte, "Review of Immanuel Kant, Perpetual Peace: a Philosophical Sketch", D. Breazeale (trans), *The Philosophical Forum, Königsberg: Nicolovius, 1795*, [second 1796], vol. xxxii, n.4, 2001, p.319.

Regarding the process of justification of private property, in the *Metaphysics of Morals*, namely in the section on the *Doctrine of Right*, Kant explains how to move from a hypothetical natural condition of common possession of all (not yet property!), one where each has a right to all and things do not belong to anyone in particular (*res nullius*), to one where I can claim something as a property for myself and exclude all others from interference. The *Innate Right to Freedom* allows to us the freedom of movement and bodily integrity. First, it guarantees one's bodily space, so that any infringement violates my innate right to freedom. But, secondly, when it comes to the appropriation of external objects, it prompts the formulation of the *Postulate of Practical Reason.*[100] It is at this juncture that Kant introduces the concept of permissive rights with regard to property. By permissive/provisional rights Kant accounts for the possibility of rightful possession. This is far from the Lockean strategy of labour as a means of private appropriation, or, by consent to a contract as in Hobbes. Certainly, this view is also very far from Columbus' first occupancy title, not to speak of the use of force by the *conquistadores.*

For Kant, the entry point to rightful possession (and next to private property), occurs through permissive rights as accounted for in the *Postulate of Practical Reason.*

The *Postulate* affirms that: "'it is a duty of right to act towards others so that what is external (usable) could also become someone's'".[101] Here Kant is not referring to an object of choice on which I exercise "*physical* power to use".[102] There is a distinction to be made between holding an object under one's control – as an act of power – and having "*a capacity*"[103] to control it. In the latter case I'm allowed to "*think* of something simply as an object of my choice".[104] This represents "an a priori presupposition of practical reason to regard and treat any object of my choice as something which could objectively be mine or yours".[105] The postulate, concludes Kant, "can be called a permissive law (*lex permissiva*) of practical reason, which gives us an authorization that could not be got from mere concepts of right as such [. . .]."[106] What the postulate authorizes is to think as possible to hold all others under an obligation of non-interference which they would not otherwise have. It is starting from such *Postulate* that one can next to move to a rightful condition of private property.

100 On the positioning of the postulate see B. Ludwig, "Der Platz des rechtlichen Postulats der praktischen Vernunft innerhalb der Paragaphen 1–6 der kantischen Rechtslehre", R. Brandt (ed.), *Rechtsphilosophie der Aufklärung*, 1982, pp.218–232. For a wider reconstruction of the difference between 'Sittengesetz' and 'Rechtsgesetz', see W. Kersting, "Sittengesetz und Rechtsgesetz – Die Begründung des Rechts bei Kant und den frühen Kantianern", R. Brandt (ed.), *Rechtsphilosophie der Aufklärung*, Walter de Gruyter, Berlin, 1982, pp.148–177.

101 Kant, "The Metaphysics of Morals (1797)", 6:252, p.406.

102 Kant, "The Metaphysics of Morals (1797)", 6:250, p.405.

103 Kant, "The Metaphysics of Morals (1797)", 6:250, p.406.

104 Ibid.

105 Ibid.

106 Ibid.

Permissive rights and the *Postulate* for their justification mediate between *the possibility* of external appropriation in space and time and a rightful condition of appropriation in accordance with the law. Permissive rights disconnect property from spatio-temporal physical determinations, paving the way for the construction of a civil condition.

With regard to the justification of private property, Kant claims that unilateral appropriations and exclusion of all others from interference should be imaginable a priori in view of the possibility of instantiating, next, a general obligation of all to respect one's possessions. Indeed, it would be a contradictory statement to maintain that I can appropriate something due to my inherent freedom and that I cannot appropriate the same due to the equal freedom of all others. Provisional *a priori* appropriation should allow unilateral possession (*possessio phaenomenon*) by postponing the instantiation of private property (*possessio noumenon*) to the institution of the civil condition. This explains why Kant affirms that "Possession in anticipation of and preparation for the civil condition [...] is *provisionally rightful* possession, whereas possession found in an *actual* civil condition would be *conclusive* possession".[107] Indeed, the assumption holding all others under obligation remains unilateral without being yet a generalized one. Only after the creation of a civil republican order under the vestige of an omnilateral *a priori* will, does it become possible, next, to move to a full condition of distributive justice governed under the premises of the *Universal Principle of Right* according to which "the free use of [one's] choice can coexist with the freedom of everyone".[108]

Once entered into a rightful condition, permissive rights show also an all internal constitutional-legal capacity to prompt reforms. The possibility for republican constitutional states to progress towards higher standards of normative legitimacy depends on their internal political capacity to reform the existing standards.[109]

This is the work that for Kant is absolved by the "*moral politician*",[110] a person who adopts a correct approach to public authority in so far as he "takes the principles of political prudence in such a way that they can coexist with morals".[111] For the moral politician, then, provisional rights are a concession – not an exception – from strict obligations. Derogation to peremptory rights is therefore justified only in view of contingent, prudential reasons, which nevertheless only postpone the purported practical object to a specific time of realization. Such postponement bears retroactive effects to the justification of the adopted provisional measure. In other words, prudential decisions derogating reforms to future action are justifiable only if considered as contingently necessary steps for the safeguarding of the already gained civil thresholds.

107 Kant, "Metaphysics of Morals (1797)", 6:257, p.410
108 Kant, "Metaphysics of Morals (1797)", 6:230, p.387.
109 On the reformative function of permissive right see Brandt, "Das Problem der Erlaubnisgesetze", , pp.85–86.
110 Kant, "Toward Perpetual Peace (1795)", 8:372, p.340.
111 Ibid.

Finally, and most importantly, the domestic and international context in which Kant introduces the notion of provisional rights is the one related to the natural law context and not the one regarding the derogation of reforms in an already established civil condition. Provisional rights, therefore, help, in one case, in entering the civil domestic condition, whereas in the other case, they prompt approximation towards a cosmopolitan condition.

If, in the case of domestic republican reforms, it holds true that constitutional progressions proceed contingently, but steadily, towards the approximation of the mandates of the original contract (so that whoever put himself outside a system of law can be coerced through force and punished), the case is different with regard to the international progression of states to an international civil condition. Here, coercion cannot be exercised against states since they "have already outgrown the constraints of others".[112]

Accordingly, the view for which public authority should direct itself towards the greatest approximation of the idea of an original contract is to be extended, internationally, under the premises of Kant's "sort of contract"[113] among nations. The hesitancy with which Kant appeals to the international transferring of this notion is due probably to the view that nations cannot be coerced, as can be individuals, to leave the state of nature.

In later sections, I develop in full the strategy that Kant had presumably in mind when he refers to the idea of a cosmopolitan constitution and of the cosmopolitan right to visit. For the present purposes, though, I assume that all transitory institutions accompanying the progression towards a peaceful condition (i.e. the *Amphictyonic League*, the *Kongreß*, the *Völkerbund*, etc.) are the product of provisional laws presented as *Preliminary articles* 2-3-4 in *Toward Perpetual Peace.*[114]

These articles allow for the postponement of full compliance with strict laws in the name of consideration of current political circumstances.[115] As reminded earlier, these laws apply at the interstices of the domestic and international state of nature where only natural law holds.

Provisional rights and laws are indeed at full work in Kant's *Toward Perpetual Peace.* This writing is strictly connected to the *a priori* structuring of the law presented in the *Metaphysics of Morals.* Even if *Toward Perpetual Peace* was published before, to some extent Kant developed both works in parallel. Conceived in the form of a peace treaty, *Toward Perpetual Peace* is organized around a distinction between preliminary and definitive articles which contain – in the same practical application of preliminary articles – a division between peremptory and provisional laws, as exposed in the *Rechtslehre.*

112 Kant, "Toward Perpetual Peace (1795)", 8:355, p.327.

113 Ibid., 8:383, p.348. Translation partially modified.

114 Ibid., 8:344, p.318 ff.

115 As Ellis notices: "Kant's concept of provisional right deals with exactly this problem of applying universal principles based on ideals of justice to a world that will never achieve them". Ellis, *Kant's Politics*, p.116.

In general, the division between preliminary and definitive articles allows some leeway in the remedy of practices contrary to peace. Some of the provisional cases include the consideration of states in terms of personal patrimony (*Preliminary article* 2), that is, in terms of the acquisition of states by family inheritance. For Kant, the exchange or purchase of states represents a violation of "the idea of the original contract",[116] yet, such practice is provisionally authorized if conducted in compliance with prudential reasons.

The moral politician is the one capable of assessing the relevance of prudential consideration with regard to the ultimate object of practical political reason: the duty to approximate the regulative standards of the world (state) republic. The result is that, for Kant, what would never be allowed in a civil condition, such as the practices of inheritance of states, would be nevertheless tolerated along the transition from the natural to the civil condition.

In addition to personal patrimony, other cases of provisional rights mentioned in *Toward Perpetual Peace* include standing armies (*Preliminary article 3*) and the possibility of resorting to debt-financed wars (*Preliminary article 4*). Both cases present serious problems of acceptability under a strict-right/law perspective. In the former case "standing armies is itself the cause of an offensive war".[117] In the latter case, financial borrowing for the continuation of war represents a concrete impediment to peace.

Unfortunately, Kant does not give us a precise indication of how to interpret the relation of provisional rights to strict laws in the international sphere. As an interpretive attempt, one could suggest that concretely adopted practices, in an imperfect world, are admissible only *in so far as* they allow "reforms in keeping with the ideal of public right",[118] such that it is constructed "a lawful constitution based on principles of freedom".[119] The political rationality of the moral politician reveals two sets of capacities: the normative ability to keep faith with the practical regulative ideals of reason and the capacity to provide a realistic evaluation of the appropriate moment for introducing effective reforms.

From all such dynamics, it appears that Kant's political reformism remains in a constantly unresolved tension between an ideal – *a priori* model – the *noumenal* world – and a pragmatic – *a posteriori* reality – the imperfect dimension of a *phenomenological* world. As a result of the application of the Kantian maxim: "Always leave open [. . .] the possibility of entering a rightful condition",[120] pragmatic-reformative politics justifies provisional rights as 'second best' approximations to *a priori* conclusive rights.

It is not by chance, therefore, that also at the institutional level Kant opts for the league of states (the *Völkerbund* or *Föderation*) as a second best option – what

116 Kant, "Toward Perpetual Peace (1795)", 8:344, p.318.
117 Ibid.
118 Kant, "Metaphysics of Morals (1797)", 6:350, p.487.
119 Ibid.
120 Ibid., 6:347, p.485.

he defines as a surrogate solution – in order to secure a realistic staring point to progress towards peace.[121]

Provisional rights and international transitional entities are strictly connected notions in the progression towards a global rule of law and peace. As I have explained, in Kant, a legal and institutional asymmetry always remains unresolved – as it is evident in the distinction between the *in thesi* and *in hypothesi* alternatives, where what is desirable in ideal terms is distinguished from what is feasible pragmatically. It is along this institutional asymmetry and legal discontinuity that the construction of a regulative global cosmopolitan constitution establishing transitional lines of progression becomes the feasible substitute for the positive realization of a world state republic.

In these concluding paragraphs, I attempt to bring about an overall characterization of the relation between provisional principles and the regulative ideas of reason.

First of all, in the preparatory works of the *Doctrine of Virtue* Kant affirms that the "*Lex permissiva* is the law by which something is permitted according to natural law that is forbidden by civil law",[122] so that theft is admissible if caused by starvation in accordance to a natural law perspective even when it is ruled out under a positive law scheme.

In the *Vigilantius' lectures notes* (1793), Kant defines the *leges latae* in terms of the totality of the "laws of rights",[123] excluding the possibility of a dynamic shift from provisional to peremptory norms. This multiplicity of uses has raised a number of interpretive puzzles. The suggestion here is that since neither the *Vorarbeit zur Tugendlehre* nor the *Vigilantius' lectures notes* express Kant's final design of the system of right, it would seem inappropriate to consider these works as a disconfirming proof of a unitary interpretation of *Toward Perpetual Peace* and the *Metaphysics of Morals.*[124]

Thus, in order to defend a unitary interpretation, I begin from the consideration that a regulative function of the world (state) republic manifests itself

121 "There shall be no war between myself and other states, although I recognize no supreme legislative power which secures my right to me and to which I secure its right, it is not understandable on what I want to base my confidence in my right, unless it is the surrogate of the civil social union, namely the free federalism that reason must connect necessarily with the concept of the right of nations." In Kant, "Toward Perpetual Peace (1795)", 8:356, p.327–328.

122 "*Lex permissiva* ist das Gesetz wodurch etwas nach Naturgesetzen erlaubt ist was nach Civilgesetzen verboten ist", I. Kant, "Vorarbeit zur Tugendlehre", I. Kant, *Handschriftlicher Nachlaß Vorarbeiten und Nachträge*, xxiii, p.385. Available online at: https://korpora.zim.uni-duisburg-essen.de/kant/aa23/Inhalt23.html (accessed on 28.08.2019).

123 I. Kant, "Kant on the metaphysics of morals. Vigilantius' lectures notes", P. Heath and J.B. Schneewind (eds.), *Immanuel Kant. Lectures on Ethics*, Cambridge University Press, Cambridge, 1997 [1793], 27:536, p.295.

124 One might add also that the defence of a unitary interpretation complies with the Occam's razor principle according to which one should never make more assumptions than the minimum needed.

as a resource for solving the (apparent) contradiction between provisional and peremptory rights.

The contradiction consists in opposing two types of propositions: one, holding that domestic and interstate relations are arranged on contingent bases (the position held by Kant's political moralist for whom morality is subordinated to the interests of politics); the other, considering, instead, that in virtue of peremptory rights one should create a positive world (state) republic all at once (what Kant categorizes in terms of moral despotism, in so far as law totally excludes politics).[125] To this contradiction, the idea of a regulative world (state) republic allows for a justification step-by-step, that is, along political progressions.

This interpretive possibility is drawn from Kant's discussion of the regulative idea of reasons in the theoretical domain as something capable of bringing a *conjunction* of the multiple into a unity (Kant uses the term *Verbindung* as a translation of *conjunctio*).[126] Regulative principles are concerned here with the formal *a priori* anticipation of experience. Yet, they consider existential relations and are not therefore purely *a priori* principles.[127] They provide, instead, a dynamic unity of the temporal sequence for the determinations themselves. Regulative principles furnish, rather, the overall conditions wherein experience can be thought of. If constitutive principles define the domain of possible knowledge, regulative principles justify a transcendental order in reference to which empirical knowledge can be ordained.

In the *Transcendental Dialectic*, as seen, Kant illustrates extensively the unifying function of the ideas of reason with respect to orientation in thinking.[128] Regulative ideas provide not a concept of the object but a rule for the intellect.[129] This is the kind of unity connected to the multiplicity of phenomena, something based on a regulative use of the ideas realizing "the experience as a system (die Erfahrung als ein System)".[130]

When transferred to the practical domain, the regulative domain reveals its links with the pragmatics of historicity. Whereas the experience of the whole is given only in relation to the regulative realm, its justification proceeds along

125 On the distinction and analysis between 'moral politician', 'political moralist' and 'moral despotism', see J. Weinrib, "Permissive Rights and the Dynamism of Kantian Justice", *Law and Philosophy*, 33(1), 2014, pp.105–136.

126 On the properties and functions of the constitutive and the regulative in Kant's theoretical philosophy see A. Aportone, "Funzioni Costitutive e Regolative nella 'Critica della Ragion Pura' di Kant", *Rivista di Storia della Filosofia*, 45(4), 1990, p.700 ff.

127 Aportone, "Funzioni Costitutive", p.707.

128 O. Höffe refers to a double (opposite) direction for the orienting function of regulative ideas: one towards an interconnected legislation and the order towards the diffusion of a plurality of objects. See O. Höffe, *Immanuel Kant*, Verlag C.H. Beck, Munich, 1988, p.164.

129 Kant, *Critique of Pure Reason*, A645/B673, p.607.

130 Aportone, "Funzioni Costitutive", p.719. My translation.

historical directives through principles and maxims of actions. Here the ultimate goal of practical reason, peace, is postponed to future realization and not dismissed on merely pragmatic considerations – as it would be the disgraceful case of Kant's political moralist. The presupposition of a regulative unity solves the tension between necessary and contingent laws by orienting judgments under a systemic ideal framework of reason.

Part 4

Juridical constructivism and the cosmopolitan constitution

§8 Thinking political, thinking cosmopolitan

Kant's pessimism on human anthropology is famously captured by the idea that "out of such crocked wood as the human being is made, nothing entirely straight can be fabricated".[1] Yet, Kant believes at the same time that "the human race is constantly advancing with respect to culture (as its natural end) it is also to be conceived as progressing toward what is better with respect to the moral end of its existence, and that this will indeed be *interrupted* from time to time but will never be *broken off*".[2]

It is within such a conceptual framework that, as I will show in detail here, the regulative role of the world (state) republic leaves open for the possibility, at least, *to hope* that one day peace will be possible among human beings.[3] Whereas morality does not take into consideration the contexts for the application of its own imperatives (indeed, it must be applied universally and without exceptions), politics operates contextually, admitting exceptions only whenever the juridical command is not immediately instantiated. For Kant, non-ideal normativity is necessary to understand what is equitable in political contexts informed by universal standards of morality.[4]

The consequences of such position in political rationality are straightforward.

They amount to: (a) the recognition of the validity of permissive laws which allows for a qualified derogation from the peremptory character of right as such (what I have termed more in general 'the transitional'); and (b) a general scheme of public reasoning, which proceeds along constitutional lines, so that it must be

1 Kant, "Universal History", 8:23, p.113.

2 Kant, "On the Common Saying", 8:309, p.306.

3 This point is well captured by G. Marini when he distinguishes in Kant between "theological chiliasm" and "philosophical chiliasm". The first is represented by the unification of the visible churches in the bringing about of the empirical conditions for realizing "the supreme good on earth", while the second is the "republican peace in this earthly life". We can only realistically hope for the latter, particularly on the basis of adoption of a teleological judgment. In G. Marini, "Kants Idee einer Weltrepublik", P. van Tongeren, P. Sars, C. Bremmers and K. Boey (eds.), *Eros and Eris. Contributions to a Hermeneutical Phenomenology Liber Amicorum for Adrian Peperzak*, Springer, Dordrecht, 1992, p.133.

4 On the notion of the 'non-ideal' in Kant, see Horn, *Nicht Ideale Normativität*, p.324.

possible to define cosmopolitan issues in such a way that "a violation of right on *one* place of the earth is felt in *all*".[5]

Kant's construction of a cosmopolitan constitution is meant to provide principles for the structuring of public reasoning along the task of reflecting upon international justice and approximating peace among nations.[6] For Kant, to consider the world (state) republic as a regulative ideal allows for the possibility to envision the unity of the international society of states and the law of nations, thus legitimizing international relations in transition from a state of nature to a federation of states. Without such an idea of global unity of the law, neither an exit from the natural condition, nor an adjudicative point of view, can be shared between foreign citizens and the states, nor among the states themselves. The ideal role of an international state with republican features structuring all legitimate parameters of just relations provides for the legitimate conditions of interstate relations in the progress on international peace and justice. For Kant, this remains an asymptotic process realizable indefinitely in the tension between the theory of the law and the practice of politics.

Compliance with the postulate of public right means for Kant to instantiate a civil condition.

The point becomes, next, to consider that if one does not wish states to surrender to an unstable and negative condition that is always in "constant danger of its breaking out",[7] as the league of states, then it should be posited that some sort of gradual and positive transformation of interstate relations is realizable instead, and assume, accordingly, a cosmopolitan constitutional framework for international law.

The unity of international law helps in stabilizing interstate relations, not to mention providing a scheme of international justice. The institutional form of such legal unity is the world (state) republic. Since a supraordinate power – the positive instantiation of a world (state) republic – is not a feasible option from the point of view of the states, unity of international law is to be regulative. Indeed, only a regulative interpretation of such an idea of a world state could save both a progressive understanding of interstate relations and a non-empirical understanding of a republic.[8] This conceptual thread appears to represent to individuals

5 Kant, "Toward Perpetual Peace (1795)", 8.360, p.330.

6 On a precious study on this matter, both textually accurate and philosophically challenging see G.W. Brown, *Grounding Cosmopolitanism: from Kant to the Idea of a Cosmopolitan Constitution*, Edinburgh University Press, Edinburgh, 2013; see particularly, pp.59–83.

7 Kant, "Toward Perpetual Peace (1795)", 8:357, p.328.

8 This point has been missed by those interpretations that, while recognizing a transitional aspect in Kant's cosmopolitanism, have nevertheless considered the world (state) republic as a concrete ultimate state of realization. As for instance, among others, G. Cavallar: "In thesi, that is, according to reason, the world republic is the ideal and should be the ultimate goal; in hypothesi, under given circumstances and conditions, the federation or league of states establishing a permanent state congress for initiating or instituting public coercive right is the second-best option and should be an intermediate goal [. . .]". In Cavallar, *Kant's Embedded Cosmopolitanism*, p.50.

more faithfully the way in which the mandate of the postulate of right commands leaving the lawless condition of the state of nature.

Perhaps, one might be sceptical as to whether an idea of unity for international law is required at all. Legal pluralists would contest this point and argue that there is instead an irreducible multiplicity of jurisdictions whose legitimacy is all internal and never transposable in an overarching supraordinate principle. Yet Kant, in so far as he mentions a plurality of transnational political entities, shows himself to be supportive both of a plurality of states and of a multiplicity of transnational entities. The point, nonetheless, is that the legitimacy conditions of all such actors respond to the same unitary presupposition: an omnilateral *a priori* will, which only justifies the rationale of exiting a lawless condition by resorting to a notion of authority.[9]

This bears important implications among which is the idea that one cannot be content with a "surrogate"[10] solution, such as that of a league of states. Therefore, a transitional interpretation should be embraced where states are expected in the long term to engage in a cognitive shift, *creating and interpreting* international law 'as if' it has to respond to the requisites of a world state-like republic. This move appears crucial. It provides necessary criteria to states for conceiving their mutual relations along global public constitutional lines without having also to embrace the idea of a positive and coercive international state of states.

Perhaps an alternative description of such a conceptual shift consists in considering the league of states as an entity responding to the commands of a hypothetical imperative of the kind: 'if you want x, do y!'

It follows that the league of states becomes legitimate only in so far as it exhibits an unsolved tension with the idea of right. However, in order to accomplish such a command, the league of states has to be and not to be, that is, it has to show a *telos* pointing beyond itself. This is the transitional outcome to which the negative element of the league of states gives rise in Kant's league of states. One should disambiguate here the significance of the notion of a *telos* when adopted in connection with the approximation of peace. Such finalistic directionality, indeed, can be neither a causal nor an eschatological idea of a political end, but rather a standard defining a counterfactual scheme of public reasoning and argumentation for interstate and cosmopolitan relations. The felicitous expression "Völkerbund als Weltrepublik"[11] should indicate a regulative way of looking at interstate law transformations, rather than describing a positive transformative

9 Kant, "Metaphysics of Morals (1797)", 6:313, p.457.

10 Kant, "Toward Perpetual Peace (1795)", 8:357 p.328.

11 Geismann, "Kants Rechtlehre", p.377. This interpretation comes closer to the one advanced here even if it does not explicitly formulate an 'as if' thesis for the role of the world (state) republic. Unfortunately, the author has abandoned this view, and in later writings he has adopted a standard idea of an institutional progression from a league of states to a positive instantiation of a world (state) republic. In Geismann, *World Peace* (accessed on 27.2.2018).

Moreover, the Kantian textual evidences brought forth as evidence of the suggested interpretation appear to contradict the suggestion that is made (in Geismann, "Kants Rechtlehre", note 57, p.377). Here, Kant refers to the utopianism of the thesis of philosophical instantiation from the league of states into the world (state) republic. The regulative trajectory seems to better capture Kant's cosmopolitan framework when he considers states as "work[ing] toward establishing it [peace] and the *constitution* [*Konstitution*] that seems the most suitable to that end [emphasis added]".[12] Plurality is here safeguarded.

Regulative ideas, Kant observes, are of a special kind since "even though one may never concede them objective reality (existence), are nevertheless not to be regarded as mere figments of the brain".[13]

As a result of the asymptotic movement that is generated by the regulative framing of politics within the idea of a world (state) republic, the overcoming of the state of nature among states can never be completely reached. It is true that in *On the Common Saying*, Kant claims that "such a universal state of nations will thereby be ushered in, and so to assume that it is possible *(in praxi)* and that it *can be*".[14] Yet, this possibility should be interpreted only as something *in thought* and thus in coherence with the regulative function it has been identified for the *Völkerstaat*. Furthermore, the transformation of the universal state of nations into a regulative one occurs in the same year of publication of *On the Common Saying*, namely,in the *Religion within the Boundaries of Mere Reason* (1793). The same idea will be forcefully reaffirmed also two years later in the writing *Toward Perpetual Peace* (1795).

In this latter writing, Kant transforms his earlier views by suggesting that a regulative notion of the international order can have a cognitive function in granting the unity of the international order in terms of a rational idea. This takes the form of a multistate confederation (*Völkerstaat*) or the equivalent of a world (state) republic (*Weltrepublik*). In either case, both entities in their conceptual status are only heuristic ideas conceived in analogy to a notion of progress when reflecting along a presumable "purposiveness of nature".[15] As the purposiveness of nature "is in fact indispensable for us",[16] it nevertheless accompanies itself "only for the reflecting power of judgment".[17]

It appears, therefore, plausible that an association might be established between the reflectivity of judgment and the political conceptualization of the transnational arena. Similarly, the guiding idea of a world (state) republic appears to be a necessary heuristic tool in conceiving the lawless condition of a state of nature. In this respect, heads of state and their legislatures presuppose a rational

and religious chiliasm while he does not yet suggest a counterfactual interpretation of the world (state) republic, Kant, *Religion within the Boundaries*, 6:34, p.57.

12 Kant, "Metaphysics of Morals (1797)", 6:354, p.148. The condition of approximation is considered by Horn in his work *Nicht Ideale Normativität*, pp.312–313, where he also considers that the non-ideal character of approximation means that men are not called to confront each other merely through morality but through "a state finalistic order, ('a master')", p.313. However, as often noticed, this remains only a regulative ideal.

13 Kant, *Critique of Pure Reason*, A 569/B 597, p.552.

14 Kant, "On the Common Saying", 8:313, p.809.

15 I. Kant, *Critique of the Power of Judgment*, P. Guyer (ed.), Cambridge University Press, Cambridge, 2000 [1790], 5:414, p.283.

16 Kant, *Critique of the Power of Judgment*, 5:398, p.269.

17 Kant, *Critique of the Power of Judgment*, 5:379, p.250.

unity between state and international law, so as to embrace a political conception of a world (state) republic. Only on the basis of such presupposition can heads of state proceed *reflectively* into the construction of a legitimate international order.

For Kant, thinking politically is to express a particular type of rationality, one that is not categorical, like that of the moral imperative or of the universal principle of right, but rather one that is non-ideal and contextually sensitive. Thinking politically is to think comparatively through confrontations of possible situational outcomes.[18] Due to this conceptual characterization, it is not surprising that, whereas Kant clearly distinguishes between moral and juridical rationality, assigning to each a principle, he does not see politics as distinctly defined by a dedicated *a priori* principle, but rather as contributing to define practical rationality more generally.

Certainly, in *Appendix I* of the writing *Toward Perpetual Peace* (entitled: *On the Disagreement between Morals and Politics with a View to Perpetual Peace*), Kant introduces the role of political rationality in order to supply a solution to the theory/practice problem. Thinking politically is to bring about a coherent whole between *a priori* principles of morality and *a posteriori* contingency of a given reality. This means that when it comes to thinking politically, 'moral oughts' presuppose 'political cans'.[19] For Kant, if one admits that nature is not just a mechanism that politics is called to tame, but that freedom and morality have a place in our cooperative lives, then: "it must be granted that the two ['the concept of right with politics'] can be united".[20]

Furthering this point, Kant argues that "a *moral politician* [is someone] who takes the principles of political prudence in such a way that they can coexist with morals".[21] Political rationality in this sense strives to bring about the ideals of morality into the impure world of conflicting and apparently irreconcilable interests. It follows that political thinking is always entrapped into a tension with morality and right, in so far as it strives to realize emancipatory trajectories of freedom within history.

18 On the non-ideal character of political thinking Horn notices: "Das Politische ist das Feld nichtidealer Verhältnisse *par excellence*, in dem man 'nach besten Kräften' oder 'im Rahmen des Möglichen' Güter wie äußere Freiheiten, Sicherheit oder Wohlstand herstellen oder erhalten muss." In Horn, *Nicht Ideale Normativität*, p.326.

Horn also insists correctly on the comparative function that political rationality engages in when deciding upon different scenarios: "Im Feld des Politischen ist man typischerweise mit einer von zwei Gefharen konfrontiert: enteder einem moralischen Utopismus Raum zu geben oder aber zynischen Realismus. Wünschenswert wäre jedoch ein Mittelweg; die politische Realität verlangt nach nichtidealen Lösungen, die gleichwohl normative gehaltvoll sein sollten." In Horn, *Nicht Ideale Normativität*, p.321.

19 "Morals is of itself practical in the objective sense, as the sum of laws commanding unconditionally, in accordance with which we *ought* to act, and it is patently absurd, having granted this concept of duty its authority, to want to say that one nevertheless *cannot* do it." In Kant, "Toward Perpetual Peace (1795)", 8:370, p.338.

20 Kant, "Toward Perpetual Peace (1795)", 8:372, p.340.

21 Ibid.

Nevertheless, Kant considers misleading to conclude that the divergence of the ideal from the real suffices to supply a justification for "the pretext that human nature is not *capable* of what is good [. . .] as reason prescribes"[22] and therefore to "*make* improvement *impossible*".[23]

To be sure, the conflict holds only *subjectively* – "in the self-seeking propensity of human beings"[24] – but not *objectively* – that is, "in theory".[25] Politics is subordinated to realizing the conditions set by the principle of right, namely, by that principle which considers that right actions must agree with a universal law.[26] The contrast here is between the *a priori* status of the postulate of public right (the "*exeundum esse*" command) and practical reasoning as a form of political prudence. The latter is evidently positioned within *a posteriori* conditions.[27] The hiatus between the ideal and the real that is to be filled by state politics provides a justificatory platform for transitionality as permissive laws.

As an interpretive hypothesis, this fulfilment of an *a priori* postulate of public right might be considered as generating hypothetical imperatives (of *prudence*). However, regardless of whether the search for (juridical) peace is categorically 'commanded' or hypothetically 'advised' – whether it is a question of morality or of prudence – its achievement is *possible* only if thinking politically amounts to reflecting under the premises of an idea of right, but reasoning concretely throughout readily available options. The type of prudence that Kant often associates with the political should, therefore, not be confused with "expediency",[28] nor with "something intermediate"[29] resulting in "a pragmatically conditioned right".[30] For Kant, instead, the prudential attitude to politics implies an "homage to morals",[31] so that when it creates a conflict between the two: "morals cuts the knot that politics cannot untie".[32] Yet, the transformation of social reality by politics has to proceed in compliance with a normative legal standard, one which

22 Ibid.
23 Kant, "Toward Perpetual Peace (1795)", 8:373, p.341.
24 Kant, "Toward Perpetual Peace (1795)", 8:379, p.346.
25 Ibid.
26 Kant, "Metaphysics of Morals (1797)", 6:230, p.387.
27 This position is also supported by the forceful remarks expressed by Geismann: "Only a short-sighted judgment of so-called prudence can come to the conclusion that the disregarding of rules of Right is advantageous. Kant pleads in favour of Right as the supreme principle of all political maxims because any other principle (like the 'State's welfare and happiness' [the famous-infamous 'reason of State']) would a priori make impossible world peace as the guarantee of the external freedom of everyman with regard to all others. Also and especially prudence, if it be really prudent, 'must bend its knee before Right'. Right is, in the moral as well as in the prudent sense, the basis of all prudent politics", Geismann, *World Peace*, p.30 (accessed on 27.2.2018).
28 Kant, "Toward Perpetual Peace (1795)", 8:380, p.347.
29 Ibid.
30 Ibid.
31 Ibid.
32 Ibid.

grants that "the right of human beings must be held sacred",[33] despite any brutality manifested by power.

This three-pronged structure defines the form of operation of political-practical reason. The normative and prudential aspect of political reason facilitates the grasping of what realistically *can* be done with regard to what ultimately *ought* to be done, political wisdom is connected to the idea of a gradual reform of institutions and the law. Here it is clear that the relation between morality and politics refers to the theory/practice problem. The point at stake is that whereas the moralist adopts "measures prematurely",[34] the prudent politician when subordinating action to morality brings "experience [. . .] gradually [. . .] onto a better course".[35] The function that politics plays in social reality, therefore, is one that makes possible a realistic utopia, one where the morality of the law is institutionalized in the political life of a community of people. If politics falls in between brute reality and the idealizations of law and morality, then, its domain turns into being neither a mere objectivity of the status quo nor an abstract ideal; it becomes, rather, the domain for the normativity of the transitional – a condition of gradual transformation of reality. It is under this light that the fracture must be placed between what is right *in thesi* and what is instead possible, but suboptimal, *in practice*, as famously formulated by Kant.[36] Besides the transitionality aspect linked to the idea of permissive laws, the theory/practice dichotomy opens up to the understanding of 'the political' in terms of a critical non-ideal normativity – something in between realism and utopia. This also reflects the specificity of the concern of the political, namely, the question of 'what is possible?' *vis-à-vis* the duties connected to the moral and juridical sphere of 'what ought to be done?'

In this respect, for Kant, states' practical rejection of what is correct for an idea of right should not pave the way to *Realpolitik*. In rejecting the idea of a (private) reason for the states, Kant grounds the pragmatic-critical attitude of political reasoning in the interplay between the pure principles of right and the circumstances of reality. This view emerges clearly from Kant's conditional proposition "if all is not to be lost",[37] when he introduces the suboptimal alternative between the "the *negative* surrogate of a *league*"[38] and "the positive idea *of a world republic* [*Weltrepublik*]".[39] Note here that the opposition is not simply one between two possible institutional configurations; it is rather between *a positive,*

33 Kant, "Toward Perpetual Peace (1795)", 8:380, p.347. Here the expression refers to the right in general that belongs to human beings with no substantively specific reference to a contemporary notion of human rights.

34 Kant, "Toward Perpetual Peace (1795)", 8:373, p.341.

35 Ibid.

36 On this distinction see Kant, "On the Common Saying", 8:276, p. 280: "what sounds good in theory has no validity for practice. (This is often expressed as, this or that proposition does indeed hold *in thesi*, but not *in hypothesi*)".

37 Kant, "Toward Perpetual Peace (1795)", 8:357, p.328.

38 Ibid.

39 Ibid.

law-giving and law-enforcing world republic, on the one hand, and a *negative*, war-confining entity lacking statehood qualities as the league of states. Kant had already traced such distinctions when explaining that only if it were possible to establish a perfect analogy between the domestic and the international realm by introduction of public coercive laws within the international sphere, would it then also become possible for states to enter a civil condition. However, since from the subjective perspective of states, this move amounts to a contradiction of the same idea of international law as a domain characterized by autonomous states as its subjects, then a dichotomy would arise between an ideal and a non-ideal juridical order whose incongruence remains a task for the political to solve.

Following such distinctions, Kant justifies what later Rawls refers to as the difference between ideal and non-ideal theory in political justice.[40] In an ideal scenario, agents are cooperative, whereas in non-ideal contexts they are mostly not, even if not completely so. Yet for Kant – and this is a crucial difference from Rawls – *republican states* are also under a not-fully cooperative scheme regarding their mutual relations under an international state of nature. It is only once a cosmopolitan constitution is instantiated through the regulative presumption of a world (state) republic – as a *lingua franca* among foreign nationals and nations – that it becomes possible to establish also an overall scheme based on terms of fair cooperation.

The cosmopolitan constitution is the ultimate level of instantiation of the global civil condition. Certainly, for Kant, this is a condition valid *a priori*, but its realization not only has to surrender to the fractioning of temporal stages, but it also has to take into consideration the free will of sovereign states, which can never be coerced externally. Accordingly, the attempt to realize immediately and positively the *a priori* ideal of a world (state) republic is doomed to fail. "*Nature wills* [. . .] otherwise"[41] and it will keep nations separate because of "*language* and of *religion*".[42]

The conditions Kant poses for the political realization of the world (state) republic as something right *in thesi* are important for understanding the type of normativity that he conceives as binding for the international law community. First, the community of peoples coexists within a "*status iuridicus*" which in turn "must proceed from some kind of [regulative] pact [*aus irgend einem Vertrage*]",[43] as according to the already discussed transformation of Wolff's global covenant.

40 On this distinction see J. Rawls, "Non-Ideal Theory", *The Law of Peoples*, Harvard University Press, Cambridge, Mass., 2000, p.89 ff. As C. Horn acutely points out, justice under non ideal conditions is equal to "Gerechtigkeit unter (stark) suboptimalen Bedingungen festhalten lässt". In Horn, *Nicht Ideale Normativität*, p.321. Yet, following my previous remarks, I would extend Horn's observation to conceiving international justice as a whole under non-ideal conditions and not only to the relation between liberal and decent states on the one hand and all other states, on the other.

41 Kant, "Toward Perpetual Peace (1795)", 8:367, p.336. On this point cf. also Geismann, *World Peace*, p.21 (accessed on 27.2.2018).

42 Kant, "Toward Perpetual Peace (1795)", 8:367, p.336.

43 Kant, "Toward Perpetual Peace (1795)", 8:383, p. 349. Translation modified.

Being 'a sort of' compact is all important. It establishes a difference of coercion between the domestic and international orders whereby the latter "need not (like that from which a state arises) be based on coercive laws but may, if necessary, be a condition of *continuing free* association".[44] The starting point for realizing such endless effort of continual improvement is that of the league of states. Now, however, its significance is no longer one opposing a supposedly correct practice vs. the utopianism of idealizations of politics. Instead, the league of states is too, like the world (state) republic, an entity which upholds itself appropriately because it realizes "the harmony of politics with morals".[45] Thus, one must still see such a 'surrogate' solution as one characterized by necessity, springing from a transitional concept of right and based on the presupposition of an accord between law and politics.

§8.1 Kant's legacy and the idea of a transitional *ius cosmopoliticum*

At the end of the eighteenth century, when Kant elaborated his major political writings, not many would have thought of history as a cosmopolitan project (see the initial sections of the book). Kant, however, dedicated nine propositions to elucidate his views in the *Idea for a Universal History with a Cosmopolitan Aim*.[46] Scepticism in this respect is referred to by Kant with the Abbé de St. Pierre's and Rousseau's "ridiculed"[47] cosmopolitanism because they believed its realization was imminent. For Kant, instead, "universal world history"[48] should be rather understood in terms of "a regular course of improvement of state constitutions".[49]

44 Ibid.

45 "Thus the harmony of politics with morals is possible only within a federative union (*which is therefore given a priori and is necessary by principles of right*) [emphasis added]". In Kant, "Toward Perpetual Peace (1795)", 8:385, p. 351.

46 Kant, "Universal History", 8:15–8:31, pp.107–120.

47 Kant, "On the Common Saying", 8:313, p.309.

48 Kant, "Universal History", 8:29, p.118.

49 Kant, "Universal History", 8:29, p.119. On the relation between Kant's "theoretical" and the "practical" thesis of philosophy of history that is reflected also in the role of the progression towards perpetual peace, Wood notices: "It is important to distinguish between two quite different (and largely independent) theses that Kant maintains here. The first thesis [. . .] is a wholly theoretical one: Under the guidance of heuristic or regulative principles of reason, we should attempt to make sense of human history as a process involving an unconscious and unintended teleology of nature [. . .] whose ultimate end [. . .] also includes the creation of a perfectly just civil constitution and a peaceful international order among states. [. . .] A second thesis [. . .] is a practical or moral one: As human beings, we have a duty to work together toward devising and realizing the end of a perfect civil constitution administering justice among human beings, and to this end we are also required to seek an order guaranteeing peace among states [. . .] The first (theoretical) thesis is in no way dependent on the second (practical or moral) thesis. [. . .] Yet there is one connection between Kant's theoretical theses about history and his practical ones. [. . .] The fact that, according to a teleologically conceived theoretical philosophy of history, a natural purposiveness leads toward an ideal civil constitution and toward perpetual peace between nations – and even

The cosmopolitan ideal represents indeed a long-term project. As discussed in earlier sections, this is due to the fact that Kant not only thinks that it is contradictory to "*justify* an offensive war"[50] by recourse to principles of law, but also that "what holds in accordance with natural right for human beings in a lawless condition [. . .] cannot hold for states in accordance with the right of nations (since, as states, they already have a rightful constitution internally and hence have outgrown the constraint of others [. . .])".[51] I have already claimed that it is by attempting to solve such conundrum that the hypothesis of a 'transitional' interpretation of Kant's cosmopolitanism gains legitimacy. Yet, even though there are already some transitional interpretations of Kant, a question remains in regard to what might have been the most legitimate transnational arena compatible with Kant's notion of state sovereignty.[52]

In the following sections, I will defend the idea that Kant's argument relies on a distinct view of the 'transitional' character of cosmopolitan law which defines a normative space that avoids the danger of a world state. According to this suggested interpretation, the relation between cosmopolitan law and its institutional instantiations is explained by the function that the former plays as a 'freedom generating' advancement. Among those which are most relevant to the argument I offer here, both Kleingeld and Brown are worth mentioning.[53] However, my interpretation differs from these in important ways. Whereas Kleingeld attributes to Kant's change of mind the institutional shift from a weak non-coercive league to a coercive state of states and Brown emphasizes the practical implementation of cosmopolitan law as a form of legal transition, I will rather attempt to reconstruct and explain how the multiple institutional entities Kant refers to are to be considered as part of a single global constitution. This hypothesis justifies the idea of an inherent form of pluralism as embedded in the transitional character brought about by cosmopolitan right.

---

more, the factual reasons why it does so – constitutes part of the reason why we have a moral duty to place an ideal civil constitution and perpetual peace among the ends of our action. [...]", in A. Wood, "Kant's Philosophy of History", P. Kleingeld (ed.), *Immanuel Kant. Toward Perpetual Peace and Other Writings on Politics, Peace, and History*, Yale University Press, New Haven, Conn., 2006 [1795], p.254 ff.

50 Kant, "Toward Perpetual Peace (1795)", 8:355, p.326. Kant defines in the same paragraph Grotius, Pufendorf and Vattel as "sorry comforters". On the role that morality plays in Kant for maintaining "the possibility of peace" see P. Capps, "Natural Law and the Law of Nations", A. Orakhelashvili (ed.), *Research Handbook on the Theory and History of International Law*, Edward Elgar, Cheltenham, UK, 2011, pp.88 ff.

51 Kant, "Toward Perpetual Peace (1795)", 8:355, p.327.

52 Certainly, Fichte could be mentioned as the first to suggest a 'transitional' interpretation of Kant. Fichte, "Review of Immanuel Kant", p.319. For contemporary approaches to Kant's cosmopolitanism see also P. Kleingeld, *Kant and Cosmopolitanism. The Philosophical Ideal of World Citizenship*, Cambridge University Press, Cambridge, 2012, p.7 ff. and Brown, "Cosmopolitan Legal Theory", p.430.

53 See, in particular P. Kleingeld (ed.), *Immanuel Kant. Toward Perpetual Peace and Other Writings on Politics, Peace, and History*, Yale University Press, New Haven, Conn., 2006 [1795], p.7 and Brown, "Cosmopolitan Legal Theory", p.430 ff. For the notion of the *Verkehr* see Kant, "Metaphysics of Morals (1797)", 6:352, p.489 ff.

This is also the pattern towards the achievement of international peace as a solution of the potential conflict among states through legal means. The most important point, here, is that such a condition not only embeds a trajectory of progressively legally binding configurations beyond the state, but also a form of synchronic transitionality whereby functional differentiation does not raise uncontestable and conclusive claims of authority. Given this scenario, the regulative interpretation of the *Völkerstaat* (multistate confederation) is what I will consider Kant's most intriguing element of originality for our contemporary time.

Cosmopolitan right, as a component of public right, follows from Kant's *Universal Principle of Right* according to which "Any action is *right* if it can coexist with everyone's freedom in accordance with a universal law, or if on its maxim the freedom of choice of each can coexist with everyone's freedom in accordance with a universal law."[54] On the basis of this assumption the resulting political duty combines moral constraints with prudential reasons: "I can indeed think of a *moral politician*, that is, one who takes the principles of political prudence in such a way that they can coexist with morals, but not of a *political moralist*, who frames a morals to suit the statesman's advantage".[55] It follows also that the institutional realization of perpetual peace, even if subjected to a moral standard, is sensitive to political considerations and therefore cannot occur all at once. In the *Doctrine of Right* of the *Metaphysics of Morals*, Kant says that a full legality for the international level cannot be brought about through revolution since this would contradict – by entirely nullifying – the previous juridical status. Instead, he refers to a progression: "by gradual reform in accordance with firm principles".[56] It is to such a gradual process of political, legal, and ultimately institutional reform that I refer with the use of the term 'transitional'.

Indeed, there are at least two different senses in which it is possible to speak of transitional law and of its impact on institutions. A first contemporary sense is related to the transformative role of law concerning regime transitions as, for instance, in the highly debated cases of authoritarian regimes turning into democracies.[57] A second sense concerns democratic transitions towards transnational integration. This latter is the transitionality aspect in Kant I analyse here, one, where the multistate confederation (*Völkerstaat*) represents a normative 'reference point' – as a regulative idea of reason – for assessing the institutional progression towards a cosmopolitan condition. I suggest, therefore, that Kant's view of transitionality is particularly interesting in virtue of the non-ideal character of cosmopolitan law that it defines. As I will argue, this is the condition where the enforcement of cosmopolitan law occurs in the absence of a world government.[58]

54 Kant, "Metaphysics of Morals (1797)", 6:230, p.387.

55 Kant, "Toward Perpetual Peace (1795)", 8:372, p.340.

56 Kant, "Metaphysics of Morals (1797)", 6:355, p.492.

57 A seminal work on this notion of law transitionality has been the work of R. Teitel, *Transitional Justice*, Oxford University Press, Oxford, 2000.

58 The debate on ideal vs. non-ideal theory has been quite extensive. Rawls himself considers that "non-ideal theory presupposes that ideal theory is already on hand", Rawls, *Law of*

This leads to a further point: the problem of feasibility. The suggestion is that it is possible in Kant to trace a distinction between a long-term feasibility standard, according to an overall view based on an orienting ideal principle, and a short-term feasibility standard for foreseen advancements. The first are considerations of feasibility for a political theory, whereas the second are feasibility issues connected to political decisions.[59] Indeed, the idea according to which a scenario should be considered where all principles can be maximally realized confuses the question of justification of principles or simply as it is here argued – of regulative and counterfactual orientation – with the question of the comparative adjudication of principles along given circumstances.

The purported distinction between ideal and non-ideal principles finds its equivalents in the distinction between ideal and non-ideal institutional configurations. It seems that also in this case a clear-cut separation of non-ideal institutions – as means to an end – and global ideal institutions for full compliance is untenable since the proposed ideal end, as it appears from Kant's rejection of a world state republic, is not a desirable empirical result to realize. Again, it is rather the case that comparing alternative normative and institutional configurations according to an orienting standard is what cosmopolitan law should aim to do. From a more normative perspective, the unsettled condition of transnational constitutionalism is the result of the competition of different constitutional meta-agreements of the kind of the 'more-or-less' vs. a Westphalian 'all-or-nothing' constitutionalism.[60] Kant suggests a multiplicity of options that represent stages of progression of cosmopolitan law. Indeed, he had in mind a plurality of transnational arrangements that have been often overlooked. For example, what he calls *Völkerstaat*, which I have translated as 'the multistate confederation', presents features that make it differ from both the league of states or federation, for which he uses the words *Völkerbund or Föderation*, as well as from the "*permanent congress of states*" (*Kongreß*).[61] That this is for Kant a particular type of institutional configuration is also clear from its definition of the Congress as "an *association* of several *states* to preserve peace"[62] and which only can grant a true and long-lasting condition of peace as "the assembly of the States General at the Hague".[63] This seems a weaker form of organization than the league of states, one characterized by a voluntary congress (*Kongreß*) built with the purpose of maintaining peace and with the possibility for each state to leave the union at any time.

Peoples, pp.89–90. My point is, instead, that in the transnational sphere there is not an (ideal) end-result to be reached so that legitimate claims of authority are not defined on a legal and institutional hierarchy.

59 Cf. J. Culp, *The complementary understanding of the relation between ideal and nonideal theory*, Ma Thesis, Bern, 2008.

60 Consider also the contemporary idea of post national constitutionalism as a "form of practical reasoning". For a contemporary parallel with Kant's views, see N. Walker, "Taking Constitutionalism Beyond the State", *Political Studies*, 56(10), 2008, p.525.

61 Kant, "The Metaphysics of Morals (1797)", 6:350, p.487.

62 Ibid.

63 Kant, "Metaphysics of Morals (1797)", 6:350, p.488

Yet, the normatively loaded institutional typology that Kant considers as the most important is the *Völkerstaat*. My proposal to translate the term *Völkerstaat* as 'multistate confederation' is grounded on the conviction that this captures more accurately the 'state' element and the 'plurality' component of the confederal setting. Also it coheres with the remark by Höffe for whom, when Kant speaks of the right of nations (*Völkerrecht*, *ius gentium*), he is not interested in the rights of peoples as *gentes*, that is, as homogenous and blood-related ethnic groups but rather as "civitates".[64]

As widely discussed already, the *Völkerstaat* represents the only regulative standard available in the non-ideal sphere, which analogously to the world republic (*Weltrepublik*), its counterpart in the classification of the forms of government, cannot be empirically realizable. With this move, Kant abandons the hypothesis of a domestic analogy.[65] The world republic differs from the "universal monarchy"[66] and this latter is categorically excluded by Kant even as an ideal option. These terminological distinctions are clear in the famous passage of *Toward Perpetual Peace* where Kant draws a distinction between the ideal and the non-ideal (what is right in *hypothesi* – in practice – and what is right *in thesi* – in theory),[67] and rejects what is ideally desirable – the *Weltrepublik* – in favour of what is practically feasible – the *Völkerbund*.

Yet, even once the league of states is established, it remains the requirement for states to exit a lawless condition. It is this burden that compels states to regulate their relations in accordance with *a regulative ideal of coerciveness*, that is, *as if members of a Völkerstaat*.

Accordingly, when referring to the multiple institutional instantiations of international law, the word *Völker* indicates a state component. Other translations obscure this aspect, as for instance Kleingeld's "state of peoples",[68] even if several textual evidences are provided.[69] For different but equally relevant reasons, Reiss' translation with "international state"[70] does not capture an essential feature of the *Völkerstaat*, namely, the already mentioned plurality of the states included in the confederation. The pluralistic aspect of states/peoples involved in the multistate confederation would be lost in this latter case, whereas it remains crucial in the terminological distinction between *Völkerstaat* vs. *Weltrepublik*. Also the notion of the *Völkerstaat* relies on three different conceptual components grounded in the history of ideas as, respectively, Rousseau's republicanism,

64 O. Höffe, *Kant's Cosmopolitan Theory of Law and Peace*, Cambridge University Press, Cambridge, 2006, p.190.

65 Kant, "Toward Perpetual Peace (1795)", 8:357, p.328.

66 Kant, "Toward Perpetual Peace (1795)", [8:367], p.336.

67 On the interpretation of the theory/practice distinction, see note 7, Kleingeld (ed.), *Immanuel Kant*, p.81.

68 Kant, "Toward Perpetual Peace (1795)", [8:354], p.78.

69 P. Kleingeld, "Approaching Perpetual Peace: Kant's Defense of a League of States and his Ideal of a World Federation", *European Journal of Philosophy*, 12(3), 2004, p.305.

70 I. Kant, "Perpetual Peace: a Philosophical Sketch", in H.S. Reiss (ed.), *Kant Political Writings*, 2012, Cambridge University Press, Cambridge, 2012 [1795], [8:354], p.102.

Hobbes' idea of a unity of the state and, finally, Wolff's normative hypothesis of a pact among nations.[71]

In the following paragraphs I present an interpretive thesis of Kant's cosmopolitanism as divided into two sections. In the first section I reconstruct and defend Kant's idea of a multiplicity of transnational configurations, that is, constitutional stages disclosing a wider variety of institutional options than scholarship has traditionally considered.

In the second section, I argue in favour of a transitional reading of cosmopolitan law both as a way to further institutional transformation and as an expanding notion of rights in itself. It follows that the ultimate aim of the paper is to reconstruct the hypothetical contours of how legal reasoning should be conducted at the transnational level. This does not require specifying also which cosmopolitan categories of rights should be derived from what I consider, at the end of the essay, as the quintessential notion of Kant's cosmopolitanism: the *Verkehr* (interrelation).[72]

§8.1.1 Institutional progressions: the regulative role of the multistate confederation

One preliminary element favouring a transitional reading is provided by the use of the preposition '*zu*' (toward) in what is Kant's most important writing on cosmopolitanism: *Toward Perpetual Peace.* If interpreted as indicating 'movement' and not as 'to the advantage of' or as a 'dedication to' peace, then, the '*zu*' refers to a condition of approximation of peace.[73] Starting from the title, then, Kant puts the emphasis on the transitionality aspect of achieving peace as well as on the ever fulfilled duty for its achievement. The emphasis on the transformation over the end-result of the process indicates that he considered the transnational as subjected to institutional legal pluralism not resorting to one single institutional fixation. As I argue, the reason for such unsettlement relies on the parasitical role that transnational institutions assume for the cosmopolitan transformation of the state. To illustrate this point, confront the following two models:

A. End-result interpretations

Kant presents the alternative of *either* the league of states (*Völkerbund* or *Foedus Pacificum*) *or* the world republic (*Weltrepublik*).[74]

71 See J. Ritter, K. Gründer, G. Gottfried (eds.), *Historisches Wörterbuch der Philosophie*, Band 11, Schwabe Verlag, Basel, 2011, p.1091.

72 See Brown, *Grounding Cosmopolitanism*, 2013.

73 On the linguistic distinction of these two meanings, see Kleingeld's note in the translation of Kant's *Perpetual Peace*, in Kleingeld (ed.), *Immanuel Kant,* note 1, p. 67.

74 Kant, "Toward Perpetual Peace (1795)", 8:357, p.328. On the (implicit) reliance of cosmopolitan theories on assumptions of "stateness" see W. Scheuerman, "Cosmopolitanism and the World State", *Review of International Studies*, 40(3), 2013, p.440.

B. Transitional interpretation

Kant defends a progressive advancement of cosmopolitan transitionality starting from the congress of states (*Kongreß*),[75] moving to the league of states (*Völkerbund*)[76] or the federation (*Föderation*).[77] The further advancement from this condition is regulated by the regulative role played by the multistate confederation within the non-ideal sphere (once the positive instantiation of a world republic is excluded as unfeasible option). As noticed, the multistate confederation/world (state) republic (*Weltrepublik*) performs instead a regulative role, that is, as a regulative idea of reason.

The difference between end-result *vis-à-vis* transitional interpretations is that in the first case it is assumed that there is only one optimal institutional outcome, whereas in the second case there are a number of constitutional stages which lead to a plurality of coexisting transnational configurations regulated 'as if' part of a multistate confederation. All in all, what I attempt to prove is that it seems possible to trace in Kant a hypothetical progression of institutional configurations at the transnational level. This starts from the least advanced configuration of the congress of states (*Kongreß*), characterized by the lack of a common constitution and by states' voluntary-only inclusion and opt-out. It then moves towards a more advanced form of interconnection as with the *Völkerbund*, characterized by the presence of a common republican constitution with voluntary membership but with no real possibility to opt-out. The league of states is defined by some legal enforcement but with no allowed interference into the internal affairs of the states.

According to the interpretation suggested here, stricter constitutional enforcement is to be understood as a regulative model based on the ideal of a *Völkerstaat* and combining a harmonization between a common constitution and a legal-constitutional autonomy of states. One difficulty in what might initially appear

75 "By a *congress* is here understood only a voluntary coalition of different states which can be *dissolved* at any time, not a federation (like that of the American states) which is based on a constitution and can therefore not be dissolved", Kant, "The Metaphysics of Morals (1797)", 6:351, p.488. On the historical reconstruction of what Kant had in mind with the congress of states see Byrd and Hruschka, *Kant's Doctrine of Right*, p.204 ff.

76 "A league of nations in accordance with the idea of an original social contract. is necessary, not in order to meddle in one another's internal dissensions but to protect against attacks from without. 4) This alliance must, however, involve no sovereign authority (as in a civil constitution), but only an *association* (federation); it must be an alliance that can be renounced at any time and so must be renewed from time to time". Kant, "Metaphysics of Morals (1797)", 6:344, pp.482–483.

77 When Kant describes the characteristics of the Federation he seems to refer to be puzzled between a weaker and a more advanced legal condition: "Nations, as states, can be appraised as individuals, who in their natural condition (that is, in their independence from external laws) already wrong one another by being near one another; and each of them, for the sake of its security, can and ought to require the others to enter with it into a constitution similar to a civil constitution, in which each can be assured of its right." In Kant, "Toward Perpetual Peace (1795)", 8:354, pp.325–326.

as a coherent progression of constitutional phases is that no specific example is provided on what comes after the league of states.[78] Kant seems rather interested in defining the normative space wherein this occurs, as with: (a) the realization of a lawful condition among states and (b) the coordination of states' wills within a lawful constitutional condition (*constitutio*). Both features are subjected to 'degrees of constitutionalization' since, as he says in *Toward Perpetual Peace*: "for some *rightful* constitution or other, even if it is only to a small degree in conformity with right, is better than none at all".[79] Particularly in the first case, Kant faces the problem of reconciling the loss of an internal legal condition which is regained at the transnational level. Since the notion of constitution as a rightful condition cannot be disjoined from the law and from its enforcement, the constitutional advancement requires institutional enforcement. Yet in the process of explaining the institutional progression towards the multistate confederation there is no explanation of why states should move from an interstate dispute resolution (as in the congress of states Kant mentions with reference to the assembly of states-general in The Hague) to an initial form of constitutionalization of international law as in the case of the league of states. What can be inferred is that the voluntary union of the Congress which "can be *dissolved* at any time"[80] is a weak even if an essential step to "deciding their disputes in a civil way, as if by a lawsuit, rather than in a barbaric way (the way of savages), namely by war".[81]

For the present purposes, I restrict myself to the assessment of the transformative function of cosmopolitan law and to its enhancement of stability at the global level. The dynamic aspect of Kantian cosmopolitanism not only indicates the desirability of a linear progression towards peace as a way to regulate state-relations lawfully but, more importantly, it defines a permanent tension among the institutional elements of global constitutionalism. Even if often implicitly, it is also the case that some of the most recent scholarship adopts a transitional reading of Kant at the domestic level, as in the case of Benhabib's idea of "democratic iterations"[82] and "jurisgenerative politics".[83] Yet, Benhabib's analyses focus on the ways to reconcile the democratic will of the majority (Kant's *First Definitive Article* of *Toward Perpetual Peace* concerning the republican nature of state legitimacy) with standards of cosmopolitan justice (*Third Definitive Article*), but

78 As Klabbers claims: "Fragmentation, verticalization and constitutionalization form the holy trinity of international legal debate in the 21st century, and made a sustained appearance in the well-known Yusuf and Kadi cases". In J.P. Klabbers and G. Ulfstein, *The Constitutionalization of International Law*, Oxford University Press, Oxford, 2009, p.1. For the philosophical debate consider J. Habermas, "The Constitutionalization of International Law and the Legitimation Problems of a Constitution for World Society", C. Cronin (ed.), *Europe: The Faltering Project*, Polity Press, Cambridge, 2009, pp.109–130.

79 Kant, "Toward Perpetual Peace (1795)", 8:374, Note*, p.341.

80 Kant, "Metaphysics of Morals (1797)", 6:351, p.488

81 Ibid.

82 S. Benhabib, *Another Cosmopolitanism*, R. Post (ed.), Oxford University Press, Oxford, 2005, p.49ff.

83 Ibid.

not with cosmopolitan progressions at the international level.[84] While Benhabib's account provides an insightful explanation of the mediating role of cosmopolitan right into the domestic democratic sphere, she leaves out the role that cosmopolitan right plays in the transition from free states towards both a federal arrangement (*Second Definitive Article*) and, as I suggest, the regulative ideal of a multistate confederation. Accordingly, my interpretive thesis aims at extending Benhabib's jurisgenerative thesis.

§8.1.2 Kant's ius publicum *and the idea of a transitional* ius cosmopoliticum

For Kant, public right – *ius publicum* – represents a bulk of interconnecting spheres of laws articulated internally into domestic right (civil constitutional law) and externally into international right – *ius gentium* – and cosmopolitan right – *ius cosmopoliticum*. Respectively, they all regulate the relations: (1) between states and individuals (domestic right) (2) between states themselves (international right), as well as (3) between states and non-citizens (cosmopolitan right). Public right as a whole is for Kant grounded on *a priori* reason and not on an empirical, positivist view of rights; *a priori* reason represents "the sum of conditions under which the choice of one can be united with the choice of another in accordance with a universal law of freedom."[85]

Accordingly, the notion of public right is constructed on the model of the categorical imperative and particularly on the idea of a submission of one's maxims as if one were "a law-making member in the universal kingdom of ends".[86] For Kant, public right is also what generates a constitution (*constitutio*) as a 'rightful condition' of a unifying will within the three areas of public rights already mentioned: the domestic, the international, and the cosmopolitan. In the case of the Kantian cosmopolitan right to freedom of movement, public use of reason, free trade etc., legal progression is provided by the realization of an idea of human beings as moral agents and, thus, from the perspective of the protection of the human innate right to freedom. Particularly, in the case of cosmopolitan right, freedom is linked to the idea of an original condition of a right to receive a location on earth.[87]

84 As Benhabib claims: "The distinguishing feature of the period we are in cannot be captured through the *bons mots* of 'globalization' and 'empire'; rather, we are also facing the rise of an international human rights regime and the spread of cosmopolitan norms, while the relationship between state sovereignty and such norms is becoming more contentious and conflictual (IV). Such conflicts render starkly visible the 'paradox of democratic legitimacy', namely, the necessary and inevitable limitation of democratic forms of representation and accountability in terms of the formal distinction between members and nonmembers (V). This is the core tension, even if not contradiction, between democratic self-determination and the norms of cosmopolitan justice." In Benhabib, *Another Cosmopolitanism*, p.17.

85 Kant, "Metaphysics of Morals (1797)", 6:230, p.24.

86 I. Kant, "Groundwork of the Metaphysics of Morals (1785)", 4:438, p.87.

87 As Brown notices: "These principles [of freedom and of original common possession] are synthetic a priori truths related to a condition of right and do not exist as facts, but as a

In §62 of the *Metaphysics of Morals*, Kant discusses the third section of public right, namely, cosmopolitan right.[88] The argument presented proceeds quite distinctly and it is therefore worth reconstructing its main steps. First of all, Kant reminds us that cosmopolitan right is not philanthropy, but a proper public right. As for its content, it consists of "the possible union of all nations with a view to certain universal laws for their possible commerce".[89] The word 'commerce' corresponds to the semantically wider notion of *Verkehr*, better translated as 'interrelation'. Since the term is used to explain the more inclusive content and scope of cosmopolitan right, its interpretation cannot be limited only to commercial activities. Kant's argument proceeds to the deduction of cosmopolitan right on the bases of a geographical consideration. The argument is the following: from the general premise of an original right to freedom and in order to make sense of the lawfulness or unlawfulness of our actions, the notion of an *original* community (of *commercium*, but not of common ownership) of universal relations for possible physical interaction and consequently for potential right-acquisitions should be postulated. This community embeds the notion of an originally united will which is also an *a priori* notion for the deduction of rights. It is from the unity of the general will that the *a priori* deduction of cosmopolitan right as a right to enter a potentially universal set of relations can also be inferred. Indeed, from this *a priori* perspective Kant measures the extent to which the peoples of the earth have already entered into a universal community, so that the "a violation of right on *one* place of the earth is felt in *all*".[90]

Difficulties arise, however, when trying to define what counts as the best institutional order for a rightful condition and it is here that the idea of an inherently transitional notion of cosmopolitan law, not resorting to a final end-state configuration, finds its explanatory plausibility. Within the context of transnational actors, Kant's cosmopolitan law realizes two interconnected goals: (1) it favours the institutional advancement of a legitimate cosmopolitan condition as with a multistate confederation; and (2) it provides the transnational legal standards for the legitimate exercise of power. These two aspects are inherently related in so far as the redefinition of the institutional constellation is the result of transformation brought about by cosmopolitan law. In the *Metaphysics of Morals*, Kant says that while "*perpetual peace*, the ultimate goal of the whole right of nations, is indeed an unachievable idea",[91] there is, nevertheless, a duty to favour "continual *approximation* to it".[92] It seems that Kant foresaw a particular role for specific transitional legal advancements towards peace as grounded primarily on

concept of reason which alone yields a principle making it possible for individuals, families, nations or states to use land compatibly with principles of right." In Brown, *Grounding Cosmopolitanism*, p.58. See also Brown, "Moving from Theory to Practice", pp.430–451.

88 Kant, "Metaphysics of Morals (1797)", 6:352, p.489 ff.

89 Ibid.

90 Kant, "Toward Perpetual Peace (1795)", 8:360, p.330.

91 Kant, "Metaphysics of Morals (1797)", 6:350, p.487.

92 Ibid.

the political duty to realize each individual's original right to have a share on earth "in a thoroughgoing relation of each to all the others *of offering to engage in commerce* with any other".[93]

As already introduced, Kant presents different institutional options. In *On the Common Saying*, he observes that as it has been the case historically with large states, the "condition of universal peace is still more dangerous to freedom".[94] Accordingly, this should prompt states not "to enter a condition that is not a cosmopolitan commonwealth under a single head but [that] is still a rightful condition *of federation* in accordance with a commonly agreed upon *right of nations*".[95] Only a federation (*Föderation*) is suggested as a legitimate institutional arrangement worthy of pursuing; similarly, in *Toward Perpetual Peace*, Kant refers to "a universal monarchy"[96] as "a soulless despotism [. . . which] finally deteriorates into anarchy"[97] and rules out the "positive idea *of a world republic*"[98] suggesting, instead, the "*negative surrogate* of a *league*"[99] (a *Völkerbund* or a *Foedus Pacificum*), as a starting option.[100] In this respect, the dilemma that Kant faces consists in reconciling his idea of a universal legislation with the independence of states' sovereignty. Since states cannot be coerced, due to the fact that this would endanger their autonomy and the indivisibility of their powers, only the uncoercive constraint of a league of (republican) states granting a cosmopolitan right to visit could be legitimately admitted. But as Kleingeld observes: "Kant does not actually write that the concept of a state of states [*Völkerstaat*, my addition] is contradictory. Rather, he claims that there is a contradiction between the concept of a state of states, on the one hand, and a fundamental 'presupposition' of international right, on the other."[101] According to this reading, Kant wants apparently to formulate a normative standard for the unity of international order as something that goes beyond bilateral or multilateral separatenedess of the states, as with the case of international law. Yet, this does not commit, necessarily, to an interpretation for a transition towards the realization of 'a state of states' or, as I prefer to call it, 'a multistate confederation'.[102]

93 Kant, "Metaphysics of Morals (1797)", 6:352, p.489.
94 Kant, "On the Common Saying", 8:311, p.307.
95 Ibid., p.308.
96 Kant, "Toward Perpetual Peace (1795)", 8:367, p.336.
97 Ibid.
98 Kant, "Toward Perpetual Peace (1795)", 8:357, p.328.
99 Ibid.
100 Wood has drawn attention to the distinction in Kant of three institutional models, see Wood, *Kant's Philosophy of History*, P. Kleingeld (ed.), *Immanuel Kant. Toward Perpetual Peace and Other Writings on Politics, Peace, and History*, Yale University Press, New Haven, Conn., 2006 [1795], p.251.
101 Kleingeld, "Approaching Perpetual Peace", p.312.
102 Contrast this perspective with that of Kleingeld (ed.), *Immanuel Kant*, p.7. Here the author defends a coercive state made of a plurality of federated states. On the idea of a "state of states" as a factual hypothesis see also Kleingeld, "Approaching Perpetual Peace", p.305 ff.

For the sake of the argument let's recall again Kant's famous paragraph of *Toward Perpetual Peace.*[103] Here he says: (1) states, in analogy to individuals, have to exit a lawless condition of the state of nature and establish a regime of legal enforcement through a *Völkerstaat* (2) yet, since the *Völkerstaat* leads to an ever expanding state ultimately including all peoples of the world, and since this contradicts states' view of international law (3) what is ideally desirable is not empirically so, and therefore (4) only the realization of the negative surrogate of a league of states remains a viable option.

The formulation of a *regulative* function played by the *Völkerstaat* arises *vis-à-vis* the *negative*, that is, non-enforceable law as with the league of states and the *positive*, legally enforceable – and yet unfeasible – world republic.

This reading finds some confirmation in the optimism Kant had shown two years before the publication of *Toward Perpetual Peace* with the writing titled *On the Common Saying*. Here, he defined the *Völkerstaat* as "it is possible *(in praxi)* and that it *can be*",[104] but this possibility should be interpreted only as something *in thought* and thus in coherence with the regulative function it has been identified to the *Völkerstaat.*

This view is in line also with what Kant affirms with regard to the general aim of perpetual peace in the *Rechtslehre* for which: "we must act as if it is something real, though perhaps it is not; we must work toward establishing perpetual peace and the kind of constitution that seems to us most conducive to it (say, a republicanism of all states, together and separately)".[105] The way in which the regulative idea translates into a political duty is in accordance with limited but progressive institutional reforms which maintain an unresolved asymmetry between the universal scope of cosmopolitan law and its contingent transnational institutionalization. It is the mismatch between the universal validity of

103 "[States] accommodate themselves to public coercive laws, and so form an (always growing) *state of nations (civitas gentium)* that would finally encompass all the nations of the earth. But, in accordance with their idea of the right of nations, they do not at all want this, thus rejecting *in hypothesi* what is correct *in thesi*; so (if all is not to be lost) in place of the positive idea *of a world republic* only the *negative* surrogate of a *league* that averts war, endures, and always expands can hold back the stream of hostile inclination that shies away from right, though with constant danger of its breaking out.* (*Furor impius intus – fremit horridus ore cruento.* Virgil)`", Kant, "Toward Perpetual Peace (1795)", 8:357, p.328. While often overlooked by scholars, in the German text the terminological distinctions are clear: "[States]sich zu öffentlichen Zwangsgesetzen bequemen, und so einen (freylich immer wachsenden) *Völkerstaat* (*civitas gentium*), der zuletzt alle Völker der Erde befassen würde, bilden. Da sie dieses aber nach ihrer Idee vom Völkerrecht durchaus nicht wollen, mithin, was in thesi richtig ist, in hypothesi verwerfen, so kann an die Stelle der positiven Idee einer *Weltrepublik* (wenn nicht alles verlohren werden soll) nur das n e g a t i v e Surrogat eines den Krieg abwehrenden, bestehenden, und sich immer ausbreitenden *Bundes*, den Strom der rechtscheuenden feindseligen Neigung aufhalten, doch mit beständiger Gefahr ihres Ausbruchs [. . .][emphasis added]", I. Kant, *Zum ewigen Frieden* [1795] Königsberg, http://philosophiebuch.de/ewfried.htm (accessed on 3.6.2014),

104 Kant, "On the Common Saying", 8:313, p.309.

105 Kant, "Metaphysics of Morals (1797)", 6:354, p.491.

cosmopolitan law and its non-ideal institutional implementation that is relevant for understanding Kant's idea of the normativity of law at the transnational level.

Why does such asymmetry remain unresolved? According to the textual interpretation here advanced, this is because Kant changed his mind on the extent to which he could pursue the analogy between individuals and states, on the one hand, and states and the multination state confederation, on the other. Indeed, the departure from a lawless condition by individuals entering into state-relations and the overcoming of an international state of nature by these states through the formation of a transnational arrangement does not reflect Kant's definition of analogy "which surely does not signify, as the word is usually taken, an imperfect similarity between two things, but rather a perfect similarity between two relations in wholly dissimilar things".[106] The counterfactual relation, and not the analogy between the two spheres in the real vs. ideal opposition, frees space to a transitional advancement beyond the *Völkerbund.* In the case of the transnational sphere, states in fact possess already a constitution and meet a minimum standard of a rule of law. It follows that there is no duty to abandon completely the domestic condition but only to *supplement* this with cosmopolitan obligations. Since the multination state-like confederation cannot be imposed on already legitimate sovereign states, this remains a regulative tool for advancing the league model.

Thus, also according to a transitional reading of cosmopolitan law, the inclusion of the *Völkerstaat* under *ideal* circumstances means that Kant admits a legitimate institutional progression of the *Völkerbund.* Since the *Völkerstaat* remains entrapped within the two extremes of the institutional negative surrogate of the *Foedus Pacificum*, on the one hand, and the undesirable realization of a world state republic, on the other hand, the only role the *Völkerstaat* can be said to play is that of representing the counterfactual hypothesis of a transitional progression of the league of states towards a more coercive framework for realizing peace.

How can the multistate confederation arguably advance the minimal constitutional stage of the league of states? It might be argued that whereas in the first case the condition of legality is mostly maintained by states' equal worth on the basis of converging interests (self-protection) and political features (republican nature), in the second case, compliance to international law principles is realized by states 'as if' they were juridical subjects of a multistate confederation. The legal interdependence of states is interpreted as regulated by a form of transnational jurisdiction 'as if'.

That Kant had in mind this more advanced phase of constitutionalization of international law is part of his reasoning in the *Metaphysics of Morals* where he refers to the relations set by international law as "merely provisional"[107] and where "Only in a universal association of states (analogous to that by which a people becomes a state) can rights come to hold conclusively and a true condition

106 I. Kant, *Prolegomena to any Future Metaphysics*, G. Hatfield (trans.), Cambridge University Press, Cambridge, 2002, [1783], pp.146–147.

107 Kant, "Metaphysics of Morals (1797)", 6:350, p.487.

of peace come about".[108] The remark on the provisional aspect of international law links this with the transitory character of international law, that is, the previously addressed distinction into peremptory and provisional rights. Furthermore, it shows again the irrealizability of a positive world state, as when he concludes that: "if such a state made up of nations were to extend too far over vast regions [. . . it] would finally have to become impossible, while several such corporations would again bring on a state of war".[109] It is for such reason that "perpetual peace, the ultimate goal of the whole right of nations, is indeed an unachievable idea".[110] We can therefore only aim at a "continual approximation to it [as] a task based on duty and therefore on the right of human beings and of states".[111]

The more advanced case of international constitutionalism that the regulative function of the multistate confederation is expected to bring about thus implies: (1) a recognition of a legal constitutional core and a hierarchization of the legal sources; (2) the adoption of a standard of coherence and uniformity in the application of the law; and (3) an interpretation of legitimate sovereignty as dependent on states' capacity to comply with principles of international law as a form of anti-colonialist state equality.

My interpretation departs here from Höffe's reconstruction of Kant's sovereignty based on an "overly simple alternative: either full sovereignty or none".[112] It is rather more sympathetic with the view advanced by Flikschuh whereby "a state which claims immunity from international juridical coercion on the grounds of its juridical sovereignty domestically is *for that reason* juridically obliged to enter into rightful relations with other states".[113] Yet, what I suggest, is that the Kantian puzzle and the ideal of a coercive multistate confederation finds a solution in the view of states as self-interpreters and self-enforcers of international and cosmopolitan principles, namely, 'as if' generated by an act of universal co-legislation. It is on the bases of such an assumption that the apparent contradiction to which Kant seems to fall prey, that of states not willing to enter a multistate confederation even if ideally desirable, can be explained. The question that remains open, nonetheless, is which institutional subjects are most capable of advancing a process of global constitutionalization of international law, as for instance in the case of third party arbitration between states with international courts or transnational networks. Kant remains silent on this point.[114] While the structural transformation of the Westphalian system had only been initiated in the

108 Ibid.
109 Ibid.
110 Ibid.
111 Ibid.
112 Höffe, *Kant's Cosmopolitan Theory*, p.197.
113 K. Flikschuh, "Kant's Sovereignty Dilemma: a Contemporary Analysis", *The Journal of Political Philosophy*, 18(4), 2010, p.488.
114 For an interpretation of Kant which foresees the requirement of international courts operating in view of distributive and commutative justice purposes – international and cosmopolitan law – see Byrd and Hruschka, *Kant's Doctrine of Right*, p.210 ff. For a recent discussion of the compatibility of the Kantian framework with the contemporary arising of

previous fifty years, Kant can still be said to have captured the normative terrain of this trajectory by formulating the legitimacy conditions for the *cosmopolitan state*.[115]

As noticed, Kant had in mind several transnational phases in which to embed the constitutional advancement of international law. The question becomes then how to understand such distinctions as part of a unified picture for the institutional progression at the transnational level. If we follow a 'transitional' reading, as the one suggested, the configurations identified here exemplify an incremental set of options for institutional progression backed by an increment of cosmopolitan rights. As a whole, cosmopolitan right represents a principle of law aiming to realize the transitional move towards a constitutional condition referred to by Kant in the concluding paragraphs of the *Rechtslehre*.[116] The suggestion of gradual reforms shows Kant's attempt to isolate a process of constitutionalization at the transnational level that presents itself as being different from the revolutionary events of America and France. Accordingly, Kant's idea of constitutional progression toward perpetual peace shows the distinctiveness of cosmopolitan constitutionalism as a process to be assessed on its own terms and as something which cannot be simply equated to state constitutionalism.

Let me recapture the transitionality aspect of Kantian cosmopolitan law and conclude with a remark on Kantian cosmopolitan legacy in Habermas and Benhabib. Since for Kant the constitutionalization of international relations through cosmopolitan law occurs in *stages*, it becomes possible to account for the transition from the federation (*Föderation*) or league of states (*Völkerbund*) as a surrogate solution to the too often overlooked Kantian idea of a multistate confederation (*Völkerstaat*). Taken as an 'as if' organizational paradigm, the multistate confederation becomes the legal interpretive framework for advancing the project of a confederation of a plurality of states without resorting to the positive instantiation of a world republic. In addition, the multistate confederation, by providing a formal standard for the regulation of interstate relations, *transforms* the same legal relations of the federation by advancing the constitutional project.

To illustrate this point, I refer to how the Kantian 'as if' legal reasoning can be further interpreted – to paraphrase Habermas – "with the benefit of two hundred years".[117] There are two alternatives that can be referred to by this form

---

international courts see A. Føllesdal, "Kant, Human Rights and Courts", A. Føllesdal and R. Maliks (eds.), *Kantian Theory and Human Rights*, Routledge, London, 2014, p.193 ff.

115 On the historical legal reconstruction of European common laws and a prerequisite for the notion of cosmopolitan state see P. Glenn, *Legal Traditions of the World*, Oxford University Press, Oxford, 2010 and P. Glenn, *The Cosmopolitan State*, Oxford University Press, Oxford, 2013. On a recent legal and philosophical understanding of the same theme see M. Kumm, "Constitutionalism and the Cosmopolitan State", *Public Law and Legal Theory Research Paper Series, Working Paper No.13-68*, 2013, available on-line at: http://ssrn.com/abstract=2338547, pp.1-28 (accessed on 21.1.2014).

116 Kant, "Metaphysics of Morals (1797)", 6:355, p.491 ff.

117 J. Habermas, "A Political Constitution for the Pluralist World Society?", *Journal of Chinese Philosophy*, 34, 2007, pp.331–343.

of symbolic constitutionalism interpreted along regulative lines. One is the idea of monist constitutionalism – as with a monist republican world state model annihilating all internal states' constitutional differences – and the other is the idea of pluralist constitutionalism – as with the idea of a multistate confederation model legitimating internal pluralism.[118]

If monist constitutionalism was the right option to choose, then, the enforcement of a strictly hierarchical standard of world constitutionalism would transform the regulative standard of the 'as if' into pure legal positivism. On the contrary, according to the suggested interpretation, for Kant there is not a world-state hierarchy of legal norms that is to be maintained but a standard of coherence and harmony between a *plurality of constitutional systems.*

Let me illustrate this point with some contemporary legal examples. In this respect, it is worth considering the controversy between the UN and the EU in the Kadi case.[119] Kadi was a Saudi national accused of terrorism and subjected to special sanctions according to the Security Council Resolution 1267 under Charter VII of the UN Charter. The EU had to freeze his assets and comply with the UN resolution. Both the Court of First Instance and the European Court of Justice considered the issue and came up with opposite conclusions. The Court of First Instance upheld a monist position according to which international obligations hold priority over domestic ones and where the court has no authority to review the Security Council's regulation. The court saw itself as hierarchically subordinated in a global system of laws: "the Court reasoned [. . .] to act *as if* the EU and by implication domestic courts of other countries are already organs of a cosmopolitan legal order and global legal-political community whose core values and institutional structure are already constitutionalized [emphasis added]".[120] The European Court of Justice, instead, held a 'pluralist' position on the Kadi case and concluded that his rights to due process were violated. The Court held that states were bound to the rule of law and that no state could avoid review. The Grand Chamber of the ECJ assumed a distinct – regional domestic – constitutional understanding of the EU for its review of international law. It assumed that, in view of the priority of respect of its fundamental principles, it could not comply with the requirements set by Security Council regulation. At the end, it upheld a pluralist view for the interpretation of legal orders.[121]

If these are the alternatives allowed by a hypothetical update of Kant's transnational advancements, then, one is in a vantage point to provide some insight *from within* to what Habermas sees as the "incomplete"[122] element of Kant's

118 For the monist and dualist vs. pluralist constitutionalism, see J. Cohen, "Constitutionalism beyond the State: Myth or Necessity? (A Pluralist Approach)", *Humanity: An International Journal of Human Rights, Humanitarianism, and Development*, 2(1), 2011, pp.127–158.

119 Case C–402/05 P and C–415/05, P. *Kadi and Al Barakaat International Foundation v. Council and Commission* [2008] ECR I–6351.

120 Cohen, "Constitutionalism beyond the State", p.139.

121 Cohen, "Constitutionalism beyond the State", p.140 ff.

122 Habermas, "Political Constitution", p.331.

cosmopolitanism. Indeed, if the model of the *Völkerstaat* is adopted as a regulative tool for individual and interstate constitutionalization, it becomes possible along Habermasian lines: (a) to construct a 'multilevel system' as a pluralistic form of legitimate power and capable of transforming the sovereign indivisibility of the 'we the people' of the Republics; (b) to construct a constitutional arrangement "of a world society without world government";[123] and finally (c) to progress along a "temporal pattern of incremental advances in the constitutionalization process, initiated and backed by governments rather than by citizens".[124]

Consequently, also Benhabib's insights into the jurisgenerative process of incorporation of cosmopolitan law into the domestic domain can be expanded and connected to a non-domestic (cosmopolitan) sphere of citizens' rights. In this respect, there is full continuity between Kant's and Benhabib's cosmopolitan theory in so far as the right to hospitality is "situated at the boundaries of the polity".[125] Yet, if the Kantian project is advanced further in the direction of the constitutionalization of international law, then, the same legal categorization of 'the right to hospitality' becomes part of a global constitutional project. As Kant puts it: "In this way distant parts of the world can enter peaceably into relations with one another, which can eventually become publicly lawful and so finally bring the human race ever closer to a *cosmopolitan constitution* [emphasis added]".[126]

As mentioned earlier, the interlinking of different jurisdictions did not go unnoticed by Fichte's *Review* of *Toward Perpetual Peace* when he emphasized the 'intermediary condition' of the federation of nations [*Völkerbund*]. My suggestion is that to speak of an intermediary condition leads to either an interpretation of cosmopolitan law as grounded on an end-state view or, alternatively, to a transitional reading. The argument, therefore, has consisted in showing how it is possible to argue for a transitional reading as an intrinsic aspect of Kant's international and cosmopolitan law. The transitionality of cosmopolitan law is in Kant only sketched but it certainly grounds the trajectory of institutional progressions presented here. It seems that only within such a forward-movement governed by transitional cosmopolitan law does it become possible to explain Kant's constitutional project as well as to provide further insight into Habermas' cosmopolitan theory.[127] Indeed, that process which would not also be compatible with some degree of enforcement through transnational regulating agencies would be

123 Habermas, "Political Constitution", p.333.

124 Ibid.

125 S. Benhabib, *Transformations of Citizenship. Dilemmas of the Nation State in the Era of Globalization*, Koninklijke van Gorcum, Assen, 2001.

126 Kant, "Toward Perpetual Peace (1795)", 8:358, p.329.

127 J. Habermas, "Kant's Idea of Perpetual Peace, with the Benefit of Two Hundred Years' Hindsight", J. Bohman and M. Lutz-Bachmann (eds.), *Perpetual Peace. Essays on Kant's Cosmopolitan Ideal*, The MIT Press, Cambridge, Mass., 1997, pp.113–154; J. Habermas, "Does the Constitutionalization of International Law Still have a Chance?", C. Cronin (ed.), *The Divided West*, Polity Press, Cambridge, 2006; Habermas, "Constitutionalization and Legitimation Problems", pp.109–130.

a rather unsatisfactory form of constitutionalization of the entire system of international law. The problem remains of advancing constitutionalization without renouncing to a minimally acceptable democratic standard also at the transnational level. This condition also seems to be endorsed by Kant's *First Definitive Article* of *Toward Perpetual Peace*, particularly in the concern expressed for the requirement of the republican nature of a self-legislating confederal body and not only within the units of which it is composed. The jurisgenerative process of law production considered by Benhabib at the domestic level should, thus, also be included and replicated at the transnational level given that the constitutionalization of international law must proceed through a democratic interaction among states and along a hypothesized set of legitimate confederal arrangements. Kant had not foreseen all of the implications and institutional options opened by his sketch, even though the legal dynamism he drafted allows both an incremental view of cosmopolitan right as well as an ordering of interstate relations on the basis of the regulative role of a multistate confederation.

§9 Constructivism in cosmopolitan law

Kant's right to visit

Constitutionalism in global law has gained significant momentum in recent years, benefiting from a truly interdisciplinary debate among international law scholars, political theorists and legal-political philosophers. It is hard to believe, though, that this has been the outcome of a simply fashionable academic thinking. Rather it seems the case that post-1989 international relations have profoundly changed the way states act in relation to new conceptions of legitimate sovereignty, authority, and state powers, in particular the democratic rule of law and respect for human rights. As a result, academic interest in global constitutionalism has followed the course of development of new jurisdictional events: from the end of a bipolar world to the emergence of a plurality of regimes. These developments have also raised the question of whether national and international law should be conceived as integrated elements of one single constitutional framework and, furthermore, what degree of pluralism it should allow.[1] However, one could hardly claim that also as a *political project* the cosmopolitan ideal is anything new. Limited to modern times, cosmopolitanism was a project of the Abbé de St Pierre and Rousseau whose utopianism was reminded to us by Kant, as I have recalled in the previous sections.[2]

Kant began his reflections bearing this legacy in mind, while aiming to relaunch cosmopolitanism as a serious philosophical framing for understanding the legitimate relation of the individual and the state and, ultimately, for the achievement of a gradual approximation to peace. Kantian insights, as sketchy as they are, help to explain nevertheless several of the contemporary issues of constitutionalism that we are now facing. Kant is neither a blunt natural law philosopher nor just a positivist legal thinker. He is, as I claim, a legal constructivist. As in the

1 Selecting from the burgeoning literature on the topic I suggest M. Kumm, "On the Past and Future of European Constitutional Scholarship", *International Journal of Constitutional Law*, 7(3), 2009, pp. 364–400; Walker, "Constitutionalism Beyond the State", pp. 519–543; P. Dobner and M. Loughlin (eds.), *The Twilight of Constitutional Law: Demise or Transmutation?* Oxford University Press, Oxford, 2010.

2 Kant, "Universal History", 8:27, p. 116. For a comprehensive reconstruction of this debate until Kant see Cavallar, *The Rights of Strangers*, 2002.

more recent case of Rawls,[3] the starting point of legal constructivism for Kant is a conception of rational agency marked by freedom and equality as the basis of a procedure of justification of the law. With regard to the procedure, it is only with the protection of a formal condition of right that autonomous beings can be enabled to bring their aims together into rational union. This allows for the exercise of external freedom in view of the requirements of the *Universal Principle of Right*, making possible a transition from a 'provisional' to a 'conclusive' ownership under an *a priori* civil constitution (since for Kant "conclusive acquisition takes place only in the civil condition"[4]).

Kant's cosmopolitan constructivism unfolds from the role that the right to visit plays in linking republican states and peoples among themselves into a cosmopolitan constitution. Yet, not surprisingly, this requires an *a priori* justification. To this purpose, the idea of a synthetic unity between the *possessio phaenomenon* (as physical possession, i.e. *occupatio*) and the *possessio noumenon* (possession according to a juridical standpoint), as realized by an *a priori* "originally united will",[5] justifies the notion of cosmopolitan authority.

The basic idea here is that first-order principles of right are, at least provisionally, valid as they are agreed upon by all members of an initial condition of choice (as exercises of external freedom). It follows that the coerciveness of any system of law depends upon a procedure of justification that specifies the conditions of validity for external acquisition. For Kant, the peremptory justification of the provisional character of unilateral appropriations is understandable under the idea of a synthetic *a priori* will from which both private and public rights are held together. In so far as such originally united will allows such shift, it also defines the authority of the law.

Legal constructivism takes form starting from the move from the provisional to the peremptory possession, that is, from the *a priori* synthetic unity of an originally united will. The latter is in turn grounded on a concept of cosmopolitan authority, that is, on *a priori* obligation of juridical coercion. The cosmopolitan right to visit arises from the move from the *possessio phaenomenon* in unilateral external acquisitions to peremptory possession according to public right. In such respect, the cosmopolitan "right to visit"[6] stands as a limiting

3 See in particular J. Rawls, "Kantian Constructivism in Moral Theory", *The Journal of Philosophy*, 77(9), 1980, pp. 515–572.

4 See Kant, "Metaphysics of Morals (1797)", §15, p. 416 ff. On a different interpretation of the role that 'a community of rational beings' holds with regard to the mediation between Kant's ethics (Categorical Imperative) and Kant's philosophy of right (*Universal Principle of Right*), see H. Pauer-Studer, "'A Community of Rational Beings': Kant's Realm of Ends and the Distinction between Internal and External Freedom", *Kant-Studien,* 107(1), 2016, p. 125. Unlike Pauer-Studer I argue that this mediation is of a regulative and not of a constitutive type.

5 Kant speaks of the role of a "will that is united *originally* and a priori", one "that presupposes no rightful act [rechtlichen Akt] for its union", and which grounds, as I argue, a non-contractual obligation to enter into a civil condition. Kant, "Metaphysics of Morals (1797)", §16, 6:267, p. 418.

6 Kant, "Toward Perpetual Peace (1795)", 8:359, p. 329.

clause to peremptory appropriation, that is, as a generalized guarantee of non-exclusion from territorial accessibility. It maintains a constructivist element in so far as it realizes a constitutionally justified unification of juridically differentiated domains. Cosmopolitan law, therefore, brings into legal effectiveness the synthetic *a priori* unity of peremptory possessions under the coercive force of an originally united will. For Kant the notion of cosmopolitanism embraces two dimensions: one concerning the general international order that is required for perpetual peace (and primarily the interstate relations of international law) and the other concerning the cosmopolitan right in a strict sense, that is, the third section of public right.[7]

In the following sections, I examine therefore a particular relation that Kant establishes between "the right to visit"[8] and the generation of a global rule of law – what is called alternatively a "cosmopolitan constitution" (*Weltbürgerliche Verfassung*), a "cosmopolitan commonwealth" (*Weltbürgerliches gemeines Wesen*)[9] or, in the *Critique of the Power of Judgment*, "a cosmopolitan whole" (*Weltbürgerliches Ganze*).[10] Here, I pursue an argument grounded on textual evidence, but arguably extensible beyond Kant's writings. A connection between the abovementioned concepts is evidently established in the following passage:

> *this right to hospitality [or to visit]* – that is, the authorization of a foreign newcomer – does not extend beyond the conditions which make it possible to *seek* commerce with the old inhabitants. In this way distant parts of the world can enter peaceably into relations with one another, which can eventually *become publicly lawful* and so finally bring the human race ever *closer to a cosmopolitan constitution* [emphasis added].
>
> (I. Kant, "Toward Perpetual Peace (1795)", 8:359, p. 329)

Kant's legal constructivism answers to the general question of how to establish a cosmopolitan civil condition on the basis of a synthetic *a priori* foundation of the law.[11] Furthermore, the idea of a cosmopolitan constitution reflects a process of progressive constitutionalization of international law, starting from the adoption

7 On this distinction see Mori, *La pace e la ragione*, p. 144.

8 Kant, "Toward Perpetual Peace (1795)", 8:359, p. 329.

9 See, for "cosmopolitan constitution", Kant, "Toward Perpetual Peace (1795)", 8:307, p. 304 and 8:359, p. 329. For the occurrence "cosmopolitan commonwealth", see Kant, "On the Common Saying", 8:311, p. 308. In the following sections I quote different English editions of Kantian works. The choice will depend on the version I find most adequate to the point I intend to elucidate.

10 Kant, *Critique of the Power of Judgment*, p. 300.

11 See the parallel for moral and political constructivism in L. Krasnoff, "How Kantian is Constructivism?", *Kant Studien*, 90(4), 1999, p. 385. This seems also the strategy endorsed by Forst's "right to justification" as the most "fundamental moral demand that no culture or society may reject", in R. Forst, *The Right to Justification: Elements of a Constructivist Theory of Justice*, Columbia University Press, New York, N.Y., 2014, 209 ff.

of a domestic 'civil constitution' and then converging towards an incipient transnational arrangement identifying peremptory norms (*Foedus Pacificum*).[12]

Based on these premises the "right to visit"[13] establishes a relation with domestic constituencies. In other words, it creates a constitutional connection among previously autonomous jurisdictions. The rational engagement of different peoples in peaceful relations follows from a constructivist role played by the cosmopolitan right to visit – something, as Kant considers, that is not simply equivalent to a moral sentiment of philanthropy or virtue.[14] In turn, the overall structure of Kant's cosmopolitan constructivism assumes that a system of rights is valid if it fulfills the standard of a normative theory, one based on the grounding concept of equal freedom as "the only one innate right",[15] of humanity and thus realizing the presupposition of the *Universal Principle of Right* (*Allgemeines Prinzip des Rechts*).[16]

Each domestic jurisdiction has to strive not only internally but also externally towards the realization of peace as an approximation of the idea of reason "to which no object given in experience can be adequate – and a perfectly *rightful constitution* among human beings is of this sort – is the thing in itself"[17] and this is also the task of the "moral politician"[18] in aligning the critical demands of cosmopolitan citizens with the requirements of public use of reason set by a *Universal Principle of Right.*

Taken together, these components contribute to a general 'transitional' scheme for Kantian cosmopolitan constitutionalism, one which accounts for why (a) Kant can claim that "each of them [states], for the sake of its securing peremptorily possessions as rights, can and ought to require to others to enter with it into a constitution similar to a civil constitution",[19] and one where (b) the constitutional level established by the '*league of nations*' (*Foedus Pacificum* or *Völkerbund*), is in continuous approximation with the ideal of a republican multistate confederation (or 'state of nations', *Völkerstaat*).[20]

The notion of a transitionality, i.e. political approximation to peace, is not a spurious notion to Kant's system of thought. On the contrary it derives from the overall systemic partition between theoretical absolutely prescriptive disciplines where right is together with ethics a component of morality, on the one hand,

12 Kant, "Toward Perpetual Peace (1795)", 8:356, p. 3273. In the following sections I use 'cosmopolitan' and 'global' constitution(alism) as synonymous terms.
13 Kant, "Toward Perpetual Peace (1795)", 8:359, p. 329.
14 Kant, "Toward Perpetual Peace (1795)", 8:358, p. 328.
15 Kant, "Metaphysics of Morals (1797)", 6:237, p. 393.
16 Kant, "Metaphysics of Morals (1797)", 6:230, p. 387.
17 Kant, "Metaphysics of Morals (1797)", 6:371, p. 505.
18 On this point see M. Koskenniemi, "Constitutionalism as a Mindset: Reflections on Kantian Themes About International Law and Globalization", *Theoretical Inquiries in Law,* 8(1), 2007, p. 9.
19 Kant, "Toward Perpetual Peace (1795)", 8:354, p. 326.
20 Ibid.

and politics as "doctrine of right put into practice".[21] All this structure of reasoning, which will be unpacked in the following sections, makes of Kant a relevant starting point also for our contemporary understanding of a global (or cosmopolitan, as Kant calls it) constitution.

§9.1 Starting points for a constructivist justification of cosmopolitan right: on the inherent connection between (external) freedom and possession within the original community

Kant's idea of an original community reinterprets in ideal-normative terms the traditional conceptions of Grotius and Pufendorf of the *communio primaeva* as well as later criticisms in Achenwall's *Elementa Iuris Naturae*.[22] For Kant, the *communio fundi originaria* is *not* similar to the *communio primaeva* "one that was *instituted* and arose from a contract by which everyone gave up private possessions",[23] since the 'factual' understanding of the original community is mistaken. This is because a community regulated by features of identity and property relations is a non-starter, as it is the community of the mine and thine (*communio*).

Kant introduces the conditions under which something can be acquired originally by referring to the idea of an "*original* community of land".[24] Given the limited and spherical shape of the Earth, individuals cannot disperse and must instead relate to each other in a condition of free interaction (*communio fundi originaria*). Since all nations are *originally* members of a community of the land and since the community of the land is not a legal community of ownership but rather a community of possible physical *interaction* (*commercium*), everyone is in "a thoroughgoing relation of each to all the others *of offering to engage in*

21 Kant, "Toward Perpetual Peace (1795)", 8:370, p. 338.

22 See, respectively, Grotius, *Law of War and Peace*, and Pufendorf, "Law of Nature and Nations", C.L. Carr (ed.) and M.J. Seidler (trans.), *The Political Writings of Samuel Pufendorf*, Oxford University Press, Oxford, New York, 1994 [1672]. See also, G. Achenwall and J.S. Pütter, "Elementa Iuris Naturae", G. Achenwall and J.S. Pütter, *Anfangsgründe des Naturrechts*, J. Schröder (ed.), Insel, Frankfurt, 1995 [1750]. For Kant 'community' is primarily, even if not uniquely, a pure concept of the understanding. As Milstein notes, this illustrates a form of relation rather than a sociological or a political concept. This relation of interaction is characterized by reciprocal causality, one where the affirmation of one member implies the denial of all others and vice versa. See B. Milstein, "Kantian Cosmopolitanism beyond 'Perpetual Peace': *Commercium*, Critique, and the Cosmopolitan Problematic", *European Journal of Philosophy*, 1(21), 2010, p. 121. The disjunctive relation between a member and the original community can be understood only on the presumption of an original unified concept of possession which considers the totality of human beings. It is only on the premise of an original form of interconnection among all individuals that a disjunctive relation of interaction among all members is established.

23 Kant, "Metaphysics of Morals (1797)", 6:251, p. 405.

24 Ibid.

commerce with any other [. . .] without the other being authorized to behave toward it as an enemy because it has made this attempt".[25]

Originally, all human beings are "in a possession of the land that is in conformity with right",[26] namely, to the right to "be wherever nature or chance [. . .] has placed them".[27] This is what is also described in *Toward Perpetual Peace* as the "right of possession in common of the earth's surface",[28] from which follows the disjunctively universal right for each to have a place on Earth.[29] For Kant, the original appropriation is never an appropriation of a *res nullius* but of something *already* occurring within a domain of possession in common of the Earth (one that is not of common property). The exit from the state of nature is therefore grounded on the shifting from a provisional to a peremptory possession which can only take place within an established system of coercive (public) rights. I have mentioned in earlier sections what is the transitional role of provisional laws to the presumption of legitimate possession. This shift is what allows also the move from a *possessio phaenomenon* to a *possessio noumenon*, that is, possession in accordance with right. In order to justify a move to a civil condition, Kant has to introduce the idea of an originally united will on the base of which the original community constitutes itself as a coercive authority. In this way the will of the original community performs a transition from a state of nature regulated on the base of a private – natural law – type, to a civil condition structured by publicly proclaimed, and therefore positive, laws. Lacking the presupposition of an already 'rightful act', as it would be, instead, if the original condition of common possession had juridically valid features, the coercive character of an originally united will articulates a system of positive legal duties enforceable towards all. In such a way, the omnilateral dimension of an originally united will constitutes a response to unilateral appropriations within the state of nature. From a conceptual point of view, the analytical justification of unilateral appropriations of the will based on an innate right to freedom (as a coordination among different wills), is synthetically subsumed within a notion of authority that legislates *a priori*. You must "leave the state of nature and enter into the civil condition".[30] Such authority enacts a coercive obligation that commands omnilaterally.

Perhaps not surprisingly, from the original community unfolds also the justification of establishing rightful terms of interaction both from the relation of the citizens with the states and from the relation of states among themselves. A distinct set of reasons applies to the connection between an original community and the formulation of a cosmopolitan right to visit. Kant's argument for the justification of the cosmopolitan right assumes, on a preliminary basis, that we

25 Kant, "Metaphysics of Morals (1797)", 6:352, p. 489.
26 Kant, "Metaphysics of Morals (1797)", 6:390, p. 521.
27 Kant, "Metaphysics of Morals (1797)", 6:262, p. 414.
28 Kant, "Toward Perpetual Peace (1795)", 8:358, p. 329.
29 I. Kant, "Vorlesungen Rechtslehre" [23:323: 26–30; 23:320: 20–23] and [23:321:14–16]. Quoted in B.S. Byrd, "Intelligible Possession of Objects of Choice", L. Denis (ed.), *Kant's Metaphysics of Morals: A Critical Guide*, Cambridge University Press, Cambridge, 2010, p. 108.
30 Kant, "Metaphysics of Morals (1797)", 6:264, p. 416.

are all endowed with an original right to freedom as non-domination.[31] Freedom for Kant is either internal – related to virtue – or external, that is, connected to an interpersonal obligation for agents to comply with the *Universal Principle of Right* for which "Any action is *right* if it can coexist with everyone's freedom in accordance with a universal law, or if on its maxim the freedom of choice of each can coexist with everyone's freedom in accordance with a universal law".[32] Coexistence of free choices requires that formal constraints on justice are defined in terms of standards of 'interpersonal consistency' and 'demands for universality'.[33] Freedom and particularly 'external freedom' is equal to independence, that is, to be an equal subject of self-determination. External independence from the mastery of others, from control, follows from the postulate of 'giving laws to oneself' of the Categorical Imperative.[34] As a result, a reciprocal coercive authority of legal obligations is ultimately derived from respect for everyone's freedom.

In addition to these formal constraints, material limitations apply. Unlike internal freedom, external freedom is subject to space boundaries, that is, to the shape of the Earth as a condition for social formation and demands for justice in circumstances of moderate scarcity ("determinate limits"[35] and "spherical shape"[36] of the earth). As noted, for Kant there is a necessary connection between external freedom and the possession of external objects, so that if I were denied a place on Earth my original right to freedom would also be infringed. The original right to external freedom justifies therefore my right to 'a place on earth' – what for Kant is a disjunctively universal right, that is, a right to be here or there. In Kant, the

31 Kant, "Metaphysics of Morals (1797)", 6:236, p. 392.

32 Kant, "Metaphysics of Morals (1797)", 6:230, p. 387.

33 As Pogge puts it: "If persons were to embrace [. . .] 'what seems just and good' (Rechtslehre 312), then a social order ensuring interpersonal consistency would once again not be achieved. Different schemes for achieving mutual consistency will be mutually inconsistent [. . .] Kant's later theory of justice sees its task then in pruning further the set of consistent systems of constraints – ideally down to a single one [. . .] The first step in this reduction is taken through the other component of pure practical reason's formal aspect – the demand of universality. One person should have a particular external freedom only if that same freedom is enjoyed by everyone." In T. Pogge, "Kant's Theory of Justice" (reprint from: *Kant Studien*, 79, pp. 407–433), B.S. Byrd and J. Hruschka (eds.), *Kant and Law*, Ashgate, Aldershot, 2006/Routledge, Taylor and Francis, London and New York, 2016, p. 413.

34 As Ripstein synthesizes this point: "Interference with another person's freedom creates a form of dependence; independence requires that one person not be subject to another person's choice", in A. Ripstein, *Force and Freedom: Kant's Legal and Political Philosophy*, Harvard University Press, Boston, Mass., 2009, p. 15.

35 Kant, "Metaphysics of Morals (1797)", 6:352, p. 489. With regard to T. Pogge's 'lexical hierarchy' of Kant's principles of justice, two formal and one material {FP-1} Consistency{FP-2}Universality{MP}Enlightenment, I would add a fourth element concerning the 'circumstances of justice' as the material constraints on justice. I would suggest calling this {MC 2} Geographical/Resources Scarcity. See Pogge, "Kant's Theory of Justice" (reprint from: *Kant Studien*, 79, pp. 407–433), B.S. Byrd and J. Hruschka (eds.), *Kant and Law*, Ashgate, Aldershot, 2006/Routledge, Taylor and Francis, London and New York, 2016, p. 414.

36 Ibid.

legitimate acquisition of an external object depends on the possibility of "taking control of it [*occupatio*]"[37] and this, in turn, requires the recognition of having a place on Earth. As one moves from original acquisition to property and from a state of nature to a juridical state, the general recognition of a place on Earth shifts into a cosmopolitan right not to be refused hospitality whenever one's life is endangered if returned ('the right to visit' as *non refoulement*). This rationale shows how for Kant there holds an inherent connection between the innate right to freedom and the idea of possession of the Earth given in common.

The interactions within an original community of *commercium* grant to its members the possibility to put forward reciprocal requests. Relations of this type define a community that is radically different from that regulated by property relations (*communio*). However, a community of common possession lacks features of freedom-guarantees and social stability. For Kant, the state of nature, and with that an original community of interaction, though not necessarily unjust (*iniustus*) because allowing a system of private rights expressed in the natural law form, is certainly "*devoid of justice* (*status iustitia vacuus*)"[38] due to the non-peremptory character of the law and the absence of a "judge competent to render a verdict having rightful force".[39] As a result, in order to defend the right to externally acquired objects, as well as for these rights to be granted a peremptory status, a form of coercion is required. It would be contradictory to claim rights to external objects without at the same time holding others to a duty of compliance. "Hence [Kant concludes] there is connected with right by principle of contradiction an authorization to coerce someone who infringes upon it".[40] In this way, Kant justifies the duty to enter into a juridical condition as a dimension regulated primarily by a coercive authority acting on the base of a system of rights. Indeed, since my right to intelligible possession (*possessio noumenon*, "possession *merely by right*")[41] is implicit in an *a priori* united will,[42] I assume that my rights to property "do not depend on social approval".[43] Intellectual possession of external objects is based on an originally united will that is given *a priori* and which legislates necessarily, not contingently: "But the *rational title* of acquisition can lie only in the idea of a will of all united a priori (necessarily to be united) [. . .]".[44] The subjective right to a particular possession on Earth holds only in so far as this becomes a generalizable interest for all other members (*Principle of External*

37 Kant, "Metaphysics of Morals (1797)", 6:259, p. 412.
38 Kant, "Metaphysics of Morals (1797)", 6:312, p. 456.
39 Ibid.
40 Kant, "Metaphysics of Morals (1797)", 6:231, p. 388.
41 Kant, "Metaphysics of Morals (1797)", 6:259, p. 412.
42 Kant distinguishes between three types of possession (empirical, as a concept of the understanding and as intelligible possession); Kant, "Metaphysics of Morals (1797)", 6:245, p. 401 ff. Where the first two categories pertain to the notion of having control over something, either directly or indirectly, intelligible possession pertains to the legal requirement that others should not interfere with my possession.
43 B.S. Byrd, "Intelligible Possession". p. 94.
44 Kant, "Metaphysics of Morals (1797)", 6:264, p. 416.

Acquisition). What follows is an obligation to divide the Earth in accordance with a will "that commands absolutely",[45] namely, a coercive authority as a concept grounding *a priori* the idea of a "civil constitution".[46]

If this is the case, then, also my duty to be part of a civil order is linked to securing everybody's rights through the coercive force of the law. It is with a view to securing my *provisional* rights to external objects that the right to coerce others is upheld. The originally united will, in so far as it justifies coercive laws through an omnilateral will, also defines a general *standard of public authority* of a *cosmopolitan* nature. It is indeed from the presumption of "possession of the land [. . .] as possession of a part of a determinate whole [. . .] to which each [. . .] has a right"[47] that cosmopolitan right as right to hospitality is ultimately derived. The cosmopolitan character of the authority of the originally united will consists therefore in assuring that each individual is conferred a peremptory right to territorial occupancy under a system of law. The cosmopolitan right to visit is 'co-original' to the peremptory will of this authority since, in so far as it commands the division of the Earth, it assigns to each the right to territorial visit in the name of an original possession of the earth held in common.

As it appears, indeed, it is from the acceptability of an original appropriation that it follows that those who are excluded by territorial seizure must be compensated through the allocation of a qualified right – the right to visit – in order to respect their original right to have a place on earth. I define the right to visit as establishing state obligations to individuals that are excluded from a legitimate appropriation of land under the legislation of an *a priori* united will. Such will establishes a synthetic *a priori* unity of coercive rights in a context of limited availability of land and resources. A legitimate appropriation of land in circumstances of limited resources demands that others are left with comparatively undiminished opportunities to an original appropriation of the Earth.

This understanding reformulates the Lockean clause of appropriation, as famously defined with the "enough and as good left in common for others".[48] But, more generally, it responds to a fundamental problem discussed in the natural law and concerning the way in which to justify negative externalities of territorial appropriation by establishing obligations towards the exclusion of third parties. This was indeed also the problem of Grotius who allowed for interference

45 Kant, "Metaphysics of Morals (1797)", 6:263, p. 415.
46 Kant, "Metaphysics of Morals (1797)", 6:264, p. 416.
47 Kant, "Metaphysics of Morals (1797)", 6:352, p. 489.
48 J. Locke, *Second Treatise of Government*, 1982 [1690], §27, p. 18ff. With regard to Locke, if the 'enough and as good' clause is interpreted as a sufficiency, rather than as space left for a restrictive interpretation of the compensatory principle for cosmopolitan public authority. As Waldron acutely remarks with regard to Locke: "In §27 the rather ambiguous logical connective 'at least where'; the meaning of 'at least where' may differ, but surely reading of it is as a connective introducing a sufficient where Q' seems to me to be most naturally rendered as than as 'If P then Q'; the words 'at least' indicate that whenever Q obtains, there may also be other circumstances even though Q does *not* obtain." In J. Waldron, "Enough and as good left for others", *The Philosophical Quarterly*, 29(117), 1979, p. 321.

with private property in cases of necessity by non-members.[49] For Locke the enough and as good represents a 'factual circumstance' and it is not a restrictive standard for original appropriation. Accordingly, when money is introduced, as with civil society, Locke appeals to a natural duty "to preserve the rest of Mankind"[50] in response to the "spoilage proviso".[51] Following the suggestion here proposed, Kant seems instead to hold that cosmopolitan public authority justifies the entry into a system of public right on the basis of the maintenance of a restrictive standard of an original appropriation of the Earth. In contrast with the general Lockean natural law 'duty of preservation', the cosmopolitan right to visit leaves unaltered the possibility of interaction by members of an original community. Accordingly, the institutionalization of a juridical authority within a state comes to depend not only on an inner-boundary but also on an outer-boundary lawful relation. Both elements, together, define states' territorial rights in accordance with a cosmopolitan standard of the law.[52] Unlike a permissible principle for territorial rights,[53] a compensatory theory of cosmopolitan law considers that states are peremptory jurisdictional entities, but where the reduction of opportunities they create for legally excluded members is acceptable only on the ground of the respect of a minimal threshold that guarantees a place on Earth to state's non-members.

It follows that the instantiation of a public authority is not only required for the purpose of constraining, under the law, unilateral appropriations of the will through the creation of states, but also in view of compensating, as it were, those subjects who are excluded from such appropriations. Due to the limited size of the Earth, territorial exclusion is omnilaterally acceptable only if state authority is held under an obligation to allocate a cosmopolitan compensatory measure. From this it results that states have the right to rule. Therefore, they may reasonably expect others to accept territorial/jurisdictional exclusion not only if (a) they establish a rule of law and a system of justice on their territory, but also if (b) they allow foreign visitors to enter their territory on the basis of publicly justifiable reasons for compensating what would be, otherwise, a unilateral appropriation of the land.

49 See A. Pinheiro Walla, "Common Possession of the Earth and Cosmopolitan Right", *Kant-Studien*, 107(1), 2016, pp. 160–178.

50 Locke, *Second Treatise of Government*, §2, p. 1; also in Waldron, "Enough and As Good", p. 325.

51 Waldron, "Enough and As Good", p. 319.

52 This view therefore integrates the purely domestic conception of state's territorial rights legitimacy advanced by A. Stilz, "Nations, States and Territory", *Ethics*, 121(3), 2011, p. 572. The author explicitly recognizes that the rights to territorial jurisdiction are "limited by *external legitimacy conditions* that constrain how the state should exercise these rights when their exercise affects foreigners", pp. 573–574.

53 As Ypi in her otherwise well-conceived argument argues that "permissive principles justify states of affairs incompatible with the idea of 'right' only provisionally and conditionally", in L. Ypi, "A Permissive Theory of Territorial Rights", *European Journal of Philosophy*, 22(2), 2012, p. 290 ff. The problem I see with this account, in so far as it relies on a Kantian argument, is that the 'permissible' justifies an act of the will in a condition deprived of law, as with the unilateral exercise of the will (*lex permissiva*).

A crucial question arises at this point: what sort of institutional progression is generated by the Kantian originally united will and how does it connect to state sovereignty and more in general to a cosmopolitan order? These remarks also help framing under a constructivist form the institutional aspects of cosmopolitan approximation. I consider that Kant conceived of the role of a republican confederation of states in terms of counterfactual guidance and not as an empirical condition to be realized.[54]

The idea of a positive instantiation of a cosmopolitan republic would be plausible only if it were the case that Kant's concept of an originally united will justified a shift beyond a lawless scenario on contractarian terms. In other words, only if there was a constitutive global covenant as a way to move from the original condition would it be possible to conceive the idea of world sovereignty and a global state.

However, as already mentioned before, this can be only a 'quasi-contract', that is, a hypothetical rational idea of a cosmopolitan covenant.

Kant's objective is to explain the idea of an 'original acquisition' to an external object. Were it simply an acquisition within the civil condition, a domestic contract would be the way of transferring property. Similarly, were something originally mine, it would not require external appropriation.[55] But these are not sufficient cases for Kant, since the problem of instability of possessions reappears in the case of international potential turmoil. As noted above, the distinctive element Kant introduces into the debate is that the *communio fundi originaria* does not represent an historical event but it is rather a rational idea that we have necessarily to presuppose if we want to make sense of the legitimacy of a civil condition. Yet, this condition has to fall under regulative conditions of freedom.

For Kant "the concept of freedom cannot hold as a constitutive but solely as a regulative".[56] Accordingly, unilateral choices find mutual coordination only 'as if' they fell under the regulative standards of a general (*a priori*) united will. All the argument developed so far justifies the view that, for Kant, the unification of the unilateral wills appeals to a form of public authority that is inherently cosmopolitan – a prerequisite to understand also the *a priori* nature of the constitutional form.[57] In this respect, it is the originally united will that confers legitimacy on the appropriations of the individual unilateral wills and not the other way around, that is, through historical contractual agreements.

As showed in the initial sections, Kant reinterprets regulatively and in cosmopolitan terms the Rousseauian '*volonté générale*' in terms of the co-legislating

54 In contrast with Scheuerman, I do not consider that for Kant the realization of a republican confederation was just a matter of time. See Scheuerman, "Cosmopolitanism and the World State", p. 419, in particular, p. 440.

55 Flikschuh, *Kant and Modern Political Philosophy*, p. 154.

56 Kant, "The Metaphysics of Morals (1797)", 6:221, p. 376.

57 One significant exception in this respect is Flikschuh, *Kant and Modern Political Philosophy*, pp. 168 ff. as well as K. Flikschuh, "Elusive Unity: the General Will in Hobbes and Kant", *Hobbes Studies*, 25(1), 2012, in particular pp. 36 ff. There it is argued for a notion of a 'general united will' as a form of coercive public authority which legislates in the name of a common possession of the Earth, not by means of a social contract.

activity among equal members.[58] For Kant Rousseau's conception of the general will does not suffice to account for the transformation of a multitude into a unity of self-legislating constituent people. Sovereignty in this regard, as for Hobbes, pertains not to the people alone but to the ruler and to the state as a community. Unlike Hobbes, though, Kant does not accept the idea that coercive authority is justified simply because a multitude has transferred authority to it. On the contrary, he holds that coercive authority is subjected to a concept of legitimacy. As a result, the notion of an originally united will lays down a standard of legitimacy for coercive authority. A multitude of interactive individuals can be thought of as a community of right only in so far as an originally united will is *presupposed a priori* as a unifying concept, so that the sum total of individual actions is accountable to a standard of a cosmopolitan public authority within a civil condition. This means that the absence of an antecedently constituted people, which in Hobbes justifies the rejection of a democratic standard, is reconstituted in Kant based on the notion of an originally united will, one of equal deliberating members as for Rousseau, where real citizens take part in town assemblies. Unlike Rousseau, though, Kant believes that an association of equals is not a society, because there is no "*commander* (*imperans*) and the *subject* (*subditus*) [. . .] it rather *makes* one".[59] This is where Kant envisages conferring a distinctively legitimating form of the authority of an originally united will to state's sovereignty. The originally united will represents a more fundamental concept, one that justifies, *a priori*, a civil condition from which individual sovereign authority within the state derives legitimacy while ceasing to be arbitrary coercive forces.

The absence of a rightful condition reappears at an international level in the relations between states. Also with regard to states' *external relations* there is a duty to move beyond the state of nature and to comply with the principles of public right. However, since for Kant cosmopolitan peace requires embracing a rule of law, it may be asked: on the basis of what reasons should states be obliged to move to an external condition in compliance with a global rule of law?

Consider an *a contrario* argument. In the absence of a scheme of (distributive) justice among states, one that for Kant would result in a civil condition and therefore require an impartial adjudicator, solutions could be sought only on an individual basis and with the use of force. This would eventually undermine the internal juridical condition of republics. For instance, it is imaginable that as a result of unregulated controversies between states, at least some citizens would lose their possessions and ultimately their freedom.[60] It could be argued, then,

58 Flikschuh, "Elusive Unity", pp. 21–42.

59 K. Flikschuh, "Elusive Unity", p. 32.

60 This is mentioned by Kant in various ways in his writings, as in the *Seventh Proposition* of Kant, "Universal History", 8:24, p. 114, where war is said to prevent human enhancement; or in I. Kant, "*Conjectural beginning of human history* (1786)", G. Zöller and R.B. Louden (eds.), *Anthropology, History and Education*, Cambridge University Press, Cambridge, 2011, 8:120, p. 173, where even preparation for the war is said to exhaust the internal resources of the state.

that it is only in so far as interstate external relations are regulated by principles of public law that it would follow that internal conditions of states could be lawfully maintained.

All in all, it seems that it is possible to conclude that in Kant the peremptory command to enter a civil condition is due to the practical and reflexive character of an originally united will that is given *a priori*. Such will establishes that in a condition of common possession of the Earth any unilateral appropriation ceases to be arbitrary and provisional only when it recognizes the peremptory force of an omnilateral will. Such obligating force is not based on a contractualist form of political obligation but is, instead, postulated *a priori* through the idea of common possession of the Earth – a dimension that is normative in itself. This interpretive strategy does not push us back to a natural law interpretation of Kant's theory of political obligation. Instead, it allows for a justification based on two strands of account, namely (1) on the view of a preservation of a cosmopolitan dimension for entering a civil condition (which would instead be lost if a state's formation was to follow from a state of nature), and (2) on the view of a constructivist relation holding between the authority of an originally united will and the exercise of external freedom granted through a cosmopolitan right to visit.

Public authority, so conceived, obliges individuals to exit the state of nature and to be displaced along a general system of rights. The non-conditional character of an originally united will, as a non-contractualist justification, defines public authority in terms of an *a priori* synthetic unity. The type of public authority attached to the omnilateral will is inherently cosmopolitan because it claims that any legitimate territorial seizure is bound to recognize the cosmopolitan right to a qualified territorial accession by non-members.

This scheme of justification of public authority authorizes also the shift from provisional to peremptory possession. Indeed, the rational *a priori* assumption of a cosmopolitan authority starting from an original condition frames such relation in terms of a *gradual* and *transitional* progression, rather than a 'one-go' move. This means also that the idea of a cosmopolitan constitution that results is primarily an *a priori* concept in so far as it realizes the *a priori* unity of liberty and right. Once the *a priori* scaffolding of Kantian cosmopolitan authority is clarified along these lines, it remains to show how such a framework is realized within a practical implementation of the law and in view of the determination of a global constitution. I will attend next to this point.

§9.2 The 'right to visit' as a constructivist principle of cosmopolitan law

In the following section I contend that the cosmopolitan right to visit instantiates a variety of substantive claims: from claims to *non-refoulement* when one's life is endangered, to demands of transnational commercial agreements. The right to visit, in this regard, is characterized primarily by the possibility 'to be heard' left open to state citizens when travelling as visitors to a foreign country.[61] In so far as it aims at preserving within a dialogic medium a 'response-triggering' process, the right to visit seems to be better understandable in terms of a general 'right to be heard'. Since new claims are introduced in a foreign public sphere, the right to visit performs a constructivist role with regard to its contribution in enlarging patterns of public reasoning and in stabilizing an overall rightful condition.

I divide this paragraph into three subsections: first, I clarify in what respect the right to visit is justified from the perspective of a common possession of the Earth; second, I group a plurality of right-claims along a spectrum including 'negative' and 'positive' demands of interaction, i.e. from claims 'not to be' rejected when visiting, to commercial demands of exchange of goods etc.; third, I consider how the right to visit proceduralizes the divide between natural and positive law, laying out a constructivist agenda for the cosmopolitan constitution.

To start with, the cosmopolitan right to visit represents a conditional clause for the peremptory division of Earth commanded by the authority of an originally united will. But in so far as a peremptory authority is institutionalized, either in terms of a state authority or in terms of a transnational authority of some sort, it follows that a positive system of law is enacted. Thus the procedural character of the right to visit accommodates within itself content of specific domestic and transnational claims. Kant speaks of two forms of citizenship: one which belongs to the authority of one's state and another which regards individuals as "citizens of a universal state of mankind (*ius cosmopoliticum*)"[62] [Bürger eines allgemeinen Menschenstaats]. The latter can be thought only by recognizing an authoritative force to the originally united will, one which would command first and foremost recognition of the right to visit as a universal right (a man who remains without access to a piece of land due to prevention from interaction must be protected!). The entry into a civil condition and, therefore, into a sphere regulated by peremptory rights is strictly dependent on widespread observance, within juridical systems, of a universal right to visit due to an original right to have a place on Earth. Observance of such a right is not only due to incorporation of cosmopolitan law by individual state authorities but also by any transnational entity that is instituted beyond the state itself. There is yet an asymmetry here between the two. Indeed, whereas fulfilment of cosmopolitan right, within states, is complete when the obligations of the right of *non-refoulement* are satisfied, the same is insufficient to justify full cosmopolitan right enforceability beyond the state level. In the latter case, the cosmopolitan constitution is realized by approximation through interstate contracts.

Kant's logic of the rational synthetic unity between property and freedom within the original condition also requires that transnational entities bring about peace according to a general condition of law. In this respect both the domestic

61 See Niesen when he claims that: "The subjective *cosmopolitan* right thus appears to constitute a third category of subjective right to communication", in P. Niesen, "Colonialism and Hospitality", *Politics and Ethics Review*, 3(1), 2007, p. 92.

62 Kant, "Toward Perpetual Peace (1795)", note *, 8:349, p. 322.

and the international plane enjoy the same system of law validity, even if they diverge with regard to legal enforceability and constitutional implementation. Due to the constructivist role of the notion of cosmopolitan right (as a right to visit), there occurs a transition from a formal and merely analytical validity of international law securing a non-belligerent coexistence among states, to a conception of peace grounded on a synthetic unity between access to property and freedom under the general guarantee of cosmopolitan law. The transformation into peremptory rights of provisional possessions includes both states among themselves (as proprietors of domestic goods), and individuals as "*citizens of the world*".[63]

However, this rationale of the Kantian cosmopolitan argument has gone largely unnoticed.

As far as the second point is concerned, namely the plurality of content-related meanings of cosmopolitan claims, in general the debate among scholars has been split among those who have understood the right to visit as derivable from an innate right to freedom,[64] and those who have based it on a more property-oriented understanding of "the mine and the thine".[65] Whereas, for instance, Benhabib equates the cosmopolitan right with the right to *non-refoulement*,[66] others define it as a right to commercial exchange.[67] By means of a textually oriented analysis, Byrd and Hruschka suggest that Kant changes his mind after writing *Toward Perpetual Peace*. In particular, they consider whether in the *Metaphysics of Morals*, *Doctrine of Right*, the right to visit is included as an element of international law (rather than of cosmopolitan law).[68] As a result of this apparent shift, the two scholars argue that the cosmopolitan right to visit is better understood in terms of a collective peoples' right to freedom of trade.[69] Others, like Bohman, advance an interpretation emphasizing the role of the cosmopolitan right to visit in terms of a critical exercise of public reason.[70] Kant's apparent

63 Ibid.

64 Kleingeld, "Kant's Cosmopolitan Law"; S. Benhabib, *The Rights of Others: Aliens, Residents, and Citizens*, Cambridge University Press, Cambridge, 2004.

65 As Byrd and Hruschka put this point: "securing the mine and thine [. . .] can be done only in a juridical state, only in a state of distributive justice, only in a situation of a *lex iustitiae* [. . .] Provisional ownership is not secured, but instead preliminarily legal possession [. . .] earth's surface must be divided before any individual has a property claim to secure", in Byrd and Hruschka, *Kant's Doctrine of Right*, pp. 138–139. See also Flikschuh, "Kant's Sovereignty Dilemma:", pp. 469 ff.

66 Benhabib, *The Rights of Others.*

67 Byrd and Hruschka, *Kant's Doctrine of Right.*

68 Byrd and Hruschka, *Kant's Doctrine of Right*, p. 208.

69 Ibid. On this restrictive interpretation see also K. Flikschuh, *Kant and Modern Political Philosophy*, Cambridge University Press, Cambridge, 2000, p. 476.

70 "In the cosmopolitan case, the supreme coercive power of public right in the state is replaced by the initially very weak power of the public opinion of world citizens, that is, the power of a *critical* public", in J. Bohman, "The Public Spheres of the World Citizen", J. Bohman and M. Lutz-Bachmann (eds.), *Perpetual Peace: Essays on Kant's Cosmopolitan Ideal*, MIT Press, Boston, Mass., 1997, p. 180.

change of mind or ambiguity is diffused once we consider, as has been indicated before, that cosmopolitan law bears two different senses: one general and another technical. Under such lenses, all these interpretations testify rather to a semantic openness of the notion. This being the case, then the hypothesis of Byrd and Hruschka's semantic reduction of the '*Verkehr*' (*commercium*, interaction) to a notion of 'trade' cannot be held consistently. Indeed, both in Kant's texts and in Grimms' dictionary '*Verkehr*' means not only 'commercial interaction' but also 'contact' – a more socially oriented meaning.[71] Therefore, as it appears, the right to visit in so far as it is reflective of the interactional element of the original community, incorporates a variety of claims. In all these instances, the right to visit is justified on the basis of a general presupposition of individual inclusion into the society of human beings, that is, as a necessary condition to have a place on Earth and thus to have a right to freedom. It assumes, that is, that one can be a visitor only as a member of a foreign society. Recursively, the moving beyond a lawless condition justifies the view of a general individual attribution of (world) citizenship. A system of rights can be established together with a rightful condition only if individuals enjoy the status of equal citizenship under general principles of reciprocity and universality of rights.

In §62 of the *Metaphysics of Morals* (*Doctrine of Right*), Kant defines the cosmopolitan right as the capacity to commerce with all others:

> each has a right to make this attempt without the other being authorized to behave toward it as an enemy because it has made this attempt. – This right, since it has to do with the possible union of all nations with a view to certain universal laws for their possible commerce, can be called *cosmopolitan right (ius cosmopoliticum)*.
>
> (I. Kant, "The Metaphysics of Morals (1797)", 6:352, p. 489)

What Kant affirms here is that interpersonal relations should be seen primarily in terms of capacities and, only then, as rights. Kant distinguishes between the *privacy* of interpersonal relations, as a capacity, and the *publicity* of the cosmopolitan right as an element of cosmopolitan law. He also considers cosmopolitan right as an individual right of foreign nationals not to be treated as enemies, thus resulting in universal laws that regulate the intercourse among nations. Note here the recursive use of the word "people" [*Volk*].[72] This explains why Byrd and Hruschka argue for the cosmopolitan right in terms of a collective right.[73] However, this reading leaves unanswered the question as to why Kant considers on an equal plane the individual-collective 'human being', as in the case of when he refers to "a human being (or a people)"[74] [*Der Mensch* [. . .]

71 See J. Grimm and W. Grimm, entry '*Verkehr*' in *Deutsches Wörterbuch*, 16 Bde. in 32 Teilbänden, Leipzig 1854–1961. Quellenverzeichnis, Leipzig 1971, Bd.25, Sp.625–637.

72 Kant, "Toward Perpetual Peace (1795)", note *, 8:349, p. 322.

73 Byrd and Hruschka, *Kant's Doctrine of Right*, p. 208.

74 Kant, "Toward Perpetual Peace (1795)", note *, 8:349, p. 322.

(*oder das Volk*)]. This use is intelligible only based on the premise of an original community by virtue of which we are individual citizens of a "universal state of mankind"[75] [*allgemeinen Menschenstaats*]. The cosmopolitan right, as a condition of "universal hospitality",[76] bridges the multidimensional gaps between individuals, peoples, and states. The status of world citizenship, when projected onto the political plane, refutes any definitive assimilation within a specific jurisdiction even within a comprehensive world state since, as Kant says, whereas a world republic is an unrealizable ideal, a world monarchy would soon turn into a "soulless despotism".[77] The more geopolitically connoted expression "nations on the earth" [*Völker auf Erden*][78] testifies to the relations that the cosmopolitan right also establishes between individuals and peoples.

In view of ordering the multiplicity of meanings mentioned above, it is worthwhile recalling that the cosmopolitan right to visit spans across a 'negative' and a 'positive' polarity. With regard to the negative side, the cosmopolitan right takes hospitality as a minimum threshold for protecting life as a precondition for legitimate possession. However, preservation of life must be obtained "without a crime".[79] Today this right is captured by the notion of *non-refoulement* as Benhabib has rightly pointed out. Like the right of a foreign national not to be turned away in the case of mortal danger, the right to visit reflects the core of Kantian cosmopolitanism rooted in the universal entitlement to a place on Earth. It is thus a peremptory command issuing directly from the authority of the originally united will.

Moving to the third and final point, the relation between content-related claims arising from a universally valid right to visit and their reception within legal systems as positive laws testifies to a Kantian conception of an existing internal link between natural and positive law. Kantian cosmopolitanism establishes indeed a connection between a critical-political dimension in the exercise of the cosmopolitan right to visit and the form of rationality of any positive juridical system as a whole. This contributes to explaining the proper constructivist characterization of Kantian cosmopolitanism and his departure from a natural law scheme. Kant attempts to reinterpret the natural law framework of the 'common possession on earth' and 'the right to visit' as elements of a global system of law. By virtue of their earthly affiliation, as original members of a community on Earth, individuals are entitled to submit requests for hospitality to contingently

75 Ibid.
76 Kant, "Toward Perpetual Peace (1795)", 8:357, p. 328.
77 Kant, "Toward Perpetual Peace (1795)", 8:368, p. 336.
78 Kant, "Metaphysics of Morals (1797)", 6:353, p. 489.
79 As Kant makes this general point: "For to preserve my life is only a conditional duty (if it can be done without a crime); but not to take the life of another who is committing no offense against me [*der mich nicht beleidigt*] and does not even *lead* me into the danger of losing my life is an unconditional duty", Kant, "On the Common Saying", 8:301, p. 299. On a similar point see A. Pinheiro Walla, "Common Possession of the Earth and Cosmopolitan Right", *Kant-Studien*, 107(1), 2016, pp. 160–178.

formed positive jurisdictions.[80] However, as a right grounded in an original condition, the cosmopolitan right to visit remains in perpetual tension with positively given jurisdictions. There seems to be here a bi-univocal relation between natural and positive law. Whereas natural law establishes a distinct standard for the validity of positive law, its content as a right can be articulated only within a positive system. Kant notes that the lack of compliance of positive law with natural law is "Like the wooden head in Phaedrus's fable, a merely empirical doctrine of right is a head that may be beautiful but unfortunately it has no brain".[81] For Kant, there is an appearance of law also when moral normative validity is lacking; but in the absence of moral justification, positive law is defective law.

Taken together, the positive-constitutive and the natural-law character of the cosmopolitan right to visit tend to subordinate the domain of international law to the legitimate demands of individuals as world citizens. Coordination among states by means of international law is justified only when individual requests remain mindful of standards of equality and non-discrimination, thus resulting in further integrations between different legal domains. I turn next to the assessment of how this view of the law impacts on the construction of a cosmopolitan system of state-relations that would hopefully lead to peace.

§9.3 Thinking cosmopolitan through the 'critical' public use of reason

In this final paragraph, I consider how a cosmopolitan public use of reason realizes the Kantian ideal of freedom as independence within a process of constitutionalization of international law. In particular, I explain how a progressive trajectory of human emancipation is realized by the capacity to give oneself universal laws as a citizen of a *cosmopolis*.[82]

As argued, the right to universal hospitality, the negative-limiting definition of the right to visit (the right 'not to be treated with hostility'),[83] is explicitly connected by Kant to an original community on earth:

> this right [the *right to visit*], to present oneself for society, belongs to all human beings by virtue of the right of possession in common of the earth's

80 For a different position on this point see A. Pinheiro Walla, ibid. The author quite rightly argues that Kant abandons Grotius' traditional view on needs as grounding elements for the common possession on Earth. However, while she establishes important connections with the right not to be refused when in danger of life, not much is said with regard to the positive 'interactional' aspect of Kant's right to visit, namely, the right to submit communicative demands that lead to the formulation of transnational legal principles.

81 Kant, "Metaphysics of Morals (1797)", 6:230, p. 387.

82 On the link between autonomy and public reason in Kant, see O. O'Neill, "Autonomy and Public Reason", M. Timmons and R.N. Johnson (eds.), *Reason, Value, and Respect: Kantian Themes from the Philosophy of Thomas E. Hill, Jr.*, Oxford University Press, Oxford, 2015, pp. 119–134.

83 Kant, "Toward Perpetual Peace (1795)", 8:359, p. 329.

> surface on which, as a sphere, they cannot disperse infinitely but must finally put up with being near one another; but originally no one had more right than another to be on a place on the earth.
>
> (I. Kant, "Toward Perpetual Peace (1795)", 8:359, p. 329)

Cosmopolitan right, in so far as it is connected to the original community of Earth, derives its mandatory force from an *a priori* commanding will which proceeds to the division of the Earth held in common.[84] Since the unity of the will has an original character, any factual arrangement is constantly subjected to a check of legitimacy with regard to the maintenance of a condition of interaction.[85] This inherent tension within the original condition is evident also in Kant's characterization of the cosmopolitan order which remains a project in search of a long-standing approximation towards peace. Consider the following passage:

> If it is a duty to realize the condition of public right, even if only in approximation by unending progress, and if there is also a well-founded hope of this, then *the perpetual peace* that follows upon what have till now been falsely called peace treaties (strictly speaking, truces) is no empty idea but a task that, gradually solved, comes steadily closer to its goal (since the times during which equal progress takes place will, we hope, become always shorter).
>
> (I. Kant, "Toward Perpetual Peace (1795)", 8:386, p. 351)

The achievement of peace implies the persistence of an unsolved tension between a cosmopolitan ideal and its positivist instantiation. This should come as no surprise since the original community represents a normative concept: "a practical rational concept which contains *a priori* the principle in accordance with which alone people can use a place on the earth in accordance with principles of right".[86] It follows that authority arising from an originally united will establishes that the cosmopolitan demands through visits of another state remain always open to public assessment, even if to what temporal and juridical extent is not specified by Kant.

What appears to be the case, instead, is that the positive effects that the right to visit have on domestic legal systems may be considered as resulting from a public justificatory strategy where a cosmopolitan "right of justification"[87] places both

84 Kant, "Toward Perpetual Peace (1795)", §14, 6:262, p. 415.

85 This hypothesis diverges profoundly from Byrd and Hruschka's thesis for whom once the disjunctively universal right to a place on Earth is met, then the right to be located in a particular location disappears "and with it the right to visit that other place", see Byrd and Hruschka, *Kant's Doctrine of Right*, p. 207. Contrary to this interpretation, I consider that the availability to the cosmopolitan citizen of the right to visit prevents closure as with final-state individual geographical assignment.

86 Kant, "Metaphysics of Morals (1797)", 6:262, p. 415.

87 See Forst, *Right to Justification*", p. 203 ff.

citizens and non-citizens on the same plane of generality and reciprocity with regard to an original claim of earthly affiliation. Certainly this view is at odds with a strictly exclusionary territorial understanding of state powers. Indeed, other candidates of sovereignty could eventually replace Kant's hesitancy to shift away from a Westphalian model of the state. Yet, this does not lead necessarily to the embracement of an over inclusive idea of the state as a "trustee-of humanity".[88] For Kant, instead, the dialectic between the right to visit and the right to be a guest marks the divide between what is mandatory and what is consensual – the latter being an object of voluntary contract for the state. A countervailing standard to sovereign territorial exclusion is for Kant limited to an original right to have a place on Earth, even though the idea of *non-refoulement* can be broadened to include more than just the case of an asylum seeker's threat to her life. One's original right to a place on Earth admits also those cases where economic agreements disallow the possibility of conducting a decent life, an existence where freedoms and appropriations would be co-possible. This boundary cannot be traced *a priori* and it requires rather a public form of reasoning. Practical assessment, in turn, demands that the political autonomy of state citizens is considered in light of an external public use of reason beyond state borders, one where each is not only a 'member of a commonwealth' but "of the society of citizens of the world".[89] For this reason, continues Kant, even positive laws within the state, notwithstanding they must be obeyed, can nevertheless be criticized so that a "citizen cannot refuse to pay the taxes imposed upon him [. . .] But the same citizen does not act against the duty of a citizen when, as a scholar, he publicly expresses his thought about the inappropriateness or even injustice of such decrees".[90]

A corollary to this line of argument expands upon Kant's anthropological views on the "unsociable sociability"[91] of human nature. This approach, though, captures the problem from an *a posteriori* perspective. As the reasoning goes, it appears that in an empirical perspective, unsociable sociability motivates the perpetuation of claims of interaction in a context of moderate scarcity of land

88 As "The trustee-of-humanity model allows states to claim territory on behalf of humanity because individual states, in their capacity as territorial authorities, are conceived as co-representatives of humanity. As trustees as well as representatives, however, states cannot treat peaceful migrants with indifference." In E. Fox-Decent, "Constitutional Legitimacy Unbound", D. Dyzenhaus and M. Thorburn (eds.), *Philosophical Foundations of Constitutional Law*, Oxford University Press, Oxford, 2016, p. 135.

89 Kant, "An Answer to the Question: What is Enlightenment? (1784)", 8:38, p. 18.

90 Kant, "An Answer to the Question", 8:38, p. 19. According to Waldron this point seems to prevent any interpretation of Kant as a positivist. See J. Waldron, "Kant's Legal Positivism", *Harvard Law Review*, 109(7), 1996, p. 1535.

91 See I. Kant, "*The means nature employs in order to bring about the development of all their predispositions is their antagonism in society, insofar as the latter is in the end the cause of their lawful order*. Here I understand by 'antagonism' the *unsociable sociability* of human beings, i.e. their propensity to enter into society, which, however, is combined with a thoroughgoing resistance that constantly threatens to break up this society". In Kant, "Universal History", 8:20, p. 111.

resources. The idea of unsociable sociability also requires the public justificatory argument to be valid. The fact that further demands for legitimation are presented following justified schemes of redistributive justice, presupposes that the cosmopolitan right to visit reflects the idea that a rightful relation between individuals and states is conceived independently from constituted determinations of citizenship or, to put it differently, that historically given affiliations are under a 'corrective' scheme of cosmopolitan inclusivity. As Kant states in the *Conclusion* of the *Doctrine of Right* of the *Metaphysics of Morals*: "the rule for this constitution, as a norm for others, cannot be derived from the experience of those who have hitherto found it most to their advantage; it must, rather, be derived *a priori* by reason from the ideal of a rightful association of human beings under public laws as such".[92] Both the public justificatory and the 'unsocial sociability' argument account for establishing a constructivist relation between the 'critical-constitutional' function of the right to visit and the making of the cosmopolitan constitution. This point remains implicit in Kant's writings and it can be reconstructed only conjecturally. In the following paragraph I abandon, therefore, the pretence of a philological reading of the texts in order to pursue a purely Kantian argument.

As Kant observes, since peoples are subjected to a geographically constrained place on Earth, each must receive a share of resources in accordance with an original right to earthly affiliations. Since this condition is that of a community of reciprocal action, or commerce, cosmopolitan right allows individuals to engage in communicative interaction under the conditions of limited availability of space and resources. The cosmopolitan right regulates the relation between law and space by legitimately restricting individual external freedoms on the basis of a *Universal Principle of Right*. From the attempt to enter into differential relations, the right to visit allows the submission of claims as a foreign national to a different public sphere and, ultimately, to a different jurisdiction.

The distinction between a 'negative' and a 'positive' aspect of the right to visit finds a further grounding here. Whereas the threatening of one's life advances only an unchallengeable claim to the "moral politician",[93] that is, a claim-duty to host temporally anyone who is endangered upon return to her native land, the same does not hold for the 'positive' critical aspect of cosmopolitan constitutionalism. Whereas in the 'negative' aspect of the right to visit the limiting of an original right to equal access to a portion of land compels the moral politician to comply, the 'positive' aspect of the right to visit leaves the claims of the foreign visitor open to rejection. A striking case is that of a claim to trade. In this case nobody could demand, even from a 'moral politician', a duty to comply. Here, *the form* of the claim that is advanced (as with a capability to be heard across different jurisdictions) does not stand in a necessary relation to the violation of the

92 Kant, "Metaphysics of Morals (1797)", 6:355, p. 491.

93 Kant, "Toward Perpetual Peace (1795)", 8:372, p. 340. On this point see Koskenniemi, "Constitutionalism as a Mindset", pp. 9–36.

content of the cosmopolitan right (namely, the respect of an equal right to have a place on Earth).

It might be argued that the right to visit has only a minimal constitutional-constructive output. However, Kant explicitly rejects the idea that in a legitimate state there is no such duty. On the contrary, he urges the 'moral politician' to bring the constitution of the state into line with the principles of right. The striving of the moral politician, arguably one administering a republican state, permits understanding of a possible link between a universal right of hospitality (*Besuchsrecht*) as something which "belongs to all human beings"[94] and which is non-derogable by states, and a "*right to be a guest*"[95] (*Gastrecht*), namely a right requiring the stipulation of a "beneficent pact"[96] that is discretionary to the will of the state. Derrida speaks in this regard of the relation between a law of unconditional hospitality (*Besuchsrecht*) and the conditional laws of a right to hospitality (*Gastrecht*) in terms of an internal (progressive/emancipative) transformation of the law.[97]

The right to visit, in so far as it triggers a reply, places the moral politician under a duty to provide a justification for the demands of a foreign visitor, either in the case of a mandatory obligation of *non-refoulement*, or in the case of a discretionary acceptance of a claim. In the latter case, the domestic constitution incorporates a cosmopolitan request into a legal framework, establishing a juridical interconnection – a constitutional platform – between differently dispersed legal domains. Although it might appear as a functionalist argument at first sight, i.e. one motivated by protective measures, the rationale described above represents a truly constructivist justification for the consolidation of the cosmopolitan constitution (one realizing an original right to have a place on Earth). The moral politician has a 'duty of justification', either accepting or rejecting claims to visit so that any acceptable outcome has to be brought into line with an overall system of law.[98] One might speculate and argue that it is only if political judgment strikes an equilibrium between the external freedom of domestic and foreign nationals and the *Universal Principle of Right*, then justification is achieved. If this is the case, it also becomes possible to understand why the right to universal hospitality, in allowing for a communicative interaction among disparate legal communities, gives rise to the conditions for a state supra-ordinate rule of law.[99] In turn, the

94 Kant, "Toward Perpetual Peace (1795)", 8:359, p. 329.

95 Ibid.

96 Ibid.

97 J. Derrida, *De l'hospitalité*, Calmann-Lévy, Paris, 1997.

98 "A moral politician will make it his principle that, once defects that could not have been prevented are found within the constitution of a state or in the relations of states, it is a duty, especially for heads of state, to be concerned about how they can be improved as soon as possible and brought into conformity with natural right, which stands before us as a model in the idea of reason, even at the cost of sacrifices of their self-seeking [inclinations]." In Kant, "Toward Perpetual Peace (1795)", 8:372, p. 340. For the idea of a 'duty of justification' as a "duty that citizens have as 'world citizens'", see Forst, *Right to Justification*, p. 225.

99 On the subjects of cosmopolitan rights including not only individuals, but also states and peoples, see Niesen, "Colonialism and Hospitality", p. 98.

idea of commerce, in order to realize communicative interaction, must admit a critical use of reason in so far as the submission of individual claims as a foreigner raises an obligation to justify territorial exclusion.

These final considerations find textual support in the nexus that Kant establishes between cosmopolitan right and the standard of public use of reason as delineated in *Toward Perpetual Peace*. Kant claims that public reasoning has turned global and that legal integration among different regimes has become so pervasive that "a violation of right on *one* place of the earth is felt in *all*".[100] Following on from this, the 'negative' and 'positive' side of the right to visit can be grasped only by presupposing a critical-constitutionalist dimension of public use of reason where cosmopolitan citizens challenge 'from within and from without', so to say, public domestic constitutional standards making them porous. What ensues from this process of dialogical interaction is that the critical bite of Kantian cosmopolitan right highlighted by authors such as Bohman is only a stepping stone towards the juridification of public international relations and, finally, to the constitutionalization of public international law.[101] This progression represents, therefore, only an intermediate step towards the realization of the cosmopolitan ideal as ultimately a constitutional project achieved under public standards of reason.[102]

Furthermore, Kant is undoubtedly supportive of anti-colonialist views since any imposition by force, even of a rule of law, would create a legal void in the target population.[103] This means also that he places a global constitutionalist burden primarily on the shoulders of the visitor, as it were. It is for this reason that Kant approved the restrictions on European visitors adopted by China and Japan.[104] Several other examples of kind are on offer here, all marked by a banning of colonialist forms of domination that violate an equal standing of the people before the law. For Kant, states' signatories of voluntary contracts of hospitality (*Gastrecht*) are obliged to respect standards of external freedoms of cosmopolitan citizenship. A notion of trade-fairness applies in this case too. The agreement would turn into one not violating the cosmopolitan constraint of access to the Earth for

100 Kant, "Toward Perpetual Peace (1795)", 8:360, p. 330.

101 Bohman, "The Public Spheres" p. 180 ff.

102 Bohman emphasizes this point in his reactualization of Kant's cosmopolitanism when he asserts that: "When community-wide biases restrict the scope of such self-scrutiny, usually by leaving relevant problems of the public agenda, a new public emerges to press for public self-scrutiny and sometimes for new rules and institutions [. . .] The civil rights movement, rather than the Supreme Court, is the exemplar of the public use of reason that can be extended to cosmopolitan conditions." In Bohman, "The Public Spheres", p. 190.

103 On this point see the recent collection of essays edited by K. Flikschuh and L. Ypi, *Kant and Colonialism*, Oxford University Press, Oxford, 2014.

104 Kant, "Toward Perpetual Peace (1795)", 8:359, p. 329. As Risse observes: "China and Japan may impose restrictions only if *that* is what is required to protect their citizens from assault, that is, only if *that* is what the maintenance of charitable treatment of individuals by foreign government requires. European powers had undermined that requirement. Protection against their intrusion was needed." In M. Risse, "Taking Up Space on Earth: Theorizing Territorial Rights, the Justification of States and Immigration from a Global Standpoint", *Global Constitutionalism*, 4(1), 2015, p. 98.

humanity, for instance, one causing massive environmental devastation or resulting in severe economic impoverishment for third parties. Were these catastrophes to occur, access to Earth's resources would be prevented and an interaction-based standard of cosmopolitan justice violated.[105]

However, it remains the case that any cosmopolitan request, whenever successful, would arguably give rise to a 'constitutional crisis' and raise self-reflectivity by questioning how to relate externally with other constituencies. This would eventually lead to a transformation of the domestic constitutional system. Individual requests nudge domestic constitutions to comply with the generalizable public principles of law. Whereas domestic constitutions, *stricto sensu*, derive their legitimacy from a self-determining collective body that by definition excludes those subjects who are not recognized as members of the constituency – the people – , enactments of the cosmopolitan right to visit challenge such a self-referential understanding by introducing the possibility of interaction between non-citizens, communities, and foreign states.

New constraints of public reasoning lay down limits to strategic state behaviours with regard to external relations and hence to their use of secrecy and political expediency.[106] Publicity empowers the individual as a generalized other, that is, as a representative of an unrestricted audience in the "communication *between* audience and speaker".[107] In this way cosmopolitan law realizes an interconnection among jurisdictions.

As a result of this overall argument, it appears that the gap is closed between (a) the assumptions of a rightful cosmopolitan condition from which the cosmopolitan right to visit is legitimately enforced, (b) a specific content-related claim submitted by a visitor, and (c) a domestically defined context of public use of reason (following a "constitutional mindset"[108] as Koskenniemi defines the thinking of Kant's 'moral politician'). Integration between these three levels allows for the transnationalization of domestic public legal standards. This process completes what I have referred in the opening sections as the second part of the Kantian juridical aspect of cosmopolitan constructivism.

As observed, the outcome of the construction of a cosmopolitan public sphere by the public use of reason, while necessary and valuable, should not be regarded as the end point of Kantian cosmopolitan concerns. It is rather the *juridification* of the global public sphere that, ultimately, brings about a lawful condition between citizens and foreign states among themselves, as well as between domestic citizens. As Kant says: "The problem of establishing a perfect civil constitution

105 On the contextualization of some of these problems in the contemporary world see T. Pogge, *World Poverty and Human Rights*, Polity Press, Cambridge, 2008.

106 "Publicity has a limiting effect upon all strategic actions, both within states and between states. In the *First Appendix* to *Perpetual Peace*, Kant subjects political strategies to tests of publicity alone: if many maxims of political expediency are publicly acknowledged, they cannot attain their own purpose." In Bohman, "The Public Spheres", p. 182.

107 Bohman, "The Public Spheres", p. 184.

108 The relevant passage is Kant, "Toward Perpetual Peace (1795)", 8:370, p. 338. On this point see Koskenniemi, "Constitutionalism as a Mindset", p. 9 ff.

is dependent on the problem of a lawful external relation between states and cannot be solved without the latter."[109] Here is the link with the law: in so far as standards of public reasoning are reflected in domestic constitutionalism, the incorporation of new interactional claims gives rise to further codifications in compliance with the general principles of public law. This time, though, such norms reflect an external – cosmopolitan – perspective, filling the gap between domestic and international law. Whereas national constitutional law may be seen as the product of a domestic constituent power – a sovereign people – the cosmopolitan constitution results from a more fundamental source of legitimacy: the common possession of the Earth.

Kant seems to suggest that the construction of a cosmopolitan constitution is to be conceived along the lines of global citizenship and civil society as when he states that "the condition of peace is alone that condition in which what is mine and what is yours for a multitude of human beings is secured under *laws* living in proximity to one another, hence those who are *united under a constitution* [emphasis added]".[110] More precisely, the cosmopolitan legitimacy of the state as a subject within the international order is the result of two intersecting parameters: national constituent sovereignties for self-legislating peoples and global citizenship. For Kant, this condition is far from being unrealizable. However, if peace has to be preserved as a realizable aspiration, then, it has also to be achieved through counterfactual-regulative conditions. As Kant argues in the *Metaphysics of Morals* "we must act *as if* it [perpetual peace] is something real, though perhaps it is not; we must work toward establishing perpetual peace and *the kind of constitution* that seems to us most conducive to it (say, a republicanism of all states, together and separately) [emphasis added]".[111] For Kant, the time seemed ripe to conceive a "realistic Utopia"[112] to gain momentum.

I have proposed a constructivist interpretation of Kant's cosmopolitanism. To this end I have claimed that the right to visit represents a formalization of right-interactions among members of an original community of *commercium*. In so far as cosmopolitan right requires the justification of political decision making and territorial boundaries, it gives rise to the need for mechanisms of constitutional coordination among individuals, peoples, and states. A hierarchy of legal principles, equal protections and constraints on hegemonic states are just a few of the features relevant here.

Kantian cosmopolitan constitutionalism includes innovative elements with respect to his natural law tradition as well as to constitutional theory as such. It not only envisages a form of cosmopolitan constitution without a state, wherein the idea of a progression under the guidance of a multistate confederation (*Völkerstaat*) becomes apparent, but it also argues for a form of world citizenship without world sovereignty, one where the cosmopolitan point of view gives rise

109 Kant, "Universal History", 8:24, p. 114.
110 Kant, "Metaphysics of Morals (1797)", 6:355, p. 491.
111 Ibid.
112 The expression is taken from Rawls, *Law of Peoples*, p. 4 ff.

to a critical stance against an ultimate assimilation to a *de facto* constituency from the perspective of an *a priori* authority. It is not only the case that constitutional progression is part of the Kantian vision of a regulative function based on the cosmopolitan ideal of an original shared possession of the Earth but also, and more importantly, that the obstinate commitment to the idea of freedom as independence is not only an internal domestic resource but also a cosmopolitan liberty limited to the right to be heard in another jurisdiction.

There is a way in which great thinkers remain contemporary. This is by virtue of a continuous reinterpretation of their ideas in light of presently unsolved challenges. It is in this sense that Kant's cosmopolitan theory is relevant for guiding our contemporary reflections on the standards of legitimacy of international law. For Kant, valid law should reflect an ideal of moral freedom. Following on from this premise, public right generates a rightful condition – a constitution (*constitutio*) – at both state and international level. For Kant, public right enhances freedom not only within the state, that is, internally and in the form of domestic right (civil constitutional law), but also externally through international right – *ius gentium*. The innovative nature of Kant's thinking, as it seems, is that he claims that international law should be supplemented by one further component, one regulating primarily relations between non-citizens and states. This is the right to visit or what Kant calls also the "right to hospitality".[113] Arguably, the constitutional effects of such a right should by now be clear.

113 Kant, "Toward Perpetual Peace (1795)", 8:357, p. 328.

§10 Thinking with Kant 'beyond' Kant

Actualizing sovereignty and citizenship in the transnational sphere

The Kantian view on the legitimacy of the state cannot be disembodied from the international and cosmopolitan dimension of public law. Yet, *prima facie*, these sources of obligation generate a dialectical tension between the domestic right of state-citizens (*citoyens*)[1] and the cosmopolitan level of the right of peoples as a "*right of citizens of the world*" (*Weltbürgerrecht*)[2] or as a right of the "citizens of the earth" (*das Recht des Erdbürgers*).[3] If the state is sovereign, then its will must be autonomous. This means that at the risk of losing their sovereignty, states cannot be coerced by a heteronomous will – neither internally by an independent force, such as a revolutionary power, nor externally by an internationally independent body, as in the case of a supra-ordinate sovereignty. For Kant, however, law requires coercion, and since international and cosmopolitan rights are two of the three pillars of public law, they are enforceable rights. This conundrum is known as Kant's sovereignty dilemma.[4]

Kant uses the terms *Herrschergewalt* and *Souveränität* to define sovereignty as something primarily linked to legislative authority.[5] For Kant, sovereignty requires

1 As Kant defines this: "He who has the right to vote in this legislation is called a *citizen* (*citoyen*, i.e., *citizen of a state,* not of a town, *bourgeois*)". In Kant, "On the Common Saying", 8:295, p. 295. Alternatively, he uses "*citizens of a state (cives)*", Kant, "Metaphysics of Morals (1797)", 6:314, p. 457.

2 Kant, "Toward Perpetual Peace (1795)", note *, 8:349, p. 322. The same expression occurs again in Kant, "Metaphysics of Morals (1797)", 6:353, p. 489.

3 I. Kant, "Metaphysische Anfangsgründe der Rechtslehre", O. Eberl und P. Niesen (comm. and eds.), *Immanuel Kant Zum ewigen Frieden*, Suhrkamp, Berlin, 2011 [1797], 6:353, p. 84. Kant also uses the expression "*das Recht der Oberfläche*" ("the right to the *earth's surface*"). In Kant, "Toward Perpetual Peace (1795)", 8:358, p. 329. The expression "*der Weltbürgergesellschaft*" ("the society of the citizens of the world") is used in Kant, "An Answer to the Question", 8:37, p. 18. Finally, yet another formula is used by Kant with "a *man of the world* (or citizen of the world generally)". In Kant, "On the Common Saying", 8:277, p. 281.

4 See Flikschuh, "Kant's Sovereignty Dilemma", p. 471.

5 See Kant, "Metaphysics of Morals (1797)", 6:312, p. 457, note "h". Notice also Kant's distinction between the "form *(forma imperii)*" namely 'who' has the power, if one, few, or many and the "form of government (*forma regiminis*)", that is, whether "*republican* or *despotic*" according to whether it follows a division of powers or not.

holding exclusive legislative functions: states cannot be externally coerced. This would violate the Kantian republican principle of legitimate coercion, namely the tracking of state sovereignty to an ultimate constituent will.[6] External coercion is thus incompatible with state authority as expressed by its constituent source: 'the people'. Kant's sovereignty dilemma thus poses the problem of reconciling states' autonomous will with the duty to comply with international and cosmopolitan obligations.[7] Given his views on sovereignty and enforceability of the law, Kant is not explicit on how and through which institutions states are to comply with international and cosmopolitan standards of the law. Nevertheless, he mentions the "proposal for a universal state of nations [*Völkerstaat*] to whose power all individual states should *voluntarily* accommodate themselves [emphasis added]".[8] Kant wants to give momentum to this apparently utopian project, initially introduced by the Abbé St. Pierre and Rousseau. In particular, Kant aims to provide a reason for compliance by those states determined to "never submit to coercive laws of this kind"[9] as well as their unified stand on one single "rational ground",[10] so that what "holds for theory [holds also] for practice".[11]

As referred to by the previous section it is here, however, that the problem lies. Thus, how can one reconcile this sort of divide? Kant suggests assuming a certain practical attitude, one considering that "such a universal state of nations [. . .] is possible (*in praxi*) and that it *can be*".[12] It appears here as if the theory-practice divide is solved by assuming, cognitively, the *possibility* of such unity from the state perspective. What this means is that if states *must* comply with the coercive demands of international and cosmopolitan law, then they *can* do so only by assuming a regulative role for the coercive power that an international institution (i.e. the universal state of nations), would exercise on its members. States adopt laws, judicial decisions, etc. issued by a supra-ordinate political entity only 'as if' they were externally coerced to do so. In fact, however, they maintain an always actionable opting-out reservation in regard to the demands of an international body. Suppose that international obligations are regulated and enforceable. This means that states' compliance with the commands of an external agency would occur 'as if' there was an external enforcement. In fact, though, actual enforceability is left to states' exercises of sovereign will and to their understanding of the compulsory character of non-domestic law in regulative terms.

In this fashion, I consider that Kant has manoeuvring space to conceive of the possibility for states to conform to the constitutional cosmopolitan demands adjudicated by a transnational institution such as a court of arbitration. Nevertheless, in all these cases it would remain true that none of the organs of a

6 Kant, "Metaphysics of Morals (1797)", 6:221, p. 376.
7 Flikschuh, "Kant's Sovereignty Dilemma", p. 471.
8 Kant, "On the Common Saying:", 8:313, p. 309.
9 Ibid.
10 Ibid.
11 Ibid.
12 Ibid.

transnational institution would be allowed to seek states' compliance by threat of legitimate punishment. Compliance, instead, would remain in the hands of the states themselves.

If this interpretive hypothesis is sound, then it also becomes possible to explain why Kant is in the position to maintain the idea that states will never give up their sovereignty, as well as accounting for the likelihood for their practices to be understood as advancing a global rule of law, as with the case of approximation to a universal state of nations. The 'drama' of an insoluble conflict of duties would be in such a way diffused. To be sure, there is here no logical contradiction between duties to comply with the commands of a state's sovereign will, and obedience to the commands of an international or cosmopolitan norm externally issued. As far as such order obligates in a regulative manner, enforceability requires a state's incorporation of an international or cosmopolitan standpoint 'as if' the supranational juridical order to which it belongs were directly enforceable.

Accordingly, the thesis I defend consists in identifying a regulative role for the ideal of peace towards which public international and cosmopolitan law approximate. Whereas nature for Kant provides us with the idea of a general compatibility of such mechanisms with the possibility of peace, it is only by striving morally towards peace that we might hope to achieve moral progress. Similarly, Guyer considers that the "morally motivated acts of human will"[13] complete the Kantian picture of a cosmopolitan progression which nature alone makes simply possible but not necessary. The regulative force of peace is therefore of relevance to establish the duty of the moral politician to comply with the demands of practical reason. However, as my argument goes, the moral striving towards human progression turns into the constitutionalization of interstate relations. It is the legal point which in the end interests Kant. The difference is subtle but crucial: states' motivating reasons for compliance are based on moral reason, but the reason for other state parties to create a federation to coerce is law. That is, it is because a member state violates interstate agreements (and not just the morality of such agreements), that other parties have a legal right to intervene.[14] Furthermore, in the second appendix, Kant argues that politics and morality can be reconciled among themselves only through *publicity*, and that conversely, any maxims that "*need* publicity (in order not to fail in the end) harmonize with right and politics combined".[15] This point also helps to clarify some institutional aspects of Kant's cosmopolitan project, such as the apparently enigmatic sentences of *Toward Perpetual Peace* in which Kant asserts that the realization of a *civitas gentium* (*Völkerstaat*) does not match what nations want: "they do not at all want this".[16] To argue this view, Kant draws a distinction between what is ideally right ("*in thesi*"), and what states actually reject ("*in hypothesi*").[17]

13 See Guyer, *Kant on Freedom*, p. 413.
14 For a different view on this see Guyer, *Kant on Freedom*, p. 422.
15 Kant, "Toward Perpetual Peace (1795)", 8:386, p. 351.
16 Kant, "Toward Perpetual Peace (1795)", 8:357, p. 328.
17 Ibid.

Several readings of this passage have been suggested. All in all, one can distinguish between two groups: those considering that states would never allow for external interference – so that only a non-coercive league of states would be admissible – and those considering that states would eventually embrace a global confederation, such as the universal state of peoples or, as I prefer to translate, the multistate confederation (*Völkerstaat*). Whereas the first group expresses a liberal internationalist view *à la* Rawls,[18] the second is typical of cosmopolitan theories *à la* Held or, in line with present interpretive purposes, of Kleingeld's interpretation of Kant.[19]

Liberal internationalists consider from their perspective that, in so far as democracies do not wage war with one another, this suffices to bring about international peace. Kleingeld, instead, holds that the Kantian starting assumption of a 'no analogy' thesis between the domestic and the international realm does not prevent cosmopolitan approximation and, with that, the realization of a multistate confederation (*Völkerstaat*). Differently from individuals who can be coerced to exit the state of nature even "through the *force of law*" [*Gewalt*],[20] sovereign states cannot be obliged to do so. Coercion to enter a multistate confederation would infringe upon "people's autonomy"[21] and self-determination. Accordingly, it would create a relation of subordination of an "inferior (the people obeying the laws)"[22] to a "superior (the legislator)"[23] ultimately leading to a contradiction between the 'presupposition' of international law and that of a universal state of peoples. At face value, this would also prevent the possibility of conceiving of a *plurality* of self-legislating states, such as that arising from the departure of a lawless condition characterizing the original state of nature.[24]

Kleingeld considers that the multistate confederation is a realizable ideal, even if one that is difficult to achieve. It is an ideal that can be reached starting from a league of states.[25] Coherently with such a rationale, Kleingeld aims to solve the sovereignty dilemma by claiming that for Kant a "global federation of states"[26] requires at some point a "transfer of external sovereignty".[27] The

18 Rawls, *Law of Peoples*.

19 Kleingeld, "Approaching Perpetual Peace", pp. 304–325. I prefer to translate "*Völkerstaat*" as "the multistate federation".

20 "each may impel the other through *force of law* [*Gewalt*] to leave this state and enter into a rightful condition", emphasis added on modified translation of Kant, "Metaphysics of Morals (1797)", [6:312], p. 456. In support of the reading of the term "*Gewalt*" as "force of law, ius", consider Grimms' dictionary on this entry. In Jacob and Wilhelm Grimm, *Deutsches Wörterbuch*, Bd.6Sp.4910–5095. In my reading of Kant, the exit from an original condition by formation of a generally united will justifies a reading of "*Gewalt*" as a legitimate use of power/authority rather than as unjustified brutal force.

21 Kleingeld, "Approaching Perpetual Peace", p. 310.

22 Kleingeld, "Approaching Perpetual Peace", p. 312.

23 Ibid.

24 Kant, "Toward Perpetual Peace (1795)", 8:354, p. 325.

25 Kleingeld, "Approaching Perpetual Peace", p. 314.

26 Kleingeld, "Approaching Perpetual Peace", p. 313.

27 Ibid.

problem, however, is that for Kant, sovereignty as the capacity to enforce the law is indivisible. The solution envisaged by Kleingeld would be feasible only if it were the case for Kant that a new notion of sovereignty would eventually replace the old one in the future. Unfortunately, Kant at no point suggests this possibility. We are thus left with the sovereignty dilemma unsolved.

The alternative reading, the one I have offered here, is that control of law enforcement by state parties does not prevent conditional delegation of authority to a transnational body in the form of a state-proxy authority. The conditionality of authority transfer here means that states always remain the ultimate subjects to exercise authority upon their territory, that is, to decide whether to enforce or not the commands issued by international bodies.

Let us take the case of international adjudication. What is conditionally delegated by states, in this instance, is an adjudicative *competence* that is useful to solve rather complex international issues involving two or more states. However, this requires no actual delegation of sovereign powers as with, for instance, disrupting forces for the "*monopoly of legitimate physical violence* within a certain territory"[28] – to use a Weberian definition. Enforcement of decisions remains to be ultimately interpreted and implemented by an act of will of the state. It follows that the conditional transferring of authority leaves the ultimacy of state sovereignty as well as of its power unity unchanged. I explain this point with reference to Kelsen's distinction between 'direct' and 'indirect motivation' of states for compliance with the law. Even though this explanation is far from being Kantian in a strict sense, one might take this account as strengthening Kant's view. Kelsen argues that the coerciveness of the law is not guaranteed only by the threat of punishment (indirect motivation). In addition, "voluntary obedience is itself a form of motivation, that is, of coercion, and hence is not freedom".[29] For Kelsen, one can conceive of coercion simply "in the psychological sense".[30] Differences arise with regard to the *efficiency* wherever an institutional apparatus lacks a sanctioning system. If one now substitutes Kelsen's 'psychological' character for self-coercion with a properly Kantian 'morally' motivating character of the law, then it becomes possible to understand why for Kant compliance with international law requirements is in need of a 'constitutional mindset'. This is yet another step in the construction of an argument for states' compliance with international law.

§10.1 'Constitutional mindset' and the progression towards cosmopolitan peace

These reflections provide a supply of arguments for interpreting one of the most crucial, as well as puzzling, passages of Kant's cosmopolitan theory: what I have

28 M. Weber, "The Profession and Vocation of Politics", P. Lassman and R.Speirs (eds.), *Political Writings*, Cambridge University Press, Cambridge, 2002, p. 311.

29 H. Kelsen, *General Theory of Law and State*, Harvard University Press, Cambridge, Mass., 2007 [1945], p. 19.

30 Ibid.

mentioned before with the distinction in *Toward Perpetual Peace* of what is right in theory (*in thesi*) – as in the case of the institutionalization of the universal state of peoples – and what is right in practice (*in hypothesi*) – as exemplified by the federation of states as a "*negative* surrogate of a *league*".[31]

What my interpretation suggests is that the move from the league of states does not allow for a *positive* instantiation of a universal state of peoples. The *Völkerstaat* understood as either a universal state of peoples, or as I prefer, in terms of a multistate confederation, can never be for Kant something empirically realizable from the perspective of a state's sovereignty. Instead, only a *regulative function* can be assigned to a model for global coordination of spheres of law among states in their transitional progression towards peace. In the eyes of the states, therefore, the multistate confederation would represent only an 'as if' rule for the coordination of states among themselves on the basis of the presumption of a universally shared jurisdiction.

In *Appendix I* of *Toward Perpetual Peace*, Kant explains why there is a connection between morality and politics and why morality as such constrains meaningful projects for political action.[32] Kant claims that if there were an irreconcilable conflict between theory and practice, between what we are required to do by the moral imperative and what we are in fact capable of doing in practice, this would amount "to deny[ing] that there is a [doctrine of] morals at all".[33] If we could not act in accordance with moral demands, any use of politics would become a legitimate means for advancing expediency and self-interest. This point is captured by the distinction Kant draws between the "moral politician",[34] i.e., "one who takes the principles of political prudence in such a way that they can coexist with morals",[35] and "the political moralist",[36] i.e., one "who frames a moral to suit the statesman's advantage".[37]

On the one hand, the moral politician sees the subordination of political action and legal reforms to the duties of morality. On the other hand, the political moralist disguises his personal advantage in moral terms and "on the pretext that human nature is not capable of what is good in accord with that idea".[38] Unlike the moral politician, the political moralist sees the cosmopolitan project in terms of a "*technical problem* (*problema technicum*)",[39] and perpetual peace as simply the result of the adaptation of morality to political advantage. According to the latter perspective, it is based on states' interests and in view of a cost/benefit analysis that solutions to international problems are to be sought. Kant rejects this possibility, and in the concluding paragraphs of *Appendix I* of *Toward Perpetual*

31 Kant, "Toward Perpetual Peace (1795)", 8:357, p. 328.
32 Kant, "Toward Perpetual Peace (1795)", 8:370–8:380, pp. 338–347.
33 Kant, "Toward Perpetual Peace (1795)", p. 338.
34 Ibid.
35 Ibid.
36 Ibid.
37 Ibid.
38 Kant, "Toward Perpetual Peace (1795)", 8:373, p. 341.
39 Kant, "Toward Perpetual Peace (1795)", 8:377, p. 344.

Peace, he declares that: "The right of human beings must be held sacred, however great a sacrifice this may cost the ruling power",[40] alluding to a non-managerial interpretation of the significance of the law in view of its non-instrumental value. It follows that when confronted with the question of how to construct the cosmopolitan project, the moral politician interprets this as a moral task. Nevertheless, such a task does not end, in my view, in a merely moral endeavour as Guyer has argued.[41] It leads instead to the establishment of a global rule of law, and thus to *the cosmopolitan constitution* which provides for the ordering of the sources of international law in relation to itself.[42] This moral striving of the suitable political arena that Kant presents us lays down the preconditions for the construction of a cosmopolitan rule of law. For Kant, this also means that constitutional thinking represents an instance of practical reasoning. It concerns the process of unification of public international law by means of compliance with a cosmopolitan ideal. As Kant states in the fourth thesis of Idea: "*nature employs in order to bring about the development of all their predispositions* [. . .] *their* ***antagonism*** *in society, insofar as the latter is in the end the cause of their lawful order*".[43] The lack of sociability depicted here by the word 'antagonism' gives rise to the need for domestication through the enforcement of valid laws. This process should take place not only among individuals per se and within domestic borders, but also among states engaged in warfare or aggressive behaviour (i.e. through colonization). A "cosmopolitan condition"[44] (*weltbürgerlicher Zustand*) must be instantiated, one in which a global rule of law is realized through a cosmopolitan "right to visit".[45]

With regard to Kleingeld's interpretation of the unwillingness of states to comply with transnational demands of reason, the hypothesis of a Kantian transfer of 'slices of sovereignty' to a hierarchically supra-ordinate institution, even if a federated one, appears counterintuitive. This differs from the case of the transferring of competences for interstate coordination, where implementation remains ultimately in the hands of states themselves. Transferring of adjudicative competences, for instance, can always be claimed back by states even when this might result in a breach of law. Furthermore, the potential contradiction between the dissolution of state sovereignty and the persistence of international law is diffused by a division of labour throughout dispersed juridical sources. The division between domestic and transnational adjudicative sources thus bears no substantive effect on the unity of state sovereignty as such.[46] This reading requires a corollary, namely, the idea that for Kant cosmopolitan peace represents a regulative

40 Kant, "Toward Perpetual Peace (1795)", 8:381, p. 347.
41 See Guyer, *Kant on Freedom*, p. 408 ff.
42 Kant, "Toward Perpetual Peace (1795)", 8:358, p. 329. See also Kant, "On the Common Saying:", 8:310, p. 307.
43 Kant, "Universal History", 8:27, p. 111.
44 Ibid.
45 Kant, "Toward Perpetual Peace (1795)", 8:358, p. 329.
46 This is my reading of the expression "Da sie dieses aber nach ihrer Idee vom Völkerrecht durchaus nicht wollen ". In Kant, *Zum ewigen Frieden*, 2011 [1795], 8:357, p. 29.

ideal rather than being a constitutive notion.[47] It orients stages of approximations without proposing an 'either/or' standard for legal validity. Kant's regulative function for the multistate confederation offers, therefore, a precise understanding of the validity of institutional decision making and adjudication. Overall, it provides a criterion for defining the formal unity of the law.

A further speculation on what Kant might have had in mind when sketching the institutional progressions toward perpetual peace would also consider the significance of the distinction between compulsory and non-compulsory jurisdiction. As referred to initially, for Kant right is defined by its coerciveness and coercion which, in turn, requires an enforcing agent. Thus, the dilemma of sovereignty is not solved by simply avoiding a state's delegation of legislative functions. In addition, it must tackle the problem of law coerciveness. In this case, it also seems that Kant holds a view based on *progressive stages* of legal coercion. At the end of *Toward Perpetual Peace*, indeed, he observes that "public right [. . .] must proceed from some kind of pact, which need not (like that from which a state arises) be based on coercive laws but may, if necessary, be a condition of *continuing free* association, like that of the federalism [. . .]".[48]

In the case of transnational adjudication, the problem turns into how to ground obedience to a judicial decision issued by an international body. If sovereignty is to retain any significance at all, it has to require state-consent. As we know, there are two purposes for demanding consent, either in view of compulsory or in view of non-compulsory forms of jurisdiction.[49]

Whereas compulsory forms demand that states enforce the law without a renewal of their consent once this has been initially granted, non-compulsory mechanisms conceive interstate arbitration as requiring a renewal of state consent each time. In either case, a state's refusal to comply with the law raises complex issues of international legal enforcement, but it does not set aside the duty to comply.

How does the distinction between compulsory and non-compulsory jurisdiction help in understanding Kant's sovereignty dilemma? One might argue that for Kant a non-compulsory form of adjudication would be compatible with the unwillingness of states to subordinate to supranational law-enforcing bodies. In this way, both coerciveness of the law as well as state sovereignty would be saved by admitting self-enforcement.

Under the regulative rationale for a progressive instantiation of perpetual peace, one would also consider that Kant would place a shift from non-compulsory to compulsory forms of transnational adjudication. Let us recall

47 See H. Arendt, *Lectures on Kant's Political Philosophy*, R. Beiner (ed.), The University of Chicago Press, Chicago, Ill., 1992.

48 Kant, "Toward Perpetual Peace (1795)", 8:383, p. 349.

49 See in this regard the groundbreaking work by K. Alter on the compulsory jurisdiction of international courts and their transformation of international law, in K. Alter, *The New Terrain of International Law. Courts, Politics and Rights*, Princeton University Press, Princeton and Oxford, 2014.

Kant's three-step leeway starting from an unbound Hobbesian conception of international relations and progressing towards forms of interstate relations under an inclusive rule of law. As recalled earlier, Kant mentions the case of the beginning of the eighteenth century, of the assembly of the States General at the Hague, the *permanent congress of states* [*Kongreß*], where "each neighbouring state is at liberty to join".[50] This represents a weak form of association since it lacks a constitution, and therefore, it "can be *dissolved* at any time".[51] Nevertheless, Kant recognizes that it plays a significant role in allowing the possibility for states to introduce "the idea of a public right of nations"[52] so as to allow states to solve their disputes "by a lawsuit, rather than in a barbaric way".[53] As starting points of departure, both the congress and the league of states contribute to the construction of a domestic cosmopolitan mindset. This constitutes the premise for a higher degree of state interdependence, something that would eventually lead to compulsory mechanisms of transnational adjudication. Whereas the first two phases, the congress and the league of states, are characterized by non-compulsory jurisdiction, it is only starting from the progression towards the third phase that states conceive the idea of compulsory judicial deferral to international courts. We know nowadays what such mechanisms are, an example being the *European Convention of Human Rights* and its judicial organ, the Strasbourg Court.

Indeed, even if coercion cannot be demanded by states, certainly a form of moral suasion appears to be possible, as when Kant claims that states "can and ought to require the others to enter [. . .] into a constitution similar to a civil constitution, in which each can be assured of its right. This would be a *league of nations*, which, however, need not be a state of nations".[54] Since states already do grant themselves an internal rule of law, if it holds true that internal enjoyment depends partially on the enforcement of external legal conditions, then this should also be established *among* states themselves.[55] Ergo, it appears that citizens should want, at least because of prudential reasons, to exit an interstate lawless condition by complying with a cosmopolitan rule of law.

This element also explains why Kant perceives the formation of a league of states (*Völkerbund*) as feasible, even if suboptimal, without the additional consideration

50 Kant, "Metaphysics of Morals (1797)", 6:350, p. 487.
51 Kant, "Metaphysics of Morals (1797)", 6:351, p. 488.
52 Ibid.
53 Ibid.
54 Kant, "Toward Perpetual Peace (1795)", 8:354, p. 326.
55 On the partial analogy between individuals and states see A. Ripstein: "The absence of arguments from coercion and assurance, and the corresponding absence of public law and coercive enforcement, reflect two differences between states and private persons. The first difference is that as Kant understands states. The second difference is that a state is a public rightful condition. The public nature of the state limits the purposes for which it can act to those that are properly public, that is, sustaining its own character as a rightful condition" (p. 228) and also "If the only source of conflict in a state of nature between states is generated by the indeterminacy of the right to self-defence, then the solution is a partial analogue if a civil condition, but not a civil condition as such" (p. 229). In Ripstein, *Force and Freedom*, 2009.

that the lack of an international confederation of states (*Völkerstaat*) would compromise the project of cosmopolitan peace. Furthermore, one might think that a non-compulsory form of dispute settlement would serve the purpose of overcoming a lawless scenario by 'enlightening' and 'educating' states, as it were, to solve interstate disagreements through law (by means of a legal process). This would cohere with the general Kantian view on the regulative role that the ideal peace would have with regard to history as a learning process.[56]

I propose, accordingly, to understand this point through an argument based on regulative analogy. This allows an explanation of the shift that appears in Kant between the *Metaphysics of Morals*, where he separates the power to constrain unwilling people to enter a civil condition from the possibility of coercing states, and the more conciliatory position he holds in *On the Common Saying*, where he draws an analogy between these two spheres. In this latter writing, indeed, Kant claims that as individuals enter into a *civil constitution* due to the insecurity of an "omnilateral violence",[57] for the same reasons (due to "omnilateral violence and the need arising from it [states]) states even against their will"[58] will eventually "enter into a *cosmopolitan constitution*; or else [. . .] a *federation*".[59] The entering into a transnational civil condition is here justified on the basis of a 'need' and not on deliberate coercion conducted by a transnational power. Therefore, Kant does not seem to have changed his mind with regard to the self-motivating character of the authority of states when incorporating, domestically, transnational legal standards. What remains permanently available is compliance with an *a priori*, adjudicative, and united will as a premise for grounding a general cosmopolitan condition of the law.

According to the regulative analogy I propose, the political will of cosmopolitan citizens is grounded not only on the compulsory entrance of individuals into the civil state, but also on the political request to their states for *voluntary* inclusion in a cosmopolitan rule of law. It is indeed from the presumption of a general *political will* compelling a move towards a juridical condition that each citizen of the world would *also* want the enactment of a cosmopolitan rule of law. As in domestic constitutions "the well-being of a state is understood [as] that condition in which its constitution conforms most fully to principles of right".[60] Similarly, one could argue that compliance of constitutions with standards of reason represents "that condition which reason, *by a categorical imperative*, makes it obligatory for us to strive after".[61]

Based on these assumptions, it is not difficult to imagine, therefore, that the demand for enjoyment of the cosmopolitan right to visit would pave the way to the enhancement of domestic public *fora*.[62] Here the *citoyens*, once having

56 Kant, "Universal History", pp. 107–120. See on this Guyer, *Kant on Freedom*, p. 425 ff.
57 Kant, "On the Common Saying:", 8:310–8:311, pp. 307–308.
58 Ibid.
59 Ibid.
60 Kant, "Metaphysics of Morals (1797)", 6:318, p. 461.
61 Ibid.
62 Kant, "Toward Perpetual Peace (1795)", 8:358, p. 329.

shifted their thinking to earth citizenship, would likely raise demands for the formation of a league of states (*Völkerbund*), and then request entrance to compulsory forms of jurisdictions 'as if' they were members of a multistate confederation (*Völkerstaat*). The projection of a state's self-contained civil condition into a transnational plane does not exhaust the domestic sovereign capacity of states to remain ultimate "self-enforce[rs] of [. . .] international obligations".[63] Nevertheless, the implementation of an international decision should not be conflated with the autonomy and the compulsory force of an international adjudicative institution.

What ensues from this process is the undertaking of a further step, one in which Kant's state-subjective anticipation of a community of earth citizens is followed by a *conditional* delegation of authority to a transnational body with compulsory adjudicative functions. This is the most significant shift in contemporary international adjudication, and while it was still far from realization in Kant's time, it was certainly not inconceivable.

For Kant, there is no shortcut to the achievement of a legitimate order, one derogating from compliance with both an internal and external standard of legitimacy. This means that no solution is available in the direction of a centralized institutional system, neither republic nor monarchy. Both options are to be excluded because they are empirically unrealizable or normatively undesirable.[64] Transition, instead, should be sought starting from a weak congress of states (*Kongreß*) and progressing towards a league of states (*Foedus Pacificum*). Finally, the advancement into jurisdictional structures would occur under the counterfactual guidance of a multistate confederation (*Völkerstaat*).

In the absence of further institutional details, it remains problematic to identify in Kant the alternatives to the realization of the co-dependence of all states and peoples under a common legislation.[65] However, what Kant indicates here is that the cosmopolitan constitution backed up by a regulative multistate confederation is an arrangement of a particular kind: one that needs to be appropriate to the goal that it serves; namely, the achievement of perpetual peace. Yet the movement on the progressive advancement of compulsory adjudication does not elicit the idea of a form of adjudicative pluralism, that is, the possible coexistence of compulsory and non-compulsory forms of adjudication within a single cosmopolitan framework.

In this way, state sovereignty is saved and, with that, the formal unity of the legal system. Indeed, such unity does not require a global institutional hierarchy. On the contrary, it is compatible with institutional heterarchy, or the recognition of a relative autonomy of adjudicative bodies understood in terms of functional specialization. Since the unity of the global system of law is conceived in counterfactual terms, there is no logical contradiction between global constitutional pluralism as the idea of a plurality of constitutional sources and the view of a

63 See Flikschuh, *Kant and Modern Political Philosophy*, p. 488.
64 Ibid.
65 Kant, "Toward Perpetual Peace (1795)", 8:349–350, p. 322.

formal unity of law. It follows that in the case of constitutional disagreement, there would always remain open the possibility to resort to interstate arbitration as a way to identify who is the legitimate subject of authority.[66] Given such an institutional trajectory, the question arises as to how it is possible to instantiate a cosmopolitan rule of law in the absence of a world state.[67]

As Byrd and Hruschka observe, Kant's move from a state of nature to a juridical condition first requires the postulation of a form of *iustitia commutativa* – the type of justice connected to the public market as a realm of free interactions[68] – something also realizable outside of a statehood framework.[69] However, this asks for the establishment of an interstate rule of law which would regulate property outside states' jurisdictional domain and in the absence of a world state. The regulation of the market in accordance with a general principle of right would thus have to take place counterfactually, 'as if' occurring within the jurisdiction of an international state confederation. Second, in the progression of states towards a cosmopolitan condition, incremental demands of "possible commerce"[70] are achievable only as elements of public law-giving. This could take place only in the absence of a transnationally centralized legislative power. Such a second requirement is, indeed, what Kant defines as *iustitia tutatrix*: a public law-giving process protecting rights. This is subjected to public enforceability–what Kant calls *iustitia distributiva* – and only when framed in terms of global public justice can it also be administered by an impartial arbiter, something resembling an international court of arbitration.

Once the above framework is assumed as a plausible interpretation of what Kant might agree with for the definition of the legitimacy conditions of the transnational realm, how would coordination problems among members of a federation be solved? How should one conceive forms of coercive powers exercised within a transnational entity in accordance with Kant's principles, and particularly with a 'thick' conception of state sovereignty? Perhaps a few features can be sketched. An international court operating under the regulation of Kant's cosmopolitan constitution could authorize the use of force against a member or a non-member of the federation. Yet, no state member of the transnational

66 The type of model for global sovereignty and constitutionalism that my suggested reading of Kant implies, therefore, is closer to M. Kumm's cosmopolitan pluralism than to J. Cohen's "constitutionalist pluralist conception" constructed on a dualist notion of sovereignty. In J. Cohen, *Globalization and Sovereignty. Rethinking Legality, Legitimacy and Constitutionalism*, Cambridge University Press, New York, 2012, p. 66. With regard to Kumm's pluralist theory of global constitutionalism, see M. Kumm, "Who is the Final Arbiter of Constitutionality in Europe?", *Common Market Law Review*, 36, 1999, pp. 509–514.

67 See on this point Habermas, "The Constitutionalization of International Law", pp. 109–130 as well as the debate between W.E. Scheuerman and H. Brunkhorst, respectively: W.E. Scheuerman, "All Power to the (State-less?) General Assembly!", *Constellations*, 15(4), 2008 and H. Brunkhorst, "State and Constitutions – A Reply to Scheuerman", *Constellations*, 15(4), 2008, pp. 493–501.

68 Kant, "Metaphysics of Morals (1797)", 6:306, p. 450.

69 On this see Byrd and Hruschka, *Kant's Doctrine of Right*, p. 211.

70 Kant, "Metaphysics of Morals (1797)", 6:352, p. 489.

entity could be obliged to comply with such a command since this would violate the autonomy of its sovereignty. Therefore, as each of the member states could only enter the transnational confederation of states voluntarily, similarly it could only voluntarily fulfil the commands of an international adjudicator. Whatever a state decided upon to comply with such a decision, it would act in accordance with a rightful coercion, one conceived in accordance with the laws and treaties of a transnational federation. This means that within this Kantian picture, there remains an unsolved tension: one between the non-enforceability on member states of a lawful transnational decision, on the one hand, and the mandatory compliance with transnational adjudications, on the other. This implies that, as sovereignty would be infringed upon if states were compelled to punish another state for non-compliance with a transnational command, similarly, a state's non-compliance with judicial decisions would represent a violation of the transnational law of the federation. In other words, it would manifest, illegitimately, the will of the state to withdraw from the obligations set out by the transnational entity, lacking authorization by the other members, and thus legitimizing a war against it. In conclusion, given this characterization of law, whereas international entities cannot by themselves constrain member states to comply, for Kant this role could be performed horizontally, so to speak, by co-member states acting on behalf of the whole federation.

§10.2 The 'general united will' as *a priori* idea for the cosmopolitan rule of law

Progressive legal stages of enforceable transnational justice (*iustitia*) require the interplay of a multi-layered conceptual apparatus. Given the notions displayed by Kant, it appears that a number of mediations are realized between: (a) the perspective of individuals both as state-citizens (*citoyens*) as well as citizens of the earth (*Erdbürger*); and (b) the anticipation of a necessary *a priori* authority, as with the idea of a 'common united will'. Finally, (c) the cosmopolitan 'right to visit', resulting from the liberties set forth by both (a) and (b), realizes the jurisdictional unity of the Kantian cosmopolitan constitution, providing a view that accommodates the individual 'at home' in this world. The right to visit brings together constitutional progressions by transforming distant jurisdictions into legally porous wholes.

In the following paragraphs, I discuss the relation between (a) and (b) with regard to the significance of what it means, from the standpoint of state and earth citizenship, to comply with the demands of an *a priori* originally united will.

As anticipated, the legitimacy for states to move towards transnational realms of adjudication and power-sharing relations depends on the presumption of an *a priori* role played by the originally united will. Once individuals progress towards a condition regulated by principles of law, as with the creation of states, a claim to a general united will reappears with regard to the peaceful establishment of interstate relations. State demands for a cosmopolitan rule of law are justified not only by virtue of security threats, but also because international trade undertakings and interstate cooperation require altogether the construction of a cosmopolitan legal framework.

As previously observed, Kant claims that citizens of the earth are the subjects of cosmopolitan rights among which is recognized the right to visit.[71] Furthermore, in identifying the conditions of a "rightful constitution",[72] he considers not only "*the right of citizens of a state*"[73] as well as "*the right of nations*".[74] He also speaks of "the *right of citizens of the world*, in so far as individuals and states, standing in the relation of externally affecting one another, are to be regarded as citizens of a universal state of mankind (*ius cosmopoliticum*)".[75] This bi-directional relation points to a critical tension between natural and positive law in so far as Earth's citizens are defined by the former and states by the latter. For Kant, it appears therefore to be justified to conceive both strands of law as mutually defining planes. It is by such reciprocal determination that external relations among states become regulated by an overarching legal system.

In this light, Kant's explanation of earth citizenship as a form of "citizen[ship] of a universal state of mankind [*allgemeiner Menschenstaat*] (*ius cosmopoliticum*)"[76] can also be interpreted. This is a condition where individual relations are coherent with the notion of a cosmopolitan authority used regulatively – an originally united will – presupposed necessarily *a priori*. By advancing a claim to visit, the citizens of Earth aim at transforming the protectionist strictures of national jurisdictions, ultimately creating the legal conditions for earth citizenship. In this respect, state citizenship as well as earth citizenship qualify as mutually interdependent forms of community affiliation. To be a citizen of the state is also to be a world citizen in so far as both affiliations realize an original right to freedom within a whole of rationalized institutions.

Let me illustrate this point by confronting Kant's position with an opposite view such as Schmitt's constitutional theory.[77] Whereas for Schmitt, modern constitutionalism is characterized by the never pacified antagonism between the primacy of a constituent will (the democratic system) and a constituted power (a rule of law), the Kantian notion of an original *a priori* will stands quite at the opposite end of the spectrum, subordinating democracy to a cosmopolitan rule of law.[78] For Schmitt, the democratic will can never be represented, which he

71 Kant, "Metaphysics of Morals (1797)", 6:352, p. 489 ff.

72 Kant, "Toward Perpetual Peace (1795)", 8:349, p. 322.

73 Ibid.

74 Ibid.

75 Ibid.

76 Ibid.

77 C. Schmitt, *Constitutional Theory*, Duke University Press, Durham, N.C. and London, 2008.

78 As O. Eberl and P. Niesen observe: "In Abwesenheit eines globalen Staatsvolks kann Kant sich für den übergreifenden Verfassungsbegriff nicht auf das in den demokratischen Revolutionen etablierte Prinzip verfassunggebender Volkssouveränität stützen. *Sein Verfassungbegriff für die globale Ordnung ist rechtlich-normative, aber nicht demokratisch* [emphasis added]", O. Eberl and P. Niesen (eds.), *Immanuel Kant Zum ewigen Frieden und Auszüge aus der Rechtslehre*, Suhrkamp, Berlin, 2011[1795], p. 209.

often claims by referring to Rousseau's *Social Contract*.[79] In Schmitt the relation between what comes first, whether the constituent or the constituted will, is inverted with respect to Kant's regulative account. Furthermore, for Schmitt, the constituent will is subordinated to an empirically identifiable constituent power, which is prior. In Kant, in contrast, the (cosmopolitan) general united will is anticipated *a priori* under the idea of an original contract as a rational principle (not as a 'fact'). Kant affirms that if the principle of happiness is rejected as a replacement of the principle of right, then:

> the idea of the social contract would remain in its incontestable authority, not however as a fact (as Danton would have it, apart from which he declares null and void all rights and all property to be found in the actually existing civil constitution) but only as a rational principle for appraising any public rightful constitution.
>
> (I. Kant, "On the Common Saying" 8:302, p. 301)

Next, for Kant the problem becomes one of reconciling states under the premises of a "universal state of nations".[80] Also in the *On the Common Saying*, the reasoning is compatible with that expressed two years later in the *Perpetual Peace*. Indeed, Kant reaffirms here his commitment to the unity of theory and practice cognizant, though, of the impossibility of pretending from the head of states to accept it as a positive entity. Then, how can Kant conclude this essay by affirming that: "What on rational grounds holds for theory also holds for practice"?[81]

The reply, it seems, can be only that the analogy between the domestinc and the cosmopolitan level is adopted *regulatively*, that is, in accordance to the idea of a general will and cosmopolitan contract as a regulative idea of reason.

Through the anticipation of an *a priori* general will, it follows that empirically constituted powers fall into a general concept of unity of a cosmopolitan rule of law. Unlike the Schmittian identitarian seizure of membership,[82] such unity in Kant remains open to critical demands of inclusivity. The "right to visit" testifies to the ineradicable openness of any constituted jurisdiction to the legitimate demands of cosmopolitan interaction. It follows that the concept of a general united will provides reflexive conditions that realize the constitutive unity of the polity by 'means of' and 'of' a collective body.[83]

79 Schmitt, *Constitutional Theory*, p. 272 and 289 ff. and, particularly, p. 300.

80 Kant, "On the Common Saying", 8:313, p. 309.

81 Ibid.

82 Alternatively, in terms of "identity as sameness", see H. Lindahl, "Constituent Power and Reflexive Identity: Towards an Ontology of Collective Selfhood", M. Loughlin and N. Walker (eds.), *The Paradox of Constitutionalism*, Oxford University Press, Oxford, 2007, p. 9.

83 Ibid.

If this interpretation is sound, then Kant's views are incompatible with any attempt to subordinate law to politics. On the contrary, for Kant the *a priori* original will demands a conception of the legal and the political as *united and co-dependent* concepts at the outset.

The Kantian understanding of the *a priori* regulative conditions legitimizing a historically given constituent power also provides for an indication of the debate concerning the self-reflexive character of a constituent collective selfhood.[84] Based on these normative assumptions, the construction of a cosmopolitan constitution is not simply the precipitate of a historically given constituent power as it is in the liberal constitutional processes of national jurisdictions. Unlike domestic social movements of sorts, the ultimately regulative character of cosmopolitan authority places Kant's natural right to visit into a constructivist tension with the positive laws of states. Such tension confronts opposed constituencies, such as an empirically domestic and a cosmopolitan one, out of which springs the notion of earth citizenship.

If this captures Kant's views accurately, a problem arises far beyond a textual exegesis. Indeed, were it the case in Kant of a circular movement between the constituting will of historically self-determined peoples and the notion of a rule of law, then the demands for the transnational legitimacy of an agent ('I') could be assimilated into her acting as a subject representing an *already constituted* will. On the contrary, she could act only based on an *a priori* presumption of cosmopolitan authority of a yet to be constituted collectivity.[85] Such a community, indeed, could never be constituted exhaustively and therefore it could never be represented as a whole. Renewals of claims of cosmopolitan representation unfold over time with none being conclusive.

Representation of a collective will be identified by an act of transnational agency that takes the form of a plural 'We'. The collective 'We', conceived here in terms of a double plural. Indeed, the mediation with the *a priori* originally united will generates the notion of "the right of the citizens of the earth [*das Recht des Erdbürgers*])".[86]

Overall, the formulation of a Kantian argument for the cosmopolitan constitution helps in understanding the problematic relation of representation of a transnational constituent whole. First, it avoids a simplistic dichotomy between presence and representation, as well as between constituent and constituted power.

Regarding the problem of the self-constitution of the political community, one might then wonder how this process helps to bring about democratic-like

84 For a particularly illuminating reconstruction of the debate as well as distinct position see Lindahl, "Constituent Power and Reflexive Identity", pp. 9–24.

85 See on this the passage by H. Kelsen quoted in Lindahl, "Constituent Power and Reflexive Identity", p. 10.

86 I. Kant, "Metaphysische Anfangsgründe der Rechtslehre", O. Eberl and P. Niesen (comm. and eds.), *Immanuel Kant Zum ewigen Frieden*, Suhrkamp, Berlin, 2011 [1797], 6:353, p. 84.

features within the transnational realm. It could be said that, paradoxically, a space for representation remains open when no claim aims at representing the whole – even though it is the case that such a new order is constituted only once a claim of such sort is made.[87] In the Kantian-like argument I propose here, the attempt to replace the whole never exhausts the *a priori* standard set by the originally united will. The authority of the *a priori* general will represents, therefore, an exhortation to societal emancipation by means of creating a progressive cosmopolitan rule of law, which can never pretend to be valid by resorting to an omnicomprehensive appeal 'in the name of humanity', as it were. In this regard, individual cosmopolitan agents neither only represent nor solely constitute the whole of a collectivity. The author of cosmopolitan *acts* of constitution remains therefore external to the same order thereby constituted. Only when cosmopolitan agency avoids objectification in a solidified and constituted rule of law, will earth citizenship as a whole remain open to the demands of an *a priori* cosmopolitan authority (the originally united will), which stands as a critical counterpoint against power domination.

§10.3 Double sovereignties and plural Citizenries: a rejoinder to a (virtual) 'family quarrel' between Kant and Habermas?

Perhaps not surprisingly, the dilemma between transnational sovereignty, constituent power, and transnational democratic legitimacy has been tackled recently by Habermas in his collection of essays published with the title: *The Lure of Technocracy*.[88] Under examination, here, is the relation between a European political identity and its division into national and regional constituencies. Habermas introduces a conceptual pillar of his cosmopolitan theory that goes under the notion of "double sovereignty".[89] This is the idea of a "form of sovereignty divided *at the root*"[90] which accounts for the legitimate transferring of authority from the national to the transnational level.[91] From this notion, it follows that a dialectical movement is unleashed between "*constituted components*"[92] and a "*constituting power*",[93] wherein "*citizens and states* (*that are already constituted by citizens*) can participate *on an equal footing* in constituting a supranational democracy".[94]

87 On this point see Lindahl, "Constituent Power and Reflexive Identity", p. 18.
88 J. Habermas, *The Lure of Technocracy*, Polity Press, Cambridge, 2015.
89 J. Habermas, *Democracy in Europe*, discourse for the Holberg prize at Universitetet i Stavanger, 11 September 2014, available at www.youtube.com/watch?v=0sLtM0hNnVc.
90 Habermas, *Lure of Technocracy*, p. 59. The concept had already been introduced as "*pouvoir constituant mixte*," in J. Habermas, *The Crisis of the European Union. A Response*, Polity Press, Cambridge, 2012, p. 36.
91 Habermas, *Lure of Technocracy*, p. 58.
92 Ibid.
93 Ibid.
94 Ibid.

In this section, I will claim that the Habermasian notion of an inherent duplicity of constituent citizenship could be reinterpreted in the light of the Kantian interpretation I have advanced as, namely, with the definition of sovereignty from authority. In particular, the Kantian distinction between state citizenship and citizenship of the earth helps in defining the Habermasian thesis on the internal division of sovereignty as well as illustrating the plurality of a scheme of transnational memberships.

Whereas Habermas' conception of a 'double sovereignty' goes beyond the traditional view of a purely domestic source of power for state legitimacy, Kant's idea of earth citizenship provides the conceptual template for framing the tension between a state-constrained conception of sovereignty and, ultimately, a critical conception of cosmopolitan affiliation claimed in compliance with a global principle of public law: "a principle *having to do with rights*".[95]

Why so? The reason, to employ the Habermas expression, is that "the trust among citizens that currently exists in the form of a nationally limited civic solidarity can very well develop into an even more abstract form of trust that reaches across national borders. The 'no demos' thesis obscures a factor that we must take seriously – the conviction that the *normative* achievements of the democratic state are worth preserving."[96] Habermas asks us to formulate a thought experiment: "Let us imagine a democratically developed European Union *as if* its constitution had been brought into existence by a double sovereign".[97] These two sovereignties would be the citizens of the European states (the European peoples) and the citizens of Europe. Such cofounding powers would then "be reflected at the level of the *constituted* polity".[98] However, as Habermas notices, this determines a situation of deadlock where "no longer [would anyone be able to] decide in a real sovereign manner".[99] An assumption arises spontaneously, one where the European constituent power has "already committed itself [. . .] to recognizing the historical achievements [. . .] by the nation-states".[100]

From a Kantian perspective, an initial argument would take into consideration that no empirically given *constituent power* can be postulated from outside a process of justification of a *constituent will-formation*. This means that the Habermasian conception of a double sovereignty can be conceived only in the light of a deeper notion, one resorting to the idea of earth citizenship. Habermas also seems to concede this point, as when he claims that "the citizens satisfy their two allegiances [state and EU affiliations][. . .] from the perspective *as if they had* participated in the constitution-building from the outset *as equal subjects* in their dual role [. . .]".[101]

95 Kant, "Metaphysics of Morals (1797)", 6:353, p. 489.
96 Habermas, *Lure of Technocracy*, p. 39.
97 Habermas, *Lure of Technocracy*, p. 40.
98 Ibid.
99 Ibid.
100 Habermas, *Lure of Technocracy*, p. 41.
101 Habermas, *Lure of Technocracy*, p. 44.

Yet, the regulative assumption of the Kantian originally united will also suggests more than the options envisaged by the Habermasian conception of a dual sovereignty. The former opens to inclusion different types of constituent affiliations established transnationally. Furthermore, it defines standards of legitimacy for those kinds of jurisdictional affiliations that do not require conceiving exercises of sovereignty. These include, for instance, all those transnational regimes as in the case of commercial trade agreements such as the WTO, or the case of networks as with the G8 and G20.

What a Kantian-like argument has to say here is that it is through the presumption of *the authority* of a general united will, that there follows a peremptory command to join a rightful condition of a global polity. Once the Habermasian conception of double sovereignty is reinterpreted according to this Kantian interpretive hypothesis, it also becomes possible to account for both the possibility of a *plurality* of transnational sovereignties as well as of transnational but non-sovereign supranational regimes.

By thinking in Kantian terms with "the benefit of two hundred years' insight",[102] it can be shown how the critical perspective associated with the idea of earth citizenship needs to shift away from the national realm of republican states to the burgeoning of transnational regimes. For these cases, the notion of earth citizenship expresses a pragmatic instantiation of a cosmopolitan *a priori* will.

That contemporary legal and political regimes continue to express incomplete forms of earth citizenship reflects a contingent deficit but not a normative drawback. Nevertheless, in such a plurality of regimes, even the non-ideal democratic progressions achieved under the guidance of a regulative use of a general *a priori* will show deficient arrangements in the treatment of their members. Notwithstanding significant progress, moving beyond the treatment of individuals as mere objects of concern, a comparably diffused notion of earth citizenship framed by human rights is not yet delivering a form of subjectivity fully endowed with enforceable constituent powers.

Legal and institutional integration certainly requires *some form* of transnational democratic accountability, but this does not imply an all-pervasive form of global sovereignty. Instead, there might be different means by which legitimate forms of transnational powers are realized: from the opportunity for citizens to express a critical appraisal of decisions taken by transnational bodies, to their participation as members in transnational decision-making processes. Whereas state-sovereignty provides, to a large extent, an indirect way for people to influence political outcomes worldwide, it is undeniable that decisions beyond the state level are often made by technocrats rather than by state-elected representatives pursuing a public agenda – something known in the EU context as the power of comitology committees.

102 This is the title of Habermas' first essay on Kant's cosmopolitanism. See J. Bohman and M. Luz-Bachtmann (eds.), *Perpetual Peace. Essay on Kant's Cosmopolitan Ideal*, MIT Press, Boston, Mass., 1997, pp. 113–154.

Unfortunately, the lesson handed down by Kant does not provide guidance with regard to the institutional mechanisms for realizing a positive transnational integration among peoples. The time was not yet ripe to propose viable institutional steps for the constitutionalization of international law. However, following Kant, what continues to remain valid today is that in a cosmopolitan perspective any justifiable arrangement beyond the state has to be consistent with republican ideals. With regard to such an enterprise, the cosmopolitan constitution must promote an ideal of freedom as non-domination, meaning an overall protection of individual rights from domestic and transnational domination.[103]

103 Kant, "Toward Perpetual Peace (1795)", 8:356–357, pp. 327–328.

Conclusion

Let me conclude with a remark concerning the reactualization of Kant's cosmopolitan insights. It is understood that the world of domestic law and international relations has changed profoundly. Nowadays, we certainly need new categories to reflect and understand such transformations. The relevance and actuality of Kant, nonetheless, is that of having inaugurated a modern view of international law, one that later developed through the *Charter of the United Nations* in 1945, followed by the growth and consolidation of the human rights regime. To understand the contribution of Kant, one should first underscore his challenge to a persistent dogma of his time: the impossibility of conceiving domestic and international law as one single legal system. Conversely, Kant argues for the unity of public law, notwithstanding an internal partitition into "the *right of a state*, the *right of nations* and *cosmopolitan right*".[1] We know how the idea of a unity of the law affected later reflections in philosophy of law and, in particular, how such an idea gained momentum with Kelsen's notion of a "basic norm".[2]

But for Kant, however, such unity is a matter of defining a law-internal "juristic hypothesis"[3] on the basis of a grounding cosmopolitan will (a principle of law being only its result). Furthermore, whereas for Kelsen an internal law-like grounding principle answers the question of 'what the law actually is', avoiding an allegedly widespread confusion with 'what it should be', for Kant such a separation does not seem to hold due to the validating force that the categorical imperative provides to the principle of right.[4]

Thus, it seems that the Kantian conviction for the unity of the law rests on resorting ultimately to a regulative hypothesis validating the legal system as a *whole*. The suggestion I have made throughout this essay detects the juncture between positive law and its meta-legal foundation in the Kantian justification of the reasons for abandoning a lawless condition of the state of nature. Such a step becomes possible due to a rejoining of provisional and peremptory

1 Kant, "Toward Perpetual Peace (1795)", 8:365, p. 334.
2 Kelsen, *General Theory of Law and State*, p. xv.
3 Ibid.
4 On the textual difficulties to defend such reading, see A. Wood, "General Introduction, Immanuel Kant. Practical Philosophy", M. Gregor (ed.), *Immanuel Kant. Practical Philosophy*, Cambridge University Press, Cambridge, 1999, p. xxxi.

norms into the idea of a 'general united will' regulating intersubjective relations by rights. It is by this condition that the structuring of the spheres of a general civil condition occurs and that can provide an approximation towards perpetual peace.

As Kant affirms: "If it is a duty to realize the condition of public right, even if only in approximation by unending progress, and if there is also a well-founded hope of this, then the *perpetual peace* that follows upon what have till now been falsely called peace treaties (strictly speaking truces) is no empty idea but a task that, gradually solved, comes steadily closer to its goal [. . .]".[5] It is to the understanding of the actual stage of international law that one needs to turn in order to see how progress might reasonably be achieved regarding perpetual peace.

5 Kant, "Toward Perpetual Peace (1795)", 8:386, p. 351.

References

G. Achenwall and J.S. Pütter, "Elementa Iuris Naturae", G. Achenwall and J.S. Pütter, *Anfangsgründe des Naturrechts*, J. Schröder (ed.), Insel, Frankfurt, 1995 [1750].

K. Alter, *The New Terrain of International Law. Courts, Politics and Rights*, Princeton University Press, Princeton and Oxford, 2014.

K. Ameriks, *Kant's Theory of Mind. An Analysis of the Paralogisms of Pure Reason*, Clarendon Press, Oxford, 2000.

K. Ameriks, "The Critique of Metaphysics: The Structure and Fate of Kant's Dialectic", P. Guyer (ed.), *The Cambridge Companion to Kant and Modern Philosophy*, Cambridge University Press, Cambridge, 2006, pp. 269–303.

C.A. Andersen, "*Ens rationis ratiocinatae* and *ens rationis ratiocinantis*: Reflections on a New Book on Beings of Reason in Baroque-Age Scholasticism", *Questio, Annuario di storia della metafisica*, 14, 2014, pp. 315–327.

A. Anghie, *Imperialism, Sovereignty and the Making of International Law*, Cambridge University Press, Cambridge, 2007.

A. Aportone, "Funzioni Costitutive e Regolative nella 'Critica della Ragion Pura' di Kant", *Rivista di Storia della Filosofia*, 45(4), 1990, pp. 695–721.

T. Aquinas, *Summa Theologica*, Catholic Way Publishing, London, 2014 [1467].

R.R. Aramayo, "La Plausible Impronta (Política) de Diderot en Kant", *Ideas y Valores* 66(163), 2017, pp. 13–37.

M. de Araujo, "Hugo Grotius, Contractualism, and the Concept of Private Property: An Institutionalist Interpretation", *History of Philosophy Quarterly*, 26(4), 2009, pp. 353–371.

D. Archibugi and F.Voltaggio, *Filosofi per la pace*, Editori Riuniti, Roma, 1991.

H. Arendt, *Lectures on Kant's Political Philosophy*, R. Beiner (ed.), The University of Chicago Press, Chicago, Ill., 1992.

Aristotle, *Politics*, E. Barker (trans.), Oxford University Press, Oxford, 1995.

Aristotle, *Nicomachean Ethics*, T. Irwin (ed.), Hackett Publishing Company, Inc. Indianapolis/Cambridge, 1999.

Augustine of Hippo, *City of God*, H. Bettenson (trans.), Penguin Classics, London, 2004.

B. Bachofen and C. Spector, "Le Project de la paix perpétuelle: de Saint-Pierre à Rousseau", B. Bernardi and G. Silvestrini (eds.), *Principes du droit de la guerre, Ecrits sur le Project de Paix Perpétuelle de l'abbé de Saint-Pierre*, Vrin, Paris, 2008, pp. 229–294.

S. Baiasu, S. Pihlström, H. Williams (eds.), *Politics and Metaphysics in Kant*, University of Wales Press, Cardiff, 2011.

T.W. Balch, *The Proposed International Tribunal of Arbitration of 1623, 1907*, pp. 302–311; available online at https://archive.org/stream/jstor-983742/983742_djvu.txt.

H.C. Baldry, *The Unity of Mankind in Greek Thought*, Cambridge University Press, Cambridge, 1965.

J. Bellers, "Some Reasons for an European State (1710)", G. Clarke (ed.), *J. Bellers, His Life, Times and Writings*, Routledge and Kegan Paul, London, 1987, pp. 177–220.

S. Benhabib, *Transformations of Citizenship. Dilemmas of the Nation State in the Era of Globalization*, Koninklijke van Gorcum, Assen, 2001.

S. Benhabib, *The Rights of Others: Aliens, Residents, and Citizens*, Cambridge University Press, Cambridge, 2004.

S. Benhabib, *Another Cosmopolitanism*, R. Post (ed.), Oxford University Press, Oxford, 2005.

J. Bennett, *Kant's Dialectic*, Cambridge University Press, Cambridge, 2016.

J. Bohman and M. Luz-Bachtmann (eds.), *Perpetual Peace. Essay on Kant's Cosmopolitan Ideal*, MIT Press, Boston, Mass., 1997.

J. Bohman, "The Public Spheres of the World Citizen", J. Bohman and M. Lutz – Bachmann (eds.), *Perpetual Peace: Essays on Kant's Cosmopolitan Ideal*, MIT Press, Boston, Mass., 1997.

F. Bosbach, *Monarchia Universalis. Ein politischer Leitbegriff der frühen Neuzeit*, vol.32 Schriftenreihe der Historischen Kommission bei der Bayerischen Akademie der Wissenschaften,Vandenhoeck & Ruprecht Gm., 1997.

R. Brandt, "Das Erlaubnisgesetz, oder: Vernunft und Geschichte in Kants Rechtslehre", R. Brandt (ed.), *Rechtsphilosophie der Aufklärung. Symposium Wolfenbüttel 1981*, Walter de Gruyter, Berlin, 1982, pp. 233–285.

R. Brandt, "Das Problem der Erlaubnisgesetze im Spätwerk Kants", O. Höffe (ed.), *Zum Ewigen Frieden*, Akademie Verlag, Berlin, 2004, pp. 69–86.

A. Brett, "Natural Right and Civil Community: the Civil Philosophy of Hugo Grotius", *The Historical Journal*, 43(1), 2002, pp. 31–51.

M. Brito Vieira, "*Mare Liberum vs. Mare Clausum*: Grotius, Freitas, and Selden's Debate on Dominion over the Seas", *Journal of the History of Ideas*, 64(3), 2003, pp. 361–377.

G.W. Brown, "Moving from Cosmopolitan Legal Theory to Legal Practice: Models of Cosmopolitan Law", *Legal Studies*, 28, 2008, pp. 430–451.

G.W. Brown, *Grounding Cosmopolitanism: from Kant to the Idea of a Cosmopolitan Constitution*, Edinburgh University Press, Edinburgh, 2013.

H. Brunkhorst, "State and Constitutions – A Reply to Scheuerman", *Constellations*, 15(4), 2008, pp. 493–501.

B.S. Byrd, "Intelligible Possession of Objects of Choice", L. Denis (ed.), *Kant's Metaphysics of Morals: A Critical Guide*, Cambridge University Press, Cambridge, 2010, pp. 93–110.

B.S. Byrd and J. Hruschka, Kant's Doctrine of Right. A Commentary, Cambridge University Press, Cambridge, 2012.

M. Cacciari, *Geofilosofia dell'Europa*, Adelphi, Milan, 1994.

M. Cano, *De Dominio indorum*, V.L. Pereña (trans. and ed.), *Misión de España en América (1540–1560)*, Consejo Superior de Investigaciones Científicas, Madrid, 1956.

P. Capps, "Natural Law and the Law of Nations", A. Orakhelashvili (ed.), *Research Handbook on the Theory and History of International Law*, Edward Elgar, Cheltenam, UK, 2011, pp. 61–92.

Case C–402/05 P and C–415/05, *P. Kadi and Al Barakaat International Foundation v. Council and Commission* [2008] ECR I–6351.

G. Cavallar, *Pax Kantiana. Systematisch-historische Untersuchung des Entwurfs "Zum ewigen Frieden" (1795) von Immanuel Kant*, Böhlau Wien, Wien/Köln/Weimar, 1992.

G. Cavallar, *Kant and the Theory and Practice of International Rights*, University of Wales Press, Cardiff, 1999.

G. Cavallar, *The Rights of Strangers: Theories of International Hospitality, the Global Community and Political Justice since De Vitoria*, Ashgate, Aldershot, UK, 2002.

G. Cavallar, "De Vitoria, Grotius, Pufendorf, Wolff and Vattel: Accomplices of European Colonialism and Exploitation or True Cosmopolitans?", *Journal of the History of International Law*, 10(2), 2008, pp. 181–209.

G. Cavallar, *Imperfect Cosmopolis*, University of Wales Press, Cardiff, 2011.

G. Cavallar, *Kant's Embedded Cosmopolitanism. History, Philosophy and Education for World Citizens*, de Gruyter, Berlin/Boston, 2015.

F. Cheneval, "Der präsumtiv vernünftige Konsens der Menschen und Völker – Christian Wolffs Theorie der civitas maxima", *ARSP: Archiv für Rechts- und Sozialphilosophie/Archives for Philosophy of Law and Social Philosophy*, 85(4), 1999, pp. 563–580.

Cicero, *De Officiis*, W. Miller (trans.), The Loeb Classical Library, William Heinemann Ltd., London, 1913.

J. Cohen, "Constitutionalism beyond the State: Myth or Necessity? (A Pluralist Approach)", *Humanity: An International Journal of Human Rights, Humanitarianism, and Development*, 2(1), 2011, pp. 127–158.

J. Cohen, *Globalization and Sovereignty. Rethinking Legality, Legitimacy and Constitutionalism*, Cambridge University Press, New York, 2012.

E. Crucé, *The New Cyneas*, T.W. Balch (ed.), Allen, Lane and Scott, Philadelphia, 1909, reprinted by Forgotten books, London, 2017 [1623].

J. Culp, *The complementary understanding of the relation between ideal and nonideal theory*, Ma Thesis, Bern, 2008.

Dante Alighieri, *The Divine Comedy, Purgatory*, Penguin, Harmondsworth, London, 1985 [1320].

Dante Alighieri, *Tutte le opere. Opere minori. Il convivio, Epistole, Monarchia, Questio de acqua et terra*, F. Chiappelli, E. Fenzi, A. Jacomuzzi, P. Gaia (a cura di), UTET, Torino, 1997, pp. 471–781.

S. Darwall, "Grotius and the Creation of Modern Moral Philosophy", *Archiv für Geschichte der Philosophie*, 94(3), 2012, pp. 296–325.

D. de Covarrubias, *De iustitia belli adversus indos*, Salamanca University Library, MS M.2043, also translated in part into Spanish by V.L. Pereña (trans. and ed.), *Misión de España en América (1540–1560)*, Consejo Superior de Investigaciones Científicas, Madrid, 1956.

D. de Soto, "Sumario", J. Brufau Prats (ed.), *Relecciones y Opuscolos*, Editorial San Esteban, Salamanca, vol.1, 1995 [1552].

D. de Soto, "Relección "de dominio"", J. Brufau Praz (ed.), Editorial San Esteban, Salamanca 1955 [1535].

E. de Vattel, *The Law of Nations. Or, Principles of the Law of Nature, Applied to the Conduct and Affairs of Nations and Sovereigns, with Three Early Essays on the Origin and Nature of Natural Law and on Luxury*, R. Whatmore and B. Kapossy (eds.), Liberty Fund, Indianapolis, 2008 [1797].

F. de Vitoria, "On Civil Power", A. Pagden and J. Lawrance (eds.), *De Vitoria Political Writings*, Cambridge University Press, Cambridge, 2017 [1528], pp. 1–44.

F. de Vitoria, "Commentarios a la Secunda secundae de Santo Tomas", Ediciòn preparada por el R. P. Vicente Beltrán de Heredia, D.P., Tomo III: *De Justitia*, Salamanca, 1934 [1533–4 and 1536–7].

F. de Vitoria, "On American Indians", A. Pagden and J. Lawrance (eds.), *De Vitoria Political Writings*, Cambridge University Press, Cambridge, 2017 [1537], pp. 231–292.

F. de Vitoria, "On Dietary Laws, or Self-Restraint", A. Pagden and J. Lawrance (eds.), *De Vitoria Political Writings*, Cambridge University Press, Cambridge, 2017 [1537], pp. 205–230.

F. de Vitoria, "On the Law of War", A. Pagden and J. Lawrance (eds.), *De Vitoria Political Writings*, Cambridge University Press, Cambridge, 2017 [1539], pp. 293–328.

L. Denis (ed.), *Kant's Metaphysics of Morals: A Critical Guide*, Cambridge University Press, Cambridge, 2010.

J. Derrida, *De l'hospitalité*, Calmann-Lévy, Paris, 1997.

D. Diderot, "Droit Naturel", J. Hope Mason and R. Wokler (eds.), *Diderot: Political Writings*, Cambridge University Press, Cambridge, 1992 [1755], pp. 17–21.

S. Di Liso (ed.), *Bartolomé de Las Casas, Juan Ginés de Sepúlveda, La controversia sugli Indios*, Edizioni di Pagina, Bari, 2016.

P. Dobner and M. Loughlin (eds.), *The Twilight of Constitutional Law: Demise or Transmutation?* Oxford University Press, Oxford, 2010.

H. Dreier, "Kants Republik", *Juristen Zeitung*, 15/16, 2004, pp. 745–804.

D. Dyzenhaus and M. Thorburn (eds.), *Philosophical Foundations of Constitutional Law*, Oxford University Press, Oxford, 2016.

O. Eberl and P. Niesen (eds.), *Immanuel Kant Zum ewigen Frieden und Auszüge aus der Rechtslehre*, Suhrkamp, Berlin, 2011.

C. Edwards, "The Law of Nature in the Thought of Hugo Grotius", *The Journal of Politics*, 32(4), 1970, pp. 784–807.

E. Ellis, *Kant's Politics. Provisional Theory for an Uncertain World*, Yale University Press, New Haven and London, 2005.

D. Erasmus (of Rotterdam), *The Complaint of Peace. Translated from the Querela Pacis*, The Open Court Publishing Co, Chicago and London, 1917 [1521].

L. Ferrajoli, *L'America, la conquista, il diritto. L'idea di sovranità nel mondo moderno*, Meridiana, 15, 1992, pp. 17–52.

J.G. Fichte, "Review of Immanuel Kant, Perpetual Peace: a Philosophical Sketch", Nicolovius, Königsberg, 1795, [second 1796], D. Breazeale (trans.), *The Philosophical Forum*, xxxii(4), 2001 [1795], pp. 311–321.

K. Flikschuh and L. Ypi (eds.), *Kant and Colonialism*, Oxford University Press, Oxford, 2014.

K. Flikschuh, "Elusive Unity: the General Will in Hobbes and Kant", *Hobbes Studies*, 25(1), 2012, pp. 21–42.

K. Flikschuh, "Kant's Sovereignty Dilemma: A Contemporary Analysis", *The Journal of Political Philosophy*, 18(4), 2010, pp. 469–493.

K. Flikschuh, *Kant and Modern Political Philosophy*, Cambridge University Press, Cambridge, 2000.

A. Føllesdal, "Kant, Human Rights and Courts", A. Føllesdal and R. Maliks (eds.), *Kantian Theory and Human Rights*, Routledge, London, 2014, pp. 193–202.

R. Forst, *The Right to Justification. Elements of a Constructivist Theory of Justice*, Columbia University Press, New York, N.Y., 2014.

E. Fox-Decent, "Constitutional Legitimacy Unbound", D. Dyzenhaus and M. Thorburn (eds.), *Philosophical Foundations of Constitutional Law*, Oxford University Press, Oxford, 2016, pp. 119–140.

M. Frede, *Essays in Ancient Philosophy*, University of Minnesota Press, Minneapolis, 1987.

V. Gerhardt, *Immanuel Kants Entwurf"Zum ewigen Frieden". Eine Theorie der Politik*, Wissenschaftliche Buchgesellschaft, Darmstaadt, 1995.

V. Gerhardt, *Immanuel Kant. Vernunft und Leben*, Reclam, Stuttgart, 2002.

G. Geismann, "Kants Rechtlehre vom Weltfrieden", *Zeitschrift für philosophische Forschung*, 37(3), 1983, pp. 363–388.

G. Geismann, *World Peace: Rational Idea and Reality on the Principles of Kant's Political Philosophy*, available online at www.researchgate.net/publication/27518143_World_Peace_Rational_Idea_and_Reality_On_the_Principles_of_Kant's_Political_Philosophy. Originally published in H. Oberer and G. Seel (eds.), *Kant. Analysen-Probleme-Kritik*, Königshausen und Neumann, Würzburg, vol. ii; 1996, pp. 265–319.

A. Gentili, *De Iure Belli, Libri III* [1598]; available online at https://archive.org/details/dejurebellilibri00gent/page/n4. Author's translation.

P. Glenn, *The Cosmopolitan State*, Oxford University Press, Oxford, 2013.

P. Glenn, *Legal Traditions of the World*, Oxford University Press, Oxford, 2010.

D. Gordon (ed.), *Paul's Letter to the Philippians*, Eerdmans Publishing, Grand Rapids, Mich., 1995.

Gratianus, *Decretum Gratianii*, Bayerische StaatsBibliothek [1142]; available online at http://geschichte.digitale-sammlungen.de/decretum-gratiani/online/angebot.

N. Greenwood Onuf, "Civitas Maxima: Wolff, Vattel and the Fate of Republicanism", *The American Journal of International Law*, 88(2), 1994, pp. 280–303.

M. Grier, *Kant's Doctrine of Transcendental Illusion*, Cambridge University Press, Cambridge, 2004.

J. Grimm and W. Grimm, *Deutsches Wörterbuch*, 16 Bde in 32 Teilbänden, Leipzig 1854–1961, 1971.

H. Grotius, *De Iure Belli ac Pacis*, B.J.A. de Kanter-van Hettinga Tromp (ed.), Brill, Leiden, 1939 [1625].

H. Grotius, *The Free Sea*, D. Armitage (ed. and introd.), Liberty Fund, Indianapolis, 2004 [1609].

H. Grotius, *Commentary on the Law of Prize and Booty*, Liberty Fund, Indianapolis, 2006 [1603].

H. Grotius, *On the Law of War and Peace*, S.C. Neff (ed. and annot.), Cambridge University Press, Cambridge, 2012 [1625].

P. Guyer, *Kant*, Routledge, London/New York, 2006.

P. Guyer, "Stellenindex und Konkordanz zum *Naturrecht Feyerabend*, Teilband I: Einleitung des *Naturrechts Feyerabend*", *Ratio Juris*, 25(1), 2012, pp. 110–116.

P. Guyer, *Kant on Freedom, Law and Happiness*, Cambridge University Press, Cambridge, 2000.

J. Habermas, *The Lure of Technocracy*, Polity Press, Cambridge, 2015.

J. Habermas, *Democracy in Europe*, discourse for the Holberg prize at Universitetet i Stavanger, 11 September 2014; available online at www.youtube.com/watch?v=0sLtM0hNnVc.

J. Habermas, *The Crisis of the European Union. A Response*, Polity Press, Cambridge, 2012.

J. Habermas, "The Constitutionalization of International Law and the Legitimation Problems of a Constitution for World Society", C. Cronin (ed.), *Europe: The Faltering Project*, Polity Press, Cambridge, 2009, pp. 109–130.

J. Habermas, "A Political Constitution for the Pluralist World Society?", *Journal of Chinese Philosophy*, 34, 2007, pp. 331–343.

J. Habermas, "Does the Constitutionalization of International Law Still have a Chance?", C. Cronin (ed.), *The Divided West*, Polity Press, Cambridge, 2006, pp. 115–193.

J. Habermas, "Kant's Idea of Perpetual Peace, with the Benefit of Two Hundred Years' Hindsight", J. Bohman and M. Lutz – Bachmann (eds.), *Perpetual Peace. Essays on Kant's Cosmopolitan Ideal*, The MIT Press, Cambridge, Mass., 1997, pp. 113–154.

D. Harmitage, "Introduction", R. Hakluyt (trans.) and D. Armitage (ed.), H. Grotius, *The Free Sea*, Liberty Fund, Indianapolis, 2004 [1609].

D. Heater, *World Citizenship and Government. Cosmopolitan Ideas in the History of Western Political Thought*, Palgrave Macmillan, London, 1996.

O. Hekster, *Rome and Its Empire, AD 193–284*, Edinburgh University Press, Edinburgh, 2008.

T. Hobbes, *Leviathan*, J.C.A. Gaskin (ed.), Oxford University Press, New York, 1998 [1651].

O. Höffe, *Immanuel Kant*, Verlag C.H. Beck, Munich, 1988.

O. Höffe, *"Königliche Völker". Zu Kants kosmopolitischer Rechts- und Friedenstheorie*, Suhrkamp, Frankfurt am Main, 2001.

O. Höffe (ed.), *Zum Ewigen Frieden*, Akademie Verlag, Berlin, 2004.

O. Höffe, *Kant's Cosmopolitan Theory of Law and Peace*, Cambridge University Press, Cambridge, 2006.

C. Horn, *Nicht Ideale Normativität. Ein neuer Blick auf Kants politische Philosophie*, Suhrkamp, Berlin, 2014.

D. Horst, *Moralphilosophie und Naturrecht bei Samuel Pufendorf. Eine geistes- und wissenschaftsgeschichtliche Untersuchung zur Geburt des Naturrechts aus der Praktischen Philosophie*, 22 Band, Münchener Studien zur Politik, Munich, 1972.

J. Hruschka, *Das deontologische Sechseck bei Gottfried Achenwall im Jahre 1767. Zur Geschichte der deontischen Grundbegriffe in der Universal Jurisprudenz zwischen Suarez und Kant*, Joachim Jungius-Gesellschaft der Wissenschaften e.V. Hamburg 4, 1986/2.

I. Kant, *Kant's Gesammelte Schriften*, Preuβische Akademie der Wissenschaften (ed.), Deutsche Akademie der Wissenschaften zu Berlin (ed.), Akademie der Wissenschaften der DDR (ed. until 1991) and Akademie der Wissenschaften zu Göttingen (ed.), de Gruyter, Berlin-Leipzig, 1900ff.

I. Kant, "Anthropology Collins (1772–1773) [excerpts]", A. Wood and R. Louden (eds.), *Lectures on Anthropology*, Cambridge University Press, Cambridge, 2012, pp. 11–26.

I. Kant, "Of the Different Races of Human Beings (1775)", G. Zöller and R.B. Louden (eds.), *Anthropology, History and Education*, Cambridge University Press, Cambridge, 2011, pp. 82–97.

I. Kant, "Anthropology Pillau (1777–1778) [excerpts]", A. Wood and R. Louden (eds.), *Lectures on Anthropology*, Cambridge University Press, Cambridge, 2012, pp. 257–280.

I. Kant, "*Menschenkunde* (1781–1782?) [excerpts]", A. Wood and R. Louden (eds.), *Lectures on Anthropology*, Cambridge University Press, Cambridge, 2012, pp. 281–334.

I. Kant, *Critique of Pure Reason*, P. Guyer and A. Wood (ed. and trans.), Cambridge University Press, Cambridge, 2000 [1781–7].

I. Kant, *Prolegomena to any Future Metaphysics*, G. Hatfield (ed.), Cambridge University Press, Cambridge, 2004, [1783].

I. Kant, "An Answer to the Question: What is Enlightenment? (1784)", M. Gregor (ed.), *Immanuel Kant. Practical Philosophy*, Cambridge University Press, Cambridge, 1999, pp. 11–22.

I. Kant, "Moral Philosophy: Collin's Lectures Notes", *Lectures on Ethics*, P. Heath and J.B. Schneewind (eds.), Cambridge University Press, Cambridge, 1997 [1784], pp. 11–26.

I. Kant, "Idea for a Universal History with a Cosmopolitan Aim (1784)", G. Zöller and R.B. Louden (eds.), *Anthropology, History and Education*, Cambridge University Press, Cambridge, 2011, pp. 107–120.

I. Kant, "Reflections on the Philosophy of Right", F. Rauscher and K.R. Westphal (eds.), *Lectures and Drafts on Political Philosophy*, Cambridge University Press, Cambridge, 2016 [1764–], pp. 1–72.

I. Kant, "Vorarbeit zur Tugendlehre", *Handschriftlicher Nachlaß Vorarbeiten und Nachträge*, XXIII; available online at https://korpora.zim.uni-duisburg-essen.de/kant/aa23/Inhalt23.html

I. Kant, *Lezioni sul diritto naturale (Naturrecht Feyerabend)*, G. Sadun Bordoni and N. Hinske (eds.), Bompiani, Milan, 2016 [1784], pp. 1–72.

I. Kant, *Gottfried Feyerabend. Kant's Natural Right*. Read in the Winter of the Year 1784, English Translation by L.Vinx; available online at www.academia.edu/5541693/

I. Kant, "Anthropology Mrongovius (1784–1785) [complete]", A. Wood and R. Louden (eds.), *Lectures on Anthropology*, Cambridge University Press, Cambridge, 2012, pp. 335–510.

I. Kant, "Groundwork of the Metaphysics of Morals (1785)", M. Gregor (ed.), *Immanuel Kant. Practical Philosophy*, Cambridge University Press, Cambridge, 1999, pp. 37–108.

I. Kant, "Determination of the Concept of a Human Race (1785)", G. Zöller and R.B. Louden (eds.), *Anthropology, History and Education*, Cambridge University Press, Cambridge, 2011, pp. 143–159.

I. Kant, "What is Orientation in Thinking?", H.S. Reiss (ed.), *Kant Political Writings*, Cambridge University Press, Cambridge, 2012 [1786], pp. 237–249.

I. Kant, "*Conjectural beginning of human history* (1786)", G. Zöller and R.B. Louden (eds.), *Anthropology, History and Education*, Cambridge University Press, Cambridge, 2011, pp. 160–175.

I. Kant, "Critique of Practical Reason (1788)", M. Gregor (ed.), *Immanuel Kant. Practical Philosophy*, Cambridge University Press, Cambridge, 1999, pp. 133–272.

I. Kant, "On the Use of Teleological Principles in Philosophy (1788)", G. Zöller and R.B. Louden (eds.), *Anthropology, History and Education*, Cambridge University Press, Cambridge, 2011, pp. 192–218.

I. Kant, "Anthropology Busolt (1788–1789) [excerpts]", A. Wood and R. Louden (eds.), *Lectures on Anthropology*, Cambridge University Press, Cambridge, 2012, pp. 511–524.

I. Kant, *Critique of the Power of Judgment*, P. Guyer (ed.), Cambridge University Press, Cambridge, 2000 [1790].

I. Kant, "Kant on the Metaphysics of Morals. Vigilantius' lectures notes", P. Heath and J.B. Schneewind (eds.), *Immanuel Kant. Lectures on Ethics*, Cambridge University Press, Cambridge, 1997 [1793], pp. 249–252.

I. Kant, *Religion within the Boundaries of Mere Reason. And Other Writings*, A. Wood and G. Di Giovanni (eds.), R. Merrihew Adams (intro.), Cambridge University Press, Cambridge, 1998 [1793].

I. Kant, "On the common Saying: That may be correct in theory, but it is of no use in practice (1793)", M. Gregor (ed.), *Immanuel Kant. Practical Philosophy*, Cambridge, Cambridge University Press, 1999, pp. 273–310.

I. Kant, "Toward Perpetual Peace (1795)", M. Gregor (ed.), *Immanuel Kant: Practical Philosophy*, Cambridge University Press, Cambridge, 1999, pp. 311–352.

I. Kant, *Immanuel Kant Zum Ewigen Frieden. Ein Philosophischer Entwurf. Kommentar*, O. Eberl and P. Niesen (ed. and comm.), Suhrkamp, Berlin, 2011 [1795].

I. Kant, "Perpetual Peace: a Philosophical Sketch", H.S. Reiss (ed.), *Kant Political Writings*, Cambridge University Press, Cambridge, 2012 [1795], pp. 93–130.

I. Kant, "Metaphysische Anfangsgründe der Rechtslehre", O. Eberl and P. Niesen (comm. and eds.), *Immanuel Kant Zum ewigen Frieden*, Suhrkamp, Berlin, 2011 [1797].

I. Kant, "The Metaphysics of Morals (1797)", M. Gregor (ed.), *Immanuel Kant. Practical Philosophy*, Cambridge University Press, Cambridge, 1999, pp. 353–604.

I. Kant, *The Conflict of the Faculties. Der Streit der Fakultäten*, M. Gregor (ed.), Abaris Book, New York, 1979 [1798].

I. Kant, "Anthropology from a Pragmatic Point of View (1798)", G. Zöller and R.B. Louden (eds.), *Anthropology, History and Education*, Cambridge University Press, Cambridge, 2011, pp. 227 429.

B. Kapossy, I. Nakhimovsky, R. Whatmore (eds.), *Commerce and Peace in the Enlightenment*, Cambridge University Press, Cambridge, 2017.

F. Kaulbach, *Der Begriff der Freiheit in Kants Rechtsphilosophie*, Philosophische Perspektiven Band 5, Frankfurt am Main, 1973, pp. 78–91.

P. Keating, *The function of ideas of reason in Kant's political philosophy*, PhD Thesis, submitted to the School of Philosophy, University of New South Wales, Oct. 2007.

H. Kelsen, *General Theory of Law and State*, Harvard University Press, Cambridge, Mass., 2007 [1945].

A. Kenny, "The Philosopher's History and the History of Philosophy", T. Sorell and G.A.J. Rogers (eds.), *Analytic Philosophy and History of Philosophy*, Clarendon Press, Oxford, 2005.

W. Kersting, "Sittengesetz und Rechtsgesetz – Die Begründung des Rechts bei Kant und den frühen Kantianern", R. Brandt (ed.), *Rechtsphilosophie der Aufklärung. Rechtsphilosophie der Aufklärung. Symposium Wolfenbüttel 1981*, Walter de Gruyter, Berlin, 1982, 1982, pp. 148–177.

W. Kersting, *Wohlgeordnete Freiheit. Immanuel Kants Rechts- und Staatsphilosophie mit einer Einleitung zur Taschenbuchausgabe 1993: Kant und die politische Philosophie der Gegenwart*, Suhrkamp, Frankfurt am Main, 2016.

J.P. Klabbers and G. Ulfstein, *The Constitutionalization of International Law*, Oxford University Press, Oxford, 2009.

P. Kleingeld, "Kant's Cosmopolitan Law", *Kantian Review*, 2(1), 1998, pp. 72–90.

P. Kleingeld, "Approaching Perpetual Peace: Kant's Defense of a League of States and his Ideal of a World Federation", *European Journal of Philosophy*, 12(3), 2004, pp. 304–325.

P. Kleingeld (ed.), *Immanuel Kant. Toward Perpetual Peace and Other Writings on Politics, Peace, and History*, Yale University Press, New Haven, Conn., 2006.

P. Kleingeld, *Kant and Cosmopolitanism. The Philosophical Ideal of World Citizenship*, Cambridge University Press, Cambridge, 2012.

M. Koskenniemi, “Constitutionalism as a Mindset: Reflections on Kantian Themes About International Law and Globalization”, *Theoretical Inquiries in Law*, 8(1), 2007, pp. 9–36.

P. Kleingeld, “Kant’s Second Thoughts on Colonialism”, K. Flikschuh and L. Ypi (eds.), *Kant and Colonialism*, Oxford University Press, Oxford, 2014, pp. 43–67.

M. Koskenniemi, “Miserable Comforters: International Relations as New Natural Law”, *European Journal of International Relations*, 15(3), 2009, pp. 395–422.

L. Krasnoff, “How Kantian is Constructivism?”, *Kant Studien*, 90(4), 1999, pp. 385–409.

L. Krieger, *The Politics of Discretion. Pufendorf and the Acceptance of Natural Law*, The University of Chicago Press, Chicago and London, 1965.

M. Kumm, “Who is the Final Arbiter of Constitutionality in Europe?”, *Common Market Law Review*, 36, 1999, pp. 509–514.

M. Kumm, “On the Past and Future of European Constitutional Scholarship”, *International Journal of Constitutional Law*, 7(3), 2009, pp. 364–400.

M. Kumm, “Constitutionalism and the Cosmopolitan State”, *Public Law and Legal Theory Research Paper Series, Working Paper No.13–68*, 2013, pp. 1–28; available online at http://ssrn.com/abstract=2338547

B. de Las Casas, “Apologia”, A. Losada (ed.), *Obras completas*, Alianza Editorial, Madrid, 9, 1989 [1550–1].

H. Lindahl, “Constituent Power and Reflexive Identity: Towards an Ontology of Collective Selfhood”, M. Loughlin and N. Walker (eds.), *The Paradox of Constitutionalism*, Oxford University Press, Oxford, 2007, pp. 9–24.

J. Locke, *Second Treatise of Government*, R.H. Cox (ed.), Harlan Davidson, Inc., Wheeling, Ill., 1982 [1690].

R.B. Louden, “General Introduction”, G. Zöller and R.B. Louden (eds.), *I. Kant, Anthropology, History and Education*, Cambridge University Press, Cambridge, 2011, pp. 1–17.

M. Loughlin and N. Walker (eds.), *The Paradox of Constitutionalism*, Oxford University Press, Oxford, 2007.

B. Ludwig, “Der Platz des rechtlichen Postulats der praktischen Vernuft innerhalb der Paragaphen 1–6 der kantischen Rechtslehre”, R. Brandt (ed.), *Rechtsphilosophie der Aufklärung. Symposium Wolfenbüttel 1981*, Walter de Gruyter, Berlin, 1982, pp. 218–232.

J. Madison, *The Writings of James Madison*, Gaillard Hunt (ed.), G.P. Putnam’s Sons, New York, 1900; available online at https://founders.archives.gov/documents/Madison/01-14-02-0185

B. Madley, “Reexamining the American Genocide Debate: Meaning, Historiography and New Methods”, *American Historical Review*, 120(1), 2015, pp. 98–139.

Marcus Aurelius Antoninus, *The Meditations of the Emperor Marcus Aurelius Antoninus*, M. Silverthorne and J. Moore (eds.), F. Hutcheson and J. Moore (trans.), Liberty Fund, Indianapolis, 2008 [II AC].

G. Marini, “Kants Idee einer Weltrepublik”, P. van Tongeren, P. Sars, C. Bremmers, K. Boey (eds.), *Eros and Eris. Contributions to a Hermeneutical Phenomenology Liber Amicorum for Adrian Peperzak*, Springer, Dordrecht, 1992, pp. 133–146.

I. Maus, *Menschenrechte, Demokratie und Frieden. Perspektiven globaler Organisation*, Suhrkamp, Berlin, 2015.

T. McCarthy, *Race, Empire and the Idea of Human Development*, Cambridge University Press, Cambridge, 2009.

L. Milazzo, *La teoria dei diritti di Francisco de Vitoria*, Edizioni ETS, Pisa, 2012.

B. Milstein, "Kantian Cosmopolitanism beyond 'Perpetual Peace': *Commercium*, Critique, and the Cosmopolitan Problematic", *European Journal of Philosophy*, 1(21), 2010, pp. 118–143.

C.L. (de) Montesquieu, *The Spirit of the Laws*, A.M. Cohler, B.C. Miller, H.S. Stone (eds.), Cambridge University Press, Cambridge, 1989 [1748].

M. Mori, *La pace e la ragione. Kant e le relazioni internazionali: diritto, politica, storia*, Il Mulino, Bologna, 2008.

J. Muldoon, "J. Wyclif and the Rights of the Infidels: The Requerimiento Re-Examined", *The Americas*, 36(3), 1980, pp. 301–316.

S. Muthu, *Enlightenment against Empire*, Princeton University Press, Princeton and Oxford, 2003.

S. Muthu (ed.), *Empire and Modern Political Thought*, Cambridge University Press, Cambridge, 2012.

S. Neiman, *The Unity of Reason. Rereading Kant*, Oxford University Press, Oxford and New York, 1994.

F. Neuhouser, *Rousseau's Theodicy of Self-Love*, Oxford University Press, Oxford, 2008.

P. Niesen, "Colonialism and Hospitality", *Politics and Ethics Review*, 3(1), 2007, pp. 90–108.

O. O'Neill, "Autonomy and Public Reason", M. Timmons and R.N. Johnson (eds.), *Reason, Value, and Respect: Kantian Themes from the Philosophy of Thomas E. Hill, Jr.*, Oxford University Press, Oxford, 2015, pp. 119–34.

H. Oberer and G. Seel (eds.), *Kant. Analysen Probleme Kritik*; Königshausen und Neumann, Würzburg, 2 vols., 1996.

B. Orend, *War and International Justice: A Kantian Perspective*, Wilfrid Laurier University Press, Waterloo, 2000.

A. Pagden, "The Forbidden Food: Francisco de Vitoria and José de Acosta on Cannibalism", *Terrae Incognitae. The Journal of the Society for the History of Discoveries*, 13(1), 1981, pp. 17–29.

A. Pagden, *The Fall of Natural Man. The American Indian and the Origins of Comparative Ethnology*, Cambridge University Press, Cambridge, 1990.

A. Pagden, "The Law of Continuity: Conquest and Settlement within the Limits of Kant's International Right", K. Flikschuh and L. Ypi (eds.), *Kant and Colonialism*, Oxford University Press, Oxford, 2014.

A. Pagden, "Introduction: Francisco de Vitoria and the Origins of the Modern Global Order", J.M Beneyto and J.C. Varela (eds.), *At the Origins of Modernity. Francisco de Vitoria and the Discovery of International Law*, Springer, Dordrecht, 2017, pp. 1–20.

E. Papastavridis, "The Right of Visit on the High Seas in a Theoretical Perspective: *Mare Liberum* versus *Mare Clausum* Revisited", *Leiden Journal of International Law*, 24(1), 2011, pp. 45–69.

H.J. Paton, *Kant's Metaphysics of Experience*, George Allen & Unwin Ltd, London, 2 vols., 1936.

H.J. Paton, *The Categorical Imperative. A Study in Kant's Moral Philosophy*, Hutchinson's University Library, London, 1947.

H. Pauer-Studer, '"A Community of Rational Beings": Kant's Realm of Ends and the Distinction between Internal and External Freedom", *Kant-Studien*, 107(1), 2016, pp. 125–159.

Paulus III, *Veritas Ipsa*, Secret Vatican Archive, Arm.XXXVII, 15 f.145rv, *America Pontificia. Primi saeculi evangelizationis 1493–1592. Documenta Pontificia ex registris et minutis praesertim in Archivio secreto Vaticano existentibus, collegit, edidit J. Metzler*, Libreria Editrice Vaticana, Città del Vaticano, vol.1 (2 vols.), n. 84, 1991, pp. 364–366.

W. Penn, *An Essay towards the Present and Future Peace of Europe by the Establishment of an European Dyet, Parliament, or Estates (1693)*; available on line at www.fredsakademiet.dk/library/penn.pdf

A. Pinheiro Walla, "Common Possession of the Earth and Cosmopolitan Right", *Kant-Studien*, 107(1), 2016, pp. 160–78.

T. Pogge, *World Poverty and Human Rights*, Polity Press, Cambridge, 2008.

T. Pogge, "Kant's Theory of Justice" (reprint from: *Kant Studien*, 79, pp. 407–33), B.S. Byrd and J. Hruschka (eds.), *Kant and Law*, Ashgate, Aldershot, 2006/ Routledge, Taylor and Francis, London and New York, 2016, pp. 41–68.

S. Pufendorf, "Elements of Universal Jurisprudence in Two Books", C.L. Carr (ed.) and M.J. Seidler (trans.), *The Political Writings of Samuel Pufendorf*, Oxford University Press, Oxford, New York, 1994 [1660], pp. 31–94.

S. Pufendorf, "On the Law of Nature and Nations", C.L. Carr (ed.) and M.J. Seidler (trans.), *The Political Writings of Samuel Pufendorf*, Oxford University Press, Oxford and New York, 1994 [1672].

J. Rawls, "Kantian Constructivism in Moral Theory", *The Journal of Philosophy*, 77(9), 1980, pp. 515–572.

J. Rawls, *The Law of Peoples*, Harvard University Press, The Belknap Press, Cambridge, Mass., 2000.

G.T. Raynal (Abbé), *A Philosophical and Political History of the Settlements and Trade of the Europeans in the East and West Indies*, J.O. Justamond, W. Strahan and T. Cadell (trans.), London, 1783.

G. T. F. Raynal, *A History of the Two Indies*, P. Jimack (ed.), Routledge, New York, N.Y., 2006 [1770].

P.P. Remec, *The Position of the Individual in International Law according to Grotius and Vattel*, Martinus Nijhoff, The Hague, 1960.

P. Riley, *Will and Political Legitimacy. A Critical Exposition of Social Contract Theory in Hobbes, Locke, Rousseau, Kant, and Hegel*, Harvard University Press, Cambridge, Mass. and London, 1982.

P. Riley, *The General Will before Rousseau. The Transformation of the Divine into the Civic*, Princeton University Press, Pinceton, N.J., 2014.

A. Ripstein, *Force and Freedom. Kant's Legal and Political Philosophy*, Harvard University Press, Cambridge, Mass., 2009.

M. Risse, "Taking up Space on Earth: Theorizing Territorial Rights, the Justification of States and Immigration from a Global Standpoint", *Global Constitutionalism*, 4(1), 2015, pp. 81–113.

J. Ritter, K. Gründer, G. Gottfried (eds.), *Historisches Wörterbuch der Philosophie*, Band 11, Schwabe Verlag, Basel, 2011.

J.J. Rousseau, *Discourse on the Origin of Inequality*, F. Philip (trans.), P. Coleman (ed.), Oxford University Press, Oxford, 2009 [1755].

J.J. Rousseau, "Geneva Manuscript", R. Masters (ed.) and J. Masters (trans.), *On the Social Contract. With the Geneva Manuscript and Political Economy*, Saint Martin's Press, New York, 1978 [1756?], pp. 157–208.

J.J. Rousseau, "Discourse on Political Economy", C. Betts (trans., introd. and notes), *Discourse on Political Economy and the Social Contract*, Oxford University Press, Oxford, 2008 [1758], pp. 1–42.
J.J. Rousseau, "Abstract of Monsieur the Abbé de Saint-Pierre's Plan for Perpetual Peace", C. Kelly and J. Bush (trans.), C. Kelly (ed.), *Jean-Jacques Rousseau. The Plan for Perpetual Peace, On the Government of Poland, and other Writings on History and Politics*, University Press of New England, Dartmouth College Press, 2005 [1761], pp. 27–49.
J.J. Rousseau, "The Social Contract", C. Betts (trans., introd. and notes), *Discourse on Political Economy and the Social Contract*, Oxford University Press, Oxford, 2008 [1762], pp. 43–175.
J.J. Rousseau, "Considerations on the Government of Poland and on its Planned Reformation", C. Kelly and J. Bush (trans.), C. Kelly (ed.), *Jean-Jacques Rousseau. The Plan for Perpetual Peace, On the Government of Poland, and other Writings on History and Politics*, University Press of New England, Dartmouth College Press, 2005 [1782], pp. 167–240.
J.J. Rousseau, "Judgment of the Plan for Perpetual Peace", C. Kelly and J. Bush (trans.), C. Kelly (ed.), *Jean-Jacques Rousseau. The Plan for Perpetual Peace, On the Government of Poland, and other Writings on History and Politics*, Dartmouth College Press, University Press of New England, 2005 [1782], pp. 53–60.
G. Sadun Bordoni, "Introduzione", *I. Kant, Lezioni sul diritto naturale (Naturrecht Feyerabend)*, G. Sadun Bordoni and N. Hinske (eds.), Bompiani, Milan, 2016 [1784], pp. 7–50.
H. Saner, *Kants Weg vom Krieg zum Frieden*, Munich, 1967.
W. Scheuerman, "All Power to the (State-less?) General Assembly!", *Constellations*, 15(4), 2008, pp. 485–492.
W. Scheuerman, "Cosmopolitanism and the World State", *Review of International Studies*, 40(3), 2013, pp. 419–441.
C.Schmitt, *The Nomos of the Earth*, Telos Press Publishing, New York, N.Y., 2006.
C. Schmitt, *Constitutional Theory*, Duke University Press, Durham, N.C. and London, 2008.
J.B. Scott, *The Catholic Conception of International Law*, Georgetown University Press, Washington, D.C. 1934. Reprinted by the Lawbook Exchange Ltd., Clark, New Jersey, 2007.
L. Scuccimarra, *I confini del mondo. Storia del Cosmopolitismo dall'Antichità al Settecento*, Il Mulino, Bologna, 2006.
J.G. Sepúlveda, *Democrates segundo o de las justas causas de la guerra contra los Indios*, A. Losada (ed.), *Obras Completas*, Madrid, Consejo Superior de Investigaciones Científicas, Instituto Francisco de Vitoria, 1984, Pozoblanco, Ayuntamiento de Pozoblanco, 3, 1997 [1544].
J.G. Sepúlveda, "Democrates segundo. Apologia en favor del libro sobre las justas causas de la guerra", A. Losada (ed.), *Obras Completas*, revision de A. Moreno, Pozoblanco, Ayuntamiento de Pozoblanco, 3, 1997 [1544].
S.M. Shell, "Kant on Unjust War and 'Unjust Enemies' reflections on a pleonasm", *Kantian Review* 10(1), 2005, pp. 82–111.
A. Smith, *An Inquiry into the Nature and Causes of the Wealth of Nations*, R. H. Campbell and A. S. Skinner (eds.), textual ed. W.B. Todd (text.ed.), vol.2, Liberty Fund, Indianapolis, 1981.
T. Sorell, *The Eighties: a Snapshot*; available online at https://philosophy.princeton.edu/about/eighties–snapshot

T. Sorell and G.A.J. Rogers (eds.), *Analytic Philosophy and History of Philosophy*, Clarendon Press, Oxford, 2005.

C. Stahn, J.S. Easterday, J. Iverson, *Jus Post Bellum: Mapping the Normative Foundations*, Oxford University Press, Oxford, 2014.

D. Stannard, *American Holocaust. The Conquest of the New World*, Oxford University Press, New York, 1992.

S.M. Stern, *Aristotle on the World State*, Cassirer, Oxford, 1968.

A. Stilz, "Nations, States and Territory", *Ethics*, 121(3), 2011, pp. 572–601.

R.S. Taylor, "Kant's Political Religion: the Transparency of Perpetual Peace and the Highest Good", *The Review of Politics*, 72(1), 2010, pp. 1–24.

R. Teitel, *Transitional Justice*, Oxford University Press, Oxford, 2000.

Tertullian, *Apology and De Spectaculis*, T.R. Glover (trans.), Loeb Classical Library, n.250, Harvard University Press, Cambridge, Mass., 1931.

F. Teson, *Humanitarian Intervention: An Inquiry into Law and Morality*, Transnational Publishers, Irvington-on-Hudson, N.Y., 1997.

H. Thornton, "John Selden's Response to Hugo Grotius: The Argument for Closed Seas", *International Journal of Maritime History*, XVIII(2), 2006, pp. 105–127.

B. Tierney, "Permissive Natural Law and Property: Gratian to Kant", *Journal of the History of Ideas*, 62(3), 2001, pp. 381–399.

B. Tierney, "Kant on Property: the Problem of Permissive right", *Journal of the History of Ideas*, 62(2), 2001, pp. 301–312.

T. Todorov, *The Conquest of America. The Encounter with the Other*, Harper & Row, New York, 1984.

R. Tuck, *The Rights of War and Peace: Political Thought and the International Order from Grotius to Kant*, Oxford University Press, Oxford, 1999.

United Nations Charter; available online at www.un.org/en/charter–united–nations/

L. Valla, *Discourse on the Forgery of the Alleged Donation of Constantine*, C.B. Coleman (trans.), Yale University Press, New Haven, 1922 [XV sec./pub.1517]; available online at Hanover Historical Texts Projects, pp. 20–183, https://history.hanover.edu/texts/vallapart2.html

L. Vanhaute, "Colonists, Traders or Settlers? Kant on Fair International Trade and Legitimate Settlement", K. Flikschuh and L. Ypi (eds.), *Kant and Colonialism*, Oxford University Press, Oxford, 2014.

E. (de) Vattel, *The Law of Nations. Or, Principles of the Law of Nature, Applied to the Conduct and Affairs of Nations and Sovereigns, with Three Early Essays on the Origin and Nature of Natural Law and on Luxury*, R. Whatmore and B. Kapossy (eds.), Liberty Fund, Indianapolis, 2008 [1797].

R. Vierhaus (ed.), *Eigentum und Verfassung*. Zur Eigentumsdiskussion im ausgehenden 18. Jahrhundert (Veröffentlichungen des Max-Planck-Instituts für Geschichte 37), Vandenhoeck & Ruprecht, Göttingen, 1972.

A. Wagner, "Francisco de Vitoria and Alberico Gentili on the legal character of the global commonwealth", *Oxford Journal of Legal Studies*, 31(3), 2011, pp. 565–582.

J. Waldron, "Enough and As Good Left for Others", *The Philosophical Quarterly*, 29(117), 1979, pp. 319–328.

J. Waldron, "Kant's Legal Positivism", *Harvard Law Review*, 109(7), 1996, pp. 1535–1566.

N. Walker, "Taking Constitutionalism Beyond the State", *Political Studies*, 56(10), 2008, pp. 519–543.

W.H. Walsh, *Kant's Criticism of Metaphysics*, Edinburgh University Press, Edinburgh, 1975.

M. Weber, "The Profession and Vocation of Politics", P. Lassman and R. Speirs (eds.), *Political Writings*, Cambridge University Press, Cambridge, 2002, pp. 309–369.

J. Weinrib, "Permissive Rights and the Dynamism of Kantian Justice", *Law and Philosophy*, 33(1), 2014, pp. 105–136.

H. Williams, *Kant and the End of War: A Critique of Just War Theory*, Palgrave Macmillan, London, 2012.

C. Wolff, *Jus Gentium Methodo Scientifica Pertractatum*, J.H. Drake (trans.), Clarendon Press, Humphrey Milfford, Oxford, 1934 [1749].

C. Wolff, *Grundsaetze des Natur- und Voelkerrechts*, Halle (Saale) [1754]; available online at www.deutschestextarchiv.de/book/view/wolff_voelckerrecht_1754?p=5

A. Wood, "Kant's Philosophy of History", P. Kleingeld (ed.), *Immanuel Kant. Toward Perpetual Peace and Other Writings on Politics, Peace, and History*, Yale University Press, New Haven, Conn., 2006, pp. 243–262.

A. Wood, "General Introduction, Immanuel Kant. Practical Philosophy", M. Gregor (ed.), *Immanuel Kant. Practical Philosophy*, Cambridge University Press, Cambridge, 1999, xiii–xxxiii.

L. Ypi, "A Permissive Theory of Territorial Rights", *European Journal of Philosophy*, 22(2), 2012, pp. 288–312.

Analytic index

FSC
www.fsc.org
MIX
Papier | Fördert
gute Waldnutzung
FSC® C083411

Kolibri 360 GmbH
Ferdinand-Jühlke-Straße 7
99095 Erfurt, Deutschland
produktsicherheit@kolibri360.de